HQ
1731
.Z8
S838
1982

Wikan, Unni, 1944-

Behind the veil
in Arabia

BEHIND THE VEIL IN ARABIA

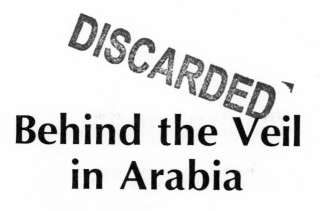

Behind the Veil in Arabia

WOMEN IN OMAN

Unni Wikan

THE JOHNS HOPKINS UNIVERSITY PRESS
Baltimore and London

The Johns Hopkins University Press, Baltimore, Maryland 21218
The Johns Hopkins Press Ltd., London

Library of Congress Cataloging in Publication Data

Wikan, Unni, 1944–
    Behind the veil in Arabia.

    Bibliography: p. 305
    Includes index.
    1. Women—Oman—Suhar. 2. Sex customs—Oman—Suhar.
    3. Marriage—Oman—Suhar. 4. Suhar (Oman)—Social life
and customs. I. Title.
HQ1731.Z8S838   305.4'2'09538   81–18622
ISBN 0-8018-2729-9   AACR2

*Dedicated to
the Women—and the Men—
of Sohar*

Contents

Preface   ix
Acknowledgments   xi
A Note on Transliteration   xiii

Part I

1. Introduction: Finding Our Way   3
2. Sohar: The First Exotic Glimpse   16
3. The Town and Its People   27

Part II

4. Segregation of the Sexes: Concept and Practice   51
5. Socialization to the Practice of Segregation   74
6. The *Burqa* Facial Mask   88
7. Women's World   109
8. Honor and Self-realization   141
9. The *Xanith:* A Third Gender Role?   168

Part III

10. Diverse Interests in Marriage Establishment   189
11. The Bride Should Be a Virgin, the Groom Should Be a Man   212
12. The Visit of an Undutiful Daughter   231
13. Portrait of a Marriage   245
14. Role-realization in Marriage   271

Appendix: A Framework for the Analysis   296
References   305
Index   309

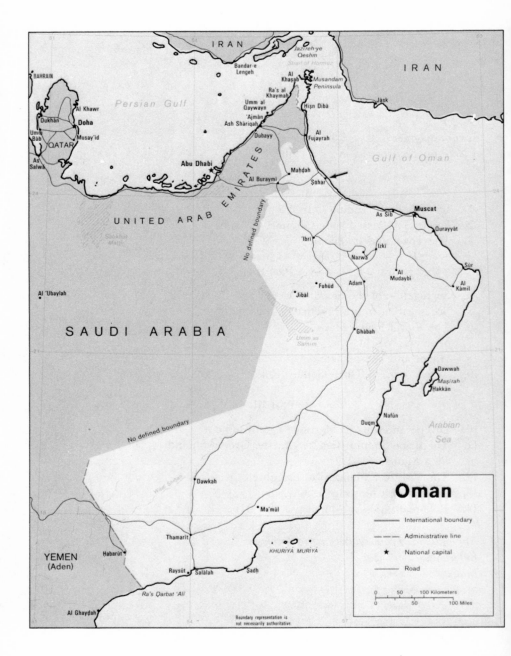

Preface

This book has been written with two kinds of reader in mind: primarily, the general reader with an interest in Arabia or in gender roles, and secondarily, my anthropological colleagues. I have tried to portray the lives of Soharis in everyday terms and to avoid words and expressions that are poorly understood beyond social science circles. I have also attempted to let the material speak, to address questions and issues that seemed to arise from the material itself, rather than problems that academic anthropology has come to judge important. It goes without saying that my account is still a subjective one. Sohar is seen through my eyes, and the material speaks through my voice. For this I make no apologies. When one human being describes another human being, social situations, or even whole societies, objectivity is, by its very definition, impossible—save where the most superficial, measurable qualities are concerned. It is my conviction that much social science would stand to gain by greater readiness to acknowledge this predicament.

While writing this book, I was often frustrated, feeling that I was pulled in two opposed and irreconcilable directions. On the one hand, I wanted to describe life in Sohar, merely to render what I saw and heard, while leaving the reader free to make his own reflections. On the other hand, I wanted to "explain" this life, to utilize my privileged familiarity with Sohar and Soharis so as to "guide" the reader on his way to an understanding, as well as to expose the inner workings of Sohari society. To approximate the latter aim, I have at times felt it useful to compare life in Sohar with that of other cultures so as to throw its distinctive features into relief. It has been a battle between the commonsensical and the anthropological parts of myself and the end product may be something of a monster: a book too academic from the general reader's point of view and too disorganized and "superficial" from the anthropologist's point of view. The conflict and resultant product may yet not be only of my own making, but arise from the failure of anthropologists generally to enter into communication with the public. The gap between anthropologists and general readers is immense, not only as between our languages, but also in our ways of thinking about the world. This I think most unfortunate. If anthropologists are to help make a better world, they must be able to communicate with that world. What is more, I think it would be most beneficial to our discipline if we subjected ourselves to the rigor of rethinking the world in everyday terms with the opportunities for new discoveries which such a venture entails; anthropologists often seem to mystify themselves, as well as their readers, by using excessive jargon. Finally, I also suspect that one can expect to grasp the lives of people more clearly by using the kinds of words which people themselves use.

To protect the anonymity of Sohari friends, all names in this book are fictitious. The photographs are likewise selected in such a way as to make identification of pseudonyms impossible.

Acknowledgments

I wish to express my gratitude to many people who, in various ways, have given me their encouragement, support, counsel, and criticism.

First and foremost I am indebted to my husband, Fredrik Barth. He shared in the field work with me, let me use freely of his notes, and spent innumerable hours tirelessly discussing every aspect of this book with me. Though the description that follows is quite different in theme and focus from his own, as will be revealed in his forthcoming book on Sohar, his invaluable participation in both field work and the analysis of field data makes this work as much his as mine.

I wish to thank the Omani authorities for their hospitality and invaluable practical help. It must indeed be rare for anthropologists to be so warmly received, yet left entirely free to pursue their work on their own conditions. In particular, I wish to thank H.E. Nassir Seif El-Bualy, H.E. Sheikh Amor Ali Ameir, H.E. Najib El Zubeidi, and H.E. the Wali of Sohar, Hamud bin Nasr.

Many persons offered us friendship and hospitality while we were in Muscat and Sohar. I owe a special debt of thanks to Leila Ingrams, Bill and Diana Peyton, and Jack and Ottley Sims. I am also grateful to Saskia and Marteen Schröder, Mr. and Mrs. Spiker, and Martha Holst. I would also like to thank the staffs of Ilaco and of Prospection for their kindness and help.

I owe a great debt of thanks to Jon Anderson for unstinting generosity with his time and knowledge in commenting on and discussing the issues raised in this book and for steering me away from innumerable pitfalls. I am also much indebted to Vilhelm Aubert, Jan Brögger, Ann Cornelisen, John Gulick, the late Margaret Gulick, Ulf Hannerz, Bill Peyton, Michelle Z. Rosaldo, and Mayling Simpson-Herbert for encouragement, counsel, and criticism of the work.

I wish to thank Wenche Amundsen, Eli Langmyhr, and Lillan Steen for their secretarial help.

The field work was financed by a grant from the Norwegian Research Council for Science and the Humanities, and the manuscript was written in the period 1976–78 while I held a stipend from them. I should like to express my sincere thanks to that organization for providing such excellent facilities and freedom to pursue my research.

I shall always be deeply grateful to the people of Sohar for sharing their lives with me and extending me their friendships.

A Note on Transliteration

In spelling Arabic names and concepts, I have tried as simply as possible to provide the nonspecialist reader with an idea of how the words are pronounced, while at the same time rendering them recognizable to one who knows Arabic. I have not distinguished long from short vowels, nor the several distinct consonants that to an untrained English ear can be grouped under "s," "t," and "h." I use the sign "ᶜ" for a guttural sound rendered in Arabic script by the letter *ain*, and "ᵓ" for the glottal stop. These are usually, but not always, indicated. "Kh" and "x" indicate a fricative quite similar to the German *ch*, and "gh" indicates another, related sound farther forward in the mouth. "Dh" and sometimes "z" indicate the soft "th" sound of English, as in "the" rather than "think." Because I have also attempted to retain such spellings as may be already familiar to the reader (for example, "Muscat" and "Koran"), this does not represent a consistent scheme for transliteration, but hopefully an acceptable compromise.

PART
1

CHAPTER 1

✦

Introduction: Finding Our Way

"But this, madam, is Oman!"

My husband, Fredrik Barth, and I, who are both social anthropologists, lived in Oman for eight months—from March to August 1974 and from December 1975 to January 1976. Six months of the time we spent in the town of Sohar, which is situated on the northern coast. It is the story of the everyday life of people in this town, and among them particularly the life of Arab women, that I try to tell in this book.

I felt immensely happy and fortunate to be allowed to do this research in Oman. For as long as I can remember, I have harbored a dream to meet the real, authentic Arabia. Oman was till 1970 a closed country, uniquely representative of traditional Arabic civilization, almost untouched by modernization. And as H.E. the Omani Ambassador to London said when we applied for visas and research permits: "These last two years we have had visits from journalists, archaeologists, architects, botanists, geologists—but I believe we have had no anthropologists so far." He could hardly have said anything more encouraging to us!

Our choice of Sohar as the place for field work followed the advice of the Minister of Information, H.E. Sheikh Amor Ali Ameir. We had expressed our preference for a larger town where people of diverse local traditions meet and mingle, and mentioned Sohar, Rustaq, and Ibri as alternatives. The Minister was terse in his reply: "Sohar is a very interesting place. Of course, so are the other places." We never regretted the decision.

Among all the many things in Sohar that made me bless again and again my good luck in being placed just here, perhaps the outstanding one was the use of the *burqa*, or facial mask, by women there. It seemed to epitomize or embody crucial features of women's identity, honor, and grace in Sohar. And in Oman, the *burqa* is worn by townswomen only in the northernmost part of the region known as the Batinah coast, of which Sohar is the major town.

3

With a population of approximately 15,000, Sohar is the third largest town in Oman. It is situated in the most fertile and densely populated region of Oman. The Batinah coast is a narrow green strip, rarely more than three kilometers wide, which stretches along by the sea from Sib in the south (a few kilometers north of Muscat) to the boundary between Oman and the United Arab Emirates in the north. Approximately one third of the people of Oman live within this region. Sohar is also the "capital" of a governorate encompassing some 22,000 people. The town has a past history of legendary splendor and grandeur and was extolled by an acknowledged geographer, Istakhri, in the tenth century after Christ as "the emporium of the whole world" (Williamson 1973). Today Sohar is a modest provincial center, but not seen as such by local eyes. It enjoys a reputation throughout Oman as a very good place. It has been chosen by several of the oil-rich sheikhs in the neighboring Gulf area as a site for new residences. And Soharis themselves, male and female, share a confident conviction that is equal to any other civilized town as a place to live.

During our first visit to Oman, we also conducted a brief six weeks' field work in Bahla, a town in the interior (see, for example, Barth 1978), and we spent, all in all, about a month in Muscat/Mattrah. These experiences served to impress upon us what aspects of life in Sohar are distinctive to it, and what traits are more generally Omani.

Statements by Soharis, as well as our own impressions, indicate that Sohar is representative of the northern part of the Batinah coast, which again is a distinctive culture area within Oman, with characteristic customs and traditions. The population, though predominantly Arab, is comprised of a motley variety of peoples, for example, Baluch, Ajam (Persians), Zidgalis—peoples who are proudly heedful of their ethnic identity and have different mother tongues, although Omani citizenship is a paramount value to all.[1] It must be stressed that my work was concentrated to the Arabs of Sohar. When in the following I use the term *Soharis*, it must be understood as a shorthand abbreviation for the numerically predominant Arab population of Sohar.

There were several reasons why I chose to concentrate on the Arabs of Sohar to the exclusion of other ethnic groups. First, among the languages traditionally spoken in Sohar, I know only Arabic, and I definitely wished to work without the aid of an interpreter, so as to facilitate easy and direct communication. (But even if I should have wished to use an interpreter, I do not know where one could have been found. An Arab *woman* with a knowledge of English at a less than exorbitant price! See my husband's difficulties in obtaining a male interpreter, forthcoming.) Many Baluch women do speak Arabic, but only in settings where they intermingle with Arabs. Among themselves, they speak Baluch. This meant that much as I

---

[1] A complete description of these groups is given in Barth's forthcoming book.

would have loved to associate with Baluchi women, to understand them I would have had constantly to interrupt their spontaneous flow of conversation so as to ask them what it was they were saying. I did not wish to play any such role of interrogator. It is a way of interrelating that corresponds poorly with both my conception of field work and my own style. Second, my husband and I decided on a division of labor. He was mainly interested in the cultural pluralism of Sohar, the relationship between the different groups of Sohar—as differentiated along ethnic, religious, and occupational lines—as well as the questions of maintenance and change of these different cultural traditions. He would move in the public world of men and take part in their important activities that were connected with economics, politics and religion. I would move among the women—if not out of necessity, at least out of deference to their manners and traditions. In consequence, my concerns would follow their concerns, the life that unfolded within the homes and neighborhoods—a life that—alas—might seem to both Middle Eastern men and their anthropological counterparts less significant because it is more limited in scope and importance than the male concerns. I did face the choice, however, of whether to strive for a more extended, but, of necessity, more superficial, acquaintance with the many, or an in-depth understanding of the few. I chose the latter course, because it suits best both my professional interests and personal inclination.

I felt immensely privileged to have had this opportunity to relate to women whose lives portray a degree of seclusion and self-containment which, even for the Middle East, is rare and perhaps even nonexistent today. I was fascinated at this chance to learn something of what the world looked like from behind those eyes and those masks. How did they regard it, how did they experience it, what did it feel like to encounter the world with a mask between it and them? Questions, so much to the fore in the West, as to *how* much subjugated they were, held little interest to me. (I deliberately say how much rather than whether, for one glimpse at an Omani woman fitted out in her shiny black *abba*—long black cloak—and startling black *burqa* would be enough to convince many Western women that she *is* downtrodden.) I had come primarily to learn about *their* lives, not to find confirmation for my own theories. I was interested in Sohari woman's experience of herself, rather than my experience of her. It soon became plain from the way these women walked, sat quietly, and talked, that they did not see their lives in terms of unmitigated subjugation—on the contrary, they questioned the merit and even the justice of ways instituted to enhance woman's life and freedom in neighboring Gulf states. Western women may bewail their "backwardness" and failure to see and seek "their own good." I have great difficulties with stereotypes and categories that purport to accommodate the lives of all women everywhere, and, no doubt, so would Soharis. Their sayings are permeated with expressions such as "Some are like this, others are like that." How foreign, no, how repulsive to their thinking would be the suggestion that all women everywhere should follow the same course!

We arrived in Oman only three-and-a-half years after the country had been opened to the outside world following years of stringent isolation. It has recently, with good reason, been characterized as "The Last Corner of Arabia." Sultan Said bin Taimur had a deep suspicion of modern trends and changes and had used his absolute power to isolate himself and his country from the world at large. Age-old traditions were maintained, and automobiles, radios, cement houses, even sunglasses were forbidden. For an estimated population of three-quarters of a million, only a single elementary school was provided (for boys), and anyone who obtained secondary education abroad was refused reentrance.

Times changed drastically, however, when Sultan Qaboos bin Said overthrew his father in July 1970 and, aided by a sudden flow of oil wealth, plunged his country into a development program that only oil-rich neighbors such as Abu Dhabi and Kuwait can rival. Hundreds of foreign experts were called in, and ambitious development contracts were signed.

Besides beginning to change the very face of Oman, these experts also brought in an entirely new style of life. Houses were constructed for them, equipped with electrical generators and every thinkable—or, as the case may be—unthinkable, convenience. Though most of them lived their "expert" lives on the edge of Omani society, they were an integral part of the scene when we arrived. The style of life they had introduced also had an inevitable effect on our own reception and position in society—though it was not till the second field trip, when we ourselves, due to my advanced pregnancy, lived like them, that we realized quite how much.

"What," the Minister of Information wanted to know, "was the purpose of our project?" We promised him that a book about Sohar would come out of it—but what kind of a book, and what use would it serve? Thinking back, we must have seemed to him even more of an anomaly than we realized. The Omani government, it turned out, was well aware of the importance of making the country known to the world and since 1971-72 had invited world-renowned photographers, seasoned journalists and travel writers, and a variety of television teams to do that job. Beautiful volumes full of color pictures and a variety of highly readable books have already appeared.[2] What is more, these authors and photographers were clearly important people, who lived accordingly and worked swiftly and efficiently. We too were experts of a kind. Yet we proposed to live for months in an ordinary Arab house, with no electricity, no running water, and no air-conditioning. We would also have no transportation. What

---

[2] See, for example, Darlow, M., & Fawkes, R. 1976. *The Last Corner of Arabia*. London: Quartet Books; Hill, A., & Hill, D. 1977. *The Sultanate of Oman—A Heritage*. London: Longman; *Oman*. Department of Information. Muscat. 1972.

for? I think now that it was not the project so much as we ourselves that did not make sense to the Minister and made him doubtful. He pointed out all kinds of difficulties that forebade the failure of our endeavor. Soharis, naturally, would extend us hospitality—that is a common virtue of all Omanis—but we would surely succumb to the hardships of local life. The heat of summer is terrible, and we would not even have a fan to alleviate the strain. There would be no hotel for us, and no available house to rent. Were we prepared to live in a tent? We suggested we might, if necessary, build a house of adobe or palm thatch. No, remonstrated the Minister; building materials were both very short in supply and extremely expensive. He had yet other objections. What would we eat? Without a car, how did we expect to get around? Distances in Sohar are great. . . . Our venture was doomed to fail. At last Fredrik, not a little annoyed at being taken so lightly, protested categorically, "We have worked many other places in the Middle East, and everywhere such difficulties have been surmountable,[3] so why not here?" Perhaps our resoluteness was finally impressed upon the Minister. His brusque expression dissolving in a cordial smile, he announced: "You will be the guests of Oman, and our government will cover all your expenses while you wait for formalities to be cleared, and transport to Sohar." All too well aware that such a wait at the cost of $80 per night (the standard rate at the cheapest of Mattrah's three hotels) would swiftly exhaust our modest research funds, I exclaimed spontaneously, "This could not have happened any other place in the world!" To which the Minister, with appropriate pride, simply replied, "But this, madam, is Oman!"

So it was. Throughout all our stay we were incessantly impressed by the unsurpassable grace and hospitality of the people.

The Minister had, however, anticipated a number of real problems, some of which only became clear to us toward the end of our field work. The most persistent difficulty was no doubt to explain to people just what kind of persons we really were, what our competence and social place might be, what we were really doing. Few understood what kind of book we were there to write—but that did not seem to matter too much. We were there with the authorization of the government. That reassured them.

A government car took us to Sohar. We were given letters of confirmation to present to the local Governor. The two-hour ride took us through a very flat and relatively colorless plain that stops abruptly along a featureless coast. The area seemed immensely monotonous as we drove through it. Sohar, though reputed to be Sinbad the Sailor's birthplace, turned out to be little more than an overgrown village, strung out along a gray beach on the Indian Ocean. On the rare clear day, such as it was when we ar-

[3] Fredrik Barth had worked previously in the Middle East among Kurds in Iraq, Swat Pathans in Pakistan, Marri Baluch in Pakistan, and Basseri nomads in Iran. I had done field work in a poor quarter of Cairo.

rived, a low line of blue mountains appears beyond the plain. Along the entire coastline is a two- or three-mile-wide strip of date orchards, but so brownish and dusty as to give the landscape a strange, lifeless appearance. The town itself, we were sad to see, lacks the simple beauty of traditional Arabic architecture and is composed in part of palm-leaf huts, in part of cement houses—in some quarters of town, abandoned and collapsing. Only occasional glimpses of colorfully dressed women in side streets would relieve this initial feeling of drabness. An imposing fort is the administrative center for the district. It had also, the driver informed us, served well into the 1950s as the population's place of refuge in times of unrest. From this fort rules the Governor, and we were appropriately taken directly to him.

In response to a telegram from the Minister (the only swift mode of communication from the government to the provinces) the Governor, Hamud bin Nasr, had already found a house for us situated in the town's center, midway between the fort and the market. It was a large cement house built around a central open courtyard. It contained five rooms, all identical. The style was typical of modern Sohari houses: plastered walls, cement floor, and wooden shutters; one floor, with a roofed veranda and access to the roof; a pit latrine and a well with brackish water. The bathroom was simply one more square, empty room, within which you splash about the water from a bucket you could fill in your well. It looked as if the house had not been in use for quite some time, for all the rooms were buried in dust. There was no furniture. The monthly rent was 100 Rials—somewhat more than $300. We balked at the price, but were assured that such were the prices in Sohar. We assured the Governor that all we really needed was a simple one-room house: the town seemed to present a great variety of alternative kinds of housing, ranging from the substantial type offered to us to simpler structures and flimsy palm thatch huts. So we asked the Governor's help in finding a more inexpensive alternative. Two days later, Abdullah, who was to become a very good friend, turned up and offered us a one-room house he owned for 40 Rials per month. The building was in such poor condition that the price seemed exorbitant. But we had no choice.

In the meantime we had been to the market to buy some bare essentials for day-to-day living: one pair of bed sheets and pillow cases; a frying pan; one cooking pot; a pair each of cups, plates, glasses, and cutlery; a primus; and a paraffin lamp. Later, when we learned Sohari etiquette of hospitality, we also bought a tray; a thermos bottle for coffee; a few bowls and soup dishes; and mocca cups. Our possessions on arrival were limited to one suitcase containing our clothes and cameras, as well as two mattresses and mosquito nets, which the driver who brought us to Sohar had encouraged us to buy in Mattrah. He doubted, he said, that such things would be available in Sohar—and in this he proved to be right. This did not mean, as it turned out, that Soharis sleep simply on mats on the floor. On the contrary, they have comfortable beds, which they buy from Dubai, along with most of the other furnishings they use for both comfort and embellishment. Restricted as we were, for both practical and financial reasons, to the market in Sohar, our home remained in consequence spartanly equipped compared to even the poorest of homes that we visited in Sohar.

Thus set up, we roamed the market and the town to get a feeling for the place and were anxious and ready to get to know the people. All our work and most of our personal sense of well-being would depend upon the quality of the relationships that we were able to establish. We had come in the hope of learning as much as possible about their life and how they subjectively experienced it themselves, and we could do so only provided they were willing to let us into their lives. As social anthropologists generally do, we wanted to rely on the method known as *participant observation*: gaining insight into the lives of others by using only ourselves as instruments. There would be no questionnaires or formal interviews. We wished to be able to truly participate in the life of Soharis, to share as much as possible in all manner of activities while making ourselves as unobtrusive as possible. To approximate this aim, we would need to learn the "rules" of the culture, the correct Sohari ways of doing things, and to observe those in our own behavior. The anthropologist is painfully aware that the ideal of true participation is merely that—an ideal. She will always remain an outsider to another culture and a foreign community. But depending upon her own sensitivity and ability to adapt, and the people's ability and willingness to let her into their lives, the anthropologist can generally move further than most in the direction of genuine participation, rapport, and empathy. And obviously, friendship with a range of members of the community is the *sine qua non* of good field work.

Fredrik and I were faced with rather different tasks. Because Sohari women observe strict seclusion and do not appear in the market or other public places, I was entirely dependent on gaining entry into private homes. Fredrik, on the other hand, could roam about the market like Sohari men do. He could linger at shops and establish contacts there. On the other hand, I was more fortunate in having a full command of Arabic. Thus I expected to be able to establish easy and spontaneous relationships once I had made contact. Fredrik planned to work with an interpreter. As it turned out, Fredrik also worked primarily without the assistance of an interpreter; this was not by choice, but because of the constraints imposed by our meager research funds—as measured against Omani prices. We simply could not afford to pay the 160 Rials ($500) a month which would secure the services of a person with a command of English—though there were many such in Sohar, because of the extensive labor migrations so long practiced by men.

Our house was surrounded, as were others in the town, by a compact wall to safeguard the privacy so valued by Soharis, so it gave no immediate access to a neighborhood. Peeping through the gate, I could catch occasional glimpses of women in colorful flowing dresses hurrying past, and, if I showed myself, they offered a friendly smile and nodded at me. But as *they* did not linger by the gate, I knew that for me to do so would not carry me very far. Our neighborhood did have a public well—that communal institution that has solved the initial contact problems of so many a female anthropologist. But in Sohar, characteristically, it was not a place where women congregated to gossip. They fetched their water and left, with only a passing graceful greeting to their neighbors. That calm, quiet self-control, that mute self-assured poise, was to prove the major obstacle all the way through to getting to know, really to know, the Soharis.

So, in the event, we both ended up roaming the marketplace and wandered aimlessly about. We lingered much at the shop of Babuji, an Indian who spoke fluent English (as well as Arabic, Persian, Baluch, and several Indian languages) and was extremely friendly. He had lived in Sohar for two years, and more than ten years in Oman. It was here that we made our breakthrough: we met the men who invited us to the wedding described in the next chapter, and we met Hamid, Babuji's shop assistant. Hamid took me under his wing and invited me home to meet the women of his family. They received me more warmly and openly than I could even have dared to dream of—they had me try on their facial masks and jewelry, and they answered freely to every question. Latifa, Khadiga, Feyza, Sheikha, and all their neighbors—the road to them was opened at Babuji's shop.

The road to a genuine understanding and knowledge of Sohari women's consciousness of themselves and their world was to prove far longer and more difficult than what this first encounter seemed to promise. And this even though the women themselves seemed to be entirely honest in their efforts to incorporate me into their lives and to share with me what they had to share. I encountered nothing but warmth and hospitality. They would vie with each other to have me visit them most often. With great tact, tolerance, and sensitivity, they would notice any doubt or confusion on my part and guide me in their ways without ever putting pressure on me to give up my own standards and conform to their conventions. In this way, they always gave me the feeling of being accepted and respected as a real person, rather than of being an anomaly, as I had expected.

My difficulty was, paradoxically, that precisely because of these qualities for which I came to admire them so and which they seemed to have developed to perfection, they had little to offer me of the kinds of things which figure as "information" in an anthropologist's notebook. Because of their tact, sensitivity, dignity, and tolerance, they did not gossip and thereby tell me about neighbors, acquaintances, and local events. They did not judge others and thereby reveal their own values. They did not chatter idly—indeed, they often hardly even talked. Their gatherings were quiet, serene congregations permeated by silence. Most of the time, each and every one would sit, introverted, gazing out into space, absorbed in her own private world, or so it seemed. Alternatively, her attention would be fixed on the embroidery of a *kummi*, or man's cap—needlework that requires both great care and concentration. Sometimes I could be present with women on visits extending for a full eight hours and be able to count the sentences exchanged between them as no more than a score. The fear of "angels passing through the room," which seems to trouble Westerners, is foreign to Oman.[4]

Under these circumstances, I had the constant enervating feeling of not knowing what was going on. What were they really thinking and feeling? And equally to my dismay, I felt that I too must always be reserved and observe tea-party manners in order to fit into their patterns—a manner of behavior that suits my own temperament poorly. I was all too conscious that I was acting a role, and I suffered from it. Later I understood that it was a role enforced upon me by my own uncertainty, rather than Sohari expectations. But this reflects the common tendency of the anthropologist—dependent as she is upon the good will of the people with whom she lives—to underestimate the extent to which they regard her as different from themselves.

With these first contacts, we very swiftly experienced a new embarrassment: the social implications of our delipidated, one-room house. The first hint of this occurred on our very first day in the house. The gracious hosts at a wedding celebration had offered to take us to the party by car. We described the location of our house in detail, and our hosts assured us that they knew where it was. Yet, when they arrived, quite a bit too late, it was plain from their bewildered expressions that they could hardly believe that this was it. They apologized for being late, saying they had been driving around the neighborhood trying to locate us.[5] As we were invited to further Sohari homes, we felt increasingly ill at ease with our own. Finally, after two weeks, we went back to the Governor and persuaded him to let us have the house that he had first offered us, but at the reduced rate of 60

---

[4] I had pondered the question of to what extent Oman is, in this respect, unique within the Middle East, or whether other Gulf states perhaps resemble it, so there might be some kind of Arab Gulf "culture area" that is significantly different from other parts of the Middle East, thus I was delighted when I recently came across a guidebook to Qatar and found that its "Customs" section opened with the subheading "Silence:" "Unlike Europeans, Arabs consider that silence is companionable. [It] is part of the indirect method of conversation" (*Dunhill Guide to Qatar*, p. 4).

[5] Indeed, before Abdullah rented the house to the next tenant, a Jordanian schoolteacher, he revamped the placed entirely, painted it, and provided it with new gate and door, a new well and toilet, and a power generator, which provided electricity in the evening. The new rent was one fourth what he charged us.

Rials ($310) per month. That he consented to this price was no doubt partly due to my skill in bargaining (developed during my stay in the slums of Cairo), but also, I think, due to his own feeling that the shelter we had found was glaringly incongruous with our position. Our shift back to the bigger house helped, but its very spartan equipment clearly continued to puzzle our acquaintances.

The truth of other of the Minister's warnings and misgivings also started catching up with us: most forcibly, the effects of the steadily increasing heat. We had thought that if Soharis could tolerate it, so could we. But even they could not. From the end of March, they could be heard commiserating, with an increasing pitch of despair, "The heat is coming, oh, now it will soon be upon us!" We thought their anxiety feigned and exaggerated; it could not be *that* bad. But it was. As May approached, the temperature rose to a high of 45°C (110°F) in the shade by day, and, with little shade and a humidity of 80–90 percent, the days were sheer torture. Sohari women adapted to the heat by rarely moving outside the immediate neighborhood between 8 A.M. and 5 P.M.; the men adapted by moving slowly and involving themselves in nothing unnecessary. We struggled on, soaked in perspiration, along the shadowless lanes. Our friends were concerned and warned us that "the sun will be upon you." We had no choice. We could not afford, or even obtain, the necessary taxis, and we had to see a number of different persons each day, or, at the least, almost every day. But if the days were only barely endurable, borne only by straining my will power to the utmost, the nights drove me to true and utter despair. A temperature around 40°C (100°F), without the slightest movement of air, made me develop the claustrophobic sensation that I could not breathe.

Our modern cement house was wholly unfunctional for this climate, because the walls absorbed the heat to such an extent that at 10 P.M. they radiated heat like an electrical oven. And, unlike many inhabitants of modern houses in Sohar, we did not have an electrical generator by night—one more incongruity of our status. Soharis slept in their yards or on the roofs of their homes. We also tried this, but were disturbed by the continual barking and fighting of the packs of stray wild dogs, not to speak of the roosters! Sohari roosters have the characteristic perversion that they crow all night through, in a perpetual cacaphony. One in particular drove me mad. It belonged to one of our next-door neighbors and at midnight, it used to climb to its roost, from where it would sit and crow directly down into our courtyard. The whole night through. I eventually went to its mistress and politely offered her an exorbitant price for her to slaughter the animal, leaving her the meat in the bargain. She accepted, and for awhile life seemed slightly more bearable with the one, strangest voice of the chorus missing. But after a few days, the racket seemed as bad as ever—and lo and behold, there, silhouetted against the night sky, was a familiar shape on the neighbor's roof. As it turned out, the neighbors had chosen merely to tie and gag the monster, and he had escaped again. In fact, all our feeble efforts to ameliorate our physical discomforts were essentially fruitless; and had not our friends Jack and Ottley Sims occasionally been so good as to come and take us to an occasional night's respite in their air-conditioned house, we would surely not have been able to persevere. At the height of summer, we were even allowed to move into the air-conditioned guesthouse of the Ilaco consultancy company for a week. Although our temporary move resulted in an additional five kilometers walking in the sun, it was only thanks to this kindness that we were able to carry on through our last weeks in Sohar in 1974.

Independent of these physical struggles, a pervasive sense of frustration threatened to overtake me. My friends gave abundantly of their company, their warmth, their selves without ever obtruding upon each other. Their company was solace for the tired mind. But for someone like myself, anxious to probe into their inner worlds and minds, their feelings and thoughts, so as to learn how they experience life and the world, they were as elusive as could be.

They were also boring. Nothing ever happened. Day in, day out, with only the most meager, unrevealing "information" recorded in my notebooks. Notes on who had been with whom, for how long, at whose places, scraps of conversation, such as who had been ill with what, and what was now the price of gold in Dubai. . . . But their thoughts, their feelings—what lurked behind the ever-present gracious façade—these remained an enigma.

Behind the gracious façade. . . . What made me think that their thoughts and feelings were behind their courteous composure and that their tact and tolerance were a mere façade? Was there any indication that what Soharis thought and felt in their private selves was in any sense *truer* than the courtesy and poise that they displayed? Today, with the insight gained from working through my notes, and writing this book, I would say no. The joys and sorrows, triumphs and defeats of Soharis are truly private, rarely even shared among the best of friends. But that does not make pretense and sham out of their behavior. Yet, this is not to say that Soharis make no such distinction. They are aware of pretenses, deception, and make-believe, as, for example, when they say that people will act *as if* they did not know compromising truths even when everyone knows, or when they are concerned about what people may think, though they know that these thoughts will never be spoken. What I failed to sense then was that, to Soharis, the "as if" is as true as the private knowledge. One's private feelings should remain private. Theirs is a society where thoughts are indeed free. One should not grope into the minds of others. What really matters is how the other acts, not what he or she "really" thinks. Tact, courtesy, and hospitality are the supreme values of this society.

The distinctive Sohari way is perhaps most clearly revealed in women's

attitude to gossip. Sohari women, if they are very close friends, will sometimes talk about women not present. But very rarely will this assume the
form of censure or criticism. It is more of a conveyance of information.
They may thus, to a considerable extent, become informed about each
others' dark secrets. But they emphatically do not traffic in condemnation
and scandal. To "carry the talk," as the Sohari expression goes, is very
shameful. During our first stay in Sohar, I too tried to conform to these
exacting standards even while deploring their consequences in the paucity
of ensuing field notes. Whatever one may think of gossip, it is certainly a
most useful source of information about people, events, and attitudes.
During my second visit, with the awareness of so little time at my disposal,
I decided to reveal my true character, so to speak. I would run the risk of
being thought a gossip by initiating gossip myself, probing and questioning and thereby getting hold of the invaluable "information." Aware of
their standards, I often felt rude and tactless. Yet it worked. And if my
friends labeled me a gossip they were—characteristically—too tactful ever
to let me sense it. It should be clear, in other words, that it was I, and not
Soharis, who initiated much of the talk that figures as gossip in this book.
I have tried to mark in the text where this is the case. Although my intuition tells me that they did not entirely dislike it, but enjoyed the spice and
variety that I thereby added to their otherwise monotonous days, I must
emphasize my own intrusion.

I realized then that I probably could have done more of this from the
start. My friends never expected me to be like them. Theirs is a world
made up of peoples with distinctly different customs—Baluch, Bedu, Indians, Egyptians, and, in their view, each set of customs is right for those
who practice it. So was mine. They found it natural that my husband and
I occasionally walked together, though for them to do so with their
husbands would be a shame. They even encouraged me to bring my husband along on visits to them and took great pleasure in his company,
though they would not dream of talking with an unrelated Arab man.
They had me try on their jewelry, *burqa*s and dresses, but never expected
me to dress as they did. My long, wide "Western" dress with long sleeves
was correct for me. What they could *not* understand was that I was so
poor in dresses and jewelry. They each had thirty to fifty outfits; I had a
meager three. They wore golden jewelry worth up to 1,000 Rials; I had
only my wedding ring.

It was partly because of these attitudes and understandings on their
part that our second visit, in 1975–76—distinctly less "participant" in its
overt form—proved both more productive and congenial than the first,
though it lasted only a third as long. We lived in a prefabricated modern
house recently vacated by other "experts," we rode in a government car,
and we were even for a brief period provided with a field assistant from the
Ministry of Information—all of them conveniences that also provided us

with an aura of importance and prestige. I suspect that it was not till then that *we* made sense to the Soharis. And we found that we gained many times as much insight during these brief two months as in the previous four. Other factors also helped us. First, I was pregnant. That may have established me as more of a "real" woman. But what is more, by *returning* to Sohar—not merely materializing, staying, and then disappearing forever as did most other foreigners—we had irrefutably demonstrated our involvement with, and perhaps even our affection for, the people of Sohar. Finally, we came direct from a six weeks' exhausting journey in India, and I was relieved just to sit and not have to talk. So I was thankful for—and therefore more receptive to—their gentle and low-key nonverbal communication, their gestures, glances, and silences. Perhaps they felt that I was more in tune with them; perhaps *they* felt more accepted.

When we left the second time, they did not ask whether we would return, but when. And would I bring the child?

CHAPTER 2

✦

Sohar: The First Exotic Glimpse

We would have to penetrate the very quaintness and exoticism that now fascinated and challenged us.

The first and perpetual task of social anthropology is to make sense of what happens in other societies. When one is confronted with the bustle of a strange and unknown place, a myriad of events of unclear significance, where does one start?

We were loitering about the covered market in Sohar. Large but unimpressive, it is composed of more than one hundred tiny, open-fronted shops facing directly onto narrow lanes; each shop is essentially identical to the next in its small range of wares. The scene has none of the raucousness often met in the Arab world: people are conspicuously polite to each other, speak in low voices, and move gently and gracefully in the crowd. A recently burned-down section of the market, open toward the beach, serves as a parking place for the increasing number of Landrovers, pickup trucks, and cars. And here, in the glare and piercing heat of the sun, one sees the motley variety of people one would expect in a Middle Eastern market: villagers and townsmen, Bedouins on shopping trips, Indian merchants, fishermen, laborers. Men, dressed in immaculately white long shirts and embroidered caps—the usual Omani garb—dominate the scene, while women are almost totally absent.

We had joined the crowds and were wandering aimlessly; here we could watch activity and wait for something to happen. Three very well-dressed young men, in brilliantly white flowing robes and white headcloths with black goat-hair circlets in the Gulf style, were busy shopping and talking, and we picked up the comment that they were provisioning for a wedding. So we sought them out and were immediately invited to come; they were sorry that we had no tape recorder for the music and singing, but we could photograph and join the feast. In the typically gracious Omani way, they offered to fetch us later in the afternoon.

They were late to fetch us and offered excuses for having been delayed by the festivities, and we headed quickly toward their village of Salan so as not to miss more of the proceedings. The bridegroom's parents' home lay picturesquely on the sandy beach; it was a very substantial and well-built house with an open-arched veranda inside a large compound. Both house and fence were very clean and whitewashed. Numerous cars were parked outside. A large crowd of at least three hundred adults, mixed Baluch and Arabs, as well as droves of children, were gathered. There was a conspicuous segregation of the sexes, and the scene was highly spectacular. Outside the compound, under a palm awning, were the men, standing or sitting in the sand, dressed in their *dishdasha*s (snow-white ankle-length shirts with long sleeves) and picturesque head gears, turbans, skullcaps, or the usual Arabian headcloth. They were silent and poised.

Inside the compound, all the women and most of the children were sitting on brightly colored straw mats. They were dressed up in flamboyantly colored clothes and much gold and some silver jewelry: necklaces; ankle rings and bracelets; rings in their noses, on toes, and on fingers; and very beautiful gold decorations attached to their face masks (*burqa*s). This was our first chance to observe these masks at close quarters, and we were entirely fascinated: The masks differ in size and shape and color; some hide most of the face, while others just cover the cheeks, upper lips and lower part of the forehead; some are straight, others heart-shaped over the

The groom with his friends on the second day of the wedding festivities

cheeks; some have a curved nose, others a straight one. They all glowed in black with a golden purple or reddish sheen in the leatherlike material, and they gave the women a strange, deformed appearance, like crouching vultures. It was as exotic a scene as one could wish for.

Dancing and singing were in full swing, both in the male and female arenas. Outside the compound, two facing lines of male singers, accompanied by drummers, entertained a highly attentive but extremely quiet male audience. They sang a long sequence of different songs, each with conventionalized mimicry and graceful, coordinated movements. Sometimes the two lines sang alternately and moved and postured differently; for example, the one line crouched over walking sticks, lampooning Englishmen, while the other stood erect. The female singing inside the compound was much more repetitive, in both melody and movement. The two facing lines of women swung to the rhythm of a small band of male drummers and advanced and retreated in a highly standardized manner, sometimes sitting, sometimes standing arm-in-arm. The drum accompaniment was sensitive and melodious, and the drummers turned back and forth as alternate lines took up the song.

From time to time, male spectators came and threw coins in a big tray, thereby having their own praise sung by the women to the same repetitive

Male musicians and female singers at a wedding

tune. The singers went on and on and on in their high-pitched voices, without tiring. The audience also persisted in its poised, quiet, attentive manner. People hardly even spoke to each other. The money-throwing was the only sign there was of behavior drawing attention to the self. The quiet style and formality of such a large gathering on such a festive occasion was indeed remarkable and impressive.

Encouraged by our hosts' invitation freely to photograph the proceedings, we went ahead eagerly. The women withdrew, saying "No, No"; male relatives would have cut their throats had they been photographed. We argued that we had the men's permission, but the women's fear proved stronger. However, when the camera was packed away, they conversed freely and eagerly with us, showing much less modesty in movement and demeanor than we had expected.

Sometime during the proceedings, a friend of the groom offered to show us the nuptial hut, where the couple would spend their wedding night and the following seven-day honeymoon. It was built of date fronds, very tight and neat, approximately nine feet by six feet. The floor was covered with several layers of reed mats, with a red Persian carpet on top. A blue-and-white striped cotton sheet was stretched across the ceiling. Along the walls were large and small soft pillows in many colors. Above these pillows was a double, close-packed row of mirrors; above them again, the walls were decked with colorful dresses folded so as to display their embroidered necklines. From the ceiling were suspended bracelets, necklaces, ankle rings, and bits of vividly colored material. The jewelry, which was largely borrowed from relatives of the groom, was hung there "to make the bride happy." A general effect of opulence was achieved. Through a curtained hole in the wall, one directly entered the nuptial bed, which had covers and pillows in many colors. It was screened from outside by curtains, which gave a strong feeling of privacy. Everyone seemed confident of its beauty and not at all embarrassed by the intimacy of its purpose.

We were told that a couple, after entering the hut on the wedding night, spends the next seven days there, with no duties. They are attended by a female friend of the bride's mother, the *mikobra*, who accompanies the bride to her new home and stays there for the honeymoon period to provide support for her through the difficult transition period. She serves the couple food and water, washes their clothes, and takes care of their needs in every way "to make the honeymoon luxurious and successful."

Some of these customs were told to us spontaneously; and we could be interested in, and ask about, them, but hardly collect systematic information here in the middle of a wedding party. But even later, when we learned the details of expected procedure at a wedding—how much does such knowledge tell you about what it is like to be a fourteen-year-old girl fetched by strangers and placed in a nuptial hut together with a man she has never seen, or what it is like for the inexperienced husband, or how all that happens, ritually and intimately, determines the future life of the couple? Likewise, we knew that, in the crowd around us, some people were Arabs, some Baluch—but which were which, and what difference did it make? To get answers to such questions, we would have to penetrate the very quaintness and exoticism that now fascinated and challenged us. At least here we were *among* them, with an opportunity to see customs being practiced in real life and to observe some of the public attitudes and reactions. So we stayed on, trying to stretch our empathy to the utmost and to be as good company as possible to hosts and guests.

The singing finished around 11 P.M., and we were invited to come back for the main wedding, which was the next day around 2 P.M. Here was an inconvenient collision: one of our few other contacts, Abdullah, had already promised to take us to something or other the next afternoon—we had not understood what, but it had something to do with poetry, verse, or recitation. We wanted to see the wedding, but did not want to loose Abdullah's good will.

It may be easy enough to make the first, tentative contacts with people in a foreign environment. To act so that these contacts mature into real relationships is much more difficult and requires sensitivity to unfamiliar expectations and correct intuitions about what is desired and respected by others. To show our interest toward both Abdullah and our wedding hosts, and not disappoint either, we decided to separate next day, one going with Abdullah and the other to the wedding. So it was arranged that I would be fetched again by our hosts, around 2 P.M.

As it turned out, we both waited fruitlessly, Fredrik at the appointed meeting place, and I at home. Finally, I decided to find my way to the wedding by myself, and hired a car to drive me the few miles to Salan. The wedding seemed so splendid, I convinced the hosts that they should also fetch Fredrik, whom they found waiting resignedly in an empty date orchard.

On this, the culminating third day of the wedding celebration, there were even more people, even more beautifully dressed and bejeweled. Several women wore splendid golden jewelry on their foreheads. The little children had their hands and scalps decorated with *hennah*, a red, propitious paste. A lot of cars were parked outside the compound: Landrovers, trucks, and several taxis. Singing went on as it had the day before, but perhaps with even greater enthusiasm and intensity. About 4:30 P.M., the crowd got ready to go and fetch the bride, who lived in a village about a twenty-minute drive along the beach. The groom and his male friends were active in organizing the procession. Most guests, both men and women, were to participate, with all the males in the first cars and trucks, and the women in the tail end of the procession. Only a few years ago, this was all done by camel, but today such processions are fully motorized in Sohar. The groom was very attractively dressed, with a prominent silver dagger, dark-red *hennah* on hands and feet, and a white cap with a gold pattern (*kummi*). With much shouting, the procession got underway; the groom drove the first car, decorated with green banners and Omani flags. We were given places in a Landrover and joined the caravan. Arriving at the bride's home, we found a large crowd of guests—perhaps 150 people, mostly women. And who should prove to be in charge, apparently acting as the bride's guardian, but our friend Abdullah! This truly amazed us, for he had seemed such an excellent and enthusiastic informant and good friend and had volunteered to take us to the first wedding he knew of, yet had feigned utter ignorance of this one when we told him about it after our first day's invitation! Confronted with us, however, he greeted us with apparent approval and claimed just a moment ago to have sent his daughter to fetch us. Only later did we find the explanation of his bizarre behavior: the bride's guardian is ashamed on the occasion of her marriage, reportedly because of its sexual aspects. Therefore the marriage guardian pretends ignorance of the wedding, and when, as usually is the case, he is the bride's father, he even stays completely away from the whole affair, claiming that he has urgent business elsewhere and leaving the bride's mother in charge. As the bride's mother's brother, Abdullah did choose to be present at the festivities, but was too embarrassed to speak about the wedding.

The groom's male convoy gathered outside the bride's family's com-

At the gates of the bride's house, the guests await the bride's arrival (the groom is at the left, the bride's guardian in the middle)

pound while the women were admitted inside. I was taken in to see the bride, but all I saw was a shapeless bundle, completely hidden, except for hands and feet dyed with *hennah*, under a large green shawl and a black, long cloak (*abba*). The bride sobbed loudly, and Abdullah explained that she was afraid of what would happen that night, because she never saw the groom or any of his relatives, among whom her new home would be. She would live far away from her parents and relatives and would be dependent upon her husband's permission to visit them. We thought to ourselves that she also must be terrified of the impending sexual consummation of the marriage. Indeed, my friends later gave vivid accounts of the fighting and screaming that takes place when a terrified bride tries to defend herself. Reportedly, this frequently takes a form in which the consummation finally takes place without the groom having seen his wife's face.

The bride's mother was also crying. "Because she will lose the daughter's assistance in work," said Abdullah. Time and again we were struck by how consistently Soharis deemphasize emotions and prefer to dwell on more practical and impersonal aspects of relationships.

After much confusion and milling around, the women got ready to lead the bride out. They formed a tight ring around her and held a green shawl above her; she crouched under it while they covered her on all sides so that nobody could catch even a glimpse of her body as she was put into a waiting car. Approximately thirty to forty female friends followed her to Salan, to return again after a short stay and a meal.

There was much chaos around the return procession; apparently all the men should have gone first, then the women, but one car of women had gone off too soon and had to be called back. The procession drove very slowly through the town of Sohar, not along the beach, as it had come. The route and speed were clearly adjusted to show off to a maximum number of spectators, and with maximum effect. The next day we heard a number of people exclaiming; "Did you see, there must have been thirty cars!" And some added, "What an enormous bride price the groom must have paid!" (We later learned that he had paid approximately 2,500 Rials, or $7,500.)

On arrival at the groom's house, the bride disappeared from view; she was reportedly taken inside. The party continued, with female and male singing. Occasionally during the song, close female relatives of the bridegroom circulated and offered water or served tea and coffee; the men helped themselves outside the gate to water placed there, and adult male guests were likewise served tea and coffee. After awhile, the groom was taken outside to be shaved; he sat on the sand, with a group of singing men and boys around him. He was wearing a green sash, just like the one that had covered the bride. Green is the color of good fortune, we were told. Finally, a number of men started with a new set of songs: one line of

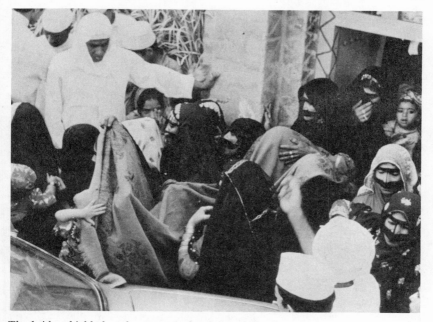

The bride, shielded under a green shawl, leaves her home

singers faced another line of men with big tambourines (plain, without rattles). Others made fires of dry palm leaves, to heat and tune the tambourines. Thereupon, the whole crowd of men, women, and children collected; and the groom, surrounded by his close friends, stood up; he was chanted to (and teased?) and looked a bit sheepish. Then a woman appeared with an incense burner, later with a tray and a bundle on her head. The crowd went outside, and a slow, three-part procession started: (1) men and boys carrying date-palm fronds, alone and en masse, and one or two carrying fire in burning fronds; then the tambourine men and singers, surrounded and followed by the big crowd; (2) the groom and his close friends, holding his hand and chanting continuously, accompanied by more of the crowd; (3) then finally the women, in a solid group, around drummers and dancers continuing their song, with many men and children spectators around them. At intervals the tambourine men would stop and sit down, then the fire would be lighted, the other two groups would also pause, all would sing for awhile in their respective places, and then move on. The effect was very picturesque: we moved slowly along the open coast in the sunset, with men carrying palm fronds, the light from the fires, the white figures of the men, the tambourines and the chanting, the smoke of the incense, the phalanx of black-cloaked women with their grotesque masks.

After moving, with pauses, for a long distance (maybe one kilometer) and time (maybe one hour), we finally arrived at a small, simple mosque, built inside the ruins of an old fort. A group of boys had been sitting waiting for us, silhouetted against the sky, on the ruins of one of the towers. Our arrival was timed just for sunset, as the *muezzin* (prayer leader) was calling to prayer. He continued his chant, and men went quietly to prayer without reacting to the racket of the crowd. Incense was passed before the crowd, so we could wave it toward our faces. The woman carrying the tray sat down, with a couple of other women, and laid out the clothes from the bundle. Fresh date fronds were cut and laid in a pile by the mosque well. Then the groom stripped, except for a loincloth, and was soaped and washed in water from the well. The clean clothes, including a golden knife and sandals, which had been carried in the bundle and laid out, were fetched, and the groom walked over with his friends to where the old woman was sitting on the carpet and carefully dressed in the new clothes. In the gathering darkness, the procession then returned in the same manner as we came, but by another route, along the beach.

By the time we arrived back at the groom's house, there was complete darkness, apart from the near-full moon in the partly overcast sky. Along the way, we were served coffee and again offered incense. The singing continued as we reentered the house. Then food was offered, finally, in fifteen to twenty big trays—first for the men outside, then a second round for the women inside. The groom and his friends ate last.

The meal consisted of very good spiced rice and a bit of meat, with water to drink, then sweet tea, then coffee. After eating most of the guests departed. Meanwhile, the bride was reported to be in the care of the *mikobra* and other women, perhaps inside the nuptial hut. We were told the groom would be led to the hut around 10–11 P.M., with only his closest relatives and companions present. They would all eat sweets and then retire, locking the nuptial hut from the outside while the groom locked it from the inside. After this, the marriage would be consummated.

We had the exhilarating feeling of having made a "scoop" at this wedding: the scene was so exotic and beautiful; we were among this graceful, pleasant crowd, sharing their interest in events of great importance to them; we had been terribly busy for two days and had profuse notes on strange customs and unique pictures on our films. Yet, "participating" in such a wedding, in the marginal position as a guest, cannot really help you so much in understanding Sohar in the sense of knowing what life is like for the local person. A wedding is a highly stylized and controlled affair; and Omanis have such extreme grace, tact, and self-control that very few revealing, discordant, or even spontaneous notes ever break through the polished surface. Perhaps the most important achievement was our implicit acceptance and our introduction to a large public, as well as the personal contacts that we had made. As it turned out, however, neither the groom nor his family and friends later played much of a role in our life in

Sohar—but the effect of this wedding as our debut party might still have been, indirectly, of importance. Several times later, we met people who said they recognized us from this wedding.

The actual material we had collected could only serve as a basis for formulating questions that might lead us deeper into Sohari society and culture. We might use—indeed, in the characteristic fashion of field anthropologists, we did use—this material as a starting point to collect detailed accounts of other weddings and other major life crises and ceremonies, in order to learn their symbolic elements and meanings in a more systematic way. Such symbols express underlying premises and values in a culture. We might also try to uncover some of the interests, passions, conflicts, and accommodations behind and beyond these polite and proper forms.

Bride prices have been high and are the object of haggling; but the Sultan had announced, only a month before this wedding, a reform banning all bride-price payments over 300 Rials ($900). Rumor had it that this payment had been much higher (possibly as much as ten times the legal amount) and that the groom might have had his in-laws called before the Wali (governor) to answer charges of extortion. Had this very expensive bride been chosen for her (reputed) beauty, family connections, wealth? Why did the bride's family accept this particular groom, and what effective bond did the marriage create for the future: would the two houses now be close, with intervisiting, gift-giving, social support? What part did the guests play, particularly the many Baluchis? What was their attitude to the differences in custom that were affirmed in this wedding? Indeed, the groom's mother was herself Baluch, but had assimilated to Arab ways since she had married an Arab. Had *she* been the male parent, then Mubarak, the groom, would have followed Baluch marriage customs instead, with standardized gifts in gold given to the bride herself, rather than bride price money presented to her father; with the nuptial hut in the *bride's* home, and the ritual procession one where the groom moved there; with no public proof of virginity after the wedding night; with only a three-day honeymoon. . . . Did these cultural differences merely serve to mark the fact of belonging to groups with different historical origins, or did they reflect, or even create, differences in social life between Arab and Baluch in the relations of spouses, in the organization of kinsmen, in the individual's position in local society?[1]

The anthropologist in the field is constantly troubled with multitudes of both specific and general questions that arise from every event she notices—while she is also aware of not even noticing or knowing about so much of what is happening around her. The understanding she can achieve, though she tries to systematize and check it, must always remain

[1] These are matters that are extensively treated in Barth's forthcoming book.

both incomplete and subjective: it can only reflect what she has managed to notice and what she has understood of its complex and multiple significances and contexts. And in seeking to present these results, she is simultaneously drawn in two opposed directions: first, of reporting real events and live persons; second, of expounding generalities, societal rules, and standards of custom and understanding that individuals must command and apply to manage their lives in the society. In the subsequent chapters, I shall try to do something of both of these, in the hope that it all adds up to a portrait of the way of life of real, living people in Sohar today.

CHAPTER 3

✣

The Town and Its People

The capital is Sohar which is on the sea; here reside many sea merchants who trade in ships with other countries. It is the most populous and wealthy town in Oman and it is not possible to find on the shore of the Persian Sea nor in all the land of Islam a city more rich in fine buildings and foreign wares than Sohar.

—Istakhri, ca. A.D. 950

The glamor of which this geographer speaks is long since gone. A matching description today, ten centuries later, would have to be incomparably more modest. Though still a town of merchants, Sohar is the end point rather than the hub of trade: small shopkeepers obtain the cheaper industrial products of the outside world from agents in larger neighboring centers (especially Dubai and Muscat), while some are also engaged in the export of dried limes to the Gulf and of poor quality dates to India. Apart from the local fishing vessels, a ship hardly ever anchors off Sohar's beach, which indeed provides no sheltering harbor. And none of the small fleet of trading *dhows* still plying the Gulf of Oman is owned by Soharis. Sohar has no place in the oil developments that have produced Oman's recent, and by no means spectacular, wealth; and though it is still one of the large centers of Oman, it obtains its share of this activity, and wealth, only indirectly, through the heightened level of development, commerce, and employment within the country as a whole.[1]

By the standards that today obtain in "the Persian Sea," Sohar is a backwater; and this fact is also clearly reflected in its undistinguished architecture of poor palm-frond huts (*barastis*) and small, unattractive modern cement buildings, intermixed in a styleless confusion, as noted in Chapter 1.

In consequence, for the newcomer to the scene with a vision of what an ancient and traditional Arab town should look like, Sohar at first sight can hardly fail to disappoint. For beauty in architecture, handicrafts, and local manufactured goods are no longer what distinguishes it. Its beach by the Indian Ocean is brownish-gray, not white, and littered with much garbage, including human feces, for it functions everywhere as the public

---

[1] Most matters treated in this chapter are handled much more fully in Barth's forthcoming book.

The town of Sohar, viewed from center and northward

toilet for males. Landrovers and cars use the beach as their main throughway, ploughing deep furrows in the sand. The oppressive heat, satiated with humidity, lays a near perpetual haze over the land. The date palms, of which there are many thousands in a belt lining the beach and extending two to three kilometers inland, stretch on in monotonous repetition along 250 kilometers of coast and lend little life and color to the drab landscape.

This is partly because the Arabian date palm, *phoenix dactylifera*, lacks the fresh green color of its near relative in the Mediterranean area, *phoenix canariensis* with which Europeans are more familiar. But chiefly responsible, I think, are the ever-present Landrovers and cars, which swirl masses of dust and sand onto the foliage, where, from a nearly total absence of rain, it settles and accumulates. Sohari tracks and roads were intended for pedestrians, donkeys, and camels. And much as Soharis admire and desire everything modern, residents all along the main throughfares bewail the discomforts that follow: "We cannot sit in our own compound yard for a moment without being covered with dust."

What Sohar lacks in physical, natural, and architectural beauty is amply compensated by the beauty of the manners of its people. Their grace and dignity are a source of continual human and aesthetic delight. The children are also of disarming physical beauty, and indeed most of the women, for the one lucky enough to observe them at close quarters. The men, too, impress with their fine features and graceful movements. Finally, the interiors of the homes, decorated with simple but colorful gaiety, are also a source of joy to the eye.

If Sohar today, from the outsider's point of view, is largely lacking in distinction, this is not a judgment shared by its inhabitants, who perceive

the town as a source of conscious pride. They regard it as second in importance only to the capital area of Muscat-Mattrah, with respect to size of
population, in importance of commerce and industry, and for the fame of
the fort. In fact, Sohar ranks only third among Omani cities in most of
these respects. But because the second most important city, Nizwa, is
located in the interior, and the people of the coast still tend to view that
region as a country all to itself, (which indeed it was until 1959), the
Sohari conviction has some basis in fact.

Soharis see further evidence of their city's distinction in its being
chosen as the site for the first hospital built on the coast outside of
Muscat. The first primary school outside the capital was also located in
Sohar, as was the second experimental farm in the country. Last, but not
least, the ruler of the world's wealthiest nation (per capita), the Sheikh of
Abu Dhabi, has built a summer palace at Sohar. And the present governor
of Sohar thrives so well there that he has abandoned the brand new official
residence and built his own private one, indicating to this subjects that he
intends to stay on forever, even though it is a governor's obligation to
transfer whenever and wherever his ruler, the Sultan, commands.

Sohar owes its prominence to several factors, but one outweighs all
others in importance: its location by the largest valley of the upper
Batinah coast, the Wadi Jizzi. In a dry country, water is the source of all
life, and, pure desert regions apart, a drier place than the Batinah coast
can scarcely be found. According to official Omani statistics (Ministry of
Information 1972), Sohar has an average monthly rainfall of zero for eight
months of the year. Two other months have scarcely more rainfall: March
figures with 1.8 mm., and December with 3.6 mm. Only January and
February have rain to reckon with, respectively, 11.7 and 20 mm. Even
this can hardly be relied on; for example, during the twenty days of
January 1976 that we spent in Sohar, it did not rain a drop. Add to this a
fierce heat, notorious among experienced travelers—and even among the
Bedu of the Arabian desert—as the worst on earth: Muscat is infamous
among Arabs under the name of "Hellish Muscat," and Sohar, though
less notorious, has its ample share of this hellish climate. Only during two
months of the year does the average monthly maximum—in the
shade—drop below 30°C—and, for the rest of the year, it hovers in the
vicinity of 40–50°C. Add to this a relative humidity of around 90 percent,
and at least an inkling of the discomforts of the climate will be felt.

Whoever might imagine, as we initially did, that the local people are so
accustomed to this heat that it does not bother them, is wrong. As May
approaches, Sohari women go into a kind of hibernation, where they, for
fear of sunstroke, hardly move through the shadowless lanes and sleep
much of the day. It is no exaggeration to say that they dread the sun,
which is perceived as the cause of a host of illnesses, ranging from
stomach ache to trachoma. Entire families move their beds out into the

streets during the summer months of May through September in order to take advantage of the slightest night breeze. The better traditional houses are specially built with air vents and large windmill-like structures to create ventilation, whereas the owners of modern cement houses sleep on the roof.

Giyen such a setting, the need for water to replenish both human beings and soil becomes all the more understandable. The Wadi Jizzi, which enters the sea only two kilometers to the north of Sohar's town center, does not carry a perennial stream, but its ground-water flow still makes the coastal plain around Sohar the best-watered on all the coast (Williamson 1973). Whereas ancient settlements depended on elaborate communal irrigation systems for cultivation,[2] Soharis have, since the eleventh century, increasingly drawn their water from innumerable wells, located in a narrow coastal strip seldom more than three kilometers wide. Close by the beach, fresh water is obtainable only one and a half meters below the surface, and, further inland, rarely more than six meters. Modern cultivation is limited to this narrow strip, and "to fly over the Batinah is thus to see a narrow stream of green, the cultivation of dates, limes and lucerne, almost always immediately by the seashore, stretching the whole length of the coast" (*Oman* 1972). This coast is the most populous region of Oman; it has an estimated population of 150,000. Sohar is its richest town.

Sohar has other geographical advantages: it is located midway between Muscat and Abu Dhabi, and between Muscat and Dubai—only two hours' ride along excellent roads from three capital centers of commerce and culture. Most Sohari men travel frequently to these places, for both business and pleasure. About 25 percent are labor migrants in Abu Dhabi or Dubai. Of the women, only one in twenty has ever traveled beyond Sohar and then usually only on a day's visit to assist a man in his dowry purchases, attend a wedding, or secure special medical services. A few of the old women have undertaken the pilgrimage to Mecca.

However, these things may soon come to change as Sohar's nearness in travel time to neighboring centers is a new phenomenon: only a few years ago Muscat was seven days away by camel along insecure roads, or, worse, an unpredictable number of days by *dhow* across an uncommonly rough sea. Sohar, and its whole way of life, is bound to change dramat-

---

[2] These ancient irrigation systems, known in Oman as *falaj* (plural, *aflaj*)—the Persian *qanat*—are "at least two thousand years old and one of the most important heritages of Oman" (Dept. of Information). Briefly, the *falaj* system is a method of obtaining water for irrigation by tapping the ground water on the flanks of a mountain through a system of wells and tunnels, and then channeling the flow underground to the cultivated land. Some of these channels stretched as far as seventy-one kilometers inland; they ensured that much of the season's precipitation was distributed over the agricultural land instead of running to waste in the sea, and were remarkable for their absolute reliability: even during the longest period of drought, the flow in the *aflaj* never fails, though it may slacken. Immense sums of money must have been spent on these irrigation schemes, which were probably introduced to Oman by the Persians some two thousand years ago.

ically as ever more modern equipment and appliances are introduced with revolutionary speed.

Such then is the setting for the community that constitutes "home" for the people we wish to understand. But before trying to enter into the small and subjective worlds of individual women and men, it is an advantage to have a picture of some, at least, of the major features of organization and composition of this community, and of its physical layout. In the following, I shall try to outline, very briefly, the formal political and geographical organization, the physical features of the houses and compounds that constitute the main scene for women's lives, and the different kinds of persons and groups that make up this complex and cosmopolitan community (for a more complete description, see Barth, forthcoming).

THE PATTERN OF SETTLEMENT

In the town, most homes are located in a narrow belt less than half a kilometer wide between the sea and the palm groves and extending three to four kilometers along the coast. The town is not densely populated.

In the center of this settlement, along the seashore, are the two main pillars of the town: the fortress with the governor's offices, and the market. The post office, municipality building, customs house, cafés, and two gas stations are also located in this core area of town, which is a male arena, generally inaccessible to women. A three-kilometer-long road, as yet unpaved and very bumpy, connects this center with the point where the main highway between Muscat and Abu Dhabi intersects with Sohar. As you enter Sohar from this highway, the Wali's official residence is located first on your right, followed by the police station and the brand new hospital; a sign on your left announces the way to the experimental farm. This area was once entirely the habitat of the least prestigious persons of Sohar, the Bedu and the Zatut—the latter a small despised outcast (see pp. 43–44). The Bedu are still present; their homes stand out by the absence of secluding fences. But as a consequence of the decision to locate all the new official state buildings here, which to the inhabitants of Sohar truly signify development, the area as a whole is taking on an entirely new character, superseding in prestige the older settlements along the sea. So whereas before the reign of Sultan Qaboos, all urban settlement was on the sea side of the palm gardens—and the closer to the sea, the more prestigious—during the past few years a new zone of more dispersed settlement is extending even wider on the inland side of the gardens, and partly within the gardens themselves. This area is also favored by a markedly less humid climate, considerably reducing the strain of the heat in the summertime. It is here that the Sheikh of Abu Dhabi, amongst other persons of prestige, has built his summer palace.

Along the coast, north and south of the town proper, are strung similar, almost contiguous communities of satellite villages in a seemingly endless pattern of settlement and gardens. Many, perhaps most, Sohari wives originate from these distant villages, just as it is there that many young Sohari brides go in marriage.

Though there are no clear indications where one village ends and another starts, the villagers themselves know full well, and each village has its separate name. Four villages to the north of Sohar and a whole series to the south lie within the governorate of Sohar. All in all, they extend about thirty kilometers along the sea.

THE WALI

The town of Sohar is formally divided into administrative units called wards, numbering up to 3,000 inhabitants. There are five wards in all, each with a Sheikh as its formal head. The duties of the Sheikhs are to try to settle internal disputes, to represent the central authorities, and to serve as a link between the people and their government. But our impression is that their word counts little and that their advice is rarely sought. For above them all rules the Wali. It is he who calls the turn.

The Wali of Sohar is the effective ruler of a population of approximately 22,000 people, 7,000 of whom live outside the town proper. Although this highly distinguished—and impressive—official strongly insists upon his own role as merely that of the loyal servant of the supreme Sultan, whose decisions in all matters he merely seeks to carry out, there is no denying by Soharis, or by ourselves, that the Wali wields immense authority.

In consequence, a close examination of his role, and the administrative apparatus that he controls, is a key to understanding the town's formal organization. This also provides basic premises for interpersonal life at the intimate, face-to-face level (Barth, forthcoming, provides a fuller analysis).

The Wali represents the state and is accountable to the Sultan in person, whose close relative he may be. Previous Walis of Sohar have also often been members of the Al Bu Said dynasty. The Wali's administrative seat is the fort. Here he holds court six hours daily, six days a week, assisted by a deputy Wali, judges who are knowledgeable in Islamic jurisprudence, and some three score soldiers of the Beni Omar tribe (tribesmen from interior Oman with no affinities or loyalties to the population of Sohar). The Wali's task is to keep law and order, and this, in Sohar, means mainly to settle interpersonal conflicts that are brought to him by plaintiffs. They are numerous: according to the Wali's own estimate, approximately two hundred cases are brought to him for settlement each month. They cover all facets of life: marriage, divorce, inheritance, business disputes, trespassing, rights of way, and so forth. Only murder cases are always referred directly to the Sultan for judgment.

The great number of such complaints might be taken as an indication of a high level of interpersonal strife and struggle among Soharis. However, such judgments can only be made on the basis of an assessment of all the conflict-resolving mechanisms in use. We shall return repeatedly to the striking reluctance of Soharis to censure each other in face-to-face relations; public opinion is not created and mobilized as a control against offenders; personal displeasure leads to withdrawal, noninvolvement, and, in extreme cases, to being on nonspeaking terms. But some of the criticisms and conflicts that are suppressed in personal relations surface in the formal forum of the Wali's court. One is indeed tempted to generalize that no issue is so intimate, and no disagreement so small, that it may not be brought before the Wali for settlement. Thus, the control and enforcement that in many societies takes place on the interpersonal level, in the actors' daily milieu, are transferred in Sohar to the formal political system and judged from above. This reflects an extremely centralized basic model of society and the state among Omanis: the framework of rules and the authority to enforce the rules, derives from the ruler and, ultimately, from God. Within this set of rules, each man should be free to pursue his own affairs and realize what capacities he has. As our friend Ali said: "Look how God made your hand, he gave you five fingers, but each a little bit different: one long, one short, one thick, one thin. People are the same way—every one of them different. Each has his own character."

The image repeatedly used to express the view of the state in relation to individual activity is that of cultivation. As our friend Abdullah put it: "A country is like a garden: if you put control over it and have a strong wall and gate and lock, all the plants prosper; if there is no control and no walls, animals come in and spoil it, thieves steal from you, nothing will grow correctly in your garden."

Despite the impressive edifice of the fort itself, there would appear to be only a flimsy material or military basis at the Wali's disposal from which to create such a position of unchallengeable central authority. The Sohari view is that much has depended on the personal qualities and competence of each particular incumbent Wali. Of previous Walis, the most respected was characterized as a man so strong and severe that no one dared to speak against him, and everyone feared to present cases unless they were sure of the rightness of their claim. The present Wali, Hamud bin Nasr, described the qualities conducive to effective rule as follows: honesty (*amana*), sincerity (*ikhlass*), and refusal to accept bribes. But when we asked him to exemplify the mode of exercise of a Wali's authority by telling us about some critical problems he had confronted, and how he had handled them, he answered with deliberation: "To speak thus about one's own acts is shameful for an Omani; and besides, what I might consider I had done well, others may feel I did poorly. Persons differ; one can never satisfy everyone. It is up to each man to act in accordance with his personality [ilwahid ᶜala shakhsiyyitu]."

COMMERCE AND PRODUCTION

The classic Islamic town is built on three main pillars: the mosque, the seat of formal administration, and the marketplace. Although Sohar has a central Friday mosque, this does not occupy such a central place in the community, for the population, as we shall see, is divided among a number of different congregations with separate mosques. It is questionable whether the mosque should be regarded as a pillar of the town. The two others, however, are definitely basic, though they largely figure only indirectly in women's lives.

As previously noted, the market consists of about one hundred tiny, open-fronted shops, which primarily sell an identical, small range of wares. Prominent among these are material for women's clothing, perfume, sweets, simple household utensils, and tinned foodstuffs of modest quality and quantity. Household articles in common use are often not available in Sohar, but must be bought from Dubai; for example, cushions, women's black cloaks, and their jewelry. We found only two craftsmen operating in the whole of Sohar: an old smith and a rope maker. Apart from the local-style male headdress—the kummi—and beautiful embroideries made by Baluch women and not for sale, Sohar is wholly devoid of locally produced crafts.

The mainstays of Sohari diet are fish, rice, a few vegetables, dates, and canned fruits; fresh fruit is eaten on more prestigious occasions. Only the fish, some vegetables, and dates are locally "produced"; the fish is auctioned at a daily fish market. Fresh fruit, imported from Dubai, sells at sky-high prices (for example, three dollars for a kilo of oranges in 1974).

The shops in the market and the stalls at the vegetable and fruit market are individually owned or rented, by members of a wide variety of different ethnic groups, the identities of which I shall later enumerate, with specific reference to how they figure in women's lives (for a complete description, see Barth, forthcoming). Suffice it to note here that, in terms of occupational differentiation, the striking feature of Sohar is the prevalence of individual mobility and the lack of occupational monopolization by any ethnic group. Only one ethnic group is occupationally specialized: a Hindu community of merchants of the Bhatia subcaste whose association with the town, in some cases, goes back two or three generations, though with business and family roots in Bombay. Although all are merchants, they own only a small fraction of the shops; adjacent shops selling the same goods may be owned by Arabs, Baluchis, and Ajam (people of Persian origin).

As previously noted, 25 percent of Sohari males above the age of twelve are gainfully employed outside of the town, mainly in Abu Dhabi and Dubai. For the remaining males, the three leading sources of employment are agriculture, fishing, and transportation. Agriculture is the main source of income for approximately 30 percent; an additional 30 percent earn some income from it as a subsidiary occupation. Approximately 25 percent are employed in transportation, factories, or construction; 15 percent are full-time fishermen. Though Sohar appears to be primarily a trading center, only some 3 percent are actually shopkeepers. It is worth noting that women also contribute to the economy indirectly through household production, most of which is for home consumption. Over 50 percent of the household units consume the greater part of their vegetable and animal production themselves. However, no less than 50 percent of all married women in Sohar also produce some income by sewing or embroidering at home. (For a concrete description of the tasks performed by women, see Ch. 7.)

Sohar has also a small municipality organization (*baladiya*) that employs a few men. Its duties concern the physical control of buildings (post office, cafés, clubs), roads and lanes, garbage disposal, and spraying to keep down a dangerous mosquito population.

THE MILIEU OF WOMEN

All the main spatial divisions and institutions noted so far do not enter into the normal lives of Sohari women. Women's lives unfold in the homes and in the adjacent narrow lanes and back streets. Market, mosques, and all main thoroughfares are off-limits, except where the latter cannot be avoided, such as for a visit to the hospital or the fort. But then the woman is required to make herself as nearly invisible as possible, by donning a black, sacklike cloak reaching from the top of the head to the ankles (*abba*), and by screening her face by a mask (*burqa*). A man is required to show respect by turning his face to the side when they pass.

When women present their complaints to the Wali, seclusion is likewise secured: whereas male plaintiffs present themselves in the Wali's main office, women crouch invisibly on an outside veranda and voice their complaints through a hole in the wall.

Each individual woman's space of movement is far more limited than the above description could indicate. Each should keep to her own home and to those of her very close neighbors, altogether some five to ten houses. With them, she may exchange visits freely with no need of her husband's formal permission. But as it is prestigious to *be* visited, and to offer hospitality, rather than to be the guest, women tend to spend most of the day at their own homes in the company of children and such co-residents as there may be; for example, a mother-in-law, mother, or sister(s)-in-law. About 65 percent of married women live in households of more than one nuclear family.

Epitomizing women's seclusion and the narrow horizon of their world is their own reference to these wards and villages as "my country" (*baladna;* literally, our country), a usage that the men find bemusing. The men regard themselves as the proud citizens of Sohar, or Oman, depending upon the place of origin of the other person to whom they are speaking.

Let us look in some detail at these homes, which provide the scene for most of the activities of women. Each home is surrounded by a wall, generally made of palm fronds, but tightly woven to block all vision. (Walls of concrete are a modern invention, which so far only a small minority has been able to afford.) The wall encloses a compound of one or more main houses, with a roofed terrace, a small outdoor kitchen, and a spacious yard of clean, light sand, which is regularly sifted and replenished. A primitive bathroom and a toilet (usually just an enclosed area with sand) are located out of view in the backyard. For better-off families who own a private well, it is situated here too. Neighboring women are allowed to help themselves freely from it. The main house generally consists of two or three small rooms, depending upon the size of the family. In 1974, more than 90 percent of all houses were *barastis*, made of palm fronds. A year and a half later, maybe 50 percent of these had been wholly or partly rebuilt in concrete. Concrete houses have become major symbols of prestige and most Soharis become affluent and thus can afford one. A measure of women's say in these matters may be reflected in the fact that it does not seem to be material affluence as such, so much as the competition for prestige in the close neighborhood—among women—which is the main inducement to such modernization.

Every compound has a roofed platform at the entrance, just inside the gate, where the menfolk may receive their unrelated friends, without bringing them into the inner areas occupied by women. The more affluent may have a separate room (*majlis*) for this purpose. But it is our impression that these guest arenas are seldom in use. Men prefer to meet their friends at the market, in clubs, and in cafés.

The interiors of the houses are the women's domain; women receive their friends either on the roofed sitting platform outside or in the bedroom inside. The floors of both are covered with colorful plastic mats (made in Japan), and the walls are lined with them as if wallpaper. This gives a cozy and intimate effect and makes the room tight against wind and dust. The furniture is very sparse, but adequate by Omani standards of beauty and functionality: a row of gold-embroidered cushions, manufactured in Dubai, lines the main wall opposite the entrance. (Women generally prefer machine-made things to home-made ones.) They provide comfortable rest for the back. Against one of the short walls stands the bed, against the other, one or two green clothes chests. Some homes also have a large cupboard with mirror-lined doors. Soharis delight in mirrors, and the long wall opposite the entrance is usually decorated with seven to ten mirrors of identical size and shape, each with a color picture of Sultan Qaboos at the top. Women also like to own a few decorative bowls and plates, which are placed in wall niches and are used for hospitality. Otherwise, the only purely decorative items in a house are likely to be a color picture of the Sheikh of Abu Dhabi, and perhaps one of a Western model, both valued highly enough to share a place with Sultan Qaboos on the main wall. The outsider is impressed with the beautiful simplicity and functionality so characteristic of Sohari homes.

Homes generally depend upon kerosene for light and fuel. Sohar did not have, throughout our stay, an electric power plant, and probably no more than one family in a hundred has gone to the considerable expense of an electrical generator, to operate a fluorescent tube and, less frequently, a fan. We often felt that their functional use may have been secondary to their show-off value. Whenever I visited Fatima, the only one of my friends whose home contained this luxury item, in the evenings, the generator was invariably "having a rest," and I was happy to chat with her in the dim, quiet, relaxing light of a paraffin lamp instead of in the unsociable, glaring light of a neon tube, discordant with, and far too powerful for, a tiny room. The generator itself is also clearly antisocial in the Omani setting, for it makes such a noise that Omanis, as quiet and soft-spoken as any people imaginable (their speech, especially that of women, often resembles a whisper), have to strain themselves considerably to hear and be heard.

The kitchen is very simple, with walls on three sides only and a corrugated iron roof as shelter against the sun and rain. Wooden boxes serve as shelves for a small selection of pots and pans, plates and saucers. In 1974, all the women we knew used charcoal for fire. A year and a half later, a few had become the lucky owners of *butagaz* stoves (gas burners with no oven), which were always discreetly placed in view of visitors.

Every item in these homes has been bought by the men; the women have only a vague idea of the range of selection from which items are picked, as they have never set foot in the market. However, they seem quite content with the material surroundings that their menfolk create for them, as indicated by the assured pride with which they display their possessions.

A proud wife in her kitchen

RESIDENCE PATTERNS

About two thirds of all married Arab women live in a compound that houses others than those in their own nuclear family (that is, their own husband and children). It is common to term such forms of residence *joint* or *extended.* Coresidents are most frequently close kin of the husband, his father and/or mother, or one or more of his married brothers. Sometimes the wife and children are placed in the custody of the wife's parents during the husband's prolonged absence. Sharing a courtyard, however, need not entail sharing a kitchen, a sitting platform, and so forth. Often each nuclear family will have its separate dwellings, and the families will often eat separately and do not pool their resources (from income and produce). This is because coresidence is *not* a preferred family form, either from the male's or the female's point of view, for autonomy is too highly valued by both sexes (cf. Chs. 7 and 9). Coresidence is regarded as an unavoidable accommodation to the problems stemming from the labor migration of males for employment outside of Sohar: how to secure protection for women and children. It is the women, in the Sohari view, who are especially in need of protection (see Chs. 4 and 13).

Of those families who live in separate residence, only one in ten has no adult male present. In these cases, however, the wife is no longer young, or she has one or more teen-age sons who can be relied upon to guard her.

About half the women who live in joint or extended residence may be said to share a household with persons other than their own nuclear family, in that they pool their resources and eat together on a regular basis. This is most often done when one or more of the coresidents is single; for example, a widowed or divorced mother-in-law or father-in-law.

Relatives not sharing the same compound do not commonly live within the same neighborhood or even the same ward. They are generally spread throughout a wide geographical area and visit each other only rarely. It is not uncommon for mother and married daughter to visit only once a month or even for one brief day each year. Adult brothers may visit as infrequently, though chances are they will run into each other at the market more frequently. Cooperation, company, and help are sought by women from neighbors, by men from friends. Kinsmen seem to rank second by the preference of both sexes. Men, when they marry, prefer to take an unrelated bride from another ward or village, so as to steer clear of involvement with kinsmen and in-laws (see Ch. 10).

CULTURAL AND SOCIAL DIVERSITY

Sohar of old is described as a highly cosmopolitan town with, among other foreign elements, "a large community of Jews, engaged in commerce, money lending and the manufacture of baked bricks. . . . In the market much business was conducted in Persian" (Williamson 1973, p. 13).

Today it is no less cosmopolitan, though the Jews, reported by Wellsted, in his *Travels in Arabia* (vol. 1, p. 231), to consist of some twenty families in the nineteenth century, have disappeared from the scene. In the market today, most business is conducted in Arabic, which, among half a dozen other languages, is the predominant one; it is also the one lingua franca that all residents need to command. However, other languages are important enough so that ambitious Hindu merchants try, from self-interest, to learn them all in order to converse with each customer in his own language. A few master all the languages traditionally spoken in Sohar: Arabic, Baluchi (an Iranian language), Persian, Zidgali (a separate language that is related to the Indo-Arian group), as well as English and their own Gujerati/Kutchi and Hindi. Many ordinary men pride themselves with their command of three or four languages, whereas Arab women are content to know their mother tongue only and leave it up to their Baluchi friends to learn Arabic, which they usually do.

No East African languages are used in Sohar: apparently systematic efforts were made to stamp out such languages among slaves, and trade and contact with East Africa have been too limited in Sohar to introduce Swahili, which is used widely in inner Oman.[3]

Each of the above languages is the mother tongue of a distinctive ethnic group: that is, populations who share a history of common origin and a distinctive cultural tradition. True Arabs constitute approximately a little more than half the population of Sohar; Persians and Baluchis, each less than one third; and the other groups, only small numbers (see Barth, forthcoming).

Today Sohar embraces, apart from these ethnic groups, many other identities and cultural traditions that differentiate its population: most important are religious communities, ex-slaves versus others, and Bedu versus townsmen, as well as differences of wealth and occupation. Representatives of all these various groups may be found intermixed in local neighborhoods, and all form a part of the world of local women.

In the neighborhood where I made my most intimate ties, the most important distinction was between Arab and Baluch. The Baluch differ from the Arabs in such things as women's costume, wedding customs, and family and tribal organization. They have been present for centuries in Oman, though immigration has continued till recently, and a few of the older Baluchis arrived in their youth. Many of the families have traditions of how and why they originally came (most came from Makran, on the Iranian-Pakistani coast), but these traditions can rarely be given firm historical authenticity and dates. The port of Gwadar on the Makran coast, held for two centuries by Oman, facilitated such immigration. Today Baluchis are found in all major occupations in Omani society. To the foreigner's eye, the men are physically undistinguishable from Arabs. But a Hindu merchant friend claimed to be able to identify them and, when we challenged him, proved his claim. The women stand out strikingly, with their elegant, flowing dresses in brilliant colors and with beautiful embroideries, an inner black shawl that covers *all* of the hair, and *burqa*s larger than those of the Arabs. They also have characteristic jewelry; for example, a large silver nose ring that perforates the nasal septum, and a pendant hung in the hair, both of which may only be seen by the husband. The Baluch also seemed to me more spontaneous, vital, and noisy in their behavior. Some communities in Sohar, for example, Salan and Záffran, are composed of a majority of Baluchis, and everywhere they are numerous, but intermingled with Arab neighbors. My closest Baluch friend, Aisha, for example, associated much more with her Arab than with her

---

[3] Swahili is also spoken widely in the capital area of Muscat-Mattrah, for a large number of the civil servants are Zanzibaris who know Swahili and English beautifully, but hardly any Arabic. Because they are generally well educated, they have obtained responsible positions with the ministries, although many of them are really strangers to Oman.

Baluchi neighbors, though both categories lived next door. And on the
$^c id$—Feast—it was with the former that she used to eat the festive
meal.

Baluchi women definitely consider themselves superior to Arabs and
volunteer three main reasons. First, the bride price is presented to the
bride herself in the form of gold jewelry, not, as among Arabs, to the
bride's father as money. Second, the husband abstains from sexual intercourse from the sixth month of his wife's pregnancy, whereas Arab
husbands demand their right up to the last day. Third, after the child is
born, Baluchi husbands show patience (*yusbur*) for forty days before they
resume sexual relations, whereas among Arabs—in the words of Arab
women themselves—"out goes the baby and in goes the man."

Other customs that are regarded by Soharis as distinctive between
Baluch and Arab include the following. Among the Baluch, the groom
settles with the bride's parents, whereas among Arabs, the bride goes to
live with the groom's parents. The Baluch have no virginity test, Arabs do.
Baluchi women assume the *burqa* on puberty, Arabs do so on marriage.
The Baluch marry in the summer, Arabs do so in spring. The Baluch
spend three days only in the bridal hut, Arabs spend seven days. The
Baluch enter the bridal hut at sunset, Arabs do so at midnight.

Although Arab women acknowledge Baluchi women's claims to pride,
they nevertheless consider themselves superior, as might be expected since
theirs is an Arab nation. Many present-day "Arabs" are, however,
Baluch by origin, although not all are aware of this—to them—
disreputable fact. Thus I remember my close friend Latifa's surprise and
distress when her uncle revealed, in a discussion with my husband about
their family background, that their family had originally been Baluch;
their ancestors had come from Makran. In a tone of voice and a facial expression begging for consolation, she asked uneasily, "But they *are* good
people, the Baluch, aren't they?"

Another ethnic group, the Ajam (a traditional term for Persians and
used generally for the local Farsi-speakers), also mixes and mingles with
Arab women, though they tend to reside in special wards. Nearly all
Ajams are Shiah by religious persuasion, rather than Sunnis, as are the
majority of Arabs and Baluch; Ajams are consequently somewhat more
isolated because of their use of separate mosques and community houses.
There is a clear antagonism between the men of these distinctive sects.
However, the women of all ethnic groups seek out the Ajam at *Moharram*
(the month of commemoration of the martyrdom of Hussein, son of Ali),
because they believe this ceremony to be conducive to health and fertility.
Ajam men are centered around the market community, mainly as merchants and middlemen. Their customs are largely like those of Arabs, and
the female dress distinguishable only in minor matters of style.

Zidgalis form a scattered minority group of probably eight to ten families in Sohar. They have their own language, akin to Kutchi and the language of Sind. Their name indicates that they originated from Sind, though they themselves claim Arab descent, originally from the area of Asir in southwest Arabia. Arabs in Sohar generally regard them as similar to Baluchis.

As previously noted, Sohar also has a community of Hindus, which is composed of some fifteen families or fifty persons. But as they all live in a compact neighborhood, by the market (where they have their private wells, holy cows, and so forth) and do not intervisit with the local population, they do not figure in Arab women's lives. I doubt even if most Arab women have ever caught a glimpse of them. Arabs—both men and women—refer to these families as *Banyans*, in contradistinction to "Indians," who to them represent the nurses and doctors at the hospital, whom they frequently meet, but only in this limited capacity. When women were asked what they thought of these Indians, so important in their lives, they stoically replied, "They are like us; some are good, some are bad."

This is merely the short list of ethnic groups present and regarded as traditional today. New categories are ever appearing on the scene: Pakistani migrant laborers, Egyptian and Jordanian schoolteachers, American, British, Canadian, and Dutch development experts.

Another dimension of diversity is that of religion and ritual, though here again it affects the men's lives more than the women's. There are three different kinds of mosque in Sohar: ordinary Sunni, Ibadhi, and Shiah, but as women are debarred from these public places, they do not emphasize such distinctions.

Ibadhism is in a sense the national religion of Oman, though in Sohar Ibadhis are only a minority of perhaps 10 percent. Ibadhism, which constitutes an early and classical schism within Islam, is found only in a few places in the Muslim world (for example, Tunisia and the inner Sahara), but is predominant in inner Øman and is the religion of the ruling Al Bu Said dynasty.

Among Sunnis, all four schools of law are represented, but their mutual attitude is one of supportive holism, rather than communal separation. Despite slight differences in ritual, Ibadhi and Sunni may also pray together and intermarry, whereas Shiah have separate mosques and neither allow non-Shiah into these nor permit marriage with non-Shiah. While some language groups are religiously homogeneous, most are divided: the Baluch are Sunni, most Ajam are Shiah, but so are some Arabs, whereas other Arabs are Sunni or Ibadhi.

Within the category of Arabic speakers, a number of groups are distinguished. Every person belongs by descent to one or another of several hundred named tribes. Though we found little evidence among the men that these tribes mean much today, we were surprised that many, if not most, women did not even know the name of their tribe. (This is bound to change, however, as the hospital *requires* that all patients, including female ones, specify their tribal identity.)

Far the most important differentiation within the Arab-speaking group, from women's point of view, is that between ex-slaves and persons of free origin. Although slavery was legally abolished in Oman a generation ago, it continued to flourish in Sohar until about twenty years ago, and freed slaves and their descendants form a recognizable population and subculture. Their Negroid features are conspicuous; the women's clothing, though cut in the style of free Arab women's, is garish by comparison; their manner of speech and gestures are both more loud and direct. They are generally more vivacious and spontaneous than "free-women." However, in all circles and neighborhoods, "free" women and ex-slaves visit each other *as if* they were one of a kind.

Nonetheless, there were occasions when free women could not refrain from informing me of someone else's slave background, or that so-and-so had once been their own family's slave, adding, to make sure I understood, "We owned her like one owns an animal." We heard no evidence from the slaves themselves that they had been poorly treated, rather they said that they had been "like family members." Yet some ex-slaves felt the stigma sufficiently never to acknowledge their background. Others, particularly those whose former owners are of the highest-ranking families, proudly referred to their "family tie"; for example, by referring to the Wali as "my uncle" (ᶜ*ammi*), or claiming their tribal identity as Al Bu Said. But when, on one occasion, I naively repeated the latter claim to my friend, Latifa, she abruptly put the ex-slave in her place: "That is nonsense. She is not *an* Al Bu Said, she *belongs to* [*maᶜa*] the Al Bu Said. Ex-slaves have no tribal identity of their own."

From a man's viewpoint, the most fundamental differentiation within the Arab-speaking category is perhaps not even that between freeman and ex-slave, but between Bedu and settled; these are locally viewed as two completely distinct and antagonistic cultures. The basis for this antagonism goes back for centuries, but its concrete manifestations are only all too vivid in the memories of present-day Soharis: the Bedu were responsible for raiding, looting, and abducting hundreds of Sohari citizens, mainly young children, to the slave markets of Buraimi, from where only two ever returned (see Barth, forthcoming, for a concrete case).

Through centuries, various Bedu tribes conducted surprise raids, even on the town itself. At present, the nomadic Bedu are a peaceful lot and only marginal and temporary participants in the settled society of Sohar, whereas the local Bedu tribes are themselves settled, as previously noted. My guess that men regard them with more contempt and concern than women do is based on the fact that the Bedu reside in the country, where women rarely, if ever, move. They are not part of women's daily life.

Among the Arabic speakers is also a very small, low-status group, the Zatut (singular, Zutti). They were traditionally smiths and performers of ritually polluting services, such as circumcision of boys and girls. They are said to have been sharp hawkers, but not dishonest. Soharis believe that the origin of their low status is that they were wandering people and supposedly unable to inhabit houses. They also married for love. Today, however, Sohari stress that the Zatut are indistinguishable from respectable people: "Now they have become so civilized that they work in proper occupations, live in houses, and marry Egyptians."

A distinction strongly stressed in many parts of the Arab world, that between town and village, is in Sohar emphasized only rarely, and mainly by the urban elite of Muscati origin. Yet there is no doubt that the town citizens are proud that theirs is a town with an urban, centralized settlement. Deprecatory remarks about the more dispersed villages, "where there are no *harah*s [wards], just one house here and another there," were sometimes heard.

Crosscutting most of the distinctions emphasized so far are clear differences in wealth and lifestyle. Monthly incomes range, under the present conditions of prosperity, from minimal salaries of 30 Rials ($100), determined by governmental decree, to incomes of 300 Rials ($1,000), for the most prosperous merchants. The husbands in most of the families I knew had monthly incomes of approximately 100–150 Rials, which seemed to represent an average income. Whereas a decade ago one would have met genuine poverty among a considerable fraction of Sohar's population, today even the poorest seem well situated, as measured by their own standards and needs for food, housing, clothing, and even jewelry. In pursuit of these incomes, there is much occupational mobility, competition, and the rising and falling of social fortunes. Thus, if one looks into a sample of shops in the marketplace, one finds some that were recently established on loans and the accumulated savings in another occupation, others that have been inherited from a father or other relative. In the fish market, the fishermen landing fish are Arab and Baluch, some ex-slaves, some not. One auctioneer is a former shopkeeper, the other is a former sailor. Most of the fish buyers are former fishermen, shopkeepers, or cultivators, and they expect to move on to other occupations in due course. Characteristically, persons rise in influence and esteem through acquiring education, administrative careers, and wealth (Barth, forthcoming, treats these matters in detail).

Few of these differences of language, religion, and wealth constitute important bars to intermarriage. Fathers of prospective brides do not look to the wealth per se of a specific suitor, but rather to the amount of bride price he will offer. Differences in mother tongue are important, but far from insurmountable, as seen by appreciable frequency of intermarriage across the language boundary Arab/Baluch. Children that issue from such intermarriage assume the ethnic identity of the father. The one barrier that is nearly insurmountable is that between Shiah and Sunni or Ibadhi. The reluctance to marry a "free" Arab girl to an ex-slave is diminishing, but still very great. But it does happen that a (previously) married woman falls in love with an ex-slave, and in that case, people say, her family is powerless to prevent the union. (This is a telling example of women's position and influence, despite all such paraphernalia as veils and cloaks!)

OVERVIEW

So we see in this small rambling town by the Indian Ocean a startling cultural diversity: in language, dress, custom, belief, ritual, personal law, and life expectations. The mere discovery of such pluralism raises the question of how do differences in culture and background appear to color the lives and relationships of Soharis—and particularly the women?

Such differences do not serve as constraints on friendship and companionship. Men and women both associate and form companionships without regard to cultural differences. Baluch, or slave, that is irrelevant. What matters is, for the men, the individual personal qualities of the other; for the women, proximity (See Chs. 7 and 8). As one man, Said, expressed it: "No one can say these people are good, those people are bad. When a person does a bad thing, then you can say *he* is bad. Each person must be responsible for himself." My husband's sometime interpreter, Ali, made the point, in another way, that it is the individual who counts. About the Bedu, he remarked: "Their *customs* are bad: they do not wash, but wear the same clothes day out and day in, eat from the same soiled saucers, etc. As *persons*, on the other hand, they are good: they do not steal, do not lie, do not meddle in each other's affairs. In fact, they are much better than those 'civilized people' of Sohar!"

The striking way in which cultural differences are handled in interaction is by the exercise of tact, politeness, and tolerant manners in all face-to-face social encounters, irrespective of status and background. As might be expected, however, people's actual attitudes are more complex and ambivalent, and certainly more difficult to uncover and document. Combing through my field notes for sentences that shatter the polite surface and reveal some of the conflict and negative attitudes that coexist with the tolerance, I came up with few items:

1. An old Arab grandmother once remarked about the Ajam as a group; "To our face they treat us nicely, but behind our backs they call us dogs."

2. A five-year-old Arab girl once remarked that the Hindus (employed at the hospital) were an irresponsible lot and was immediately reproached by her embarrassed mother.

3. An ex-slave of the Al Bu Said family, on hearing that the most active and attractive *xanith* (transexual) was an Ajam, burst out, "Well, of course he *would* be an Ajam! These Ajams, they have no manners—honor [*axlaq*]."

4. An Arab father remarked that not for a million Rials would he give his daughter to a Zidgali. He would prefer a slave, a Hindu, even a Christian. . . . !

What is the more remarkable is that even quite innocuous disparaging remarks that fall are regularly "neutralized" by an immediate positive addition, seemingly unconnected to the preceding criticism. Numerous examples will be offered throughout this book.

What truly distinguishes Sohari society, and the women as much as the men, is, to my understanding, their remarkable struggle—and success—to treat everyone, irrespective of status and background, beautifully.

Perhaps the most vivid illustration of Sohari tolerance was expressed by our friend Abdullah in his correction of my husband:

> Abdullah, waxing nostalgic about the old days and ways, described with great pleasure the traditional joys of picnicking under the date trees as the first dates ripened in the summer, some youths climbing the tall trees to collect fresh dates while others crushed coffee with a rhythmic, melodic beat in the mortar. But now, he said, young people no more have time for this, they would rather have old dates beside them than climb the trees for fresh ones, they buy Pepsi Cola and want motorcycles instead. But my attempt to commiserate on the changing quality of life brought an immediate clarification: "No, no each way is good—for those who practice it" (Barth, forthcoming).

THE HISTORICAL PERSPECTIVE

This chapter opened with a glimpse of Sohar's grandeur in the tenth century. Noted too has been its renown as the "emporium of the whole world" and the reputed home of Sinbad the Sailor. Comparing this with its undistinguished present, a general question—though marginal to my main theme—wants an explanation: From where sprang the splendor, and what caused its decline?

With regard to the Sinbad tradition, Phillips observes that "there is no evidence that a sailor named Sinbad ever existed, although he is and was a very real person to seamen of the Orient. The tradition that Sohar is the home of Sinbad probably indicates nothing more than the city's former importance as a seaport from which many fearless seamen set out in days of yore" (1971, p. 65).

They traveled far, these sailors, for Sohar's one-time splendor was due to its favored location with respect to the trade in luxuries and spices between the Far East and India on the one hand, the Near East and Europe on the other, and with East Africa. The ports of the Omani coast were ideally located for the overseas trade, governed by the monsoons. Passing from the Near East with the northeast monsoon, Sohar was the last landfall before India, and therefore it was here that they would provision for the month-long voyage. Normally, on their return voyage, Oman would be the first landfall, for boats sailing direct into the entrance of the Gulf risked being shipwrecked on the rocks of Ras Musandam, still known as "the Cape of the Graves of the Indians."

As regards the trade between East Africa and India, the Omani coast was again ideally located, for the monsoon route between the two goes along the South Arabian coast, and thence along Africa to Zanzibar. Sohari merchants were particularly active in this trade. The commodities that they sought out were, in the words of a contemporary, "items in demand in their own country and in China, such as ivory, tortoise shell, leopard skins, ambergris . . . and African slaves who were vigorous and suitable for hard work" (Williamson 1973, p. 14).

Within one hundred years of this peak of prosperity, in the tenth century after Christ, Sohar was dramatically reduced, its area shrunken to a mere eighteen hectares (Williamson 1973, p. 19). The dominant position in the Indian Ocean trade passed to Kish and Hormuz on the south Persian coast, and a succession of other Omani towns, starting with Qalhat and ending with Muscat, took over as the major ports on the Omani coast. But Sohar continued, though with fluctuating success, to participate in this international trade. When the Portuguese in 1506 first anchored off its shore, they described it in the following words: "The population of Sohar is very large, the town being very beautiful and containing very good houses. . . . The fortress is so large that it requires more than a thousand men for its defence. . . . This place Sohar contains more nobles than any other place along the coast" (quoted in Yule 1903, p. 340).

And when, in the middle of the eighteenth century, the rest of the Omani coastline was subjugated by Nadir Shah's Persian armies, it was in the fort of Sohar that the defenders withstood and from there that the founder of the present Al Bu Said dynasty counterattacked and reestablished Omani independence.

We need not enter deeply into the turbulent and changeable history of Sohar, or into the geographical, political, and economic factors that can explain these perturbations. What is more important as a background for the present study is an awareness that such a history lies behind the present town, and the continuity of settlement, trade, cultivation, and, no doubt, many institutional arrangements and general cultural traditions that connect the present with this past.

In Sohar, we are not confronted with an overgrown village, recently integrated into a larger market and developing some urban features. On the contrary, we must be prepared to recognize an ancient, cosmopolitan city, and a population with a sophisticated, traditional urban culture. Their pride in their own identity, their urbane manners, and perspective, as well as the particular forms of a number of their institutions, take on a new meaning against this background. And, particularly to our appreciation of the nature and qualities of the small worlds of Sohari women, it adds an intriguing and challenging perspective.

PART
2

CHAPTER 4

✤

Segregation of the Sexes: Concept and Practice

The Prophet said, "After my disappearance there will be no greater source of chaos and disorder for my nation than women."

—**Al-Bukhari, 1868**

Segregation of the sexes is a prominent feature of the Sohari social scene. Women are conspicuously absent from all public arenas, such as the marketplace, main roads and mosques. On a busy market day, it is rare to see more than a solitary old widow doing her week's provisioning, probably because she is alone and has no male to do it for her. All other women shun the market, recoiling from the mere thought of the *fadiha* (scandal) it would be for them to set foot there.

In the Middle East today, the Batinah coast and inner Oman are perhaps the only major areas where this is true, and thus the extent of segregation and seclusion of women which is practiced there would seem unrivaled elsewhere, with the exception, perhaps, of Saudi Arabia and parts of Afghanistan. Women's participation at large ceremonial occasions, such as weddings, where men are also present, is likewise governed by strict rules of seclusion. The whole Sohari world, in fact, is divided into male and female spheres, roughly commensurate with the public and private domains. Essentially all public space is the exclusive domain of men. Trespassing is shameful, and breaches are rare. Violations of these rules create, in the worlds of women, scandal and chaos (*fadiha*).

The only truly common ground where closely related females and males may meet in an informal atmosphere, is the domestic scene of home and family life. But sexual segregation is so fundamental to life in Sohar, and to the constitution of man and woman as persons, that it pervades the home as well. Men and women will often eat apart, sit apart, and they will always receive their guests in segregated spots, shielded from view from the other sex. Division of labor along sex lines is carefully set out and only uncommonly is there any cooperation in joint tasks by the spouses. Only in the true privacy of the home, when just the very closest family members are present, can spouses truly address their attention to each other and interact spontaneously. But so separate are their worlds that

51

men who are regularly resident in Sohar spend no more than three waking hours a day at home, one of which may even be used for siesta, and labor-migrating males are often home no more than thirty days a year. It is considered shameful for spouses to appear together in public. When they go together to visit a relative, they will either walk separately and apart, the women being accompanied by other kinswomen or neighbors, or they will seek the privacy provided by a car.

Even when spouses have enjoyed a long and happy marriage, their worlds remain remarkably separate, and the information that each has of the other's concerns and activities remains limited indeed. This is as it should be, by Sohari values, and reflects both mutual respect and noninterference in the rightful domain of the other. Thus one day, when I visited Rahmeh, the wife of our sometime landlord Abdullah, she was mending the shirt of her son Saleh. She commented that she had to do it by hand because they no longer had a sewing machine. Abdullah has taken it, as well as another that he had bought, to two Indians whom he had brought to Sohar from Bombay to work for him as tailors. They share the income. I asked Rahmeh:

"Have you seen the shop?"

"No, I have never in my life been to the market, only ridden by car

A family together at mealtime

through the outskirts of it. You know, it is shameful and scandalous for a woman to go to the market."

"These Indians, are they married?"

"I do not know."

"Have you ever seen them?"

"Yes, once when Abdullah brought them here to take the measurements for new clothes for us to wear to the feast."

"How much do they charge for a dress?"

"I do not know ... maybe Abdullah doesn't pay them at all...?"

Hence, the actual practice of segregation in Sohar is one that creates for men and women truly distinctive worlds. Even between closely related persons of the opposite sex, and married spouses, the range of places and occasions in which they meet and interact are few. Between all other persons of the opposite sex, and on all other occasions, segregation produces either a categorical separation in space, or very strict limitations on behavior, dress, and use of space which effectively keep them apart.

The men's world is by far the larger. A man may not step inside the homes of other men, without formal invitation or explicit prior announcement; otherwise, the world lies open to him. The women's world, on the other hand, is strictly limited. Essentially, every woman is confined to her own home, and to those of her closest neighbors at such times as when the men of those homes are absent. To move outside of this immediate neighborhood, a woman should have her husband's permission, and its only legitimate purpose is to visit close relatives, situated at a distance, where again the same constraints are observed. But a woman may be even further restrained, as her male guardian has the right to veto her movements outside of her home and sometimes exercises this right. He may refuse her access to her friends and even to her parents, beyond the legal minimum of letting her visit her parents once a week if they live close, once a fortnight if they are far away. But many women are not aware of their legal rights and, for this or other reasons, do not benefit from them.

Wherever males move, their clothing is the same: a white long shirt (*dishdasha*), which reaches to the ankles and covers all of the arms. On the head, they wear either an Omani *kummi* (a small, white cap embroidered in gold), or a Arabian Gulf sheikh-type headcloth. The females' attire, by contrast, is composed of a variety of different items, which, added to the basic dress expresses increasing modesty and provides progressively greater protection against the public world. Thus a woman covers herself more decently the farther she moves away from the hearth of her home. She always, day and night, wears a knee-long dress, with a slightly swung waist, a wide skirt, and long sleeves; she wears ankle-length pants underneath. Her hair and neck are always covered by an inner, tightly wrapped head scarf (*leeso*). Not even for marital intercourse is the dress removed, whereas the *leeso* may or may not be. It is the husband's prerogative to savor such a beautiful and intimate aspect of his wife as her hair. Only for the purpose of washing and drying her hair does the woman otherwise doff her *leeso*.[1]

Within the secluded compound of the home, the woman is safe from the view of a male stranger and thus may uncover her face by pushing the *burqa* to the top of her head (in the way that we might a pair of sunglasses not in actual use). Walking to the gate to bid someone farewell, the woman pushes her *burqa* into place so as not to show her face to any passing male. When only one step outside the gate, the woman enters an entirely different stage, the public domain, and must don her top head scarf, the *wiqaya*. Finally, when visiting outside the closest neighborhood (that is, outside a radius of approximately eighty yards), she must cover her body with the long, black, heavy *abba*, an all-enveloping cloak, made of artificial satin and measuring a total of six yards, which effectively erases all bodily contours, revealing only the feet, hands and face;[2] and she must hide her face behind the *burqa*. Fully dressed in this manner, women resemble black, tentlike bundles, and fathers like to tell about the time when they met, but did not recognize, their own daughters, so well disguised were they. Rules of sexual modesty further require that the woman makes her presence in public as brief and unobtrusive as possible. She must make her way through little frequented back streets and paths, taking care to turn her head away in case she must pass a man. When women must pass through the town's street or byways, rules of decency likewise require that men take no notice of their presence by looking at, greeting, or in any way interacting with them.[3]

Some few public places and occasions form partial exceptions to the general rule that women should stay away from public places and enter them only with the expressed permission of their husbands. These are: the new hospital, the Wali's court and special localities at religious ceremonies. On such occasions, the woman should be accompanied by other women for protection and occupy a segregated space while there.

A typical scene throws the discrepancy in standards for males and females into glaring relief: the coastline in Sohar functions as a main thoroughfare for cars as well as the public toilet for males. I have ridden along

[1] Many Islamic countries that no longer use the veil regard head-covering as obligatory. Michael Fischer remarks, in an instructive article on Persian women, that "it is interesting that the head-scarf remains so important, for it indicates to many people that the rules of head covering are symbolically more deeply rooted than as mere rational signs of modesty" (1980, p. 297). He also notes that "anthropologists have long speculated about symbolic connections between head hair and pubic hair. See Hershman (1974) for a recent review" (p. 213).

[2] To the observer, the wearing of the *abba* seems an oppressive measure during the five hot summer months, when the day temperature rarely drops below 100°F, the air is saturated with 90 percent humidity, and Soharis suffer considerably.

[3] Fischer makes some intriguing remarks about a behaviorally different, but functionally equivalent, pattern of eye contact and movement in Iran's public streets (1980, p. 297).

Women during a formal visit, wearing the abba

with women, who were scarcely visible behind layer upon layer of clothing, and passed within inches of squatting men with their genitals in full view, as they lifted their tunics up under their armpits—in deference to a Muslim taboo of pollution from bodily excretions. With a keen eye for bawdiness, the women have burst into unrestrained giggling, despite strenuous efforts to exercise the self-control called for because of the presence of a male, the driver, in their company. But the object of laughter has displayed no sign of embarrassment, only annoyance at the disturbance.

MUSLIM CONCEPTIONS OF MALE AND FEMALE

What is the basis for such distinctive behavioral standards for males and females? What attitudes toward, and conceptions of, the natures and positions of men and women find expression through the above practices?

Let us first seek to relate these attitudes and practices to the precepts of Islam. Oman, as a Muslim country, situated in the Arabian heartland, isolated from most of the world for centuries, and ruled for the past half-century in entirely autocratic fashion by a conservative eccentric who despised all things modern, may well be expected to adhere closely to traditional Islamic law; and such is indeed the case. Islam perceives the male and female as different kinds of human beings, with complementary, not competing, roles in society. The male is considered, superior, physically, morally, and intellectually:

> Allah has preferred the one sex over the other in the matter of mental ability, and good counsel, and in their power for the performance of duties and for the

carrying out of divine commands. Hence, to men have been confined prophecy, religious leadership, saintship, pilgrimage rites, the giving of evidence in law courts, the duties of Holy War, worship in the Mosque on the day of assembly. They also have the privilege of electing chiefs, have a larger share of inheritance and discretion in the matter of divorce.

So writes the thirteenth-century commentator Baydawi, whose word is respected by Sunnites to the present day (quoted from Levy 1965, p. 99). He failed to mention, for some reason or other, another, most essential, privilege of men—that of polygamy: "Marry of the women, who seem good to you, two, three, or four, and if ye fear that ye cannot do justice (to so many) then one (only)" (Quran 1:3).

The Islamic tradition—the accumulated rules and understanding of the *ulama* (religious scholars of Islam)—has thus conceptualized females as morally weak and irresponsible. Whether this is in line with the intentions of the Quran is a different question, to which we shall return shortly. It stands beyond dispute that the Quran found its interpretation through *men* who, in most cases, were not "neutral," but proponents of specific political and economic interests.[4] Lacking the spiritual and mental strength of men, women are regarded neither fit nor equipped for public tasks. And as the physical and animal side dominates women's nature, it would seem that their presence in public life would represent a threat to community order and morality: The Prophet said: "After my disappearance there will be no greater source of chaos and disorder for my nation than women" (Al-Bukhari 1868, quoted from Mernissi 1975, p. 13).

As a protection for the Muslim community of religious believers, women must be constrained and protected by men, the responsible upholders of law and moral order; they must be secluded by physical and symbolic means, walls as well as veils; and they occupy the status of minors all through their lives, in that, no matter how old, a woman must have a male guardian.[5]

In this capacity, women are charged with full responsibility for housework and child-rearing, duties that entail the potentialities of a considerable measure of influence, and even of power, in the life of the family. They have no economic responsibilities, however, and are entitled to be fed, housed, and clothed by their male guardian, be he a father, husband, son, brother, or a more distant kinsman related in the paternal line.

[4] Nawal el Saadawi cites, in a fascinating book, the following intriguing observation about Aisha, the favorite young wife of the Prophet: "She even went so far as to challenge him in relation to some of the Koranic verses which descended upon him from Heaven. When, in one of these verses, Allah permitted Mahomet to marry as many women as he wished, she commented with heat: 'Allah always responds immediately to your needs' " (1980, p. 131).

[5] For an interesting discussion of the significance of such ideas among men in a Moroccan town, see Rosen 1978.

Though a woman may possess a large personal fortune, she has nevertheless a legal right to be provided for by a man, who alone must worry about earning a living. In return, her guardian male may request absolute obedience and submission, that is, *respect* (*ihtiram*).

With these conceptions of fundamentally different male and female natures, and of the roles consistent with them, goes a set of clear-cut constraints on the female's "presentation of self in everyday life," to borrow an apt phrase of Goffman's (1959). She should, first and foremost, show modesty:

> And tell the believing women to lower their gaze and be modest, and to display of their adornment only that which is apparent and to draw their veils over their bosoms, and not to reveal their adornment save to their own husbands or fathers or husband's fathers, or their sons or their husband's sons, or their women, or their slaves, or male attendants who lack vigor or children who know naught of women's nakedness. And let them not stamp their feet so as to reveal what they hide of their adornment. And turn unto Allah together, O believers, in order that ye may succeed. (Quran 24)

The need for modesty on the part of women, and the containment of their self-assertion to a small domestic circle, are doubtlessly basic features of Islam. However, the justified extent of this containment and segregation, and the reasons for it, are less clear. Scholars have never ceased to debate which aspects of the position of women have their ideological foundation in the Quran—the actual word of God—and which represent an accretion of man-made social institutions. In an intriguing book, *Beyond the Veil*, the sociologist Fatima Mernissi argues the latter view:

> Paradoxically, and contrary to what is commonly assumed, Islam does not advance the thesis of women's inherent inferiority. Quite the contrary, it affirms the potential equality between the sexes. The existing inequality ... is the outcome of specific social institutions designed to restrain her power: namely, segregation and legal subordination of the woman to the man in the family structure ... the whole system is based on the assumption that woman is a powerful and dangerous being. (Mernissi 1975, pp. xv–xvi)

Mernissi cites the Muslim feminist Kacem Amin, who, in his attempt to grasp the logic of woman's seclusion and the basis for sexual segregation, came to the conclusion that they are devices to protect men, not women:

> If what men fear is that women might succumb to their masculine attraction, why did they not institute veils for themselves? Did men think that their ability to fight temptation was weaker than women's? ... Preventing women from showing themselves unveiled expresses men's fear to lose control over their minds and fall prey to *fitna* (disorder, chaos, also a beautiful woman) whenever they are confronted with a non-veiled woman. (Amin 1928, quoted from Mernissi 1975, p. 4)

The Egyptian author and physician Nawaal El Saadawi argues along the same lines, in her fascinating book *The Hidden Face of Eve*, but wholly without the reservations and question marks of Amin! She writes:

> It is easy to understand why segregation and the veil were imposed upon women at a later stage of Islam, whereas in the earlier stages women were allowed to move about freely and expose their faces for all to see. Even today some of the Arab countries still maintain the customs that developed in later Islamic society. Segregation and the veil were not meant to ensure the protection of women, but essentially that of men. And the Arab woman was not imprisoned in the home to safeguard her body, her honour and her morals, but rather to keep intact the honour and the morals of men.
>
> In addition, the fact that men felt the need to prescribe such customs, and to keep the women away from participation in normal life seems to explode the myth of the powerful male and the defenceless and weak female. The tyranny exerted by men over women indicates that they had taken the measure of the female's innate strength, and needed heavy fortifications to protect themselves against it.
>
> To my mind, Islamic culture rests on the above premises, namely that woman is powerful and not weak, positive and not passive, capable of destroying and not easily destructible, and that if anyone needs protection it is the man rather than the woman. (El Saadawi 1980, pp. 99–100)

Justice cannot here be done to the lucidity and comprehensiveness of the arguments of either Mernissi or El Saadawi. The reader interested in the subject should consult the original works themselves. Suffice it here to note that the question of whether the female is inherently weak and passive or powerful and hence destructive, fascinating though it is, may be debated endlessly; both sides will find support in the Quran and the Hadith (sayings of the Prophet).

SOHARI CONCEPTIONS OF MALE AND FEMALE AND THEIR SOCIAL GENESIS

Islam is basic to the constitution of Omani society, and Islamic conceptualizations of male and female and their segregation in social life have affected both thought and practice over the centuries. However, in my endeavor to interpret and understand the way of life and the outlook of real, living people, I am not seeking answers in what constituted the logical bases or rationale for the institution of segregation once upon a time, or in the minds of thinkers in other places. We want to know what segregation means to people in Sohar today, as a vital, forceful institution that channels their everyday life. Although there seems to be a close congruence between Muslim ideals and Sohari realities, it does not follow that Muslim theories and Sohari folk understandings converge. Very different, even contradictory, ideologies may be at the base of similar overt behavior. (Leach 1954, is a brilliant demonstration of this.) Likewise, we would be wrong to think that this congruence occurs because the terrain has been fashioned on the map. Sohar was a society long before Islam. Like all religions, everywhere, Islam in Sohar fell upon cultivated ground, so to speak, rather than virgin land. It took hold in a society that was already structured according to specific values and conceptions about people, land, and life which gave the country a flavor and style very different from, say, the Egypt or Morocco of the time.[6] Islam had to accommodate itself to this particular setting. Unfortunately, as regards male-female relationships in the Oman of the time, little is known. But we do know that the basic features that distinguish Sohari women today have considerable antiquity, as evidenced by the British explorer W. G. Palgrave, who, reporting a visit to Sohar in 1863, observed: "But in Oman the mutual footing of the sexes is almost European, and the harem is scarcely less open to visitors than the rest of the house; while in daily life the women of the family come freely forward, show themselves, and talk like reasonable beings, very different from the silent and muffled status of Nejed and Riad" (1865, vol. 2, p. 330). Thus, to learn about sexual segregation and the seclusion of women, Sohari style, we must ask questions such as: How, then, do men and women in Sohar today actually formulate their views on segregation? Do they, for example, voice ideas on the relative equality or inequality of the sexes? Do they have views on whom segregation is protecting, males or females?

Let us first ask to what extent Arabs in Sohar are actually familiar with Muslim ideology. Every Friday, from the twenty-odd mosques in Sohar, *imam*s (Muslim religious leaders) summon the men to sermon, prayer, and the worship of God, before whom all are equal without distinction of rank, class or race. But women are not invited to join. They should individually turn their souls to God within the private confines of their homes. Thus men, through the Friday sermon and also from Koranic school, are given the opportunity to familiarize themselves with God's literal message, whereas women, because of illiteracy, as well as inattendance at the mosque, are hard put to do so. We may therefore expect men's expressed views to adhere more closely to the official Muslim ideology, according to which women are inferior to men and in need of their protection and guidance. However, I will argue that any differences between men's and women's views on sexual segregation reflect first and foremost the fact of segregation itself, and their diverse life situations resulting from it. Forums and occasions where men and women can meet in an informal atmosphere to chat and exchange their views are only marginally developed. Informality is precisely what society, through segregation, discourages or bans. All topics related to segregation are furthermore

---

[6]For a brilliant discussion of how Islam has evolved differently in two very different settings, Morocco and Indonesia, see Geertz 1968.

touchy topics, sexuality being their very basis. On the rare occasions when adults of both sexes—wives and husbands, mothers and sons, sisters and brothers may mention themes with a sexual referent (most notably prostitution, male or female, and perhaps only in response to the anthropologist's inquiries), they are notably shy and bashful. Living the greater part of their lives in worlds that hardly meet, men and women have little chance to influence and modify each other's views. The barriers to interaction across the sexual boundary may even be so categorical that males and females remain ignorant of each other's views, to the extent that they do not even know them to differ.

Men in Sohar rarely volunteer explicit verbal evidence of their views on women's nature and intergender relationships. Only once did my husband or I hear them spontaneously speak about women; otherwise it happened only in response to our inquiries (see Ch. 13). Even among their peers and equals, they seem reticent and reserved, striving toward a performance of gracefulness and style that honors the integrity of others and offers offense toward no one, women included. To praise women would be incompatible with their sense of modesty, to derogate them would be inconsistent with their sense of pride. However, we did elicit some views by direct questioning. Furthermore, people communicate their values not only through verbal utterances, but through their actions as well. It even is a tenet of much social science that the latter offer the more reliable clue, because behavior (including mimicry, gestures, facial expressions) is less subject to the actor's conscious manipulation than are words. (See Goffman's distinction between impressions given and impressions given off, 1959.) Our total evidence on men's views is scanty, but what we know springs from the above two kinds of sources.

Women are much more explicit and direct in voicing their views. Female standards of elegance and style do not call for the same degree of formal restraint and control in all encounters, but focus such on situations of interaction with men and the hostess-guest relationship. In their intimate circles of friends and relatives, women may, within bounds, relax and indulge in banter, sensational stories, and diffuse criticism. Matters of sex are here favorite topics.

Let one example serve to juxtapose men's and women's different styles and expressed attitudes to topics concerning sexuality.

Questioned why they marry their daughters off at the early age of thirteen, men explain that "otherwise she will be too old" (implicitly, and no one will want to marry her—an assumption that is not testified to by facts), or they say "such is our custom," or, most commonly, they extol the qualities of their son-in-law (to be), declaring him the perfect husband for their daughter, "with whom she will be very happy." But the women spontaneously exclaim, "Why do you think the fathers are in such hurry to marry their daughters off? Well, of course, because they fear for their chastity!"

Men are strikingly reluctant to admit that they need fear for their own daughter's chastity or wife's fidelity. The morality of women in general is a different matter. Asked why they veil their women, do not dare to leave them living alone, forbid them access to the market, even in distant towns where local women customarily go (like Mattrah), men give a variety of pragmatic reasons, with one ingredient in common: a conspicuous nonreference to the issue of female sexuality. Often the reasons given seem like clear evasions or rationalizations. One discussion we had with Ali, my husband's closest acquaintance and best informant, may illustrate the point. His wife, Fatima, had told us that Ali had refused to let her go to the market in Mattrah, when they lived there. I asked him why, and the discussion proceeded as follows:

"She could not go in Mattrah, though it is the custom there, because she would lose her way."

"Why can't a woman go here in Sohar?"

"Because she does not know prices and would be cheated; other people should do it for her: her father or father-in-law or brother-in-law, as I have authorized them to do. A woman should be relieved of such chores. And mind you, she has her own money and makes decisions, just has them to do the actual buying." He hesitated a moment, then said, "Perhaps after having a couple of children she can go."

"How can she if she never learns; does giving birth to children give wisdom?"

"But she is so young, only thirteen or fourteen years old; perhaps when she is eighteen, or twenty, or twenty-four, she can go...."

Because our relationship with Ali seemed very solid and mutually honest, and I wished to discover whether other considerations lay behind all this, I finally confronted him with my own intuition as a point-blank question. He hesitated briefly, and then answered:

"Yes, that is the way here, you cannot trust a woman, her judgment and reliability." And abruptly, switching to impersonal generalization, "They are afraid for their wife's faithfulness—not because it happens so much any more, but it still does happen."

"Why does it happen?"

"The wife wants something like all the neighboring women have. The husband says no, I will not—cannot give you three Rials for that [the price of an Arab woman's dress]. So the wife becomes angry, goes and does bad things to get the money. I don't involve myself in such things, but many men are looking for the opportunity."

Ali here expresses a view common to Sohari men: that women are materially demanding and morally irresponsible, *therefore* prone to sexual misconduct. Any danger inherent in the woman's sexuality as such is not emphasized. However, the moral irresponsibility is seen as an innate weakness, for which the woman cannot be blamed. It is up to her menfolk to guide and constrain her, and, should she default, they, not she, are responsible. It is their honor that suffers. (For verbatim statements, see Ch. 8.)

The women, however, hold a different view. They explicitly deny the idea that material satisfaction necessarily insures a woman's sexual stability: "When a woman goes with the men, it is because she *wants* that thing [sexual intercourse]!" They also draw a sharp distinction between illicit intercourse, as caused by a woman's love for one man, versus her desire for many men. The first one acts from love (*hubb*), they say, the other *bitxannith* (prostitutes herself). The first they regard as legitimate, saying, "It is impossible that two who truly love each other can stay apart"; the second they regard as shameful. The men however, regard both as illegitimate. In contrast to the men, women also emphasize the woman's sexuality as a factor in her behavior. Thus they may say, "If an old maid [a girl above age sixteen or seventeen] *bitxannith*, the Wali will punish her *father* for not having married her off before!"

In this statement, women express clear Islamic thinking, which is explicit on the point of women's sexual needs and their right to have them satisfied. Yet their reasoning is wrong, because Islam operates on the principle that women's sexual needs arise with marriage, not puberty. Although marriage in Sohar is supposed to coincide with puberty, Islam, to my knowledge, makes no concession to a girl whose fate is otherwise and ordains severe punishment should she fornicate. Yet, I wonder what the Wali of Sohar would have done, should he be presented with a case of an unchaste "old maid"? Sohari women's conviction that he would be understanding and forgiving with the girl, and punish her father, I consider a clear expression of their faith in the inherent justice of their system, which should consider the specificness of each case rather than abstract moral principles. As the women see it, a woman is entitled to consideration and respect, a view to which their experience testifies.

On the role of the men in sexual matters, men and women also differ in their views. Men are inclined to cast the male in the role of the hunter, and the woman as his easy prey because of her inferior physical strength, mental ability, and moral judgment. Ali phrased it this way: "A woman's bad actions spring from her lack of education [that is, knowledge and understanding]. Maybe she is going along the road, a taxi stops, the man says, 'Where are you going?' offers to take her, but drives into the desert and forces her to have intercourse. How can a woman fight a man? He is stronger...."

The women, however, stress the initiative of the female herself, and the subtle tactical maneuvers with which she steers the course toward the fulfillment of her desires. To take an example, one day, as a group of friends returned from a car ride, the comment was voiced, "Did you *see* Sheikha, the way she maneuvered to place herself beside Suleiman [the driver]!" The same Sheikha, who is known, though not acknowledged, to be a prostitute, was also said to be "so tactical that when her husband tells her he will bring his friends home, she exclaims, 'Oh, no, don't do it, I feel so shy!' And who are they, his friends? Some are her paramours!" As women see it, a woman is inherently capable of resisting or acquiescing to the invitations of a man despite her physical and mental inferiority. The view that the male is physically and intellectually superior, they do not dispute.

Thus Sohari men, in keeping with their exposure to official Muslim ideology, emphasize the theory of the female's passive nature. The women, however, voice the opposite view—that the female's sexuality is an active and potentially disruptive force. The discrepancies between the male and female views are readily understandable as a consequence of segregation itself: women have intimate knowledge of females. Their mutual interaction is a many-faceted one, in which the female stands forth as a rounded person in her own right, with the power to initiate, consummate, and break off actions according to *her* will. Through these encounters, I think it inevitable that women come to experience each other as active and vigorous agents. But the men can have little knowledge of the other sex. Such limited knowledge as they have is further acquired mainly through encounters where the man occupies a position of uncontested authority relative to the female. No wonder the female's passive and subordinate qualities come to dominate the male's view of her, or at least his view of women in general, as opposed, perhaps, to *his* particular woman! At the same time, the man's awareness that he does not understand women, combined with his knowledge that some women do practice fornication and adultery, causes him fear and insecurity. Though particular men in particular situations may, of course, be equally unpredictable and cause comparable fear and insecurity, I would argue that there is a qualitative difference in the relationship if one truly believes that this very important other is of a fundamentally different nature than oneself and is both moved by passions and insensitive to reason in ways different from oneself. The man must wonder how many are the women who have fallen, and, more importantly, who are they? How is he to know or recognize the tell-tale signs of poor character or latent, incipient tendencies? He is painfully aware of his own vulnerability in the matter: should a woman of his, a daughter or wife, go astray, his honor will suffer considerably. What then is more natural for a man, indoctrinated since childhood that women are not to be trusted, than to seek protection and consolation in those external safeguards that he can control: seclusion and all its paraphernalia? The near absence in Sohar of an informal gossip structure that would serve to inform the man in case his wife misbehaved makes his dependence upon her seclusion all the more urgent and complete (see Ch. 8).

As regard men's and women's views of whom segregation is protecting, they seem to agree: both the female and the male benefit. They both regard women's seclusion as a pillar for the man's honor, expressive of his ability to provide for her as well as of his autonomy and authority. And both see it as epitomizing the female's worth and value, an expression of the man's love and care for her. Thus Arab women are proud that none of their kind ever go to the market—except for an occasional old woman provisioning for a wedding—and they are slightly contemptuous of the Baluchis, whom they believe to be more frequent shoppers. (In fact, Baluchi women shun the market as fastidiously as Arab women do.) Shopping they perceive as labor, and labor they dislike. Leisure is the cherished ideal of both sexes. Women are also proud that their own husbands would never allow a friend of his to enter the house in his absence—ways of behaving that they have heard are acceptable in neighboring towns, where, equally to their dismay, the men are even said to allow their wives to ride in taxis alone. By Sohari women's standards, such behavior can only reflect lack of concern and respect on the husband's part. To the women of their own "country," seclusion is, above all, a source of pride. In other words, men and women here share basic values and understandings; and spouses have both compatible and common interests in conforming to and practicing these quite detailed conventions of segregation.

THE RELATIONSHIP BETWEEN NORMS AND PRACTICE

When I make the statement that Omani society is characterized by a pattern of extreme sexual segregation, this simultaneously refers to two different levels in people's lives and the anthropologist's analysis, the ideological and the actual. It asserts, on one level, that segregation is an imperative moral value in the Omani cultural scheme, a blueprint for behavior that brings honor and is inherently right. On another level, it asserts that the majority of Omanis do in fact act with respect to these imperatives, as evidenced by numerous observations of their daily life. But we must not be trapped into thinking that the latter is a mirror image of the former. On the contrary, the relationship between norms and practice is a very problematic one, for both the anthropologist and the people she studies. People everywhere make this distinction between what ought to happen and what does happen, but they stress it to varying degrees, depending upon such factors as their tolerance for discrepancies and deviance, and their proneness to think in concrete and specific terms versus abstract and general ones. Some people seem to depend on believing, against all discordant evidence, that the ideal is consistent with the real and is in fact realized in actual life, achieving this feat through such psychological mechanisms as selective perception and memory and biased interpretations of various sorts. Others show a keen appreciation of discrepancies, emphasizing the particular and singular in social life, rather than the diffuse and general in cultural ideals. Soharis resemble the latter, women even more so than men, which may reflect the men's stronger commitment to the moral order, of which they are the defenders and protagonists. This does not mean that women are more "realistic" in any sense, only that men have commitments that women do not have, and hence make efforts in those directions.

Soharis generally exercise a subtly developed sense of the nuances and complexities in people's behavior and the range of differences in their characters, coupled with a fundamental respect for the individuality of the other. Stereotypes and generalizations are conspicuously absent from their discourse, a fact likely to drive the anthropologist to despair at the beginning phase of field work, when she struggles for some general clues to behavior, something to grasp, and hold on to, some general formulas about "How we do things" and "Our way of life," as an entrance into the complex social world she sees about her. Such clues are rarely forthcoming in Sohar; on the contrary, the recurring phrases are, "Some are like this, and others like that," "I cannot tell, people are different." Likewise, when the anthropologist struggles to solicit their help to understand why some behave like this and others like that, Soharis are most unhelpful (and this applies especially to women). Not from recalcitrance, but from a sense of propriety and good manners. Theirs being a society that requires an acceptance, rather than a critical view, of others, it is not their way to ponder such matters. As one consequence of this, the proliferation of particular ways of doing things is given fertile ground. People are left much in peace to develop their idiosyncrasies; behaviors do not become standardized through being gossiped about and sanctioned; information about the whys and hows and wherefores of particular acts does not circulate and provide others with ready courses to emulate. It is up to each person to act as she or he sees fit, so one might say—paradoxical though it seems, in view of the gracious, well-mannered people—that this is a society where individuality truly reigns. But because, in the public domain, male-female interaction is so restricted and constrained, so circumspect and fraught with taboos, so evocative of deep-felt feelings of shyness and modesty in women and of reserve in both sexes, public social life is rather more uniform and "conformist" than what the Sohari live-let-live stance might lead one to expect, and much more so than seems to be the case in the privately shielded domains.

My observations of daily life among Arabs in Sohar have shown that most women, but not all, actualize in their behavior the various dictates of sexual segregation: Most never set foot in the market, but a very few on occasion do. Most brides turn out to be virgins on marriage; but some prove to be sexually experienced. The majority of women are faithful to their husbands, but some are adulterous, a few flagrantly so. The great majority always wear the *burqa* in the wards of town where such is the custom, but some very few go unveiled. The majority place their honor and pride in observing all the various rules of sexual modesty, but some blatantly disregard one or more, making for a wide variety in styles of personal living.

Lest the reader be misled to think that women alone violate the sexual code and follow irregular paths, let me hurry to add some observations on males: most of them exercise diligent care never to speak to unrelated women, eat with them, or look them in the eye; but some even cross the sexual border, acting as if they themselves were women (see Ch. 9). The majority of men invest their honor in their wife's sexual chastity, protecting themselves by divorce if she defaults; but some choose to disregard infidelity, living by different priorities. Most men keep away from other men's daughters and wives, never risking seductions or illicit affairs, but some are perceived as ever on the lookout and "chasing the women."

In other words, there is a great deal of variation in actual social life. When, in the following, I make broad, general statements like "Omani women avoid the market," or "Omani men avoid other men's wives," the reader should keep in mind that these are abstractions from reality, singling out the typical and common features in myriad singular acts while blurring all the nuances. They mean no more or no less than "Most Omani women . . ." or "Most Omani men. . . ." What they emphasize are what social scientists refer to as *patterns* of behavior, the general features in social life. I shall make it a point to indicate the relative frequencies implied by such general statements, whether any single pattern is made up of the great majority, or almost everyone, or little more than half of the female population and so forth. Unfortunately, lacking statistical data for most of these aspects of life—in part because they are inherently very little amenable to enumeration, in part because I have limited numerical coverage—these general magnitudes are as far as I can aspire.

I have always been more fascinated by people who evade the rules, or give them a distorted interpretation, and stake out their own, "deviant" course, in terms of cultural norms, than by those who follow the mainstream. Sohari society offers a rich variety of the former. In this book, I seek to make understandable the actions of both, by elucidating the basis upon which they act, the factors the people themselves take into consideration, and the goals they subjectively see themselves as pursuing. Thus I hope to convey some of the flavor and texture of real social life.

THE CONCEPTS OF CUSTOM,
CONFORMITY, AND DEVIANCE

When referring to those who fall outside the pattern I will avoid the terms "deviate" and "deviants," and I will avoid "conform" for those who are in the majority. My reason is not only the questionable character of an assumption that the majority are always right. More importantly, I hold that conform/deviate is an unfortunate dichotomy when used by social scientists, because it has connotations of right/wrong, normal/abnormal, reasonable/unreasonable and the like. It implies a value judgment on the actor's behavior, but thereby it postulates a false primacy for the former, as if all that is worth knowing about the latter is why they fall short. Such assumptions are more apt to obscure reality than illuminate it. We must give equal attention and equal primacy to all individual ways of behaving, striving to understand them all in the same terms—as the outcome of the individuals' pursuit of desired ends within a set of external constraints, perceived and interpreted by them in specific, subjective ways. It may then be shown that, to the actor herself, "wrong" ways of behaving may be the only "reasonable" or "normal" thing to do, given her life circumstances, as she perceives them. This perspective, as will be shown, is in close harmony with Sohari women's own conceptualizations of behavior (without thereby implying that the proof of the anthropologist's pudding lies wholly in the expressed views of the people she studies).

"Custom" is a concept with a close affinity to "conform" and "deviate"; I will avoid it. *Webster's Dictionary* defines it as "an established and general mode of action, which obtains in a community." Thus, as a scientific concept, it partakes of the same limitations. However, had "custom" constituted a significant concept for the actors in their attempts to make sense of their world, I should have had to investigate their usage more closely. As the case is, Sohari women rarely refer to it. Occasionally they may say that they act in certain ways because "such is our custom." It is striking, from the point of view of our present discussion, that they never explain or pass judgment on morally wrong ways as deviations from custom. Such concepts are not central to their way of thinking. On the contrary, when women are called upon to explain the acts of a person who fails to act honorably, they find the reasons either in the person's individual life circumstances, or, more often, in her psychological make-up (*roh ʿumr*). Honorable acts they interpret in the same terms. The analytical point to be emphasized here is that when some actors behave in ways consistent with "custom," like observing the rules of sexual segregation, this calls for explanation just as much as when the action is inconsistent with it. Both may be striving to make the best out of their lives.

WHY WOMEN OBSERVE SEGREGATION:
THE FEMALE VIEW

Basic to any adequate analysis of behavior is the people's subjective view of why they act as they do. Not that this necessarily holds the key to their behavior—people everywhere traffic in rationalizations—but it gives us one fundamental clue to the bases for their conduct and often *the* clue. How, then, do Sohari women conceptualize the reason why some women act in accordance with the dictates of sexual segregation, whereas others do not?

The Omani dialect of Arabic has terms to express the concept of sexual segregation and women's seclusion. Yet I have never heard Sohari women, or men for that matter, use words that could be translated as such. When women explain why they act in certain ways that we would recognize and characterize as expressions of sexual segregation, they proudly say *"nis-tihi"*—(because) we are shy/ashamed/embarrassed/bashful/ill-at-ease. They may alternatively use the verb *yitxayil,* with the same range of meanings. From a feeling of shyness, a woman will not let herself be photographed by a male, though she is eager to have a photo of herself; she will not sit beside an unrelated male driver, though everyone is agreed that someone must occupy that seat and that it is not shameful to do so; she will not let herself be examined by a male doctor, though she is suffering grave pain; she will not protest against her guardian's choice of husband for her, though she may resent his choice and has a legal right to object; if newly married, she is inclined to run and hide when her labor-migrating husband comes home on leave; she will keep the *burqa* on before all male strangers from Sohar—but not her own husband, "for he does not think that a woman must, and he will not go to people and say, 'I saw the woman's cheeks'; so we don't feel shy for him"—she will avoid the market in Sohar, but not in Mattrah (the trading center of Muscat), "because there all the women go, and people don't know us, so we don't feel shy."

The latter two examples point to a connectedness in women's minds between their feeling of bashfulness and shame and their fear what people might say about them. We would, however, be wrong to think the former a derivative of the latter. The two are linked, as is always a woman's choice of actions with the view she has of how her behavior will be judged by her significant others—that is, those whose opinions are most important to her (see Goffman 1959). But Sohari women do not let the opinions and attitudes of others determine their actions. They do what they themselves need to do and feel is right. To *yistihi* or *yitxayil* seems to be to experience a clear and strong emotion within oneself that inhibits the act in question.

I have provisionally associated these concepts with the shame and bashfulness arising from sexual modesty and segregation. However, it is striking that their meaning is not limited to this. Thus, when a hostess enjoins her guests to eat more, the says *ma-tstihi* or *ma-txayli* (don't feel shy). When explaining the reasons for the peculiar Omani custom of serving dinner guests separately from the hosts—even when this means that a single guest must eat in solitude—people say that they fear the guest will *yistihi* in the company of his or her hosts and therefore not eat well. When small children hide their faces rather than greet a returning relative, mothers explain their shyness as *yistihi*. In other words, though Sohari women regularly make use of the words *yistihi* and *yitxayil* to express the ideas of segregation and sexual modesty, the terms are not limited to these attitudes and practices as a *separate*, distinct institution. To my understanding, no term with a meaning *limited* to the sexual aspects of modesty figures at all in their daily discourse—a fact with profound implications for our understanding of what sexual modesty and segregation means to them subjectively.

As I see it, the basic implications are two. First, sexual modesty and segregation are self-evident; they are fundamental premises of the Sohari woman's world that she does not question or emphasize. They simply exist, in the same way as does the biological need for food, and she relates to them in the same straightforward and unselfconscious manner. Interestingly, from the point of view of this analogy, there also is no separate term referring to biological hunger only; *gaᶜana* (hungry) is a term used to refer to a hunger for prestigious material goods as well. The legitimacy of sexual segregation is not questioned by anyone, not even those women who occasionally violate it. Once in awhile, women may express wonder about what concrete forms segregation will come to take in the future, as a consequence of the government's policy of giving women more freedom (*hurriyya*). But in this they regard themselves the loyal subjects of a state authority whose rationale they do not aspire to understand; and they express much awe and some resentment, but no thrilled excitement, at the prospects of woman's new freedoms that, to their understanding, threaten to undermine one secure pillar of her whole existence.

Second, sexual segregation refers to a level of abstraction that Sohari women rarely imply—that of society itself. It pertains to an organizing principle of the very structure of society, and it thereby presupposes considerable analytical sophistication or awareness of the social order. Sohari women have neither. In addition, they do not interpret their own and other people's actions with reference to the macro-features of their society, but find the causes in the micro-features of their own little worlds. The genesis of the institution of sexual segreg   and its basic constituent—women's seclusion—has been sought in   e optimal functioning of the Muslim communal order; it has been said to have evolved as a solution to problems that his order faces. However, when women act, they do so with a view to their own privately felt interests, and their own personal problems, not those of society.

The nature of *yistihi* as a basic constituent of women's conceptual uni-

verse and a fundamental explanatory principle in their endeavors to grasp
and make sense of the world is further revealed in their seeing breaches of
the sexual code as resulting from an absence of this essential feeling.
Referring to a friend who was a prostitute, some women remarked: "See
the way she speaks to him [our driver]. *Hiyya matistihi abadan!* (She does
not feel the least bit shy!) We also speak to him, when we come to the gate
to fetch you, but we do so in a very different manner from her. We feel
shy."

Their view of what makes for the presence or absence of this feeling of
shyness is discussed below.

WHY MEN OBSERVE SEGREGATION: THE MALE VIEW

The other side to sexual segregation is the male's. The maintenance of
this institution as a social fact, as distinct from a cultural ideal, presupposes observance on the part of a majority of actors from both categories.
How, then, do men conceptualize the bases for the male's decisions to
honor or transgress the sexual code?

Men do not use the word *yistihi* when referring to themselves, but refer
to the honor to be gained from morally correct behavior, or to what people
might think (not say!) of breaches: their view is that "It is only *impolite*
men who sleep with the wives of others, men who do not care about their
reputation." It is significant that males and females conceptualize their
respective actions in service of the same ideals in such different ways; this
is a reflection of the different standards of self-presentation applying to
each. *Yistihi* has connotations of softness and weakness; such qualities are
deemed beneath a man's dignity. Thus, when a father absents himself
from his daughter's wedding, he will explain to the inquisitive anthropologists—no one else finds cause to ask—that he has urgent business in
Muscat or Dubai. Other men will confirm this version. But the women,
when confronted with the same question by the curious outsider, will explain that the bride's father *yistihi* on the occasion, therefore he stays
away. I do not know whether women are aware that in this they ascribe
emotions to men that men themselves deny having. In the absence of a
dialogue between the sexes about these acts and their motives, women are
probably ignorant of the discrepancy.

This discussion of folk conceptualizations of sexual segregation must
include a reference to the concept of ᶜ*aib* (shame), though its use and
meaning will be more fully discussed in Chapter 8. Shame is a value judgment of an act of behavior, as measured by the community's moral standards. A breach of the sexual code, like infidelity, is thus shame. Shame
characterizes the act in question, but does not seek to explain it. The concept is rarely used by Sohari men and women; this indicates their basic at-

titude to fellow beings—which is first and foremost to respect and honor, rather than to pass judgment and condemn (see Ch. 8).

PURDAH: EXTERNAL OR INTERNAL CONTROLS?

As earlier stated, many Muslim scholars, as well as Omani laymen, regard the seclusion of women as necessitated by women's dangerous and frail nature, and the fact that they cannot be trusted to exercise responsible moral judgments. Oman relies heavily upon external safeguards to secure its sexual morality. Sexual morality is judged high when the great majority of *women* refrain from illicit intercourse. The sexual acts of men do not affect the sexual standard per se; Oman is a country with a high sexual morality in that the great majority of women do observe sexual chastity. May we therefore conclude that the external safeguards serve their purpose? No, in the view of Sohari women: "If a woman desires to sleep with men, no amount of force can constrain her. Her husband may lock her up behind walls of concrete, but she will find her way." And conversely: "If a woman has no such desires, her [labor-migrating] husband may leave her for years alone, and she will be chaste."

What these women see as crucial for sexual chastity, or its absence, is the individual women's psychological makeup. It determines her disposition to feel shy. A woman's psychology is seen as a very powerful element or force in her behavior. Women's standard reaction to my questions about the reasons for other women's peculiarities of behavior was a shrug of the shoulders and the saying *rohha* or *ᶜumraha* (that's just her way, her nature). It is essential to stress that a woman's psyche is regarded as so unbending that it can be only minimally influenced by external sanctions, coercion, and constraints. Not that it necessarily asserts itself in a stable fashion throughout her life span. A woman may be chaste for years, then, for no reason apparant to her friends, become an adulteress, again become chaste, then fall again—everything *bi-rohha* (by herself). In other words, Sohari women clearly and explicitly conceptualize the woman as the source of her own sexual conduct, irrespective of the external safeguards that may surround her. A concept such as internalized sanction is obviously far removed from their folk concepts, but, as I understand them, their use of the concepts *roh* and *ᶜumr* has a clear reference precisely to the woman's *internal* controls.

MODESTY AND HONOR

A woman's individual psyche determines her disposition to *yistihi*. *Yistihi* connotes a personal feeling, so private and individual that it may be evoked in some individuals in some situations where their significant others tell them they need not feel shy. The act in question is not morally reprehensible by their society's standards. Some brief examples may serve to illustrate the point.

A group of seven women and three small children were struggling to position themselves in a Landrover. Everyone seemed reluctant to sit in the front seat beside the unrelated driver, though someone must. The old woman in charge instructed the two mothers in the group (her daughter-in-law and granddaughter) to sit in the front with their children, that that would be the most correct thing. They bluntly refused—from a feeling of shyness, as they later told me. The dilemma was happily solved when one of the others, known, though not acknowledged, to be a prostitute, smilingly volunteered.

When, by 1976, the ideology of equal opportunities for women stated that it was no longer shameful for women to go to the market; Sohari women were definite that, shameful or not, *they* would not go. "We would feel shy," they averred with self-confident pride.

Another, more traditional, situation illustrates the same point: Peddling in women's trinkets and materials is traditionally a female career engaged in by some of the older women. It is not shameful and brings rewards that are fervently desired by all: material gain. Yet only a few women (approximately one in fifty) embark on it. The majority say they would feel shy to go into unfamiliar houses.

Why do women refrain from acts that are judged morally acceptable by their society's scale of values? Because they are struggling for self-regard and social esteem in terms of *internalized* standards of style and grace; one may perhaps say dignity. To win honor, it is not enough to perform acts that are morally right or nonobjectionable. Honor is a relative concept. It implies ranking and measurement; to score highly, a person needs not only to fulfill values, but to excel in them—to do better than others. It has been mistakenly assumed by most anthropologists writing about the Middle East, as by their male informants, that honor is something only men have. Women, as far as the concept applies to them at all, are seen as passively partaking of their guardians' honor, and in danger of destroying what they have through the precariousness of their internal moral controls. Their honor thus has a passive quality about it, as have the women themselves. Women are not thought capable of acquiring honor. These assumptions are unfounded and wrong, as far as Sohari women are concerned (and, I venture to say, as far as women generally are concerned). Woman may be viewed as a passive pawn on man's stage, but she is an active actor on her own. Within her own world, she reflects and evaluates, chooses and acts and struggles for honor and esteem, as does the man within his. Different standards apply to the sexes, and the basic dichotomization of society through sexual segregation makes the sexes unaware of major aspects of each other's self-presentation and self-actualization. The male, whose world coincides with the public, large-scale arena, may well regard women as having no personal honor, because *within his world* she has not. There she is not even a person in her own right: if persons must address her, they do so by way of her son's or father's name; she herself should be invisible. But within her own small-scale world of home and neighborhood, the woman's honor is not at all a mirror reflection of her guardian's, however much he might like to think so. It depends upon her ability to excel in those valued acts of behavior that her female friends and neighbors deem worthy of merit. The man may build a platform for the woman's self-actualization and provide her with some major assets. But what really counts is the way the woman herself chooses to use these, as well as other assets that she herself may acquire, in her own personal struggle to think well of herself.

CHAPTER 5

✤

Socialization to the Practice of Segregation

"Destiny cannot be reversed."
—Ibadhi teaching, quoted in Phillips 1971, p. 83.

How do the standards of segregation become entrenched and internalized in women? To describe this, it is necessary to pay attention to child-rearing and -training practices as they pertain to both sexes, even though our main focus of interest lies with women. This must be so since, despite a pervasive segregation of the sexes, males and females interact with, and depend on, each other as members of *one* society. Both sexes participate in molding the child, and the formation of one gender role is affected by the shape of the other. Indeed, in both attitudes and behavior, one is also struck by profound common features shared by both genders as *Omanis* or, to be more precise, Arabs of the Batinah coast.

Surely, it must be in the course of socialization that these characteristic features are imparted: that delicate style of grace, tact, and humility, the quietness and control in manners and speech, the calm and gentle integrity that distinguish them, be they girls or boys, women or men. These are traits that seem to have struck all observers. Working through the literature on Oman—and, especially during the past three years, several volumes have appeared, though none with more than a very slight and passing reference to women—I have not come across one author who has not been forcefully impressed with precisely these qualities. Thus Michael Darlow and Richard Fawkes, in *The Last Corner of Arabia*, observe that they "noticed that all the British who had served in Oman for any length of time spoke quietly—it seemed to be an effect that the country had on them!" (1976, p. 15). And Alexander Hamilton, as long ago as 1721, observed: "The Muscati Arabs are remarkable for their humility and urbanity."

A psychologically informed analysis of personality development would be required to properly explain the factors most forceful in shaping and affecting the Omani self-presentation. In lieu of this, I shall have to confine myself to those aspects of child rearing which Omanis believe to play an important role in the formation of personality and temperament. In later chapters, we shall occasionally be confronted with patterns of behavior and reaction which call out for an understanding beyond that provided by pragmatic circumstances and cultural norms alone (for example, Chs. 8, 11, and 12). I trust that the reader will then more readily appreciate what at this stage may seem digressions from this chapter's major theme: how children in Sohar are instilled with the ways of segregation.

THE FIRST TWO YEARS OF LIFE

The birth of a child is a joyous occasion for the family, irrespective of the baby's sex, even though both men and women express a preference for sons. We did not observe baby boys receiving more attention than girls—except in a few rare cases where the boy was born last after a succession of girls. And, we believe, had the case been the other way around, the little sister would have been equally spoiled.

However, males being, in the view of both sexes, innately superior, the father gives ritual expression to this when he rewards the relative who brings him the news of the newborn boy with twice as much money as for news of a daughter. The amount, however, is symbolic: two Rials for a son, one Rial for a daughter. Only the most affluent families celebrate the birth of a child by killing a goat. We never observed such a feast, but were told that it likewise is more elaborate for a son than for a daughter.

The newborn is thought to be particularly susceptible to health hazards of various kinds, and so indeed it is, given the unfortunate combination of poor nutrition, poor hygiene, the oppressive climate, and the practice of various folk techniques of curing. These hazards have been partially overcome by the establishment of the Sohar hospital in 1972.

The most serious danger to the child, in the Sohari view, is "the evil eye" of envious people who may cause any and all kinds of illnesses, and even death itself. It is a measure of this fear that the infant is hidden from view from all strangers, for the first fourteen to forty days of life. When friends of the mother pay their ritual congratulatory visit a week after the birth, they are neither shown the baby nor should they ask questions about it. We discovered that sometimes such visitors were even unaware of the baby's sex.

To counteract the dangers of the evil eye, as well as those stemming from supernatural agents like the *jinn*, [1] mothers adorn children of both sexes with amulets of Koranic inscription. Interestingly, we did not come across the practice common in many Middle Eastern countries of pro-

---

[1] The *jinn* are supernatural beings who inhabit the natural world of ordinary human beings and are ubiquitous. They take on the shape of human beings, appear in human clothing, and are consequently impossible to discern.

viding special protection for the boy by dressing him in a girl's garments. (The common rationalization for the custom is that girls are less desirable than boys and consequently less prone to cause jealousy.)

In Oman, girls and boys are differently dressed from birth on, or shortly afterward. Girls wear loose, short-sleeved dresses, with long pants underneath, whereas boys wear ankle-length shirts with long sleeves (*dish-dasha*s).

The first two years of the child's life are characterized by loving, unconditional care and attention from all family members. Whenever the child is not asleep, in his mother's or in another relative's lap, on a mat by their side, or in his crib, he is carried around by his mother, astride her hip, wherever she goes. At the slightest sign of discomfort, the baby is offered the breast, as often as up to twelve times an hour, by our observations. If his mother's milk fails, he is offered a bottle of milk made from dried powder. Wet nurses are not used.

Sohari women regard the bond between mother and child as immensely personal and intimate and often express incredulity at the practice observed among expatriate Indians (nurses) and Egyptians (schoolteachers) of leaving their children in the home country in the care of another relative. Time and again, they wanted to know what I myself would do when my first child was born. On my next visit to Sohar, could I conceive of doing like those Indians and Egyptians, or would I, like them, need to have my child with me?

Swaddling is common in the winter. The baby is wrapped in a large piece of cloth that covers all of his body, except for the head and buttocks. Training the infant to control his bowel movements begins as early as between four and six months of age (bladder control is considered of less importance) and thus the buttocks must be left uncovered. The reasons given for swaddling were three: to provide warmth, to build strong bodies, and, most importantly, to prevent those uncoordinated movements of arms and legs which we consider normal in babies. However, Soharis perceive such jerking as the work of the *jinn* and fear it greatly.

A great deal of the mother's attention during the child's first two years is concentrated on protecting him from all threats to his health and well-being. Crying is perceived as the greatest danger, for it is believed to attract the attention of the *jinn*. To *jinn* are ascribed the power to inflict all kinds of evils, even death itself. They have an aversion to all sorts of noises, as do Soharis themselves, so much so that Soharis believe the *jinn* will soon disappear from town because of traffic noise from cars and motorcycles.

At present, *jinn* must be duly heeded. To reduce the risks caused by the baby's crying, mothers adopt a variety of measures: breast-feeding on demand is one response; the baby's wearing of amulets and branding with a hot iron (*wasum*) are others. But the most popular technique, applied twice daily, is to drug babies with an opiate, *soukour*. This is made from sugar and the dried flower of the poppy and thus contains morphine.[2]

From birth, the baby is fed *soukour*, once in the morning and once in the afternoon (for some babies, it is the first "food" they ever taste). The amount given increases with time, from a dose that covers the small fingernail, to one that covers the nail of the index finger, to a maximum dose that covers the thumbnail. Occasionally, this normal maximum may even be exceeded.

Soharis know full well that *soukour* is addictive. They say that babies get used to it, in the same way that men get used to smoking. Yet they do not consider the practice harmful, in view of its many beneficial effects. Protecting the baby from the *jinn* and stomach pains are some, leaving the mother in peace and with time to carry out her tasks and visit with the neighbors are others. We suspect, however, that there is a third, highly important one, which to Soharis is so self-evident that they do not find it worth mention: their own extreme aversion to noise. The world should be a quiet place, people tactful and predictable, movements silent and gentle.

THE CHILD FROM TWO TO SIX YEARS OF AGE

When the child is around the age of two, a series of changes—some of which can hardly fail to be experienced by the child as traumatic—are introduced.

Weaning usually takes place abruptly in the course of only one day. The mother starts the process late on a Thursday afternoon, by painting her nipples with *sabr* (an ill-tasting yellow paste) or pepper. The child cries desperately, and, to reduce the sense of loss, the mother keeps largely out of his view while other family members and neighbors hug him and try to distract him. If the child proves very recalcitrant, he is likely to be sent to the home of his maternal grandmother or aunts for a week or so. When he returns, he is, of course, expected still to be fussy and restless; but that, mothers say, is part of the process of growing up.

Weaning at precisely the age of two is based on a religious belief (Surah el Baqara, verse 233) that is closely adhered to in Sohar.

Shortly after the child has been weaned, *soukour* is also abruptly removed, with effects that can only aggravate his feeling of loss. As expected, this initiates a period of much crying and restlessness. The child's

[2] The poppy is crushed, sieved to remove the large pieces, and mixed with water, herbs, and sugar. It may also be mixed with water, then heated, strained, and given to the baby with a spoon. The government of Oman is trying to discourage *soukour*'s use, but in 1974 it was still openly displayed in shops. In 1976, women reported to me that they were in the process of abandoning its use, due to the availability of what they perceived as a much more effective substitute: sleeping pills obtained at the hospital.

crying is now ignored as a regrettable but necessary phase. As concerns the affects on the personality development of a two year old of the almost simultaneous removal of the breast and the *soukour,* one may only speculate, but it is reasonable to expect a person, after such an experience, to repudiate the relationship to the previously beloved one, to respond actively to detach himself so as to ease the feeling of loss that has been inflicted. The experience may even be so traumatic that, in the future, the person will fear any further attachment and seek to keep intimate others at an emotionally safe distance.

When the child begins to talk, around the age of two or three, he is expected to ask to be taken to the toilet, and he is scolded if he fails to do so. Until then, failures have been sanctioned with no more than discontent glances from the mother. After repeated mishaps, he may be threatened with spanking or the red-hot iron (*wasum*), or (since the inception of the hospital) injections.

At this point, the mother will probably be expecting her next child, and the two year old is left to the care of an older sister, a grandmother or another female relative. This need not entail a loss of love and attention, but, of necessity, it means a separation from the one person most beloved in the child's world. Soharis expect strong jealousy to result, and some women say that it is necessary to anticipate and counteract this by being progressively less indulgent as the time approaches. It would seem, moreover, that the felt need to attend to the new infant's smallest desire leaves the Sohari mother with no other possible attitude toward her next older child.

He now will be carried astride his older sister's hip wherever she goes. He is not included in play, but instructed to sit quietly in a corner and watch. If an infant does not have an older sister, a girl from the same compound or neighborhood will bring him along.

When a girl is around two years old, slight but fundamental changes are introduced in her clothing, in recognition of her passage from the baby to the girl stage and her dawning femininity. From now on, her dresses will have long sleeves and small neck openings, to cover such private parts of the body as the arms and the upper chest. She may still have her hair bare when inside the domestic compound, but whenever she is taken visiting outside of her neighborhood she must cover her head by the *wiqaya,* a gaily colored head scarf nearly long enough to sweep the ground behind her and wide enough to cover her back. Adult women always wear such scarves when stepping outside their own gate. Many two year olds were also seen to cover their hair and neck when at home with the *leeso,* a scarf tightly wrapped around the chin even though the *leeso* is not obligatory until around age five.

No parallel changes are introduced into the boy's dress style, reflecting the absence of change in the demands of physical modesty deriving from

the male's sexual development. Many mothers, however, like to emphasize their little boys' incipient manhood by dressing them with the Omani
male head cap, the *kummi,* a prime symbol of manliness.

The manner of dress outlined above is traditional in Sohar, and it had
scarcely been modified when we first visited the town in the spring of 1974.
One-and-a-half years later, slight but fundamental changes were noticeable in the female style of dress. Two year olds no longer wore the *wiqaya*
on visits outside the neighborhood, but went bareheaded. Five year olds
rarely wore the *leeso,* even on faraway visits, but left their hair and neck
bare. In school, however, it was obligatory to wear a scarf tied under the
chin (Egyptian style, worn by the Egyptian teachers).

Girls and boys mix freely together till around age six. As long as they do
not stray too far away from their home or neighborhood, they may play
together in an almost totally unsupervised way. A favorite game seems to
be "house and family"; they use shells, stones, sticks, and empty cans as
furniture and utensils, and younger siblings play the role of children. We
never saw dolls of any kind and were told that of old (until three years
before), girls used to make them from pieces of wood covered with cloth,
but that now such things were outdated. Boys sometimes would make cars
from old oil cans, fashioning wheels from can lids and pulling the cars by
a string. Girls may borrow such precious male toys, but they do not make
them themselves. Boys were also observed to enjoy catching frogs and
grasshoppers. On the whole, they show more imagination and inven-
tiveness in their play than girls—in harmony with the more versatile and
active role they are to play in adult life.

From my point of view as an observer, the most striking feature about
children's play was its absence rather than its presence, how very little of it
there was. Only rarely did children engage in playful activity. They seem
remarkably little oriented *toward each other;* more often, they would sit,
quite immobile, in the company of other children or adults. The use of objects in play was particularly infrequent. Indeed, Sohari children would be
seen perpetually "playing" with food, idly handling it, fingering it, then
slowly consuming it. It was rare to see children below the age of three
without a piece of food between their fingers, and for the older children,
food seemed to give joy and to preoccupy them in the way that toys do
Western children.

Mothers and elder sisters sometimes voiced the complaint that children
lacked the ability to become absorbed in their play, preferring the company of grownups: "Whenever any visitor comes, children lose all interest
in play; all they want to do is sit and watch." Thus, a conspicuous feature
of any gathering of women that includes someone who is not daily present
among them, is a large audience of ten to twenty children.

They may appear like rain from a clear blue sky. Once they are present,
they become an integral part of the gathering. Not that they make their

presence felt by intrusions into the circle of adults; they remain seated at the edge of it, beautifully well-behaved, the essence of which, in Oman, is *silence*. But they will not leave till the visitor has left, no matter how long the latter stays. Inaudible and immovable (qualities perfected with age, but developed to a rare excellence in four- and five year olds), they remain seated, listening but not looking, rarely succumbing even to one curious glance. I take it that they are in fact full of curiosity, or why should they be there? Yet, every child looks down at the ground before him, as if fully absorbed in his own private world. Adult women display a similar pattern.

The following excerpt from my field notes is illustrative:

January, 12, 1976: As I arrived in front of Latifa's home, a dozen children or so came running after me, yelling "Unni has come, Unni has come." Only one step inside the gate of Latifa's home, and their behavior changed as dramatically as if it were a church they had entered. Not a sound escaped their lips. Their movements became slow and protracted. Inaudibly, they slid onto the sitting platform and sat down in a circle, very close together, as if for mutual protection. For two hours they remained, motionless, silent as the grave, with their eyes fixed firm as stone to the ground. I was not able to catch one of them in one curious glance, or even in a glance at the group of women assembled. Wholly passive they remained. At one time the women's conversation turned to the topic of jewelry and prices, and Aisha Baluch suggested that we inspect the earrings of her little niece, a girl of some five years. While the girl sat still as a stone, Aisha Baluch removed the earrings, passed them around to some of the other women, they talked about where the earrings may have been bought, what they must have cost, etc. Their interest satisfied, Aisha Baluch put the earrings back into place. The five year old kept her statuelike composure throughout, not a sound, not a movement, *no* participation.

At this age, there are no restrictions on the boys' access to this basically female arena, but there are slight differences in the behavior of boys and girls. Socialized to become more active and self-assertive from an early age, boys show a slight tendency to change their position at times, to look out on the gathering, though not *at* the visitor, and they may once in a rare while even lose interest in the gathering and go off to play. But these are only slight trends, not clear differences, as far as I have been able to observe.

Children of both sexes love to follow their mother around whenever she goes visiting, and they are usually allowed to do so, except on rare occasions when they may be left at home in the care of a grandmother or older sibling. This pattern is not discarded till marriage puts an end to it for girls, and adolescence ends it for boys.

By the age of five or six, children are thought old enough to carry some responsibility and make themselves useful to the family. This draws them progressively into the segregated spheres of women and men; they are made to help their seniors with simple tasks, systematically allocated by sex according to a strict division of labor. At first, a boy will be asked to do very simple errands, such as opening or closing the gate or calling a member of the family. Later, he may be sent to buy things for his mother at the market and to collect fish spilled on the beach while sardines are being caught in fish nets. If the family owns a date-palm garden, as one third of the families do, the boy will now be encouraged to accompany elder female members to become acquainted with garden work. As a start, he may help pick up dates and other fruits. While the little boy is being socialized for his role in the outside world, the little girl has her attention progressively drawn to the narrower horizon of the home. She is asked to help with light housework and with the care of the younger siblings; she helps feed the animals and fetch firewood and water from stores within the compound. At this age, the girl is not yet compelled to do housework, but she is encouraged to observe how household tasks are done and to imitate adult women, and praised for doing so.

On the whole, children of both sexes are expected to learn by observation, imitation, and repetition more than by sanctions. If a child makes a mistake at this stage, he or she is rarely punished, but simply asked to try again or taught the correct way.

Parents are more lenient with sons than with daughters from an early age. Disobedience on the part of sons is more easily tolerated; they are allowed more free time and left to roam about with fewer restrictions. Girls are more closely supervised, in anticipation of steadily increasing restrictions as they grow older. From age four or so, boys' play can lead to exploration of places forbidden to girls, such as the market. So tabooed is this arena for girls that at no age may they accompany their fathers or other male relatives there, and they will usually grow up without having had as much as a glimpse of this fascinating place, with its stalls full of all the precious material things that figure so prominently in their lives.

FROM AGE SIX TO PUBERTY

When children reach their seventh year, the permissiveness of their upbringing is reduced. Expectations and demands increase, and compliance is more strictly enforced. Children of both sexes are given more jobs and are made increasingly aware of the importance of obedience and respect. Segregation is a pervasively implicit, and only occasionally explicit, part of the code that they learn. Mainly they are inculcated with their responsibilities toward parents and their duties toward other family members, relatives, and neighbors. They are told never to question persons older than themselves. If told to do something in a certain way, they must do it in that way. To enforce obedience, the parents, as well as the older siblings, relatives, and neighbors, start to speak loudly or harshly when correcting or instructing the children. Mothers and female members frequently resort to threats of punishing obstinacy with injections given by a nurse (or the anthropologist!), branding by hot iron, or complaints to the father. The first seems the most effective measure; children are terrified of injections, available in Sohar only since 1972. Sometimes the mother threatens with spanking, but the blow itself is almost never forthcoming. A mother may temporarily subdue her children by threats, but many children ignore their mothers. It is the father who may resort to corporal punishment, particularly with the sons. However, as far as we could observe, the father is also hesitant to administer blows and more frequently merely allots reprimands. However, his stern words carry much more weight than the mother's, and we have seen boys as old as ten burst into tears at a father's reprimand, though his words were free of invectives and there were no indications that a blow was in fact forthcoming. Boys are not ridiculed for crying.

On the whole, children behave better when the father or other male relative is around. Children will cease their noisy horseplay the moment an adult male enters the compound, become quiet, and sit correctly. This behavior is partially out of respect, but also out of fear of being reprimanded. It is also entirely consistent with the way in which the compound serves as a segregated women's area when men are absent and as a uniquely joint arena dominated by men when they are present.

Until seven years of age, both sons and daughters are mainly the responsibility of the mother and other female adults in the household. Much of the time, they are left in the care of older sisters, who play a major part in raising younger siblings. In these early years, the father rarely helps his wife with the care of the children. Bringing up children is a female task. For example, the husband will not take care of the children when his wife attends the newly instituted adult education classes, even though it is likely to be he, and not she, who insists that she goes. She must leave the children with a female relative. But he enjoys playing with and comforting the children, at his own pleasure, and making them happy with gifts and tenderness.

Fathers seem to enjoy their "irresponsible" role vis-à-vis their children in their early years, and the children seem to regard their father as much more a source of kindness than of discipline. After age seven, this relationship changes. The boy stays more and more under the authority and guidance of the father, whereas father-daughter interaction decreases. The father becomes more formal with his daughter, who becomes more shy and reserved in his presence. From now on, the father makes many important decisions on behalf of his children of both sexes; but whereas he sits down and explains matters to his son, he usually transmits decisions to the daughter indirectly through her mother.

In case of divorce, the father has a legal right to keep children who are seven years of age or older. But women say that the mother may actually keep only a child that she is nursing. A childhood spent with a stepmother is thought a most unenviable fate. Soharis insist that it is impossible for a woman to love children other than her own. Hence a stepmother will be harsh with the stepchild and, most seriously of all, "only gives him second-rate food."

Around the age of six or seven, most children of both sexes today enroll in school. Public elementary schools were introduced in Sohar in 1972. But their schools are located far apart, and the boys are taught only by men, the girls, only by women. The ideology of segregation in modern education seems that of supplying separate but equal facilities. Children spend about an hour a day on their homework, showering the same kind of love and attention on their schoolbooks that Western children are wont to reserve for their toys and pets. However, schoolwork does not free children from work responsibilities at home. Little girls, especially, enter a stage of increasing domestic responsibilities, because the time is approaching, only some six years away, when they will carry the full adult responsibilities of married women. The girl spends a good part of the day working with her mother, though the amount of work is lessened if she has an older sister who is closer to marriage and even more in need of training. Care of younger siblings falls to a girl of this age. She also assists by collecting firewood, carrying water, washing clothes and dishes, feeding animals, and milking cows and goats. As soon as she is able, she is taught the more difficult tasks of baking bread, cooking, sewing by hand and by machine, if one is available. Sewing at home is the female equivalent of male wage labor, begun at about age twelve—the same age that boys undertake paid work.

Before elementary schooling was introduced in Sohar, it was common for boys to take part-time or full-time employment at the age of ten; many embarked on labor migration and entirely supported themselves by the age of twelve or fourteen. By then, they were expected to behave in all respects like a man. Part-time responsibilities are now accepted, such as picking dates and limes, irrigating trees, plowing and planting gardens, cutting wood and alfalfa, and fishing. A few work as servants in houses after school, some are waiters, and quite a few assist their fathers in their shops. Any wages earned by the boy are handed over to the father.

From school age, boys and girls play together less frequently. Their own gender group takes on added significance as the reference group from which they take their standards and values. Boys are allowed to explore even more distant reaches, whereas girls are even more carefully confined to the home and the neighborhood. The discrepancy derives directly from Omani codifications of male and female identities. A male may make serious mistakes, yet he does not stand in danger of having his whole identity spoiled by any one fault committed. Only a female for whom he is responsible may afflict him in such a way. For a man, even transexualism carries no disastrous implications—the wrongdoer may later build up an honorable, if not exactly spotless, reputation (see Ch. 9). But a female risks irreparable damage to her reputation, and above all, to that of her menfolk, if caught once in compromising circumstances. She needs only to be seen alone once in the company of an unrelated male and people will know that "Satan was their third companion." Thus, if not a powerful person, the female is dangerous indeed to herself and others and cannot be trusted to her own judgment.

Around the age of seven, the boy starts to accompany his father to the market, the mosque, and the fields, and he is invited to join his father when he goes visiting. The father advises or instructs his son to stop the pattern he has practiced so far of following the mother around as she goes visiting and sitting with the women as they gossip. Now the boy is encouraged to sit with his father's visitors, in the male guest arena—a walled and raised platform located just inside the gate. The boy should politely listen to the men's discussions so as to develop the knowledge and understanding peculiar to them. He will also be instructed to serve coffee to the guests—a task that conventionally devolves on the youngest or lowest ranking male in a gathering. In performing this correctly and elegantly—pouring the coffee deftly into the small shallow cups, serving in the correct rank order, attending solicitously but subtly to the appetites of the guests—he has the opportunity to exhibit the Omani man's social graces in an act that is somehow felt to epitomize the men at their purest and best. He also brings whatever snacks are served and shares them with the men, while every female stays out of sight.

At this stage of development, commensal practices in many homes will be changed to accommodate the changes in self-presentation appropriate for girls and boys. If they are members of extended or joint households, children have so far eaten with the women, who eat apart from and after the men. However, a boy of seven is recognized as no longer a child, but a man-to-be, by being asked to join the men for meals. Such recognition will also be forthcoming in those few nuclear families where the father eats apart. Thus unequivocally stepping across the sexual boundary, and becoming a member of the world of males, the boy loses a child's privileges. Prime among these is the freedom to join the mother and her guests or hostess for snacks during the frequent female visits. A child may help himself to as much of the favored delights as his stomach can hold. But a boy of seven must patiently wait till the others have finished—commensality being the most intimate of acts, next to physical caresses—and consequently taboo between unrelated persons of the opposite sex. We have witnessed boys as old as ten violating this golden rule and being duly ridiculed and punished; the breach seems to have been caused by fear on the boy's part that the good snacks might be snatched away under his very nose. But these are exceptions; boys commonly compose themselves and behave like the men they are expected to be.

Although fathers command that boys keep away from women's company, boys as old as their teens side-step these commands. Maybe they find the conversation entertaining—such little of it as there is, for, as I have already stressed, Sohari women rarely indulge in gossip, and never in juicy gossip—judged by our standards. However, measured by the demanding Omani male standards, it may seem much, for men hold it beneath their dignity ever to stoop to gossip. Young boys may also find the informal atmosphere of female gatherings relaxing, as compared to the male formality.

An interesting feature of these occasions, with important effects on children's socialization, is the extent of sexual joking and chatting that goes on. Sex is a favorite topic of women. Vivid descriptions in words and gestures of manners of intercourse within and without marriage, as well as sexual aberrations of various kinds, have a prominent place in their informal gatherings. They observe no shyness for children, not even for a son in his teens. For this reason, children presumably grow up with a "natural," matter-of-fact attitude to these aspects of life.

In the event of the father's death, the boy will enter more swiftly and deeply into the male sphere of life. He will assume many responsibilities for his mother, brothers, and sisters. He will make decisions, relying on the advice of a paternal uncle or grandfather. In some cases, his father's brother will become head of the household and the boy will be responsible for the errands necessary to run the house and prepare the meals. If the father labor-migrates, all mail to the family will be addressed to the son, not the mother. The son answers his father's letters and attends to his literal instructions.

The boy's status as a prospective guardian of female relatives on the father's side, his "property rights" in them, and consequent superiority, may receive symbolic recognition long before he is ready to actually carry out such responsibilities. For example, when a boy's sister is married, he receives approximately 100 Rials ($300) from the bride price presented to his father by the groom; if his paternal cousin marries, he will receive 25–50 Rials, depending upon his age (see Ch. 10). A minor will hand over this money to his father or other male guardian of the household, because "what belongs to the son belongs to the father and vice versa." The money is nevertheless regarded as an expression of the joint rights in females of a corporation of males related in the paternal line. Sisters and female paternal cousins of the bride are presented only with a token gift of a dress or a piece of full female clothing, valued at one and one-half to three Rials in 1974.

In connection with weddings, the superior status of males is also expressed in a number of other symbolic ways, whose meaning can scarcely fail to impress the children. A joyous feature of these occasions is the music and the singing. Only men are musicians—the role demanding skill, as Omanis see it. Only females sing, and included amongst them are *xanith*s—those males who act as if they were women (see Ch. 9). But even *xanith*s—biological males—are unanimously seen as excelling women in this female capacity. Men also do beautiful recitations of poetry, something women are regarded as incapable of doing. When the groom and his guests make the solemn trip to fetch the bride, the males all occupy the first cars, and the women follow behind. The men also cook the wedding meal, in keeping with their privilege of serving as cooks on all major festival occasions. This act is strikingly symbolic of their inherent superiority, as on common days it is thought beneath a man's dignity to do even a trifling bit of cooking.

Starting out in life with a set of shared living conditions, material as well as social, boys and girls after two years of age enter paths that gradually diverge and end up in very different worlds. They are ascribed different tasks and responsibilities, complementary standards of behavior, and dissimilar outlooks on life and the world. To become an *Omani* female, not just any female, a girl is taught to present herself in a manner that is quiet and soft-spoken, modest and timid, graceful and poised, hospitable and polite, submissive and obedient, trustworthy and loyal. Furthermore, she is trained to signal the possession of these qualities by specific gestures and acts that convey such meanings in the Omani setting. The most shocking repudiation imaginable of all these qualities would be a violation of this segregation by uncovering inappropriate parts of the body, appearing in localities outside the female precincts, or intruding herself into the attention of male gatherings.

The female's transition to adult status is announced by a piece of clothing, which is the prime symbol of her change from girlhood to womanhood: the *burqa*, or mask. No one hoping to understand the relationship between the sexes can do so without a thorough appreciation of the *burqa*—its various symbolic meanings, the formal etiquette of its wearing, and its practical complexities. However, as this complex cultural symbol has never been ethnographically documented and may soon become a relic of the past, I have chosen to devote a separate chapter (Ch. 6) to it.

An Omani male should present himself as a person with the same attributes of politeness and hospitality, trustworthiness and humility, gracefulness and style. But the male manner of signaling these virtues is different from the female, and, most importantly, it should be done in the male sphere and on the diverse range of male arenas. Furthermore, males should also be assertive, forceful, and decisive. The *total* styles of self-presentation generated for each of the sexes are widely disparate.

At the age of twelve to thirteen, both boys and girls are thought mature and ready to assume full adult responsibilities. Whereas girls are then married off, boys wait an average of ten more years before they arrange for their own marriage. There are several reasons for this wide discrepancy of age. One is the father's fear for their daughters' chastity; another is the large bride price a male must accumulate before he can marry. But it does seem that men postpone their marriage longer than is financially necessary, often with the avowed motive to be free, to travel and see the world, unburdened by the weights and responsibilities of a family. We did not meet any man who had not at least been as far as the neighboring Gulf states (with the exception of one male-cum-female, a transexual); and some female friends of mine ridiculed a man whom they knew of who had not traveled and "gained knowledge," as they phrased it. Among the women, however, few had been to either Muscat or Dubai, the two largest cities, some two hours' drive away.

Whereas boys in their teens become masters of their own lives, girls become the subjects of a new and unknown master, their husband—and often of his mother too. Boys enter a stage of increasing freedom and experience; girls enter one of increasing work and confinement, but also of gratifying responsibilities and chances of self-actualization.

CHAPTER 6

The *Burqa* Facial Mask

"It is not that we wear burqa *because it is shameful to go without it, but because it is beautiful to go with it!"*

Ingeniously fashioned to cover some select parts of the woman's face in a design that serves exquisitely to enhance her individual beauty, yet properly to cover her when in the presence of strangers before whom she feels shy, the *burqa* epitomizes female modesty and pride. It is an integral part of the woman's self; like no other garment, her *burqa* she handles in complex ways, time and again every day, to communicate to the world her sense of being a beautiful, modest, and honorable woman, as well as her personal feelings of ease or embarrassment in a given situation. It is the major visible symbol of marital status: A young girl first assumes her *burqa* when, at the end of her seven-day honeymoon, she leaves her secluded bridal hut (*kille*) to take up her residence and functions in the world as a married woman. From this moment on, the *burqa* will remain part and parcel of her person, always on her body, overtly or covertly. Only as a partner to two relationships is she obliged to remove it completely off her body: before God in prayer, and before her husband at all times, when not in the presence of outsiders. Could there be a more unequivocal way of telling the Sohari woman that her relationship to her husband is a unique one?

THE DESIGN

Fashioned from black cotton material, to the front side of which an emulsion of golden, purple, or red dye has been applied, the *burqa*'s dominant black color glows with a slight golden, reddish, or bluish sheen. But these nuances may normally be appreciated only at a close distance, when they add to the general fairy-tale effect of the *burqa* itself. From a distance of roughly more than thirty feet, every *burqa* looks completely black. The *burqa* dominates the woman's face, though it covers only minor portions of it. Hidden are, as a minimum, the upper lip, the central part of the cheeks above a line extending from the corner of the mouth, the front part of the nose, and the lower third or fourth of the forehead, including the eyebrows. Left uncovered are the eyes, the upper and lower parts of the cheeks, the sides of the nose, the upper part of the forehead, and all of the chin. Thus enough of the face is visible to give the Western observer the impression that the Sohari *burqa* resembles most of all a bikini version of a one-piece bathing suit, the observer's mental image of the Arab facial equivalent of the latter being the Bedouin *burqa*: a full mask covering all of the face, with the exception of the eyes, which peer through small slits in the mask. Soharis would fervently deny this implied theory of their *burqa*'s origin; they claim an entirely different and noble affinity for it.

The *burqa* is basically face-shaped. It is fashioned from one piece, but appears to consist of two symmetrical halves connected in the middle by a protruding nose. Perhaps because of its sheer exoticity, the *burqa* nose seems, to the outsider, the most spectacular part of the mask. Constructed over a stiff stay (approximately three centimeters wide), which runs the whole breadth of the *burqa* (approximately twenty centimeters), the nose is a strikingly conspicuous feature, which underscores the *burqa*'s three-dimensional character, and thus its facelike appearance. The nose may be of strict rectangular shape—said to be the old-fashioned style, though worn also by many young and fashion-conscious girls; or it may be slightly curved at the top in a manner reminiscent of the aristocratic Iranian nose—said to be the modern style.

If I should venture a description of the *burqa* as a whole, I would liken its outer contours to a roughly rectangular shape, the lower angles of which have been transformed into curves, while approximately one half of the contents has been cut away to two eye holes; the inner contours of the lower part are lip- or heart-shaped, the upper part is straight, and the sides are slanted. The lower lip-shaped part is approximately twice as broad as the upper part and the sides. The height of the nose corresponds to the breadth of the headband. The whole length of the *burqa* corresponds to the width of the woman's face; its height, to her measures from mouth to forehead, plus approximately two to three centimeters. The rounded curves of the lower part emphasize the rounded contours of the cheeks—a highly valued aspect of feminine beauty.

The *burqa* is held in place by four strings; two attach at a level slightly above the ears, and two attach below them. The strings are tied together at the back of the head, in an elegant running-noose knot on top of the ubiquitous *leeso* (inner head scarf). Each pair of strings is either sewn onto the *burqa* itself or passes through rings, preferably of gold, fastened to it at the temple. Most women seem to possess one *burqa* of each design; the gold-adorned one is reserved for special occasions. The color of the strings is golden, possibly with red or blue entwined thread to match the tone of the *burqa* itself. The part of the *burqa* that supports the strings is

A woman wearing the Sohari-type burqa *with curved nose*

lined in order to prevent tearing. Otherwise, the *burqa* is generally unlined, which seems strange, as its color is not fast, and, in the hot, humid summer of Sohar, it stains the woman's face and hands with a strangely water-repellent dye! Whether this is also thought beautiful, I do not know. The stains appear in haphazard spots and thus do not reproduce the shape of the *burqa*; women do not seem to mind them, though they usually try to wipe them off.

A woman wearing the Bedouin-style burqa

When not in use, the *burqa* is pushed to the top of the head, as we might a pair of sunglasses not in actual use. Adorning the woman's face, the upper line of the *burqa* should connect with her hair, always parted in the middle, to make up a right-angled triangle, thought intrinsically beautiful. On festive occasions, those fortunate women who possess a *mafraq* will embellish themselves with this dazzling piece of golden jewelry, which, in brilliant contrast to the *burqa*'s black, as well as the shiny black of the women's hair, embellishes the triangle and contributes to the women's overall appearance of gold-bespangled birds of paradise.

LEARNING TO UNDERSTAND THE *BURQA*

Despite my best efforts, I clearly fail to portray the *burqa*. Indeed, it defies description. Its shape, dimensions, curves, and angles are too subtly harmonized and balanced to be verbally rendered, in the same way that a painting cannot be written. What is more important, if it could be rendered, even the most elegant and precise account of the *burqa* itself as an object of material culture would fail to capture the instantaneous visual effect of one actual glance of a real *burqa,* when worn by a living woman in a real-life context. And that, after all, is where its effect and meaning lies; the *burqa* is made to be worn.

When worn on a woman's face in an actual situation, the *burqa* fosters a rather subtle and many-faceted set of impressions, the tenor of which depends upon the interpretive key held by the receiver of the messages. His or her attitudes and perceptions determine what he or she sees. Sohari women perceive the *burqa* somewhat differently from the men; and the Western observer regards it entirely differently from them both. My husband and I were a case in point. I think our range of reactions and the difficult steps by which we grew to appreciate the *burqa* may usefully serve to contradict misconceptions and initial biases that the reader is likely to share with us; perhaps one way to arrive at something more like the Sohari view is to recapitulate our own stages of understanding and interpretation.

The *burqa* captivated us from the very beginning; we never ceased to be intrigued by the utter fairy-tale character of this ingenious and incredible screening device. But the emotional components of our fascination changed with time.

Our initial reaction was disbelief, when out of the teeming male crowd of the Mattrah marketplace, a dull and unremarkable assembly, there appeared a spectacular creature of vulture-like shape, her body all draped in black, her face distorted by a mask of a kind, composed mainly of a prominent beak-shaped nose, and bespangled with glittering gold. Spellbound, we gazed as she busily bargained with the vendor. What *was* it, this mask, intersected with empty spaces? Why *this* kind of pattern; were the central part of the cheeks more "private" then the rest? And why the beak? And what was the sense in bejeweling her face with the glitter of gold, necessarily drawing attention to it and "veiling" it at the same time?

Before this we had seen some Bedouin women with *burqa*s. They looked strange but sensible, by our conceptions. Granted the premise that a woman's face should be concealed, then conceal her face the Bedouin *burqa* did! But this other thing? We held no keys to understanding it.

Moving to Sohar, and being invited on our second day to the wedding described in Chapter 2, we had our vision invaded by hundreds of women with these vulturelike looks. Permitted (by their menfolk) to photograph them, we could stare at them as much as we liked. We thought they looked grotesque. How enchantingly beautiful were the faces of the little girls. And how enrapturing the women would have looked in all their colorful, gold-bejeweled finery, were it not for those ghastly masks. Surely they had the same delicate features and fine skin as the men and children. But their whole presence was distorted by the unflattering features of the masks. And we wondered whether this effect was intended, whether an ingenious male mind had in fact invented a device that would transform his society's treasured women into ugly scarecrows! In comparison, we felt the Bedouin *burqa* did much less violence to feminine beauty. Covering all of the face, it did not distort it. Undistracted by ghastly apertures, the spectator may imagine a pure beauty underneath. But the Sohari *burqa* interfered with vision; paradoxically, it "harmonized" so well with the woman's face that it seemed an intrinsic part of it; it conveyed the impression that the *woman* was ugly. We were repelled.

As we became personally acquainted with some women and learned of their proud attitudes, we slowly came to regard the *burqa* differently. One experience marking a turning point in our attitudes was our first invitation to a private home. The women—a dozen or so of different ages—were not the least bit shy to talk about the *burqa*. I had assumed they would be bashful and ill at ease. On the contrary, they were thrilled with my interest in it, and exuberantly proud to show it off. "Isn't it beautiful?" they asked. They encouraged me to try one on and exploded in acclamations when I acquiesced: "*Z-e-e-e-n!* [Beautiful!]" Confident of their view, they turned to my husband for confirmation. Carried away with their own enthusiasm, they daringly asked whether I would like to see them *without* the *burqa*. When I said that I would, they threw it off, in the manner of impudent adolescent girls, giggling and laughing, eager to have me confirm that they were more beautiful with the *burqa*.

More familiar, the *burqa* lost its bizarre character. We marveled at the ingenuity of its shape and the quality of its texture. Most of all, we wondered what it must feel like for a woman to wear it, both a long-married one for whom it has become an integral part of dress, and a newly married one when she wears it for the first time. What was its significance to them? What did the *burqa* mean?

It was long, however, two months or so, before I came to share Sohari women's fundamental view that the *burqa* beautifies. But as time passed, this quality of it came to dominate my perception.

But no matter how adequate my understanding of the *burqa*, I have never ceased to regard it, as an outsider, with a mixture of feelings: incredulity, repulsion, enchantment, admiration . . . fascination. The *burqa* no doubt is one of the oddest pieces of material culture ever fashioned by man.

RULES OF WEAR

The *burqa*'s manifest function is to hide the woman from view; that is, the sexually mature woman from the view of the sexually mature man who is also a potential marriage partner. Only a male with these qualities is perceived as a threat to her family's honor. As a girl's wedding is supposed to closely accompany her first menstruation, the *burqa* is not obligatory until she starts performing her marital role. Thus it becomes the most powerful symbol of wifely status. A married woman must always wear the *burqa* in every situation where she could be observed by a marriageable man. Thus the only men allowed to see her face, besides her husband, are her son, father, brother, father-in-law, father's brother, mother's brother, husband's brother, husband's son from a previous marriage (all of whom are debarred from marrying her by the Moslem extensions of incest taboos), as well as *younger* cousins on both her father's and mother's side. She need also not wear the *burqa* before slaves and *xanith*s.

WEARING PRACTICES

These are the rules; practice is more complicated. Like so much behavior in Sohar, it depends upon personal styles and preferences, generating a wide variety of particular adaptations.

One variable concerns the age and the stage at which the *burqa* is assumed. Most of the women I spoke with (approximately 70 percent) said they first wore it on their seventh day of marriage, which marks the end of a bride's honeymoon. On that day, a woman actually starts performing her everyday wifely role. But a minority (approximately 25 percent) reported having already worn it on their third honeymoon day, when, for the first time after consummation of the marriage, the bride acts as hostess to visitors from home. However, as this is an all-female group, the *burqa* is not obligatory, and I assume that what these women were referring to was not the first time they let the *burqa* cover their face, but the first time they wore it on the top of their head, for potential use. The choice of the above occasion for this manner of wear (whether initiated by the woman herself or her husband) clearly dramatizes the fundamental change of status the bride has undergone, from girl (*bint*) to woman (*horma*). So profoundly does this change affect her that it is even possible that a woman chooses to cover herself for this, her first encounter with her old friends; she is likely to feel embarrassed and shy.

Some few assume the *burqa* even earlier, before their marriage. Decisive factors seem to be the amount of time between the girl's physical maturity and her wedding, as well as her parents' personal standards of proper feminine demeanor. A girl's marriage rarely coincides with her sexual maturation, but lags behind by a year or more. Her parents may judge it a shame for her to expose her fully matured cheeks and insist that she adopt the *burqa*. One girl in twenty seems to have had this experience.

Although this book is primarily concerned with Arabs, I should mention in passing that the rule and practice among the Baluch is for girls to assume the *burqa* at puberty, before marriage. To dramatize marriage,

Baluchi women wear a very special wedding *burqa* of red color for three days.

Another variable is time, place, and occasion for wear. All women observe the rules of removal—they remove the *burqa* completely before God and their husband. And everyone, with the exception of a few flagrant prostitutes, also observes the mandatory rules of wear. Women don their *burqa*s whenever they go to the gate to greet someone, stand there talking with someone, or walk the few steps down the neighborhood path to their next-door neighbor. In short, they signal modesty in every context where they are in danger of being seen by a marriageable man. Within the safe precincts of their homes, where no stranger enters uninvited, they are usually unveiled. But as graceful conduct requires their speedy attention to knocks at the gate, they wear the *burqa* on the top of the head, ready for potential use. The same practice is followed during visits to the homes of friends and neighbors. Should the friend's husband unexpectedly enter, the *burqa* is instantly dropped into place. The same happens on those rare occasions when the woman's husband brings a friend into her presence.

What is striking about *burqa* wear is not that the *burqa* is worn where and when it should be, but that it is also worn much more frequently than need be. Women do not only fulfill society's ends by adhering to its general rules in this matter, but adapt the *burqa* to fulfill their own personal needs and ends.

They often wear it in all-female gatherings, whether in the role of hostess, guest, or informal friend. But I was rarely able to predict what a given woman would choose to do, thereby singling out the factors that determine this behavior. One day, in the company of her best friends, chatting or embroidering, a woman may sit unveiled; the next day, she may let her *burqa* cover her face. Her choice of behavior seems to depend solely upon the way she feels at a given moment—and Sohari women acknowledge the force of such feelings in influencing a person's behavior. One day, a woman may feel relaxed and secure, happy to expose herself to the world; the next day, she may be uneasy and shy, desiring to keep the world at a distance. The *burqa* gives her welcome assistance. Soharis do not connect such "moods" with particular factors in the woman's life situation; they are perceived to affect her unpredictably.

Generally speaking, one may say that degree of familiarity with the women present in a situation influences the way a woman handles her *burqa*. The better she knows them, the more likely she is to feel free and relaxed and to expose her face. However, women differ. The character of one may be such that she is normally at ease in every all-female group, another easily feels shy and recoils. She herself may have initiated the contact, and the hostess or guests may be her own relatives, yet she feels uneasy and shy. The *burqa* rescues her. It hides all traces of faltering poise, with no offense to those present. A prime symbol of feminine grace and modesty, and the woman's identification with her husband, the *burqa* projects nothing but an image of proper and honorable conduct.

Likewise, a woman may feel uncomfortable in the company of some males before whom she need not feel shy. Then she keeps on her *burqa*. For instance, we observed newly married women wearing the *burqa* before their father—a relationship heavily charged by sexual embarrassment.

Practice differs for the Baluch, who normally keep their *burqa* on at all times when outside their own home.

Hospitality, in the form of coffee and snacks, is an integral part of Sohari visits. Veiled women manage to partake by slightly tipping the head and lifting the right side of the *burqa,* exposing only the corner of the mouth. Children often eat in the same way—evidently imitating their mothers, whose style they see as the only natural one, unexposed as they are at this stage to male eating etiquette.

When sunset hides the world in darkness, the *burqa* becomes superfluous. Sohari homes are only dimly lit by one or, at most, two petrol lamps; and there are no street lights; thus the woman remains adequately protected. After the sunset prayer, women do not resume the *burqa* again, except for a rare visit to an occasional wedding.

Age is another variable. The younger women are more apt to go unveiled than the older ones. Paradoxically, though restrictions on movement and behavior decrease with old age, the very old grandmothers seem to prefer always to be veiled, even in the solitude of their homes. I take it that the *burqa* has become an integral part of their appearance—inseparable from themselves.

A fourth variable is rank. Those highest and lowest on the ladder of social esteem do not wear *burqa*s. Highest are kin and in-laws of the Sultan, some six families in Sohar. A few others (about six families) of high aspiration and Muscati origin likewise do not wear it. Slaves were traditionally forbidden to wear it; the *burqa* was an uncontested prerogative of free women—approximately 85 percent of the female population. Today, ex-slaves are free to assume the *burqa,* though I know of only two who have done so. But abolition of slavery in the 1950s triggered an exodus from Sohar, and many of these ex-slaves may have assumed the *burqa* upon settlement in other Gulf states.

Residence is also a variable. In Higra, the ward incorporating the town center, "it is not the custom," in women's words, to wear the *burqa*. For years some members of the Sultan's family representing him in Sohar have lived there, along with their great number of slaves, and, to this day, Higra has a predominantly mixed high-ranking and slave population. Thus a majority of Higra women go unveiled. A few ordinary Arab women do the same, maybe from a desire to emulate the high-ranking ones. But

A former slave who adopted the burqa *upon her liberation (the* burqa *is pushed to the top of her head)*

their number is probably no more than a dozen, and they will have a *burqa* in reserve that they put on, for the sake of politeness, on visits to *burqa* neighborhoods.

Conversely, a woman moving from a place where the *burqa* is not the custom, into Sohar, is likely to assume the *burqa*. But she will be inclined to remove it in all situations where it is not obligatory, never reaching the stage where she feels it a part of herself.

The final variable is the husband's attitude, which asserts a powerful influence. No doubt some of the in-married women (that is, women from parts of Oman where the *burqa* is not worn, for example, the capital area or inner Oman), who were mentioned above, don *burqa*s at their husbands' command. And a few may fail to discard it from fear of the husband's sanctions. In only one case with which I am personally familiar, has a man, Ali, compelled his wife to discard the *burqa* by the threat of divorce. In this he is representative of only the most modern of Sohari men at present. Yet he may have marked a path for others in the future.

A BEAUTIFYING DEVICE

Sohari women—and men—extol the *burqa*'s inherent beauty, as well as its beautifying properties. Let us see how this latter effect is achieved. I have described the style of the *burqa* as if each looks the same as every other. But it does not. The above pattern is the general base upon which every single one is fashioned. But the *burqa* is tailored and fit to each particular wearer's face, to enhance her individual beauty. Some want theirs to conceal high cheekbones, others, to convey the impression that their cheekbones are higher than nature made them. Some want to make their face look broader, others, narrower; some want to give length and height to their face, others to shorten it, and so forth. The style of the *burqa* is exquisitely fit to cater to all such beautifying needs; its curved lines and the nonfixity of size of its various parts make it even more suitable for manipulation than are cosmetics in Western culture. Thus it accomplishes what the Bedouin *burqa,* with its standard full shape, could never do. Time and again I was struck by the marvelous ingenuity of this cloaking device in beautifying not so beautiful women. I remember one case in particular, a Baluch woman of striking beauty. She seemed to have the most superbly balanced facial features, and eyes of enrapturing, magnetic beauty—when wearing the *burqa*. I was struck with surprise and disappointment, when, one day, she presented herself without the *burqa* to have her photograph taken. Gone was the wonder. She had been transformed into a woman of only ordinary good looks—her face too square, her features too coarse; but, most importantly, without the *burqa* her eyes were no longer in focus, and their radiant magnetism was gone. From this moment, I became aware that one general effect of the *burqa* is to throw the eyes into relief; sometimes it is assisted in this by the *kohl* (black make-up) that women apply to embellish their eyes. Therefore, women with unusually beautiful eyes derive a maximum benefit from *burqa* wear.

The Baluch *burqa* is of the same general pattern as the Arab, but all its parts are larger. Most conspicuously, it covers nearly twice as much of the cheeks. Older women generally prefer their *burqa*s larger than the young ones; some even cover all of the face, except for the chin.

While the male guardian often chooses all of the woman's dress materials and jewelry, she herself buys her *burqa*s. It need be so if the *burqa* shall embellish, so closely must it be tailored to the individual face. The woman buys from itinerant female vendors, who sell on behalf of a few specialist, female *burqa*-makers. The woman usually tries on ten or more before she decides on one. If she does not find a suitable *burqa*, she orders one made according to her specifications. The price for one in 1974 was one-half a Rial ($1.50).

BEAUTIFUL FOR WHOM?

"And tell the believing women to lower their gaze . . . and to display of their adornment only that which is apparent. . . ." (Quran 24). Is not this injunction in direct contradiction to the behavior of Sohari women when they adorn themselves with *burqa*s, which they have selected with elaborate care, so as to project their facial beauty? Not only do they seem to fail to display only that which cannot be hidden, they even seem actively engaged in the opposite endeavor: to foster impressions of exaggerated, more than factual, beauty. Or how else are we to understand their statements that a woman becomes more beautiful when she wears her *burqa*?

The problem becomes even more intriguing when we continue to examine the above quotation; it enjoins men to tell their women to reveal their adornment only to those categories of persons before whom the Sohari *burqa* is not obligatory. Does this mean that the *burqa* is not really regarded by Soharis as an adornment? Or why else do women not wear it before their husband, son, and other unmarriageable males? And is it at all likely that the menfolk of a strictly sex-segregated society would tolerate their women donning *burqa*s if the *burqa* really beautified?

The answer, as I see it, has two main components. Let me examine the first by comparing the *burqa* to feminine dress in the Western world.

To feel decent and honorable, a Western woman covers much of her body when she goes out in public. The Sohari woman covers body and face. Changing social conventions specify for each the manner and style of dress appropriate for different settings and situations. At the present time, a Western woman need not feel shy to show herself naked before her husband; a Sohari woman need not feel shy to uncover her face in his presence. Yet the Western woman often chooses to go about dressed, as the Sohari woman would have chosen to keep her *burqa* on, had she in fact had the option. The Western woman may, without offense to public morality, discard her bathing suit in a group of all-female bathers. The Sohari women may discard her *burqa* in an all-female gathering. Yet both of them may voluntarily choose to remain covered. Naked, they may feel shy, exposed, vulnerable and even ugly; clothed, they feel protected, proper, and perhaps pretty. As an integral part of her presentations of self, the Western woman selects her clothes with loving care and concern. So does the Sohari woman her *burqa*. Both aspire to look beautiful *and* honorable. In fact, these qualities are connected in their minds—the unseemly is vulgar and tasteless. To feel beautiful, the Western woman selects her dresses so that they will emphasize her feminine attractiveness. The Sohari woman selects her *burqa* with the same purpose. To her, the beautiful and the proper are two aspects of the same matter. Though these qualities are more clearly interconnected in Sohar, where avenues for the realization of women's mental and intellectual capabilities are so poorly developed. Feeling beautiful, a woman's self-regard is enhanced; she thinks well of herself and expects others do so too. No thoughts of being seductive to a man need be involved. To attend a woman's tea party, as well as a formal wedding, the Western woman chooses the dress that, for that occasion, will make her look her best. So does the Sohari woman, only she does not have the option of choosing the style and fashion of her dress. It is strictly conventionalized, and only its colors (if anything at all) are subject to her own choice. But the *burqa* she controls. No wonder she delights in it! And no wonder she treasures and exploits all the freedom it gives her to cultivate and embellish her own looks.

Still, we have only a partial understanding of what the *burqa* subjectively means to her. Granted that she feels so beautiful with the *burqa*, why does she not choose to wear it much more in those situations where it is not forbidden, such as among her friends? And, considering the fact that she is obliged to remove it completely before her husband, is it really likely that she means it when she says that the *burqa* beautifies? Is this not just a female way of speaking, possibly parroting male rationalizations intended to reconcile the women to their inescapable fate? Could it be that women and men both agree that women are really more beautiful without the *burqa*? Or maybe they differ in their conceptions of this, as in so many other things in life?

To take the first question first, the answer lies in the way in which objects derive their meaning and value from the way they are used. A female dress, for example, if worn frequently in an informal situation, ceases to be a formal dress. It may remain beautiful, but not formal. And this interconnection is so straightforward that I think every woman is conscious of it. Its value is reduced (though its practical value may be enhanced), and its meanings are changed: when the woman now wears it, she signals to those present a different conception of what the situation means to her and how she expects to act in it. Likewise with the *burqa*: it will retain its present meanings only insofar as it continues to be worn essentially as it is today. The *burqa* today *means* female modesty and decency. An obvious veiling device, this no doubt has always been its intrinsic meaning. Donning it, a woman presents herself as a person of those attributes. Should the women begin to wear their *burqa*s among themselves, as ordinary garments, the *burqa* would certainly lose its present meaning of *female* modesty. Gone would be its capacity to broadcast information about women's attitudes toward men. It might retain its capacity to convey messages about modesty simply, but it would be that personal kind of modesty which may be experienced by both males and females. It might further retain its capacity to symbolize the uniqueness of the husband/ wife and God/woman relationship. But only as long as the *burqa* serves as a symbol of that essential *female* modesty—which is still a major fact of life—can it retain its power to segregate female and male arenas, private and public domains, and be a mainstay of Sohari society. Should women be tempted to wear their *burqa*s indiscriminately, the *burqa* would cease to be a veiling and secluding device. And Sohari society would be strikingly changed.

The question remains whether women really mean it when they say that the *burqa* beautifies. I have no way of knowing for sure, but I am impressed by the enthusiastic manner in which they display it to the foreigner, and their confident expectation that she, too, will admire and extol it. Thus I think that women really mean it when they say that they are more beautiful with the *burqa* than without it. I understand their evaluation to rest upon two premises.

First, the *burqa* beautifies in a spiritual sense. Donning her *burqa,* the woman signals her moral excellence in a tangible way. She communicates a beautiful aspect of her person and, in the act, she herself becomes beautiful. But furthermore, the *burqa* itself—as a symbol of all things beautiful, female modesty and grace, decency, and poise—is intrinsically beautiful. Like a jewel, it adds to what is already there. No matter how beautiful the woman, it cannot fail to make her even more so. Because she and it are both beautiful.

Therefore, when the Sohari women takes off her *burqa* for her husband, as when the Western woman undresses for hers, she may feel that she becomes less pretty, yet it is certain that she gives him something that he treasures infinitely more: her intimacy. In Sohar, as in the West, its value far exceeds the value of physical beauty.[1]

MALE ATTITUDES TOWARD THE *BURQA*

I have concentrated so far on female attitudes and conceptions. But male views are equally important if we are to appreciate the *burqa*'s place and meaning in Sohari social life. How, for example, does the man relate

[1] For an interesting discussion of the "complex moral device" that the veil is in Iran, and the ways in which it is manipulated, see Fischer, 1980, pp. 207–8.

to his woman's efforts to embellish herself? Does he not feel threatened when she walks into public with a *burqa* carefully selected to enhance her beauty?

I shall venture an answer at the end of this section. Let us first listen to what some men have had to say about the *burqa*. Every man we asked characterized it as beautiful, and many men went on to stress its excellent ability to disguise. They would claim, for instance, that they could not recognize their own daughter behind her *burqa*. But they stressed this point so emphatically that we felt they were at pains to convince themselves, and not primarily us. One man, Said, a well-educated and widely traveled person, elaborated how the *burqa* also in other respects veiled the woman to her own advantage: "*Burqa* is a good thing because of Muslim modesty and also because it keeps the woman's face from becoming black from the sun. If you see two women, one with the *burqa* and one without, you will see that the one without it has burned dark from exposure."

This is a remarkable statement, considering the fact that the *burqa* covers considerably less than half of the face, often only a third, plus the fact that high-class women, who never wear *burqa*, are of lighter skin color than others. The latter is not explained by degree of exposure to the sun, no more than is the slave women's darker color. Said knows this; what then could he be trying to tell us? Maybe simply that the *burqa* is beautiful, and maybe that it has pragmatic value over and above its symbolic value. A cosmopolitan man, Said may have wanted to counteract attitudes that he expected us to share with other foreigners he had met: that the *burqa* is a senseless and oppressive relic of the past. In general, we found that men with modern aspirations felt compelled to disclaim that their women wore *burqa*s for traditional reasons. Many phrased it this way, "It is not that women wear *burqa* because it is shameful to go without it, but because it is beautiful to go with it."

But in other contexts, these same men would strongly object when I asked their permission to photograph their daughters, without *burqa*s, though their daughters were thrilled at the prospect. And a few women confided in me that they personally would like to discard the *burqa*, to become "modern." But they could never even hope to do so; the men would never let them.

Naturally, the men will not let them. For though Soharis may dispute whether it is actually shameful for a woman to show her face to men, or just contrary to custom, I think that the vast majority of both sexes agree that a woman who does so in an all-*burqa* neighborhood signals that she *might* possess qualities that the men apprehend and dread: faltering docility and failing shyness. I know of only one woman who occasionally walks as far as her next-door neighbors without the *burqa*. She is known to be a prostitute.

As noted, not wearing the *burqa* carries different meanings in Higra, the neighborhood surrounding the fortress. With a heterogeneous population, more than half of its adult women go unveiled. When an ordinary Arab woman occasionally does the same, she is not conspicuous and does not seem obstinate, especially because friendships and visiting patterns crisscross ethnic and "class" boundaries.

Yet when Ali, a young man with very strong modern aspirations, forbade his wife, Fatima, to wear the *burqa*, he encountered intense opposition from his parents-in-law, who are long-time residents of Higra. Fatima first wore the *burqa* on the third honeymoon day, when she stepped out of the bridal hut to receive visitors. Ali was caught by surprise. Absent from Sohar for fifteen years, he had failed to anticipate such "stupid" behavior from his own wife. But he had to tolerate it till evening came and the guests were gone. Then he lectured Fatima on the outrageousness of the *burqa* custom, instructing her never to wear the *burqa* again. The *burqa* was, he said, a bad and uncivilized custom of backward people. If she ever donned it again, he would divorce her. When his parents-in-law, with whom the couple lived, learned of Ali's attitude, they became furious. His father-in-law stressed the necessity of accepting the customs of the people in whose country you stay, thereby voicing an elementary value of Sohari culture. He cited Fatima's mother, Amineh, as an example. During the seven years she lived in Kuwait, where women do not wear the *burqa*, she also did not wear it, and likewise through her two years of residence in Muscat. As soon as she returned to Sohar, however, she submitted to honored Sohari ways by putting it on, even though she was unused to it and felt uncomfortable with it. Likewise, Fatima must do things the customary way. But Ali was unbending and threatened divorce. Heated arguments followed, but after one week Fatima discarded the *burqa*, and she has never worn it again.

Filled with admiration for her husband and convinced of the inherent wisdom of his decisions, Fatima seemed proud to be unveiled at the time when we first met her—a year after the above incident. She was convinced that the *burqa* was not pretty, or else it would have been worn by women in centers of fashion, like Kuwait, Bahrain, and Muscat. Ali was anxious to explain to us his rationale for rejecting the *burqa*:

> It is a bad custom, based on a misunderstanding of the circumstances of the Prophet's daughter, Fatima. She wore it to go to school, where nobody was to know who she was, because the Prophet's enemies would want to kill her. The Prophet does *not* say that a woman should cover her *face*, only her arms and legs and hair and body. But the uneducated women don't know this, and think that *burqa* is like clothing, like a blouse, and therefore they feel ashamed to show themselves without it.

As many Sohari men, besides Ali, are aware of the absence of a

Koranic injunction for the veil, yet insist on its use, Ali's behavior is not adequately explained by the above insight. In Chapter 13, I shall explore this problem. Here it is enough to note that Ali appears to hold the women themselves accountable for their adherence to the *burqa*, when surely he must know that the menfolk have the last say in this matter, as he did over Fatima. The latter may have seemed to him so obvious that it need not be said—naturally, a husband bears the blame for failing to educate his wife (see Ch. 8). But it may also be that he was consciously emphasizing the powerful influence of the female feeling of shyness and shame in shaping woman's behavior, in keeping with a view common to Soharis of both sexes, that the woman in considerable measure makes her own life—far beyond matters of *burqa* wear!

Men display no negative reactions to this feminine beautifying endeavor. There are no indications that they feel threatened. This lack of intervention may reflect their unawareness of the extent and profundity of this female interest: As women never select their *burqa*s in the presence of men, nor converse with them about the *burqa*'s beautifying potentialities, men are unlikely to appreciate fully these aspects of it, though they undoubtedly sense some of it from their childhood experiences. Maybe the men are primarily conscious of the *burqa*'s ability to project the beauty of the soul, and not the body?

However that may be, my interpretation of this male acquiescence is that it springs chiefly from a basic and shared premise of Sohari male culture: There is nothing improper about women beautifying themselves as long as they observe the reigning social conventions of propriety and decency. By these conventions, a woman with *burqa* signals moral beauty, no matter how much the *burqa* may emphasize her physical beauty. But Sohari men are not out to suppress feminine beauty as such—on the contrary—many of them even shower their women with the gold that makes them stand out and glitter among their sisters. It is propriety, not self-effacement, that should be served.

VEILING: A SOURCE OF PRIDE OR OPPRESSION?

If the preceding exposition has served its purpose, I will have given a portrayal and an explanation of the *burqa* that enables the reader to appreciate the meanings it has for Soharis themselves. In that case, I will have overcome the most difficult obstacle toward understanding: an ingrained Western conviction that veiling is inherently suppressive.

The anthropological literature on the Middle East and the Maghreb gives ample testimony that the opposite view is commonly held by the veiled ones themselves. To them, veiling is a source of pride and prestige. Mernissi, for one, writes: "The traditional women interviewed all perceived seclusion as prestigious. In rural Morocco seclusion is considered the privilege of women married to rich men" (1975, p. 84). Papanek observes that "despite its forbidding appearance, the *burqa* can be considered a liberating invention and is seen in this way by many women themselves. The *burqa* is an obvious social signal of the wearer's status as a secluded female" (1973, p. 295).

Why are such statements likely to strain the credulity of Westerners, or to be at best intellectually, but not emotionally, convincing? Partly, I think, because to our way of thinking seclusion *means* oppression. Implying constraints on movement and self-actualization, seclusion must be inherently suppressive, therefore oppressive. We simply cannot fathom that there are women who *prefer* a life of seclusion and actively seek it, far less that they actually derive pride and gratification from what appears to us as a deplorable human condition. If they do, so our line of reasoning is likely to run, then it must be because they know of nothing better; they are not enlightened and do not know their own best interest. But does lack of perspective diminish the value of an actual, subjective experience of satisfaction?

Our preconceptions of veiling are likely to be further colored by dramatic stories in the press or history books about strong-willed women boldly revolting to rid themselves of this presumed vestige of male tyranny. Outrageous depictions of accompanying male revenge serve to bolster our conviction that veiling is objectively oppressive. The women revolters experience veiling in the only natural way, so they receive our sympathy. They *make sense*—to us. But all the women in the past and present who have voluntarily adopted the veil, they make neither news nor sense to us. Thereby they fail to shake our conviction about the meaning of veiling. The senseless is poorly suited to modify "rational" attitudes.

The female initiators of women's liberation movements in Muslim countries appear rational and receive our sympathy because they resemble us. They represent the upper echelon of their society who have had Western education and come to cherish many "modern" values. They are typically almost as far removed from their traditional country sisters as we are.

Yet until the Muslim world came under the spell of Western ways, there were probably many more women who—by their own will—assumed than removed the veil.[2] The veil was a sign of pride, prestige, and upward mobility. It still is in those few remote corners of the Muslim world where traditional values reign uncontested, like east Afghanistan, some parts of Swat in Pakistan, parts of interior Morocco, several of the Persian Gulf sheikhdoms and sultanates, as well as the Batinah coast in Oman.

---

[2]Beck and Keddie note that "although it is often loosely said by people who visit only the major Middle Eastern cities or who do not know what things were like some forty years ago, that the veil is disappearing, it is our impression that currently the veil, if one considers the entire Middle East, is probably spreading" (1978, pp. 8–9).

Although the Sohari *burqa* is not unequivocally a sign of upward mobility, as high-class women do not wear it, it is clearly invested with pride and prestige, as shown by its adoption by some slave women when they partook of the privileges of free women.

The veil's value as a symbol of high status seems traditionally to derive from the fact that it interfered with a woman's work and therefore became the privilege of the well-off, who could afford servants. Peasant women rarely wore a veil, but often adopted it upon migration to a city (Cosar 1978, p. 132). Conversely, townswomen who married "down" into the peasantry commonly had to discard it (Peters 1963, p. 188). However, the type of veil widespread in Middle Eastern countries seems strikingly different from the Sohari *burqa*, and more like the Omani Bedouin *burqa* and dress, though typically fashioned of one compact piece. It is heavy and warm and considerably impedes movement. The name for it in most local languages is *burqa*.

The Sohari *burqa*, on the other hand, implies no practical constraints; it does not interfere with a woman's work in the home or the fields. Therefore, poor and rich alike have been able to wear it, whereas slaves have been forbidden to do so. It has been protected as a symbol of free status. However, to my understanding, this aspect of it makes it significantly different from the compact *burqa* and epitomizes its chief meaning and value. The Sohari *burqa* is not a signal of social rank. Golden jewelry serves to broadcast rank. Nor does it impede the woman's movement and activities. Moral rules and injunctions insure this effect. The *burqa* in Sohar is first and foremost a secluding and beautifying device: it gives tangible expression to the treasured ideal and constraints of female modesty, and the degree of shyness and reserve felt by a woman in a specific situation; and it expresses her value as a person.

The difference between the Sohari *burqa* and the compact, concealing *burqa* of many other Middle Eastern areas is highlighted by the difference in its manner of use. The compact *burqa* seems to be worn only in those situations where it is obligatory. The Sohari one is *removed* (completely) only when this is obligatory and frequently kept on the face when no rules enjoin so: it is controlled by the woman herself and serves her in her self-expression. It would seem that the Sohari *burqa* is experienced as much more an integral and cherished part of the woman's self than the compact kind of *burqa*.

To explore more fully the subjective meaning of the *burqa*, it is useful to exploit the analogy with Western woman once more. No doubt she would be flabbergasted if a woman from the South Sea Islands tried to convince her that her blouse was a symbol of male oppression and that therefore she should discard it. Equally disbelieving would the Sohari woman be if advised by a Western woman to throw away her *burqa*. The blouse and the *burqa* may both in fact serve to curb female sexuality. But if they do, their sexual aspects are simply not what women experience. To the wearer, they mean something entirely different. And it is this meaning above all that is ethnographically, sociologically, and subjectively important.

THE *BURQA* IN SPACE AND TIME

*Burqa*s equivalent to those of Sohar are found in Oman only along the Batinah coast, from Kaborrah in the south, to the United Arab Emirates border in the north. In all other parts of Oman, the settled women of towns and villages, as distinct from the Bedu, go unveiled. Sohari women say that on rare visits to the capital they "follow the custom of that country" and go unveiled too. The same holds true if they should visit the inner Gulf area of Basra and Kuwait, where *burqa*s are not in use.

But the Sohari-type *burqa* is not a parochial phenomenon, peculiar to the Batinah scene. It has a distribution today that encompasses the Gulf sheikhdoms of Dubai, Abu Dhabi, and Qatar, as well as some isolated parts of southern Persia (for a photograph from Band-e-Langeh, see Beny 1976). Until recently, it was also worn in coastal Baluchistan (Makran), which stretches from Persia into Pakistan. The origin of this type of *burqa* is, to my knowledge, not established, but Soharis cite the Makran coast as its original homeland.

The Sohari use of a type of *burqa* prevalent in the affluent Gulf states to the north, but not in the Omani capital of Muscat, is expressive of Sohar's close cultural affinity with these sheikhdoms. Significantly more men and women have visited Abu Dhabi and Dubai than Muscat; even today, when the distance to Muscat is as short as that to Dubai, Soharis continue to go to Dubai for all major purchases. Dubai sets the style for Sohar in fashions. When news reaches the women that a new style in golden jewelry is "in" at Dubai, they are anxious to exchange their old pieces for "modern" ones, displaying no regrets. But to the *burqa* they are attached. Thus, in 1974, when rumors had it that the *burqa* might soon be on its way out in Dubai, as the *ghashwa*—a black, transparent veil attached to the woman's black cloak, the *abba,* had become fashionable, the Sohari women were disbelieving. None praised the new fashion, and the most modern of Sohari women wore a *ghashwa* on top of their *burqa* for more formal visits, thereby doubly protecting and embellishing themselves.

For centuries these Arab Gulf states, as well as the Batinah coast, have had close communications with the south Persian coastal areas, the Makran coast, and the adjoining inland areas; they are all very much part of the same world and exhibit a number of the same cultural traits. A large percentage of the present inhabitants of the southern shores of the

Gulf are of Persian and Baluch origin, and it is likely that Persia, with its uniquely rich artistic creativity, set the style for Gulf Arabs in many matters of material culture, among which is the *burqa*. Many families in Sohar (approximately 30 percent) also trace their descent from the Persian Gulf towns and Baluchistan, and, indeed, the *burqa* had until recently a wide distribution in south Persia.

However, under the modernizing zeal of Iran's Reza Shah Pahlavi, orders were issued around 1930 for all men to discard turbans, and all women their *burqas*. The wearing of both was forbidden, and violators were severely punished. It is a striking measure of how closely the *burqa* is connected with the woman's expression of her own value and identity that many families chose to leave their home and country rather than discard its use. A number of these traditionalists are now settled in Sohar, where they still remember the senselessness of the imperial command. One of them recalled:

> We were much upset. Reza Shah Pahlavi wanted to change people *by force*, make everyone like the Europeans. . . . Here in Sohar we were free to pursue our own customs. Our customs were like those of Arabs of Sohar already when we lived in Bandar Abbas: *burqas*, turbans, clothes, and so forth. So that's precisely why we moved: Pahlavi banned the *burqa* and the turban; we wanted to keep those things. When today some young men want to leave their customs, and go bareheaded instead of wearing the turban, that is voluntary, with changing times, not *force*.

When, one day in the future, Sohari women choose to lay their *burqas* aside, it will also no doubt be as a voluntary act, expressing a changing conception of woman's role, a new orientation toward the world, and new standards with which to measure her worth and value. Some see this future as imminent, saying that "when Sohar becomes modern with electricity and a *korniche* [a paved road that runs by the sea], the *burqa* will be discarded because old-fashioned." And all agree that the wives of tomorrow—schoolgirls of today—will not come to wear it, "for they will work and earn a living."

CHAPTER 7

❖

Women's World

"A neighbor is better than a mother who is far away."

Women's world, that life which they create for themselves in the absence of men, revolves around visiting, hospitality—and solitude. A remarkable feature, inexplicable to most people who think they "know" the Middle East (and, indeed, women!), is their silence and self-containment. As I noted in the introduction, they may sit quietly, nearly immovable for hours on end, whether alone or in company, with no need to talk or fill the air with chatter. "Serene" is perhaps the word that best describes them. But whether this quality reflects mainly shyness or security, or both, I really do not know. I am deeply impressed with their grace and composure, but also aware of the difficulty for a Westerner to assess what silence "means," for, in our part of the world, the only people who can be quiet together are people who either do not know each other at all, or else know each other very intimately.

What stands beyond doubt in my mind is that this way of getting or being together reflects a fundamentally *accepting* attitude toward fellow human beings. I shall have more to say about this toward the end of the chapter.

Visiting is the highlight of women's everyday world, and food is the quintessence of such treasured conviviality. Like the Bedu of the desert who had to receive graciously any guest who presented himself, even should he be of a feuding family, Sohari women are under a holy obligation to treat graciously everyone (woman, that is!) who comes to their door. They themselves explain that "to say to a visitor that you would rather she had not come, however plausible your excuses, would be impossible—very, very shameful. If you did such a thing, she would parry: 'So you think I have come for the sake of the food? But why should I? There is plenty where I come from! I came solely for the sake of good company [*zena*]!' "

Visiting revolves around food, which is the reason why women say that

109

what a wife desires most in her husband is that he should be generous and let her entertain lavishly. Not to offer a visitor hospitality, though she be your closest neighbor, who drops by every day, is exceedingly rude to the guest and reflects stinginess on the part of the hostess. So it was that when Latifa offered to tell me just *how* bad the relationship between her own mother and Feyza's mother had been when they were married to the same man, what she chose to say was that her mother did not even offer coffee and dates to the co-wife when the latter occasionally dropped by! They lived in separate houses. (Coffee and dates rank at the bottom of the scale by which hospitality is measured. The serving of them is the informal minimum that is normally practiced among neighbors.) "But when father divorced Feyza's mother," Latifa continued, "mother and she became the best of friends, and mother took great pleasure in Feyza's mother."

It is hard to believe that a relationship so fraught with enmity could suddenly be transformed into amiability. What I believe Latifa to be expressing is the Sohari view that behavior should be taken at face value. Her mother's inability to surmount her hostility and to practice reasonable manners was a measure of how deep the animosity had been. Later, the two interacted with perfect observance of hospitality and good manners, so then the relationship had the appearance of a heart-felt friendship (good neighborliness). And whenever appearances coincide with propriety, it is not, in the Sohari view, for others to question behavior; people's self-presentation should be respected to the extent of being accepted at face value. In contrast to the men, Sohari women deny that there are any people whom they would not welcome at their door, discounting only the rare nonspeaking relationship. Latifa's and Feyza's mothers were not so estranged, or the latter would not have come visiting. Consequently, the obligation of hospitality held true.

Sohari women are graciously hospitable, yet careful to protect not their time (about which we are so obsessed), but their privacy and solitude. The rules are clear as to how long a visit may last, as in diplomatic protocol. Informal guests may visit only during the husband's absence and stay only until food has been served. To refuse hospitality extended would be both offensive and self-deprecatory; I have never heard a woman decline it. But I have seen the remainders of good food, which had been served in honor of a prestigious guest, being hastily removed by the hostess at the sound of neighborly footsteps at the gate.

It is revealing that the imagined retort of an unwelcome visitor should be the provocative "So you think I have come for the sake of the food?"—for, to an outsider at least, it seems as if this is precisely what women commonly do. Let us disregard for the time being the visitors proper. Neighbors of the hostess have a remarkable ability to appear the minute food has been served, as if guided by some remarkable sixth sense to smell snacks that have no odor! The hostess need not invite them to partake; in a matter-of-fact way, they will plunge in, their bodies intently leaning forward, and grasp the food with eager fingers—in a manner that seems, to the outsider, wholly out of harmony with their overall style of modesty and grace. They will remain silent, or, at most, make a rare inquiry into the place of residence of the guests. Their appetite (and curiosity?) satisfied, they will disappear as inaudibly as they came, gliding out with no word of farewell.

The visitors proper will comport themselves in a similar manner, except that they, observing the etiquette that prevails between nonneighbors, will bid their farewell with a *f'am(an)allah* (God's peace be upon you), announced at the gate, not at the hostess, as they too stride off the minute they have finished eating.

But before we delve into this complex syndrome of visiting, hospitality, and food, a sketch of the everyday context, of which it constitutes the delight, is in order.

THE ROUTINES OF AN ORDINARY DAY

Life begins at 5 A.M., when the sun rises, and a chorus of a dozen roosters, which has kept going intermittently the whole night through, bursts into a cacophony of discordant voices, to announce the beginning of a brand new day—one that, to all intents and purposes, will replicate the last, unless a formal visit to or from someone beyond the closest neighborhood will break the regular rhythm.

The day begins with prayers; then the woman sits down at the fireplace to prepare the morning meal of coffee, sweetened tea with milk, and bread baked and left over from supper the evening before. In a nuclear family of parents and children, the family members all eat together, or the wife and husband may eat jointly and apart from the children. If the family is a joint or extended one, consisting of members from several nuclear families, the pattern is for the men to eat first, the children second, and the women last. However, this does not mean that the later group eats leftovers from the previous one; the food has been predivided into appropriate portions. Around 6 A.M., the man leaves for market or work; he will not return till 1 or 2 P.M.

In the six-hour interval between then and the lunch preparations, the household duties of the women of the house—wife, daughter(s), mother— consist of the following. They wash the dishes, which are few, because family members eat and drink from the same plates and cups. They fetch water, normally drawing it from their own well, but fetching it from a neighbor's well if they are poor, or buying it from enterprising, itinerant water vendors if they are among the better off. They must fetch firewood from a nearby date-palm garden and do the laundry. Besides, there are the chickens to feed, and, in some households, a goat or cow.

As concerns the family's diet and what to buy and prepare for lunch, the woman is exempt from exerting much thought. It is for the man of the house to select and bring the foods, which tend to be quite the same day in and day out: stew made of rice, fish, vegetables, and spices. Fish are bought fresh every day, whereas rice is bought by the sack, about once every month, as are flour, sugar, and coffee. The woman's only responsibility in regard to food, except for its preparation, is to inform the man when the family runs out of a certain item.

Women generally do not regard the composition of the family's diet as their concern. Only a minority express concern for their children's needs for nutrients or desirable sweets, doubtless in response to recent modernization, and accordingly try to exert some influence over the husband's purchases.

Preparations for lunch start after the noon prayers; the preparations proper take about half an hour, and the cooking itself lasts about one hour; around 1 P.M. or 2 P.M. at the latest, the family will have its lunch. Then the husband will rest for an hour or so, before he departs for work or social activities. The women and children are once more alone for approximately six hours.

Supper preparations take little time and effort. Bread must be made, but for a family of six this scarcely takes more than about half an hour. The bread is eaten with leftovers from lunch.

Often the husband does not return before the children are in bed. Then he and his wife will eat supper alone. Around 9 P.M. or 10 P.M. at the latest, the day has come to an end.

THE UBIQUITY OF CHILDREN

Depicting women's world, without stressing the part and place of children, is to distort it severely. Children are integral to it, always on the scene, spatially limited by the same constraints, and socially sharing of the same pleasures. What is women's delight is also children's: visiting and eating. I was once so exasperated by the dozen children who always arrived on the scene, only one step behind me, and assembled in front of me in a silence more overpowering than the most thunderous clatter that I exclaimed to my friends, "Tell me, do you never feel bothered by the presence of children? Are there no times and places that you feel should be the reserve of grownups only?" They answered, "No, not at all, we don't feel shy before children. Only when a husband and wife are intimate together must they avoid the children. But we women, we don't feel shy to talk before children about anything, prostitutes and xaniths and intercourse and all that."

As characteristic as this absence of shyness is the presence of confidence and trust. Unlike children in so many cultures, those in Oman do not seem to be regarded as more indiscreet than grownups. They are expected to observe the same standards of propriety, tact, and silence as do adult women, and realistically so. Thus, on one occasion Sheikha, who was known to be a prostitute, asked me in the presence of some other women, and perhaps a dozen children, to write the name of her favorite lover, Ali, in Western script on a handkerchief for her to embroider. I was innocent of her activities at the time and became confused as to what was her husband's true name. I had thought it was Suleiman. So I asked her again and again what it was she had meant. Thus I inadvertently drew excessive attention to what became an extended exchange of misunderstandings. When Sheikha finally abandoned the attempt, it was, in the opinion volunteered later by one of her friends, because she had become concerned that one of the women present, Aisha Baluch, might "carry the talk" of my naïveté to the wrong circles. Fear that any of the children might do so was not expressed.

WOMEN'S SOCIETY

What, then, are the boundaries of any particular woman's world, and what determines its membership? There are a number of constraints which strongly influence the size and character of the social groups which

A neighborly encounter

women can join. First, the rules of segregation require that all social contacts among women, except for the handful of closest relatives and neighbors, *must* take place when the husbands are absent; that is, women's larger society springs to life only in the absence of the men, mainly 8–12 A.M. and 2–5 P.M. Second, the rules of wifely respect, which require that a woman never leave the house in the husband's presence, work to insure the same effect. Third, though closely familiar neighbors and companions can intervisit in the presence of men, shyness precludes their indulging in women's conversation. As a result, the aspects of their relationship that are distinctively female are held in abeyance if any man is present, even within the closest, most informal category. Fourth, modesty imposes limitations on the physical distance that women are able to travel unchaperoned; thus their contacts must be narrowly, locally based. Fifth, the climate works in a similar way; throughout a minimum of six to eight months of the year, the heat is so oppressive, and the fear of sunstroke so strong, that walks beyond a range of ten to fifteen minutes are very reluctantly undertaken. Sixth, high taxi fares—a minimum of one Rial ($3) for a return fare (that is, one-third the price of a female outfit)—further restrain movements. Last, but not least, though women are recognized and allowed to have a desire for companionship, this should be indulged in with moderation, and an excessively large circle of contacts would be deemed unsuitable.

In contrast to the expansive, cosmopolitan society of men, that of women is thus, of necessity, very small-scale: it is not the state, the region, not even the town of Sohar that provides its outer limits, but, for most purposes, the ward or town quarter. Women identify others, and describe their own identities, in terms of these local wards; in a manner that men find naïve and provincial they refer to their ward as *baladna* (our country).

A town quarter or "country"—to use female terminology—is a clearly demarcated section of town, sometimes separated from the next by some physical feature, such as a creek or a grove of palm trees; there is no doubt who its inhabitants are. Women recognize clear differences in the customs of the various quarters. They may compare them with remarkable objectivity, taking explicit pride in those features where their own ward excels, but according due prestige to other quarters in those respects where they are better. The following excerpt from a conversation is typical. I once asked some friends, "The Ajams, do they live in all sections of town?"

"They only live in Higra and in Hadira," answered Feyza.

"And in Shizaw," I said, "I have seen some of their houses down by the sea."

"Maybe . . ." mused Latifa's grandmother. There was a moment's silence, and she continued, "Otherwise, what characterizes Shizaw is that there are whole *harah*s [lanes] full of prostitutes and *xaniths*—*lots* of them!"

"How come," I asked, "Why just there?"

"We don't know," replied Latifa's mother, "formerly they were mostly in Hadira; maybe someone moved from there and spread the habit?"

"Have you heard," said Grandmother, "that there was a woman and her daughter there recently who went with their lovers to a hotel in Dubai? There they were observed by the daughter's labor-migrating husband, fortunately for the women, not in the company of the lovers. The mother is a widow. . . . But the husband understood the situation and divorced the wife. It cost him lots of money. Fatima, I think her name was. . . ."

"No," corrected Sheikha, "her name was Aisha."

"There was another one," Aisha Baluch joined in, "who went out one evening recently after her husband had gone to the market, and she had not come back when he came home at night; he searched for her everywhere, in vain. Not till three days later did she reappear, on her own accord. He, too, had to pay lots of money to get rid of her."

"Yes, there are indeed plenty such women in Shizaw," answered Latifa's mother.

"And in Harrit alSheikh," added Latifa, "whereas in other countries there are rarely more than one or two. Only once has it happened that a bride from our country turned out to be a woman, whereas in Harrit alSheikh and Ghel it happens a lot."

"But why are so many concentrated in Shizaw, alSheikh, and Ghel?" I asked.

My friends were unanimous that they did not know, but, to be sure I received a properly nuanced picture, stressed that there are some in *all* countries, *"lazim yikun fi* [there has to be]."

"But Ghel, for instance," explained Latifa, "their customs are different from ours [literally, our country] in many respects. Their women wear tight trousers, like the Baluch, and they still wear the *mafraj*; we ceased to do so last year, it's old-fashioned. In Ghel, it is not shameful for an unrelated man to enter the compound in the husband's absence and sit with the wife; if the husband comes home and finds them, he will not be angry. They have another custom too that is different from ours: if you come as a guest to one house, all the neighbors will invite you home for coffee, and you will go from one house to the next. It is a beautiful custom [*ᶜada zena*]. When someone from another country visits here, as you have seen, it is rare for the neighbors to invite them home."

"How are alSheikh and Shizaw in that respect?" I asked.

"They are like Ghel as regards women's modesty; for example, the husband will allow unrelated men to give the wife a ride to the hospital—unchaperoned. We regard such behavior as a shame, so we always go several women together."

"And concerning hospitality?" I asked.

"There they are like us. . . ."

The "country" of Sobara, which is the one I know best, in 1974 had approximately eighty houses, and married women were Arab and Baluch in a ratio of four to one. Eight Baluchi households mainly made up one compact *harah*; the other households were interspersed with those of the Arabs. There were four households of slave descent. The women of Sobara all know each other by name and face, as well as by the names of the children; they meet at ceremonial occasions such as weddings, birth, and death. By contrast, if you go outside the "country," a women's acquaintances beyond her relatives are few indeed, restricted to those who happened to drop by on the rare occasions when she visited distantly resident kin, or attended the wedding of some relative in another ward. (Of course, the "country" of one's parents, constitutes an exception.) The older women have a wider range of acquaintances than the younger ones. But all in all, I never ceased to be impressed with the narrowness of the female networks. On my daily visits to my friends in Sobara they would ask where I had been in the meantime, and rarely have an inkling of who they were, those other women whom I had seen. But if their menfolk heard the same information, they could always identify the place and identity of these other persons, provided I could give their menfolk's names.

Although the ward marks the outer limits of the group with which women identify as members, their active circle of companions is much smaller. The crucial concept here is that of *jiran* (neighbors). Only those living within a maximum of perhaps eighty to a hundred yards are close enough to be accessible as potential daily contacts. Women generally seem to belong to circles composed of two to seven such neighbors. If there is a tendency toward ethnic homogeneity in these intimate circles, it is only very slight. Age and wealth are likewise highly disparate; the very diversity of these circles indicates that physical closeness and convenience are major considerations in their formation. In fact, most women prefer to throw their ties no wider than three or four houses *up or down their own harah*. It is striking that the concept of *friend* (*sadiqa*; plural, *asdiqá*) is wholly absent from women's discourse, whereas the importance of neighbors can hardly be exaggerated. Only one woman, Fatima, have I ever heard use the word "friend." This is in stark contrast to the men, who value friends, but shun neighbors.[1]

NEIGHBORS AND COMPANIONS

Let three examples, which reflect very diverse life situations, illustrate the social circles of women.

Latifa's neighbors and closest companions are the women who live in

---

[1] Nancy Tapper notes, in her article on women's subsociety among the Shahsevan nomads of Iran, a fundamentally different pattern of organization among women, in which "a man's position determines to a large extent the relationships his wife will have with other camp women, and the kinds of economic cooperation she will give or receive" (1978, p. 389).

the six houses immediately next to hers, the three on her left and the three on her right. Six of these seven households make up one *harah*, whereas one, in which live Latifa's grandmother and her father's brother's wife, Khadiga, is located at the corner of the next lane (see the drawing on p. 119). Altogether, these households contain ten adult women. Eight are "free" Arabs, one is a Baluchi, and one is an ex-slave. One is old (around age fifty), five are middle-aged (above age thirty), and the remaining four range between sixteen and twenty-four years old. Two (Latifa and her mother) are affluent, four are well-situated, two are by comparison relatively poor (Khadiga and Grandmother), and two are distinctly so. Eight of the women are impeccably moral, one is a flagrant prostitute, another has a past history of prostitution. None of these differences had any effect on neighborliness. The ideal priority of neighborhood relationships over other ones is conventionally expressed in the saying "A neighbor is better than a mother who is far away—for, if I fall ill, who will do my housework and care for my children?"[2]

The epitome of their good relations, as they saw it, was that they would eat the feast meal together, each household bringing its own share to one of three successive houses in turn. They stressed that I must not think *all* neighbors did so, only especially *good* neighbors, like themselves! For instance, Feyza (Latifa's sister from the same father) eats only with her husband's family, because her neighbors are not on such good terms. Feyza lives only a stone's throw away from this group, which includes her mother, father's brother, paternal grandmother, and twelve full or half sisters (mostly children)—all of whom are also her husband's kin, because she married her mother's brother's son. This illustrates the importance of neighbors in contrast to kinsmen. Indeed, Latifa herself, who is at present the central person in this circle, proudly announced that, when she moves to her new house, seven houses down the road, she will eat the feast meal with her new neighbors, provided they practice such a pattern, and, in no event, will she share it any more with her mother and old-time neighbors! Could there be any clearer expression of the value placed on close neighbors—and, simultaneously, of the remarkable ability of these women to accommodate to changed circumstances—perhaps, in part, because of a failure to form deep attachments?

The preeminence of close over more distant neighbors ones is also illustrated by Aisha Baluch's comment that she preferred her neighbors to the women in the Baluch *harah* (which was immediately in front of hers). When, provocatively, I asked whether they were not also her neighbors, she speedily corrected this "slip of the tongue" and said yes, of course, they were. However, the basic idea seems clear: *real neighbors are those whose gates are next in line to yours.* It is they who, in time of crises, may

---

[2] For a similar attitude in a Lebanese neighborhood, see Joseph 1978.

help without violating their obligation to be ever-present in earshot of their own home. Aisha Baluch's mother lived two hundred yards away from the back of her house. She saw her only once a week or fortnight.

On my daily visits to Latifa's place, Aisha Baluch, Mariam the ex-slave, and Sheikha the prostitute would rarely fail to congregate. Grandmother was likely to interrupt her sewing for this bit of sociability, whereas the impoverished Rowda, the neighborhood clown, came in time for food and some sexual joking, then left to market her yogurt and milk. In 1974, Khadiga usually joined us. A year and half later, with a baby always ill, and an utterly strained economy due to a newly built house, she stuck to her sewing and could not afford the time. It is likely, too, that her deteriorating relationship with her mother-in-law (Latifa's grandmother) was a contributing cause of her absence. The remaining two members of this neighborhood group—Latifa's mother's former co-wife and the latter's present one—only dropped by once or twice; was that perhaps because, contrary to Latifa's statement, they did not take such great pleasure in each other after all?

Of all the other "women of the country," only five or six dropped by even once, despite the curiosity my frequent presence must have engendered. An exception was Latifa's sister Feyza, who, in 1974, showed up about twice every week, and, in 1976, only once a fortnight. The rest of the time she now fastidiously stuck to her sewing machine. Her neighbors had all in the meantime built cement houses, and she was maximizing her own chances of getting one.

The drawing sheds further light on women's society and visiting patterns. The arrows indicate whom the women of Latifa's neighborhood see daily. None undertakes more than two daily visits. Everyone (with the exception of Grandmother) sees one of the next-door neighbors. And Latifa and her mother's place constitutes the place of congregation for all. I am uncertain as to the reasons why this should be. They were clearly the most affluent, but, more important, it may have been that, uniquely in the group, the adult males of the household were perennially absent on labor migration. Add to this that on my rare visits to Sheikha's place, everyone, except Khadiga, would congregate; the entertainment was lavish, whereas when I occasionally went to see Khadiga before Latifa, only Sheikha would invariably appear—that is if she was present in the neighborhood at all. After a while, Latifa would generally turn up, a trifle annoyed, and try to push me into proceeding on to her house; alternatively, she might send one of her younger sisters to fetch me.

A second cluster of neighbors illustrates this same effect of closeness on female conviviality, and the heterogeneous character of women's social groups. Fatima, when she used to live in her parents' house, would daily meet with two or three next-door neighbors: two were ex-slaves and one was a free Arab; all three were twice to three times her own age. After

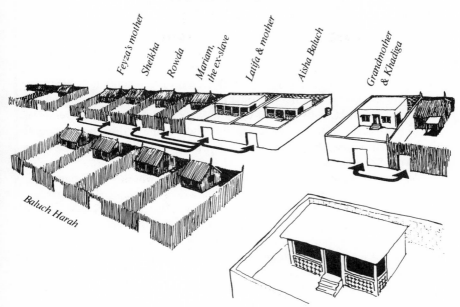

A Sohari neighborhood, indicating visiting patterns. Illustration by Viktor Eliassen.

Typical traditional dwellings

she moved with her husband to a new location, inhabited chiefly by people of Bedu origin, her husband's disapproval of their neighbors put an effective ban on her developing relations with them. With a touch of regret, she once remarked that her neighbors eat jointly during the feast, "but we eat alone, for Ali doesn't want to get involved with the neighbors." For company she stuck to two of her old-time companions who had also moved out to the new district, a five to ten minutes walk away. She met with one of them twice daily, in the morning at the friend's home and in the evening at her own, thus observing the ideal of reciprocity between equals. The other one would join them in the evening at Fatima's place.

As I said previously, Fatima is the only woman whom I have heard use the word *friend*. She characterized her closest companion, the forty-year-old widow of her mother's brother, as her "friend." Although she lived on the other side of the main road, no matter how much you stretched the term *neighbor,* it simply could not accommodate her.

My third example is Rahmeh, away in her date-palm garden; she was not wholly without neighbors, but they were beyond the reach of the eye, separated from Rahmeh and one another by thick groves of date palms. Was that the reason she never visited with them? She did conceive of them as neighbors—of a kind—as when she once told me that the neighbors had acquired television. Yet she also commented that her previous home in town had been better, because there were neighbors. Only once, during my fifty visits or so to Rahmeh's home, did she have visitors; they were distantly resident relatives who had stopped by for a rest on their way to visit her mother, who was ill. And only as an afterthought to the comment on the television did she note that these neighbors were also her relatives. The message is clear: it is neighbors, rather than relatives, who count, and from whom one's companions, if any, are apt to be drawn.

Besides neighbors, one's own children and those of the neighbors, occasional close-living relatives, and "women of the country," two further categories of person enter into women's segregated social life: they are the distantly resident woman whom one visits on rare occasions and from whom one likewise receives rare, formal visits, and the itinerant vendor, who comes by about once or twice a month.

The itinerant vendor, who is always an elderly woman, is a welcome visitor, both for the wares she sells and the news she brings. Even when women judge her prices too dear to buy from her, they take much pleasure in handling and inspecting her articles. But even more is the vendor appreciated as a source of information about births, marriages, divorces, and the like. Indeed, she seems in many ways to trade in news as much as in goods. Not that she speaks unasked, but she answers willingly the "who is who" of major social events—whereas questions about "why" are not asked.

The distantly resident woman with whom one intervisits formally on a reciprocal basis is usually drawn from the category of kinsmen and in-laws, and she is conceptualized in terms of such relationships. The relationship may extend to cousin, nephew's wife, husband's sister, and so forth. The total number of such persons is difficult to judge, for visits among them can be extremely infrequent—even between the most closely related. But it should be noted that this network is also recruited by selection from a larger category of potential relatives: visiting among kin or in-laws is not compulsory and is not practiced generally, only between some. Last, for some women, the mother may be an active member of the social circle, either because the husband lets his wife visit her alone (for example, Fatima), has placed his wife into her mother's custody during his own absence on labor migration (for example, Latifa), or the mother lives close enough for the woman to visit her readily (for example, Feyza). But frequently the mother lives too far away for the daughter to visit her, except on rare occasions when she is accompanied by her husband (for example, Khadiga and Sheikha).

Having established in some detail the social circles that compose female society, let us return to its social content—the actual behavior that unfolds in these circles, and the place of such activities in the total day and life of women. As indicated, women have about twelve hours a day for their own activities and own society. If the husband is a labor migrant, chores are further reduced, and, in a sense, women's segregated social world will extend uninterrupted through months, or even years. How do they pass the time?

FORMAL VISITS

Let us first focus on the exciting and conspicuous high points: the formal visit.

Picture a group of two to five women, cloaked in the all-enveloping black *abba*, some with a child balanced astride one hip, and another hiding shyly in the folds of the mother's cloak, entering the gate of some distant home to which they have been formally invited. They are greeted with formal constraint by the hostess(es), a ritual handshake, and *Kef ilhal?* (How are you?)—no sign of emotion is shown. Then they shed their *abba*s, and emerge as gold-bespangled birds of paradise. Their dresses are made of colorful prints, for the occasion the very best they have of Japanese nylon; shawls and scarves are of the finest and sheerest cloth; and fine gold jewelry glitters through the shawls. To carry a total of $4,000 worth in gold alone is quite within the normal range. The forehead is decorated with the gorgeous filigree *mafraj*, some ten centimeters wide, lining the contours of the *burqa*. Around the neck is a filigree necklace so broad that it covers most of the chest from throat to waist, and so heavy that

women are forced to remove it, during the worst heat of summer, to reduce perspiration. The wrists carry broad bracelets, usually filigree, and a
golden watch; most fingers are provided with gold rings, as are the toes of
the wealthier. Place all this against a background of dresses of strong and
thoughtfully composed colors, pantaloons embroidered with gold or silver
thread, headdresses of the finest lace, pitch-black hair meticulously
combed and, for the occasion, oiled to a high shine, eyes made up with the
mascaralike *kohl* so that they stand out liquid and dark behind the black,
shimmering *burqa*—and the picture is complete.

For the *burqa* is retained even in this all-female company.

A full hour of preparation will have gone into creating this apparition:
an hour of blissful expectation, with excited running to and fro to fetch
the *kohl* and oil and jewelry and all the other paraphernalia needed for
such glittering embellishment; excited indecision while trying on one outfit and changing one's mind for another—Will pinkish or bluish pantaloons best suit this many-colored dress? Rechecking that nothing has been
forgotten, bottle and a change of clothes for the baby, and sweets for the
hostess's children; struggles with the small children who resist having their
eyes made up; ready at last, the woman will move on to others who will accompany her and wait, with impatient agitation, while they complete their
own preparations. The party of women will have agreed, the previous day,
on the exact time of departure, but such punctuality is quite illusory, especially for those women whose husbands are labor migrants and who consequently need never concern themselves about times and deadlines.

Gold-bespangled birds of paradise

On arrival, the guests will be led onto the shady sitting platform or, if the hostess is set on avoiding neighbors and the heat is not too fierce, to a room inside the house. There, a rug or the best quality plastic mat is put out for the guests to sit on, along with colorful cushions against which to rest their backs. The hostess settles on the edge of this prestigious seat, with no cushion for her back, to demonstrate due deference to the guests.

The atmosphere is constrained and quiet; such little conversation as there is, is lethargic and highly conventional. Most of the time the guests and hostess sit, gazing out into space, everyone apparently engrossed in her own inner world. The topics of the sparse verbal communication are neutral: illness is by far the most prevalent one and may easily dominate the whole encounter. Prices rank second; for example, the price of gold in Dubai versus that in Muscat; the price of butter in different quarters of town. Just how formal and taciturn such visits are may be illustrated by the fact that, in summertime, it would be my common experience to be assembled with up to to six women at a time, for a full eight hours, and, at the visit's end, be able to count the sentences spoken there as no more than two score. That the women themselves endured the visit for so long I think can only be explained by the heat: throughout the months from May till September the women have a panicky fear of sunstrokes; consequently, visits outside of one's own ward tend to begin around 8 A.M. and end at 5 P.M. Such visits tend to concentrate on kinswomen, for it is only to them that the husband will agree to such extended visits. The rest of the year, the normal pattern is one of brief visits, not exceeding an hour's stay.

One example of how constrained by shyness women are at such formal visits is provided by the following episode. When we made our ceremonial visit to Mariam, on her third honeymoon day, Latifa, Feyza, and Khadiga bought two bags of candies to throw over Mariam's head as a blessing and a token of good will. On our way to visit, they remarked that they hoped no unfamiliar women would be there, because they would be too shy to perform this gesture. Mariam's mother-in-law and sister-in-law turned out to be present, and we returned home with the bags unopened.

Another example is provided by Rahmeh's ceremonial visit to an acquaintance, an old woman, who had just returned from a pilgrimage to Mecca. For days ahead of the visit (delayed because our car, which was to bring her, was out of order) Rahmeh glowed with anticipation and spoke much about the visit. This was to be one of those rare occasions when she left her solitary house in the date-palm garden. When the day finally arrived, she dressed herself and her four children in their very best attire, and, carrying a bag of candies to symbolize her joy with the safe return of the pilgrim, we set off on our grand visit. On arrival, the children threw the sweets over the pilgrim's head. Then we all sat down. Apart from the formal greetings, not a word was spoken. I found myself waiting for all the questions that I had expected Rahmeh to pour over the pilgrim's head:

about the journey, about Mecca, and so forth. Only such an active interest could explain her intense expectation beforehand, I felt. But Rahmeh did not ask a single question. And the pilgrim did not volunteer one bit of information. Their power of silence was immense. The children also remained quiet and immobile. Not till a quarter of an hour had passed did the pilgrim break the silence by asking Rahmeh about her youngest child, who suffers from a chronic skin disease. A few remarks about this illness and other children's complaints were exchanged. Then we were served snacks and left. For Rahmeh, it had been one of the great events of her year.

During a typical one hour's visit, the guests will sit for the first half hour in the manner previously portrayed, silent and poised, with only occasional spurts of conversation. The hostess then goes to fetch the food; the guests meanwhile remain silent as the grave, or at most speak in a very low whisper. As the hostess reappears with the food and places it in the midst of the circle—the number of plates and their contents being an expression of the prestige she accords to the guests, as well as her economic status—the guests' attention immediately focuses intently upon it. At the hostess's *fadlu* (please), they plunge in to the snacks, their bodies leaning heavily forward. Something about the way they grab and snatch the food, kneading it with their whole hand rather than with their fingertips only, as is common for the Middle East, gives an outsider the impression that the feel of the food is as important to them as its taste. Certainly, the overt delight they take in the food contrasts remarkably with their passive, withdrawn posture through the rest of the visit. The children help themselves with even greater abandon, and it is rare for a mother to tell her offspring "enough." Satisfied, the women drink the obligatory three small cups of coffee. Then incense and perfume are passed around, and they help themselves so generously from a choice of up to five bottles of perfume that their dresses may become quite soaked. The visit now reaching its end, they grasp some goodies for those of their children who missed the occasion, gather their *abba*s about them, and stride to the gate, with an almost inaudible "God's peace be upon you" as they disappear. There is no elaboration or acknowledgment of the hospitality received, or ceremonious leave-taking, not even a word of farewell addressed face-to-face.

Months, even years, may pass before they meet again. For example, in December 1975, I went with Latifa, her mother, and grandmother, father's brother, and the latter's wife, Khadiga, to visit Latifa's paternal cousin (her father's sister's daughter) in Zaffran, a twenty-minute ride along the coast. It was the first time in five years that these close relatives, grandmother and daughter's daughter apart, had met.

Once departing visitors are outside the gate, their mood changes abruptly, as if in reaction to the formal social pressure they have felt; they will laugh and talk, and, if there is a waiting car to provide them with protective seclusion and privacy, they dissolve into excited banter and gig-gling, like overstimulated children after a party. They will instruct the driver to take them the longest route home, through a maximum of resi-dential wards, away from the market, in the same way that they came. It seems as if all the overt excitement that preceded the visit throughout the hour-long preparations, but was suppressed during the visit proper, is again given full vent. The *fun* of the whole visit, no doubt, is acted out in the car ride to and fro; the visit's highlight may indeed be the ride, com-bined with the thrill of expectation throughout the preparations. Super-ficially, it might seem as if the visit itself constitutes a lowpoint or anti-climax in the sequence of events of which it is the ostensible core—that is, if one disregards the evident enjoyment of eating. But this is a false inter-pretation, as will be discussed more fully. And, what is more, Soharis do not break a visit into separate elements as we might; each is part and parcel of a *ziyara* (visit).

Such visits, alas, are few and far between. Generally speaking, I think a woman undertakes at most only one or two a month and receives as many.

NEIGHBORLY VISITS

It is neighbors who relieve the drabness of a humdrum life. Even Rahmeh, despite all her endeavors to appear content in her date-palm garden, was quite explicit in this: home in Higra was better because there were neighbors. And Fatima said the reason she and Ali put a quick end to their stay in Mattrah was that she had no neighbors there, only Baluch (that is, Baluch-speaking women). It was a life duller than she could tolerate.

A woman usually visits one or two neighbors a day, but sometimes none; she is likely to receive as many, either singly or in gatherings of from two to five. These everyday visits differ significantly in character from the formal ones: the hospitality is less lavish; perfume and incense do not fig-ure; jewelry is largely absent (not because the women would not like to adorn themselves, but because its weight adds to the ever-present strain of the heat); the mood is somewhat more relaxed and carefree; the topics in-dulged in are more varied and spontaneous; embroidery (that is, commer-cially oriented work) is likely to be brought along, and the sewing machine may also be used. Yet these gatherings of close neighbors have one strik-ing feature in common with the formal ones: limited conversation, long si-lences, a conspicuous absence of gossip.

The absence of gossip deserves further emphasis and perhaps corrobo-ration. This may be drawn from a seemingly unexpected source: Omani men. It is striking that, critical as they tend to be of the value and legiti-macy of an active social life among neighborhood women, they do not accuse women of being gossipy. Oman must be one of the few places in the world where men do not think of "women's talk" as synonymous with gossip or "idle talk"! Considering that males are fully aware of the extent of female leisure, how revealing is this fact of the quality of male-female relations, as well as of the character of women's society!

A comparison with women in a Western society practicing some degree of sexual segregation may serve to emphasize distinctive features of Omani women's world. Of a village in southern France, Rayna R. Reiter writes: "Women state that the activities that go on in the male domain are boring and incomprehensible. Men say the same of the gossip groups, adding that they are malicious. Each group accuses the other of wasting time in its leisure activities" (1975, p. 268). Nothing similar can be reported from Sohar. Not once did we hear a man accuse women generally of gossip and malicious talk, or of wasting time. A woman's duties are clearly demarcated. As long as she performs them satisfactorily, leisure is hers to enjoy. In fact, it is prestigious for a man to burden his wife with few duties; it reflects his ability to provide well for her.

Conversely, an Omani women stating that male activities are boring and incomprehensible, not to mention accusing men of wasting time, is beyond my powers of imagination. One may indeed wonder how women could possibly depreciate male activities when they have only the slightest idea of their content and form. In the female view, male activities are naturally superior. If they may appear incomprehensible to women, this reflects only their own ignorance, and to meddle in how men pass their leisure would be absurd. A mutual acceptance of, and respect for, the distinctiveness of the other gender prevails.

The essence of Omani women's social intercourse is not contained in its conversational aspect. For this reason, visits can well be taciturn, even essentially silent, encounters. Even in the company of close neighbors, where no special feeling of constraint or shyness prevails, each woman usually sits, silent and introverted, absorbed in her own private world—or perhaps intent on the exacting embroidery of a *kummi*. It then seems as if each woman present encloses herself in an aura of personal sacredness and is in full control of herself and her situation. The fear of awkward silences, which seems to trouble Westerners so much in social gatherings, certainly does not exist in Sohar.[3] Men, in contrast to women, appear to set some value in the art of beautiful speech, but the difference is a matter of degree only.

What the men do deprecate, and criticize women for—in fact, the only

[3] We may note that this characterization may be true only for coastal Oman. I found that women of Bahla, a town in interior Oman where we spent six weeks, were always communicative and vivacious, in a manner very different from those of Sohar.

thing they habitually criticize them for—is squandering their hard-earned money. Conversely, the most common criticism directed by women toward men is that they are stingy.

But let me not give the impression that such neighborly encounters are bland in the absence of gossip. First, seen in contrast to the eventlessness of seclusion in one's own compound—the only and perpetual alternative—*any* meeting with people tends to be an event. As Rahmeh put it, "It gives pleasure to look at people and things." To put these visits in proper perspective, let us see what life is like in their absence.

WOMEN'S SOLITARY ACTIVITIES

On my visits to the homes of Latifa, Fatima, Khadiga, Rhameh, and Sheikha—women in qualitatively very different kinds of life situations—I usually found them sitting, quite motionless, gazing out into space, a child on their lap, apparently absorbed in their own inner world; alternatively, they might be sewing on the machine or mending some clothes, but with that same statuelike composure. Periodic residence in the date-palm garden, during summer, or, in some cases, as for Rahmeh, as a permanent arrangement, is not a valued alternative. The luxuriant green growth of the orchard, with its potential for also growing flowers and shrubs, holds surprisingly little interest to Sohari women, considering the aridity of their natural habitat; such little horticulture as occurs is a male preoccupation. I met with no trace of rustic romanticism, or interest in nature, among the urban women I knew in Sohar: Rahmeh's observation that what gives pleasure is to look at people and things seemed to hold for them all.

Yet Sohari women's modesty debars them from going to the gate and observing life outside, even when footsteps are heard in the *harah*. I do not even know whether they listen for such sounds. Telling, I believe, is the response of the neighbors of Sheikha to the clearly audible noise from the cars that came to fetch her: they never went to the gate to peep. Not even when our chauffeur once stopped at Sheikha's place and lingered for five to ten minutes on his way to fetch me (the characteristic noise of our Landrover was easy to identify) did anyone in the group gathered with me at Latifa's place compromise their dignity by any sign of curiosity. It was I who finally could not desist and came back reporting that Sheikha was standing in the *harah*, without her *burqa*, flirting ostentatiously with our chauffeur. My friends responded with stoical unaffectedness.

Leisure is highly valued, but so is money and what it can buy. All but the most affluent spend some time daily producing articles for sale. Many work at the sewing machine: some, like Feyza and Khadiga, stick to it most of the time. They sew dresses for neighboring women and children.

Yet others, like Aisha Baluch and Sheikha, are rarely seen without an embroidery, a *kummi*, between their fingers.

It is an eventless life. When I returned on my second visit to Sohar, my friends exclaimed with wonder, "How you travel, while we only sit!" Most said they had asked their husbands to take them on trips to Dubai, but received diffuse promises. Those few who had traveled and had tasted a different kind of life were categorical in that they preferred it: for example, Rahmeh thought Kuwait better than Sohar because in Kuwait she could go to the market and even attend a segregated women's cinema. In her view, life in Sohar will greatly improve when women are provided with electricity and television. It goes without saying that it will be radically changed.

FEASTS AND WEDDINGS

All my female friends agreed that the most enjoyable occasions of all are the feasts (singular, *ᶜid*). The little one, following Ramadan, lasts for three days, whereas the Great Feast, the Feast of Sacrifice, which is the highlight of women's year, lasts a full five days. For both feasts, women and children dress in new and beautiful clothes; nowadays, under the present prosperity, one different outfit is worn for each of the days. The women adorn themselves with all the gold, finery, and cosmetics that

A woman sewing in solitude

they possess. For both feasts, the food is elaborate, including meat, pastry, and sweets, as well as a variety of other delights which are reserved for the major ritual occasions. The food of the Great Feast is, however, even finer than that of the Little Feast, and this aspect of the occasion is the one that women spontaneously extol when asked to tell why they regard the Great Feast as the more marvelous. In the same breath, they would stress the men's superior abilities as cooks—it being a male responsibility to prepare the Feast meals.

It is easy to see how women's restricted movement, their confinement to the world of home and neighborhood, and an uneventful daily routine intensify the value of neighbors to them, and why the women, unlike the men, should invest in proximal relations. But to give a more complete and nuanced picture of the quality of the relationship between close companions, and the reasons why such visits are so highly valued, I should emphasize that these encounters can also be considerably more eventful than I have indicated so far. Not only are they characterized by a general absence of gossip, and the frequency of long and untroubled silences, they may also be enlivened by boisterous interaction and swift repartee. This should be, and almost invariably is, practiced with due regard to strict canons of manners and politeness. But what is allowed, and practiced, within the Sohari concepts of politeness and grace that are binding on neighbors, has a more unpredictable and spontaneous character than has been described till now. Familiarity eases the constraints of shyness and gives scope for greater individual expression; and the behavior that takes place sometimes seems strangely at odds with basic courtesy as we understand it. But that which is expressed is strikingly revealing of local values. First, although gossip, in the sense of derogatory remarks, is largely absent, it is not wholly so. Second, although neighbors' marital relations are not spoken of, a striking exception is that their sexual relations, within marriage, are a favorite theme of bawdy joking. Third, avid—one may even say avaricious—profit-seeking activity in marketing co-exists with gracious hospitality. Fourth, general tact and the extolling of others' good qualities contrasts with uninhibited criticism of looks and descent. Last, but not least, the whole gathering also has marked focus and sequence, provided by the food, which constitutes the essence of hospitality. The latter subject deserves a more detailed and systematic presentation. I shall give it first.

FOOD

I asked Latifa once, "*Must* one leave the moment one has eaten?" She said, "One must not necessarily, but one should, for guests might come to one's home in the meantime." This explanation is not convincing—the guests are too few and far between. What is beyond doubt is that Soharis regard it as an essential element of good manners to depart promptly after eating. Thus it is the hostess, rather than the guests, who determines the duration of a visit. If she is not in the mood for company, she may, with every show of good manners, put a quick end to the disturbance. Conversely, a guest in a hurry may ask the hostess whether she is not going to bring the snacks soon. But only once have I witnessed this.

Some neighboring women have arranged to congregate daily for morning snacks, each bringing her share. Otherwise, the obligation to entertain rests with the hostess, who *must* serve snacks even to neighbors who drop by every day. Women are obligated to serve snacks to everyone except their closest relatives.

All snacks are ranked on a scale of prestige. In 1974, canned fruits were highest ranked; in 1976, however, they were superseded by new and more expensive items in the market, such as fresh fruits and a special kind of Lebanese cotton candy, imported from Dubai. The relationship between price and prestige is almost perfect; the more expensive an item, the more valuable it is for social purposes. Other highly prized foods are pure milk and pure orange juice. Caramels and sweets rank lower, biscuits and popcorn lower still, and dates and milk tea at the bottom. In 1975, fresh fruits, that is, oranges, grapes, and apples, cost as much as one Rial per kilo. The aforementioned are all in the category of snack. Cooked food is an altogether different thing—rarely served—and invested with very different rules and meanings.

Dates and coffee compose the traditional food of entertainment between close neighbors. Nowadays, biscuits, inexpensive caramels, and popcorn tend to be favored substitutes. Between neighbors who interact on a daily basis, or nearly so, a single dish will do. But all other visitors, even solitary ones, should be offered at least two plates, with different contents, or the hostess is thought stingy. If the guests are more numerous, the amounts or variety must be increased, up to a maximum of four plates. Three or four plates may also be offered to one or two guests when the hostess wishes to honor them.

It is for this reason that many Sohari men are opposed to women's visiting: it is an expensive activity. Such expense can be illustrated by examining entertainment.

To take some examples, among my acquaintances. Sheikha's hospitality was, during the last field work, the most lavish. On several occasions, Latifa and I were served four plates brimming with fresh fruits: apples, oranges, grapes, and bananas. Then followed a can of pure orange juice for each, accompanied by five perfume bottles. At Latifa's place, the hospitality ranged from three plates of fresh oranges, canned peaches, and caramels, to two of popcorn and caramels.

There is one exception to the correspondence between price and prestige: homemade cake is a rare and valued expression of respect. It was offered to us only once—on our first visit to a young *xanith*; the only other time I saw it was when Latifa's mother entertained some distant, affluent relatives.

The immediate departure after eating may seem the more abrupt because of the absence of any sign of farewell among neighbors. It is a silent farewell, in contrast to the arrival, which is generally announced by *Kef ilhal?* or *Kef halish?* (How are you?). There does not seem to be any normative injunction against saying farewell. My friends gave the unenlightening explanation that "It would not be wrong to say farewell, but if the hostess is busy with other things, such as a child crying, it is unnecessary." Neighbors do not say farewell, even when the hostess is conspicuously not so preoccupied, therefore one may wonder whether their mute departure immediately after eating may not be revealing of complex attitudes associated with the giving and receiving of food.

Gifts, likewise, are received formally and mutely and quickly shunted out of sight. Infrequent guests will commonly bring foods as gifts (for example, eggs, fruits, butter). The hostess accepts them as if they were of no concern to her. When the guests take their leave, she presents them with gifts in turn, which they accept in the same expressionless manner. Whether there is any feeling that the return gifts should exceed the former in value, or merely be equal, I do not know. Guests may also bring sweets for the hostess' children, in which case the neighbors, if they are familiar with the guests, will demand some for themselves, whether or not they have children.

The guests, when they leave, will take some of the offered food home for their children. I once witnessed two women, evidently well-off (as revealed by the quality of their jewelry), each drop a handful of popcorn (practically valueless) on their way out and promptly proceed to crawl about in the sand to pick it up—a dozen pieces in all—with evident concern that they not miss a single piece!

In striking contrast to hostesses elsewhere in the Middle East, a Sohari hostess will rarely urge the guests to eat. But then, there is no need to. Guests do not, from shyness or fear of the reciprocal obligations devolving on them in turn, help themselves modestly. Any such strategy would indeed fail, for helping oneself modestly carries quite other meanings in Sohar.

It was not till the end of my field work that this key to Sohari relationships was brought home to me. Latifa finally burst out, "Is it true that your people do not wish guests to eat well?"

"But of course we do!" I replied. "How could you think otherwise?"

"But you yourself eat so little," she argued; and to my confused expression, "If we ate like you, the hostess would think us stingy!"

The pieces of the puzzle fell into place for me, one of which was an episode long ago, at Mariam's wedding: Latifa, Khadiga, Feyza, Sheikha, and I were invited to visit several of Mariam's neighbors. One household was conspicuously poor. We were generously served, and I had expected

my friends to practice constraint. They did not, and I was greatly astonished, both at what I saw as their greed and voraciousness, as well as their
lack of consideration toward the hostess. However, Latifa's above statement puts the occasion into a different light; it also explains why it is not
bad manners to demand sweets; and why the dilemma for a hostess should
not be to make sure that the guests will eat well, but that they will not eat
too well.

The rules of etiquette require that approximately half of the food served
be left for the hostess's household. These rules are not observed to the letter: either much more than half, or much less, may be devoured. The
hostess may signal what she would like the amount to be in how she
chooses to serve the food and, simultaneously, how deep-felt her generosity.

Fruits may be served whole, and the hostess may leave it up to one of
the guests to set the pace for the group by letting her cut up as much of the
fruit as she deems appropriate. Chances are that she will practice suitable
constraint; there is a delicate balance between eating well to demonstrate
generosity and eating excessively, and thus gluttonously. Thus some
mothers spontaneously say that they will actively interfere and tell their
children "wait" or "that's enough" to prevent the hostess from thinking
that the children are gluttonous, as well as the child from becoming so.
When one guest in a party assumes the initiative in serving the others, one
may expect her to be doubly careful and to effectively control the consumption of the others. But the boundary between eating well and eating
greedily is flexible, as one sees when a child, as so often happens, fails to
get the message and demands a further helping for himself, necessitating
that another piece of whole fruit be cut open (to refuse a child food is
rare). Given this fresh opportunity, adult women will eat of it too!

Alternatively, the hostess herself may set the pace by cutting up as many
whole pieces as she wishes to be eaten, or by inviting the guests to share
another plate when she judges the time fit. The practice being for the
guests to eat out of one plate at a time, and not to go back to the first; thus
she may significantly affect the pattern.

I have seen a hostess cut up three-fourths of the fresh fruit served, but
also, in an extreme instance, another hostess assure that only one-eighth
of the food served was eaten—by cutting only one of eight oranges into
pieces and offering coffee to the guests once it was eaten. The latter practice is termed "to make the guests finish quickly" and is evidence of stinginess.

In neighborly gatherings, as opposed to more formal ones, the hostess
eats with the guests. During such occasions, the pace is slow and relaxed,
talking is intermixed with eating, and switching between plates is allowed.
A guest who disapproves of the quality of the food served, say dates, may,
without offense, go and fetch her own higher quality dates for the enjoyment of the whole group. The practice of immediate departure after eat-

ing may also be disregarded, though within limits. In formal encounters, on the contrary, the hostess does not eat with the guests, the guests do not talk while eating, reverting to a "previous" plate is impolite, and attention is intently fixed upon the food. In neighborly encounters, though the food is essential to conviviality, it clearly holds a far less prominent place than it does in the formal visits.

As in most of the Middle East, in Sohar food provides the most basic and central idiom of friendship and conviviality. But Sohar differs significantly in that commensality is not the *sine qua non*. Joint eating by hostess and guests is practiced only when the food involved is *snacks*, and only when the guests are close neighbors or relatives. *Cooked food cannot be shared by host and guest*, no matter how closely familiar or related. The guest would be too shy to eat at all, Soharis say. "Even after twelve years of marriage," Sheikha told me, "my parents insist that my husband and I eat by ourselves when we visit them." Even if the consequence is that the guest must eat all alone, in a separate room, it would be disrespectful to arrange it otherwise. The only exception is if the host is of clearly higher status, in which case the guest may be honored to eat with him, or her.

Cooked food is served infrequently and only to prestigious guests, who, in most cases, have been formally invited for a meal. When Latifa and her close female relatives visited their relatives in Zaffran, they were taken aback and delighted to be so honored. On no other occasion when I went visiting with women did we have such attentions bestowed upon us, whereas my husband and I were formally invited for lunch by most of our close friends. Cooked food is also featured at ceremonial occasions, such as weddings, burials, and feasts.

It is difficult to see why cooked food should be circumscribed with such special avoidance rules, when uncooked food and sweets conspicuously are not. Why are guests who devour snacks so eagerly in the hostess's presence too shy to eat even one bit of cooked food if observed by her? Why, to take an extreme but common case, can parents in the role of host eat snacks from the same plate as their daughter and son-in-law, yet cannot even be in the same room with them when treating them to cooked food?

Shyness, in the Sohari view, clearly arises out of the hostess-guest relationship, rather than the act of commensality. Thus unrelated and unfamiliar people of the same gender may freely eat cooked food together at weddings, and many neighbors do so at the feasts, when each household contributes its share.

FURTHER COMMENTARIES ON THE RULES
OF DEMEANOR AND CONVERSATION

Hospitality versus Avarice

Much buying and selling take place among neighboring women, often, but not necessarily, within a context of hospitality. For example, Latifa classifies the women who purchase dress materials from her as "guests," not neighbors. Even itinerant vendors do not visit house by house within a certain area; they go only to those few houses with which they are familiar and depend upon the hostess to gather the neighbors. The ensuing encounter, centering on the itinerant vendor, also has all the features of a social visit, including the serving of coffee and snacks, as well as a particularly rich dissemination of news and information by the vendor. For this reason, she is indeed an eagerly welcomed guest. Yet such vendors would be too shy to knock at unfamiliar gates, Soharis say.

But no seller, whether itinerant or locally resident, would be too shy to demand the maximum price that she believes she could get, even from a guest or close neighbor; and no guest would feel constrained by the situation in her style or force of bargaining. It is not bad manners to be clever at earning money, or, if it is considered so by others, the person's incentive is too powerful for her to care. Aisha Baluch was criticized by Latifa—behind her back—for selling the *kummi* for two Rials too dear, for twelve instead of the ten Rials. For this reason no neighbor will buy from her, and she must sell her embroideries through a shop in the market, Latifa explained. She herself, on the other hand, was criticized by a woman of another ward for having sold some burqas to me for too high a price.

Neighbors trade, by means of swapping, bartering, and money transaction, in a variety of foodstuffs, cloth, and items of clothing. The foodstuffs are mostly eggs, dates, and various milk products, such as yogurt, butter, and the by-product of buttermaking, *laban*. Because no fresh milk and few milk products are sold in the market, households with producing sheep or goats are at an advantage in this marketing system. Of all items of clothing, only the male *dishdasha* does not circulate within women's market transactions, as the men do not trust its making to female hands. The *dishdasha* is sewn by professional Pakistani tailors in the market. The ordering of dresses from neighboring women is preceded by much haggling, for dresses are made to order and cannot readily be sold to other customers. I myself was much astonished at the excessive prices that some of my friends demanded when I asked to buy some women's outfits. Friendship seemed to give way to avarice. This was, however, a transformation in the mode of interaction which I was consistently to observe in Sohari interpersonal relationships, but which clearly did not strike Soharis as incongruous and which left no rancor and made no change in their relationship.

Likewise, when I told my Sohari friends about life in Bahla, in inner Oman, a world as unfamiliar to them as Sohar was to me, and mentioned that the people there cannot sell the foodstuffs they produce to other townspeople (8,000 in all) because they regard foodstuffs as God's bounty, which should be freely shared, my Sohari friends were quite unbelieving. "Here you can sell *anything*," they exclaimed, "dates and milk and all!"

Their own evaluation of hospitality and generosity notwithstanding, the praxis of Bahla was beyond their grasp; they could not admire it.

As intent as women are on making a good bargain, they are as prepared to challenge the claims of others to have succeeded in doing so, where the facts do not warrant it. Revealing is the following excerpt from a conversation.

"What is the price of a sewing machine, of the kind with a stand? Sheikha, how much did you pay for yours?" I asked.

"Thirty-five Rials," she replied.

"But it was not new," Latifa added.

"Yes, it was," answered Sheikha.

Latifa said, "No, it wasn't."

"Yes, it was," insisted Sheikha.

"But how can you say that when you know yourself that a new one costs 55 Rials?" Latifa asked.

So Sheikha grudgingly must admit that hers was not, after all, brand new, but she stresses that it was just as good *as if* it had been!

The aggressive tone of this dialogue contrasts sharply with the tactful mode of nearly all other social encounters, where the parties take elaborate precautions in order to avoid criticism of each other, or questioning or challenging the other's claims. Maybe the reason why it was acceptable and appropriate is that Soharis conceptualize market relations as a clearly distinct aspect of behavior, subject to its own impersonal set of rules, rather the way Westerners regard it as inappropriate to practice tact and consideration when playing their hand in bridge.

Tactfulness versus Criticism of Physical Looks

Another aspect of the woman that is susceptible to overt criticism within these circles of close neighbors, though chiefly behind her back, is her physical features and/or descent. Women display what seems an uninhibited arrogance in denigrating the looks of others, when these do not measure up to what they regard as universally valid standards: white skin, large brown eyes, a small straight nose, and smooth hair—all features that serve to differentiate autochtones from Africans in this part of the world. Thus the only time when my Sohari friends did not stoically accept major differences in judgment between myself and themselves was when I said that I found dark skin beautiful. "But how can you," exclaimed Grandmother, "when it usually goes with a flat nose, kinky hair, and broad lips?" They made no secret of their own views. A black child would risk being labeled "slave" (*xadim*) to her face—not ex-slave, but slave. Behind their backs, people who had some physical blemish were liable to have it pointed out. Several examples have already been noted. The role of such criticism in a conversation may be seen from the following example.

Grandmother, Latifa, her mother, Aisha Baluch, and Sheikha were gathered, and I happened to mention that I had met Meimona the previous day, on her visit to her parents (see Ch.12).

"Did she wear the *burqa*?" asked Latifa, and, to my nodding affirmative, "What pieces of jewelry did she wear?" and, in the same breath, "Was she pretty?"

Grandmother said, sharply, "But Meimona is *not* pretty. She is brown-skinned."

"But she is prettier than her sister Badriya. Badriya is *really* dark," Latifa replied.

Latifa's mother joined in, "Their mother, too, is not pretty, for she, in addition, has a defective eye."

"Yes," said Grandmother, "brown skin can be pretty when the person, like Mariam [her granddaughter], has large, beautiful eyes, smooth hair, and small nose. Otherwise it is ugly."

Latifa said, "The reason Meimona had to move to Muscat no doubt was her failure to be a virgin. Her husband does not dare to leave her here."

This marked the end of the conversation. The women then reverted to self-contained peace. They remained quiet for approximately a half hour, then the encounter ended.

Modesty versus Sexual Joking

It is doubtless no coincidence that what little gossip does circulate in neighborhood circles chiefly concerns matters connected with sexuality, such as infidelity and virginity. What is surprising, given the pervasive preoccupation with sexual matters which characterizes these women, is the fact that such matters attract so *little* gossip.

Sexuality is indeed their most favored topic of conversation and provides an inexhaustible source of joking and pantomime. Women constantly tease each other about how desired they are by their respective husbands, how they enjoy intercourse, and they illustrate, with gestures and postures, how the objects of the teasing supposedly engage in intercourse. It is a striking and consistent pattern that whereas conjugal life is treated with a tactfulness so rigorous that any reference to it is avoided, this is not true of physical sexuality. Such matters are the object of unrestrained banter of the most intimate nature—but generally of an outrageous, jocular, and clearly fabricated kind and never genuinely indiscreet or vicious.

A woman who has soiled her dress cannot change it without being teased for having had sexual intercourse. If she loses weight, she will be teased for sleeping with her husband all the time. Latifa's mother was never in Latifa's bedroom with me without pointing to the bed with a lascivious twinkle in her eye and remarking, "When Latifa's husband is home, they sleep there, and Nawal [their child] sleeps with me. *Zen!* [It is good!]" A woman rarely wiped the *burqa* marks off her cheeks without eliciting "Aha! Wait till the evening [or when your husband comes home], and then he will kiss it off," and the whole gathering would burst into laughter, and maybe pantomime, and exchange "meaningful" glances.

Measured in time, talk, jokes, and pantomimes on a sexual theme occupy more than half of women's verbal and gesticulating interaction. In
this they are in no way deterred by the presence of children. As they themselves have said, they are not shy to talk about such things before children.
In the most intimate circle of neighbors, even the hostess' husband may be
present, and the conversation may yet revolve around such themes, except
that the man must make the allusions, and only his wife, among the
women, will second him. However, pantomimes will not occur in this context.

WOMEN'S NEIGHBORLY GATHERINGS: AN OVERVIEW

The distinguishing characteristic of women's neighborly gatherings
seems an oscillation between long silences—when the participants are se-
renely absorbed in their inner selves, their embroideries or sewing—and
lively, free-flowing conversations spiced with gestures, and often jokes and
pantomimes. Roughly speaking, the silences seem to pervade two-thirds
to three-quarters of the time that neighbors spend together, and talk and
jokes about sexual matters (including infidelity, nonvirginity, and so
forth), to dominate at least half of the informal conversation. Other favored topics are illnesses and prices. Neighbors may, however, bring up
any topic of their choice so long as they do not criticize the behavior of any
of the other participants (market-oriented behavior apart). The force of
this injunction was cogently brought to my attention on one occasion:
After her flirtation with our chauffeur, Ibrahim, a smiling Sheikha joined
the group of neighbors congregated at Latifa's place with a comment addressed to me, "Ibrahim says he will not fetch you today at lunchtime, but
wait til 5 p.m.!" I parried, "If Ibrahim has anything he wants to tell me,
he can come say it himself!" Sheikha took my sour pill with good grace.
But when she had left, Latifa remarked, "Had you spoken like that to one
of us, we would have become offended. But nothing touches her." Nevertheless, they never spoke like that to her.
    Two observations stand out as to what women do *not* speak about: men
figure only little, and personal names, hardly at all. The only regular references to men are indirect, in the context of sexual banter, when women
are teased about what they engage in with their respective husbands.
Otherwise, men, both individually and as a whole, are conspicuous by
their absence from women's discourse. I never heard women engage in
conversation about the nature of men, though general statements are occasionally made, such as: "Many men have no honor"; "Men are pleased
with the economic contributions that their wives make by sewing, embroidering or selling"; "Many men are stingy and do not let their wives entertain"; "Many men do not let their wives visit their parents"; "Many

men beat their wives"; and "Many fathers become shy on the occasion of their daughters' weddings." In other words, men are mentioned in the contexts where they directly impinge on the life and circumstances of women, but not as objects of interest in their own right. And particular men are very rarely described in any way, and one's own husband not at all. These features may reflect the pervasiveness of segregation and are matched among men (according to my husband's data), who scrupulously avoid references to women. Yet I think it more illuminating to emphasize another aspect of the pattern, as I shall shortly note.

Second, the *names* of women are also conspicuously absent from female conversation. When stories of a gossipy nature are occasionally reported, they open with a standard phrase, "Have you heard, there was a woman recently who . . . . or "There once was a woman who. . . ." The point seems to be the story itself, rather than the information it might provide about any particular person. The fact that someone in the group may interrupt the narrator to add, "Fatima [or Aisha or Khadiga] her name was" does not invalidate this point. The number of female names in common use in Sohar do not exceed a score; hence identifying a woman as Fatima is just a convenient means of labeling, for conversational purposes, and reveals little, if anything, of the person's true identity.

These two negative findings are most illuminating if they are seen together, as they throw into relief the small and self-contained character of the little worlds that neighbors constitute. Men hardly figure as social participants in this little world that women share, but do constitute external circumstances and affect and constrain female society. And the social circles of other women in other neighborhoods are so distant and irrelevant to life and interaction within the neighborhood group—and information about them is, in any case, so scarce and incomplete—that it is uninteresting to try to construct any comprehensive picture of persons and identities in those other small worlds.

Gossip, such little of it as there is, belongs to these neighboring groups. And because their boundaries seem definitive in the sense that women rarely belong to overlapping groups, such stories and commentaries are poorly transmitted among circles. The most a woman might do is "carry the word" on her visits to her mother's. But the mother in turn, if she passes such stories on to her neighbors, will do so by way of that cryptic introduction, "Have you heard, there was a woman recently who. . . ." In consequence, the various neighborhood groups remain effectively insulated from each other: information percolates only slowly between them. Simultaneously, the lack of differentiation within such groups, entailed by the absence of special privileged friendships that would define relations of relative exclusion and inclusion, means that all members have roughly the same information, and that this information, to the extent that it concerns identified persons, relates to members of the group, their husbands, and their children. The main exceptions are stories of a sensational nature which are public at their very inception, such as the outcomes of virginity and potency tests. The resulting homogeneity of information, noncontingency of membership and egality of rights within each neighborhood group fosters in every woman a firm sense of identification with her neighborhood circle.

CONCLUSION: BASIC SOCIAL CONFIDENCE

Insight sometimes may be had by recourse to hypothetical situations, to that which is *not*, or which actors did *not* choose to do. If Sohari women formed friendships, how would their lives change?

The answer is, of course, difficult to construct, but a comparison between the distinctive features of neighborliness versus friendship may prove illuminating. Friendships are formed on the basis of personal likes and compatibility and entail a privileged trust and intimacy. First, every friendship thus implies the evaluation of a person by the other, with the risk of her or his being found wanting, or failing in some way. It is thus subject to the continual hazard of wreckage and dissolution. Second, it is discriminating and exclusive by nature: every friendship entails the *exclusion* of others from the same privileged trust and thus a relative judgment of *distrust*—it establishes an island of greater intimacy in an ocean of greater reserve.

Neighborliness, by contrast, does not depend on personal evaluations. It arises from the objective fact of place of residence. It does not exclude anyone as a result of her personal qualities. The person is not on trial and does not have to live up to anyone's particular standards or tastes. Thus, for example, a young Sohari bride who is transferred to a new and unfamiliar setting need not undergo a period of uncertainty while she is scrutinized by potential parties to the relationship. She is manifestly a member of the neighborhood that surrounds her husband's house. Her identity is defined. She is one of them, and they cannot disown her.

This does not necessarily mean that a woman has no influence on the membership of her social circle. She can simply refrain from visiting women she does not like, and Soharis are definite that this will in turn result in their keeping away from her. They say, "It is so simple here, all you need do is not visit the person, and she will understand, and not come back" (see Ch.8). But if a neighbor is thus discreetly rejected by someone, the onus is on the woman who creates the distance, not on the woman who is turned away: the latter has not been found wanting: it is the former who has been unneighborly. The affronted woman will cast her interpretation in the mold, "She thinks I have come for the sake of the food"; that is, "*She* is stingy," not "I have been found wanting." And a person will be reluctant to expose herself to this construction.

The cultivation of neighborliness, rather than friendship, thus has a number of implications that are clearly compatible with Sohari values. It allows a woman to present herself as always tolerant and noninterfering, honorable in not seeking to sanction others by either favoring or condemning them. It secures every woman a circle of companions within the narrow confines of physical accessibility. And it provides every woman with a social identity, not as the precarious fruit of achievement, but as a secure right. The remarkable assurance and confidence that distinguish married women in Sohar can plausibly be connected with this context as its major source.

CHAPTER 8

✣

Honor and
Self-realization

"It is impossible for us to be tactless and we have no cause to...."

So far, I have focused more on the contrastive features of gender roles that set Soharis apart, and on the segregated worlds in which they unfold. Their shared features that bring them together, and the common rules of conduct that govern them both, have been noted only in passing, as in observing that the ideals of courtesy, tact, and hospitality apply to, and are cherished by, both sexes, investing life in Sohar with a pervasive quality of style and grace. Members of one society, no matter how separate their pursuits, will always partake of a host of shared premises and understandings, otherwise they could not even coexist with a bare minimum of amity. And Soharis do far better than that; they communicate and interact with striking subtlety and grace.

In this chapter, I shall discuss some basic values and premises that pertain to both sexes and profoundly shape the behavior of all Soharis. These differ in significant ways from what has been reported from other parts of the Middle East, and so should be made explicit to prevent false inferences from being made by readers familiar with the literature. Perhaps, more significantly, they raise problems in the analysis of Sohari society which are of consistent concern throughout this book.

Central in this stand the concepts of honor and shame, as used by Soharis, other Middle Eastern and Mediterranean peoples, as well as anthropologists writing on these societies. From anthropological studies of the Middle East and the Mediterranean, one gains the impression that honor, above all other considerations, is what guides and propels men in the conduct of their lives. It is the one supreme value to which all their activities should attest. And it is the ultimate measure by which others evaluate a man's actions to accord or deny him esteem. Honor has thus two aspects: "It is the value of a person in his own eyes, but also in the eyes of his society. It is his estimation of his own worth, his *claim* to pride, but it is also the acknowledgment of that claim, his excellence recognized by his society, his *right* to pride" (Pitt-Rivers 1965, p. 21).

Pitt-Rivers in the above quotation takes admirable care to speak of a person, not a man. As noted in Ch. 4, such care has been largely absent from anthropological discourse, as it often is from male Middle Eastern everyday discourse. Honor is presented as almost exclusively a male attribute. And for its description, we are given some general notions of what constitutes honorable conduct on a man's part, how his honor may be jeopardized, and what actions he would take to maintain it. For the relation of these ideological schemata to actual behavior—how necessary is the response, what consequences does its absence have,—and so forth are questions only rarely raised and answered. A Middle Eastern man apparently cannot afford to compromise, so the argument goes, unless he can do so without loss of face, that is, with no public witnesses to the disgrace.

Unfortunately for the men, it is the conduct of their women that constitutes the main threat to their honor. A man may behave in all respects honorably, but if a woman of his goes once sexually astray, his honor is dramatically compromised. Arab Muslim culture, like some others in the world, has thus encumbered the male's prospects of honor and esteem with what must seem to him a most precarious foundation, whence springs his obsessions with female chastity. To the outsider, it may seem a paradox that the female, who, in the public, male arena has no place, name, or face, is yet the source of the central preoccupation of that arena: the male competition for honor and esteem.

We have already noted and discarded the prevalent assumption that honor is an exclusively male attribute. Other assumptions deserve likewise to be contested, among them the ubiquitous one that a woman who acts dishonorably is irreparably disgraced in the act. She is portrayed as branded forever, discredited beyond all recall. In actuality, we rarely learn what becomes of her—beyond sensational and tragic cases in which the menfolk have murdered her to cleanse their own name. Yet the authors themselves admit that such solutions are infrequent (for example, Antoun 1968). Why do they not care to tell us what happened in the ordinary cases? Is her fate of so little consequence? And what became of a man's honor when he did not do what a man "must"? Why all the interest in the "shall" and "should" and so little in what *is*?

I do not think life anywhere has a quality as uncompromising as this normatively oriented anthropological discussion of honor and shame would lead one to expect. Honor may be a paramount value and ideal, but in real life there are other cherished values and priorities as well. Although the latter may appear to the outsider more trivial, and to the actors secondary, it is a commonplace insight of most people's day-to-day experience that others, if not oneself, are content to aspire to more ordinary heights. Is there any reason to believe that Middle Easterners are different? Certainly not in the case of Sohar. And often, the very literature in which such claims are made for other peoples fails to provide convincing evidence. The reasons seem clear: Real life poses obstacles to the attainment of ideal goals; individuals are unequally committed to the ideals; and the ideals themselves may be mutually incompatible or inconsistent. In order to explore human behavior, it is essential that we pay prime attention to how people actually behave—whether in pursuit of their honor, or in more mundane concerns. Only then shall we learn how they evaluate what honor and shame mean to them and what their predicaments are.

Let me therefore use a concrete case to approach an understanding of what is entailed in the concept of honor, and how it operates in ordinary life in Sohar. I choose an extreme case, in the hope of highlighting and exposing fundamental features of how a woman's action, her self-regard, and her position in society are affected by the Sohari conceptualization of honor. In presenting this case, I shall also be led to call into question some basic assumptions that are common both in social science literature and in Western everyday thought.

THE CASE OF A PROSTITUTE FRIEND

In my circle of best friends were (in 1975/76) six highly virtuous women and one flagrant prostitute.[1] Sheikha, the prostitute, a twenty-four-year-old married woman and mother of two children, was said to have embarked upon her activities in the early fall of 1975. By December of that year, she pursued her activities so blatantly that no one, except possibly her husband, could be in doubt. Toward the end of my field work, when her activities had reached an all-time peak, she would take off most mornings at nine o'clock sharp, come back at noon, go out again at three o'clock and return around five. In defiance of public morality, she let herself be picked up and dropped off by car at the gate of her house, for everyone, save her husband, to see. Her times were carefully set to harmonize with his, but as a man's movements are never fully predictable, there were occasional incidents that were fraught with tension, as when

---

[1] I shall use the term *prostitute* throughout this book to refer to a woman who practices a broad range of behaviors extending from such English concepts as unchastity, unfaithfulness, and adultery, to commercial prostitution. The Sohari terms do not make such distinctions very clearly, and the terms used most commonly—*bitxannith* (she acts like the *xanith* does) and *bitdur* (she strays)—carry a load of moral disapprobation, so I feel the English word "prostitute" is perhaps the most idiomatic translation. Sometimes in speaking to me about such women, Soharis would use the classical Arabic word *qahba*, but I am not certain that this appears in spontaneous conversation among themselves. As previously noted, women sometimes make a distinction between a woman who has an extramarital relationship because of love, and one who does so for other reasons (lust, attention, or money). Men do not acknowledge the legitimacy of such a distinction. It should be unnecessary to emphasize that the Sohari phenomenon thus in no case involves public soliciting, brothel establishment, and so forth.

one afternoon a paramour came to pick up Sheikha at her regular three o'clock hour and her husband had not yet gone to the gardens! Indeed, his presence in the home at this unexpected hour indicated to their neighbors that he himself must probably be making love with her. He looked irritated and sullen when he finally came to the gate, only to find a no less dismayed visitor. The caller tried to save the situation by acting confused and delivering his excuses for inconveniencing strangers in his search for a friend's house, but Sheikha's friends believe that her husband could not have failed to sense the mischief. And Sheikha herself was sufficiently unnerved, so she thereafter chose to leave on foot to her afternoon rendezvous.

Incidents like this, though rarely quite as nerve-racking, would stir the whole neighborhood, for everyone (even toddlers), was fully aware of Sheikha's activities. Yet no one ever said a word to her about them, nor did she mention her adventures. Sheikha and her friends in fact kept up a joint pretense, acted out to perfection, that everything was just as it should be. When she came home from her escapades, her friends could often not resist the temptation to ask where she had been, and she would answer, "With my relatives." Always the same question, and the same answer. But never was the point pursued, or any overt embarrassment caused. Indeed, to say that Sheikha's friends succumbed to temptation when they asked her "Where have you been?" is to choose one interpretation where the real situation is highly ambiguous. This question is commonly asked of any familiar person who joins a group, and to refrain from asking it of Sheikha would perhaps be more revealing than to reenact the pretense.

Once in awhile, it might also happen that our conversation in Sheikha's presence turned to the theme of prostitution and prostitutes—other, socially distant, prostitutes. They would burn in hell, averred my friends, for there is no greater sin than that. And Sheikha participated in such conversations without any reference, even of the most oblique kind, being made to her own activities, though we knew that she knew that we knew. But to as much as mention this would be bad taste and create a scandal. Indeed, to talk about prostitutes in her presence may have demonstrated tact and politeness, rather than oblique condemnation: because sexuality is a favorite topic of women's neighborly conversations, the women's studious avoidance of the theme when in the presence of Sheikha might be more conspicuous than its presence.

Only once did a situation arise that provided the children of the neighborhood with temptation so irresistible that they succumbed to it, and gave their knowledge away, to the embarrassment of both Sheikha and her neighbors. It came about like this. When she returned in the evenings, Sheikha used to let the car drop her by the gardens, at a distance from the houses, and she walked the last hundred yards—for her husband's evening movements were not as fully predictable as his workday ones. But one evening she misjudged her time and place and got off at only a short distance from where the children were playing. But if she failed to take heed of them, they more than noticed her. Yelling and screaming, they danced after her, chanting, "She has arrived, she has arrived," at the top of their lungs. The adults rushed to their gates to see what the matter was, and Sheikha was sufficiently perturbed to pause at her gate and exclaim with studied indignation, "What is all this *zeta* [nonsense, ado] when my *sister's husband* brings me home after I've been visiting at the hospital!" And she emphasized the driver's identity with special gusto. But her words were lacking in effect. As Latifa later remarked to me: "Would her *sister's husband* ever drop her at the gardens, and not at the gate?" Sheikha's other neighbors no doubt must have made the same reflection. After this incident Sheikha discontinued her activities for a full fortnight.

Despite her flagrant violation of the community's most cherished ideals, Sheikha remained an intimate member of the same little circle of neighboring women. Her immaculately moral friends in fact never sanctioned her to her face, but accepted her fully into their midst. I was most astonished, for all my reading on small-scale societies, both within and outside the Middle East, would have led me to expect a person who violated cherished moral norms to be either rejected, or at least strongly condemned, by the sinless ones. But this was conspicuously not the way of Sohar. Sheikha's friends and neighbors felt no need to avoid her, or to denigrate her, nor did they fear contamination of their own reputation through their association with her. When I, incredulous, inquired about the reasons for their lack of sanctions, and even indignation, when they had so clearly stated that what she did was shameful, sinful, and simple prostitution, they would answer: "Yes, it is very shameful behavior. And it is a terrible offense toward her husband. But it is he alone who has the right to complain about it or punish her. What reason should we have to be angry? She has done no wrong toward us—on the contrary, she is always kind and helpful and hospitable."

Taken aback by such admirable tolerance, I asked, still skeptical, "But what about your reputations? Surely you would wish to avoid Sheikha in order to safeguard your own good repute?" But my friends protested with self-confident poise: "Not at all! People know us and they know her. It is only she in this country [that is, neighborhood] who is that way at present. [There were previously two more.] All the neighbors mix with her and visit her. And she is always friendly and hospitable, does not gossip, is kind and helpful. Only in this one respect is she not good [*muzena*]". The dictum "Tell me whom you associate with and I shall tell you who you are," so often applied in Western society and ascribed to small-scale societies, is clearly not valid in Sohar.

I was in little doubt that Sheikha's escapades provided her friends with exciting divertissement and lent spice to their otherwise humdrum lives. It could hardly be otherwise. But even their barbed comments were restrained and of a good-natured kind. For instance, they might joke that they no longer needed to look at the sun to set their watches: Sheikha was even more reliable in her movements. The most daring case of public banter I can remember was when an old woman, who was the acknowledged clown of the lane (*harah*), once yelled to me, when I was seated with my friends: "If Sheikha asks you to visit her relatives with her, then don't go. That is not where she would take you!" And everyone laughed, amused and a bit embarrassed.

Indeed, this mixture of fascination and embarrassment seemed to me the most striking feature of my friends' reactions. Thus an incident like the confrontation between Sheikha's husband and the paramour, though no doubt the event of the day, maybe of the year, was not told and retold by them. It was too embarrassing. Nor were they prepared to indulge in the vivid details of Sheikha's misadventure with the neighborhood children sufficiently to tell me precisely *what* it was the children had shouted after her. They could not remember, they claimed. And even my closest friends were quite reluctant to inform me of the various incidents as they took place, although these events could not fail to preoccupy them and relieve the monotony of their day. For instance, I had been present a full three weeks during my last field work and had daily swallowed Sheikha's story that she "visited her relatives" before Khadiga one day sprang the bomb. I was commenting again how fortunate it was that Sheikha's husband had become so good to her and now let her visit her family (cf. Ch. 14), when Khadiga remarked bluntly: "Yes, now she is on the go *all* the time, *never* at home!" And to my puzzled face: "*Bitdur* [she strays]. She has become a prostitute!"

This illustrates the difficulty in obtaining data of this character, of grasping what they mean, and of presenting them correctly. To give the facts, I present a skeletonized account of conversations and reactions, yet the most remarkable fact that I wish to communicate is how *little* reaction and gossip Sheikha's behavior elicited. The pervasive self-control demanded by proper demeanor requires that one's interest in other people's lives be kept within strict bounds. And even within our relaxed circle of close friends, there were only a few times in a long succession of eventless days together that our attention turned to Sheikha's activities.

It may be necessary here to restate my general understanding of how personal information circulates in Sohari society. I argue that Soharis do not pursue gossip as censure, but that they do pass it about, with very much constraint, within their closest groups of neighbors, as information or news. They thus become informed to a considerable extent of each other's "dark secrets," but they emphatically do not traffic in condemnation and scandal.

It is also difficult to assess just how much of my friends' attention to

Sheikha's behavior was in response to my own undeniable fascination with the case, and how much they would have made of it in my absence. I certainly felt rude and tactless at times when, in the service both of social science and my own curiosity, I brought up the matter and pursued it relentlessly, and encouraged them into doing the same. I should think, however, that in my absence my friends would have reacted to Sheikha's escapades with much more of that self-contained, unperturbed dignity that is the epitome of the Omani style. (There would, of course, also be less to explain and discuss, for they would know much without talking about it.)

As time passed, Sheikha's activities developed in a fashion that we all found increasingly obvious and shameless; for example, she would stand, without her *burqa,* in the neighborhood street, talking with men in a conspicuously flirtatious way. Her behavior seemed to me so studiously blatant, so vulgar, that I took to disliking her and developed a need to censure her. Our friends, when they noticed my ungraciousness toward Sheikha, said nothing about it, but I could feel them asking themselves, wondering: Had Sheikha done me any wrong? Was she not always hospitable, friendly, and helpful?

Their own "sanctions," if one may use that word, consisted merely of never going along with her by taxi anywhere; for example, to the hospital. The reason, they explained, was that the taxi would pass through neighborhoods where Sheikha was well known, for she roamed everywhere, whereas they were not, and so she might affect their reputations. But they would never dream of telling this to Sheikha to her face. Her friends had to invent excuses, with great discretion, to avoid her company on such occasions.

THE NEAR AND THE DISTANT PUBLIC

It seemed strange at first that these women who move so confidently within the neighborhood, which in a real sense *is* their world, should be concerned at all with what anonymous others in distant places might think of them. Closer inquiry revealed that, indeed, they were not so concerned, or that they were not, for their *own* sake. It was in deference to their husbands that they cared, and for *their* reputations. Their menfolk, with good reason, were worried about "public opinion," and so had instructed their wives not to ride in a car with Sheikha alone. A *husband's* reputation might suffer gravely if his wife was observed in the sole company of a prostitute, for a man's honor is undeniably also dependent upon the behavior of his women, or rather, what is known about their behavior in the large, public world composed of a few friends, numerous acquaintances, and a host of strangers among whom men move.

But a *woman's* honor is not thus dependent. A woman is not a public

figure, and the persons to whom she looks to evaluate her worth and provide "public" recognition are not "out there" in an anonymous sea of
"public opinion." They are well-known, identifiable individuals: a few
neighbors, kinswomen, and "country women" (that is, women of her
ward). The woman is not taught to orient herself outwardly. To do so
would be counter to all she has been raised to live by. On the contrary, she
has been instilled that she be modest, polite, and hospitable—in a way
which is oriented *away* from the public. Whereas a woman in Sohar can
therefore confidently associate with all kinds of women, irrespective of
their moral qualities, secure in the conviction that "people know us and
they know her," a man is painfully aware that this is not the case with
him. He is being observed and judged by numerous people who do *not*
know him, and who form their impressions of him on the basis of only
fleeting and fragmentary glimpses. Hence the need for him to watch
carefully his own public image and that of his wife. Should she be found
wanting by the standards of his male, public world, it is *his* and not her
honor that suffers. Sohari men do not hold a woman responsible for her
own actions, but see, in her misdemeanors, the failure of the *man* under
whose authority she is.

Sohari women, on the other hand, regard other women as responsible
actors (see Ch. 4). But the moral values that are central within their world,
and by which woman measures woman, are different from those by which
man measures woman. How, then, was Sheikha's honor affected by her
sexual immorality?

SOHARI CONCEPTS AND
ANTHROPOLOGICAL MISCONCEPTIONS

Struck with the flagrancy of Sheikha's immorality, I burst out to our
mutual friends, "But does she not *care* about her honor?" Sheikha's
friends hesitated, looked puzzled, and then answered "No, she does not
care [*mayihimmha*]." I was surprised at the note of hesitancy in their
voice and expression, when they had so clearly stated that such behavior
was shameful in the extreme. Only later did I reflect that my question had
been too ambiguous to make sense to them. I had presented them with a
question that *had* no answer and that they themselves had never asked.
Their "folk explanation" of her behavior was ubiquitously *rohha* or
ᶜumraha [that's just her way, her nature]. These words are uttered much
as we might say, with a shrug of the shoulders, "God knows, man's ways
are inscrutable."

The question I had asked rated no answer. Of course, Sheikha cared!
And, just as obviously, she could not care. It all depends what you mean
by honor. It is not at all the straightforward concept that it might seem.

Had they not repeatedly told me how much Sheikha cared? "She is always kind and hospitable and helpful." Did not such behavior reflect a sincere concern about her value in her own eyes, but also in the eyes of her society?

By my way of questioning, I had inadvertently assumed that there was some primacy about sexual morality in determining a woman's honor. I had in fact assumed that the values of Sheikha's society must be a reflection of the values of society at large—of which the *men* are the protagonists. And, uncritically, I had projected a set of premises and assumptions learned from anthropological literature into our conversation. I was deep in the process of forcing Sheikha's presumed deliberations into a concept, "honor," which there is little evidence is a central preoccupation of Soharis. Just because they occasionally use the word "shame," for example, in denouncing female adultery, it does not follow that their behavior is governed by a concept of an *"honor" that depends upon avoidance of all shameful acts.* Blinded by the complex preconceptions of those all too evocative words honor and shame, I was deep in a process of distorting the genuine and authentic character of the life I saw unfolding in front of me by fitting it to alien concepts. Put otherwise, I was trying to make sense of Soharis in terms other than their own.

My friends' puzzled response deterred me. I began to pay closer attention to their concepts, reactions, and meanings.

SOHARI CONCEPTS OF SHAME AND HONOR, GOOD AND BAD

The concept "shame" is rarely heard in women's spontaneous daily conversation in Sohar and only a little more so in the men's. This is despite the fact that there are a number of acts that Soharis classify as ͨaib (shame). For instance, it is shameful for a woman to be unveiled before a male Sohari stranger, to reveal her hair to any male save her husband, to kiss her husband on her own initiative, to walk in her husband's company before darkness, to let her husband do housework, to eat before her husband does, to refrain from offering a guest hospitality, to talk rudely to a guest, to gossip, to brag, to dress nicely on the occasion of her daughter's wedding. This obviously is not a complete list, but it indicates the scope and variety of acts labeled shameful.

We should note that the concept of shame applies to acts, not people. Thus Sheikha's friends labeled her adultery ͨaib, but, of Sheikha as a person they said that only in this one respect was she *not good—muzena.* The emotion that in a woman blocks for acts that are shameful—as well as for many that are not, is, as we have seen in Chapter 4, the feeling of shyness, modesty, or bashfulness (see also below). In a man, it is his personal standards of integrity, as well as concern for his public reputation.

Soharis will say that every instance of gossip, offense toward guests, and so forth is shameful, regardless of the circumstances. Yet, when breaches occur, Soharis tend to be mercifully humane, quick to soften the impact of shame by pointing to the person's good behavior, or to some mitigating circumstances. Thus, when a widow appeared suddenly at the market one day, selling vegetables to provide for her children, she was praised by both men and women for her courage and ingenuity, and no mention whatsoever was made of the "shame" of a woman going to the market.

In the case of Sheikha, her friends showed polite disattention to her shameful behavior, whereas they were eager to emphasize how *zen* (good, nice, beautiful) she really was; for example, she was praised as always helpful, hospitable, and well-mannered. This could have been their way of saying how honorable Sheikha in fact is. Certainly, every mention of *ᶜaib* is typically followed by its negation, *zen*—as if to undo any damage done. If *ᶜaib* is one of a pair, then, in Sohar at least, *zen* would seem to be its partner.

The Sohari concept of honor—*sharaf*—I only heard used once or twice in men's spontaneous conversation, and never in women's. The male phrase was "his honor will be damaged." A couple of times women would use the word after I myself had inadvertently introduced it, as in saying about Sheikha's husband that "He does not care about his honor." They more often said, "He is lacking in character [*Malush axlaq*]." The men, too, spoke of character rather than honor, but they were inclined to be more specific, such as saying, "He is impolite," or "He is irresponsible." On the positive side, to sum up what a man should be, they simply said "He must be a *man*."

Thus there are a number of different words which Soharis use to praise or deprecate the behavior of others. In order of frequency, the most common ones are *zen* (good, nice, beautiful), *muzen* (not good), and *ᶜaib* (shame). Soharis resemble most Middle Eastern peoples who make use of the words "honor" and "shame" in that, of the two, references to the latter are far more common. Where they stand out is in *how very reluctant they are to mention the word at all.* If it is also true, as I think, that the antithesis of "shame," as they see it, is "good, nice, beautiful," rather than "honor" (in the literal sense of the term), then Soharis are remarkable in how ready they are to grant each other value. The word *zen* I would surely hear a dozen times a day, *ᶜaib*, only once a week or fortnight. This reflects, to my understanding, the basic Sohari attitude toward others, which is to honor, not dishonor, them. The person's own honor in fact *requires* that he or she honor others.

HONOR PREACHED AND HONOR PRACTICED

We cannot conclude from the Sohari nonuse of the word "honor" (*sharaf*) and their reluctance to speak of "shame" (*ᶜaib*) that the values those words express are not much at work in their daily life. Decisive is not whether Soharis make frequent use of a pair of concepts which readily lend themselves to an English translation as "honor" and "shame," but whether, in shaping their acts and giving form to their lives, they are driven by a striving to attain value in their own and others' eyes by embodying society's supreme ideals.

Caro Baroja observed, in his perceptive contribution to Peristiany's *Honor and Shame* that:

> there has been no investigation into how far they [honor and shame] may have been rhetorical commonplaces, topics of discussion in a given community where, in fact, quite other interests predominate, so that these concepts may in the end have been no more than literary affectations. It has been frequently remarked from early times that those people who make most use of the words "honor" and "shame" and other associated with them in ordinary conversation, are not those whose lives are most strictly governed by the principles which those words express. (1965, p. 81)

Soharis, as this chapter should document, make remarkably little use of these concepts, precisely because they are striving to live up to their society's supreme ideals. And we should lose little, and gain much, if we, heeding Baroja's warning, focused precisely on what the interests are that predominate in a given society, and what the principles are that find expression in its thought—and let it be of secondary importance whether people call them "honor" and "shame."

WHAT IS SHE PURSUING FOR HERSELF?

The aforementioned example of the widow who was praised for behavior that, isolated from its real life context, would be regarded as shameful, highlights the complex relationship that may exist between honor and shame. To say, as so many anthropologists seem to do, that a person who commits a dishonorable act is thereby irremediably dishonored is surely to draw a premature conclusion. Indeed, a "shameful" act may even have as its consequence to *enhance* the person's honor, as was the case with the widow. It was not that selling vegetables at the market was a last resort for her. She had at least three other options: to appear before the Wali and demand her legal rights to "social security," instituted for widows by the government; to demand her right that her closest male kinsman, related through the paternal line, provide for her; or, if she wanted to be self-sufficient, to sell her wares in the wards away from the market, as an itinerant vendor. All of these courses would be entirely honorable. Instead, she chose to run the risk of shame. And she ended up *gaining* in social esteem and, no doubt, in self-regard as well.

Could it perhaps be that Sheikha too, in pursuing her "prostitute" career, was indeed pursuing her own self-realization? Could it perhaps be that it is precisely because she *cares* about her honor that she resorted to a course labeled "shameful"? We shall gain no insight if we are content to discuss honor and shame as a partial normative system, separate from other norms of good and bad behavior. It is only by relating these concepts to other norms, and to real life, that we can hope to penetrate Sohari codes. The proper question would seem to be: What is Sheikha pursuing for herself?

Perhaps, by the priorities of women, Sheikha's behavior can make sense, even if drastically at odds with priorities of the male world *and* with the requirements of honor in an ideal sense.

Surely the "value of a person in his own eyes, but also in the eyes of his society" is neither entirely of a piece nor liable to complete destruction by a single act: it may be seriously reduced, but some value remains, and other consequences of the act may also accrue. Concepts of honor and shame cannot reproduce, in real life, their own logical and absolute schematism. Combinations of cherished ideals, when put into practice, require a far more complex accounting. A person commits many positive and some highly honorable acts, and many negative and some compromising ones—all of which have their place in the accounting.

There is no society in which sexual mores reign supreme in this respect, though societies differ as to how much weight they ascribe to sexual morality per se, and no doubt there have been times and places (and, to some extent, there still are some, for example, Saudi Arabia) where it was deemed of such pivotal importance that a person (or woman?) who misbehaved sexually was deprived of all honor and became an outcast. But Sohar is very far from this. To understand how Sheikha's notorious conduct in fact affects her prospects of honor among neighbors and "country women"—who are the ones who may grant honor to her—we must ask, for instance, how does a sexual misdemeanor somewhere else with someone else count in relation to the "misdemeanor" such as failing in reciprocal hospitality with neighboring women? A prostitute is remunerated for her services—in Sohar, in money, perfume, and so forth—assets that she may partially expend on hospitality, thus allowing her to entertain more lavishly. Sohari men, as we have seen, postulate a connection between the two when they explain unfaithfulness as if it were entirely motivated by material greed (Ch. 4). Although women protest men's understanding of its motivation, they recognize that a most tangible result of prostitution is material affluence. Thus, when I asked Sheikha's neighbors whether she made much money from her activities, they replied; "Well of course! Look at all the perfume she has. You do not think, do you, that it is from her husband?" Indeed, in 1976 Sheikha excelled among all the neighbors in hospitality, offering it so excessively that it seemed as if she were at pains to make up for the ten lean years she endured previously (see Ch. 14). However, her friends categorically denied my suggestion that hunger for material gain was what may have launched Sheikha into prostitution. To their understanding, it was impossible. There are honorable ways for a woman to earn money. If she chooses prostitution, it must be because her "nature" wills it. She desires satisfactions of a nonmaterial kind more fervently than a material one. Significantly, however, Sheikha's friends, unlike me, did not ask how and why and wherefore had Sheikha become a prostitute; such questions did not concern them. Her lavish hospitality, however, affected them, for there should be reciprocity in women's give-and-take (unless the status between host and guest is very unequal). The issue then arises whether lavish hospitality alleviates, or even outweighs, the disrepute of infidelity? It seems reasonable to assume that because hospitality may be offered in all degrees of frequency and lavishness, whereas marital fidelity is an either/or matter, the former would provide the more sensitive and interesting field of competition, and relative esteem, among women. Indeed, in Sohar, a woman's infidelity seems not to bear on her relation to other women, only on her relation to her husband and kin.

TWO SENSES OF HONOR

This line of reasoning merges honor with a general concept of esteem, and one may argue that its distinctive character is thereby disguised. Is not honor more akin to integrity, probity, rectitude—a question of good character, moral strength, high principles? In other words, is not honor better understood as a particular *kind* of esteem, and thus only one ingredient of that total repute of a person which we variously label esteem, social status, rank, or prestige?

I think that the concept of honor, as used by members of a society, may be employed simultaneously in both senses, and that Sheikha's friends attested to this dual meaning when they answered both yes and no to the question of whether Sheikha cared about her honor.

Honor, in the most restricted sense, is an ideal-like integrity, which can be lived up to, or spoiled by, a single failure. It is a particular kind of quality as measured by a supreme standard, such as rectitude or probity. It is at stake in all interaction and can be spoiled by one bad act. Women's sexual virtue is one example from Sohar.

In another sense, honor may be a measure of one's actual value as a person, as a sum of good and bad traits, judged by a conventional set of standards; that is, the esteem in which a person is held. It is the value of the person—everything about that person—which is evaluated. For example, a person is perceived as kindhearted, hard-working, but poor and unreliable in situations that require strong integrity. The person still has value, though her integrity has been spoiled by shameful acts. (Both senses of honor entail evaluations of the whole social person, not just the person's behavior toward any particular other person.)

It seems to me that much confusion in anthropological discussions of honor and shame stems from the frequent failure of anthropologists to disentangle the distinct meanings of the two. Sometimes they talk as if it were integrity they had in mind, other times as if it were esteem that they meant. Many even seem to have inferred that the two meanings are synonymous—that honor/esteem depends on moral integrity alone. Some may argue that it is not necessary for anthropologists to distinguish between the two meanings, because the people we study themselves often confound the two. But they are in the fortunate position where they need not make their assumptions clear to know what they are talking about and be understood. We are less fortunate. Whereas our informants use the concepts in the context of their everyday encounters, to interpret, evaluate, and communicate parts of their experience to others who share this reality, we elevate the concepts to the level of general models and discuss their abstract meaning in what is often a conspicuous lack of concrete context. Hence, when we speak of honor, it is essential to explain exactly what we have in mind, whether repute and esteem, or integrity and rectitude.

We must distinguish its logical form in the context of abstract moral discourse, when it partakes of a strict schematism of integrity and rectitude, and its form in the context of behavior and real life, when it measures the effect of acts on a person's esteem.

METHODOLOGICAL PROBLEMS

Serious difficulties remain. How does one ascertain the *actual* effects of so-called dishonorable acts upon "the value of a person in his own eyes, but also in the eyes of his society"? Unfortunately, "the value of a person in his own eyes" is a most elusive thing to grasp. Only slightly less so is his value "in the eyes of society." Students of honor and shame have usually been content to investigate the latter, because it is more amenable to observation. This method can be justified in terms of George H. Mead's theory of the self, which makes us aware that a person's image of himself is the reflection he sees in his fellow being's reactions to him. Alternatively, one may argue the other way round as Pitt-Rivers does, that the two commonly coincide, "considering how people extort from others the validation of the image which they cherish of themselves" (1965, pp. 21–23). However, such a procedure still leaves crucial questions unsolved. For one thing, if the two do not coincide, which is the more fundamental to a person's honor, his or her private estimation of his or her own worth, or society's view of him or her? To dwell on further complications, what is the essence of society's estimate: does it inhere in what people explicitly say, or actually do, or merely in what they think, in their hearts and minds, irrespective of whether they let it be known? But in the latter case, how could the man or woman in question, at pains to discern his or her own worth, ever discover it? Or is it at all possible to evaluate and judge the conduct of others without such judgments being effectively expressed and the behavior systematically sanctioned?

My ad hoc solution to the problem is likewise to focus on the person's value in the eyes of the society, but to do so in a way that depicts how people actually shape their acts in terms of standards of honor and shame, and why they need to take such standards into consideration. I am not merely content to elicit and note people's formal judgments devoid of context—what they *say* is honorable and what they *say* is shame. Ideals reveal their true meaning—their hold on people—primarily in how those who cherish them seek to translate them into practice. Those supreme ideals that constitute honor are no exceptions.

Sohari women would agree to a statement that female adultery and fornication are the most shameful of all acts. This is the official ideological stance throughout the Muslim world. But they would also abhor the disgrace inherent in offending a guest. To my understanding, a comparison between the degree of shamefulness of adultery and that of dishonoring a guest would be quite meaningless to them. Both acts are shameful and therefore should be avoided. To discover their relative effects in terms of the person's esteem, one must look to the *consequences* of acts. The only way to find out how and whether adultery dishonors a woman is to ascertain its real implications for the perpetrator in the value that she is or is not accorded. And these consequences must be discernible in how people relate to the adulterous one. In Sheikha's case, only to the extent that her friends and neighbors treat her, in acts, words, and gestures, with condescension on account of her adultery, does it to my mind make sense to say that a loss of honor is entailed.

HONOR AND SANCTIONS

I searched my friends' acts, words, and gestures for signs if they regarded Sheikha with disrespect, contempt, annoyance, impatience, or displeasure. There were few signs indeed, if any, that I as an outsider could detect, and I am unsure of how to interpret such few as I think I saw. When, for instance, Sheikha's friends characterize the act of female adultery as very dishonorable and sinful in the extreme in her presence, do they feel that they are reproaching her, and does she feel dishonored?

And when a man, in Sheikha's presence, endeavors to convince me of the justification of beating as a disciplinary measure, by exclaiming, "What else can a man do when he has repeatedly told his wife to stay at home, and she continues to stray!"—and his wife joins, "Yes, *many* wives do, though it is *very* shameful!"—then is Sheikha dishonored? I feel quite sure that the example was chosen with intent, but again, is an oblique verbal reproach equivalent to dishonor?

"Reprimands," if such they be, even as indirect as these, were very few and far between, probably not exceeding four or five in the course of seventy-five days (which was the extent of my field work after Sheikha had embarked upon her "dishonorable" career). During all the rest of that time—hours-long, daily encounters with her friends—Sheikha was in no way that I could discern either criticized, avoided, or otherwise censured to her face. And the conclusion lies close at hand: adultery, though conceptually the ultimate disgrace, is in reality of minimal consequence for the people it does not concern. Sheikha is hardly dishonored before her female friends. Her dishonor does not enter their relationship with her.

But is it not far-fetched to insist that honor and shame inhere fundamentally in how a woman's significant others treat her *to her face*? Is not a loss of honor entailed when Sheikha is harshly criticized behind her back, as in the following episode?

One day, Sheikha and her daughter were to accompany, as they usually did, Latifa and her sisters, mother, and grandmother on a visit to Latifa's relatives. What was unusual on this occasion was that Latifa's elder brother, Ali, with whom Sheikha had an infatuation, was home on leave and had arranged to drive the women. Norms of courtesy and respect required that the two elder kinswomen sit in front with him. But Sheikha had other ideas, and swiftly climbed up into the front seat with her daughter. Grandmother was burning with offense and later swore to her kin that she would never again in her life ride in a car with "that whore." But the culprit went unchallenged. Neither Grandmother nor anyone else reproached her, and, a fortnight later, they all rode together again. For to be rude or discourteous to Sheikha would be dishonorable to themselves.

Quite apart from the case of Sheikha, it is conspicuous that Soharis are not preoccupied with passing judgment on one another's conduct or person. Indeed, they avoid passing judgment and refrain from nearly all condemnation. Where, then, are the connections between morality, mutual sanctions, and behavior in Sohar?

Until the very end of my field work (26 January 1976), the problem continued to perplex me. Could I really believe my own eyes? Or were there perhaps sanctions so subtly expressed that I failed to discern them? I believe now that there were not. One day toward the end of my field work, my friends Latifa and Khadiga, who had daily witnessed my evident discomfiture, took it upon themselves to *explain* things to me, so as to put my mind at rest. What they said only confirmed my impression during the previous few months: They did not, indeed would not, condemn Sheikha. "You see, our customs are different from yours [ᶜ*aditna qher* ᶜ*adit-*

kum]," they said, in clear anticipation that the light would dawn in my mind. And when that magic phrase obviously failed to comfort me, they went on to explain how, judging from my behavior, they had perceived our customs to be strikingly different:

"It is *impossible* for us to be tactless and impolite to a person and we have no cause to. We *must* speak nicely to, and welcome everyone who comes to our house. To do otherwise is ʿ*aib* [very shameful]." And when I was incredulous and asked, "But what about people you do not like? Surely, you do not treat everyone *exactly* the same?" they shook their heads in forceful protest: "Yes, we do love everyone. There is *no one* we do not like," and, for extra emphasis, "*Binhibb kull innas yiguna yigahwi* ʿ*andina* [we want *all* the people to visit us and savor our hospitality; literally, drink coffee with us]."

MALE VIEWS AS UNDERSTOOD BY WOMEN

Suspecting this view to be biased and representative of only the female half of Sohar's adult community, I inquired of my female friends what their husbands were likely to have said and done, had they known that their wives frequented with a prostitute. Surely *they* would have taken action to break the relationship. My friends protested vehemently:

"But of course they already know. *Everybody* knows about her. But they treat her respectfully like we do."

"Although she is a prostitute?" I asked.

"Yes, that is no offense against *them*!" they replied.

Latifa's mother remarked that when her son Ali was home on leave, he even urged them to invite Sheikha to visit, for she was very helpful: she served food to him, washed his clothes and acted as if she were like both a wife and a mother. "She is very much in love with Ali," she added with a tinge of pride, and then, swiftly, to forestall my drawing any wrong conclusions, "but they *never* do that thing in the house. When they want to do that, they go *far* away." And Latifa commented, to be sure I would not think ill of her brother: "As you know, it is *not* shameful for a man. But it is *very* shameful for her."

Further observations revealed that my friends spoke the truth: their husbands did know, yet treated Sheikha with friendliness and respect. So I reasoned that Sheikha's husband must in fact also know. Surely some loyal friend or busybody had informed him. But my friends categorically rejected the suggestion:

"Impossible! No one would say a word to her husband! That would be shameful in the extreme—a scandal!"

And when I, still skeptical, countered, "But surely, no matter how shameful it is, there are some people here who gossip?" they looked at me uncertainly for a long while, then said,

"You mean people who 'carry the word' [*bitshil ikkalam*]? Yes, there are a few, but they are very, very few. And not even one of them would tell such a thing to her husband."

Nonetheless, they surmised that Sheikha's husband might suspect something, but that he chose to turn a blind eye. "What else can he do? He has just built a house, which, as you have seen, is not yet finished; he has not been able to afford paint for the walls and plaster for the ceiling. Divorce costs a lot of money, he must pay *ghayeb* [divorce settlement] for Sheikha and *mahr* [bride price] for a new bride. His children will have a stepmother, and that relationship is fraught with troubles. So what can he do?" Then they added, "Or maybe he really does *not* know. After all, he has never caught her in the act."

"But if he suspects things," I asked, "why doesn't he lock her up in the house as a safeguard?"

"Because that would increase the publicity of it all. And besides, she would find a way out in any case."

"But what about his honor?"

"He doesn't care about his honor [*Sharafu mayihimmu*]. He is lacking in character [*axlaq*], so he doesn't care."

"But how is it possible for a man not to care about his own honor?"

"Many men don't; Sohari men are lacking in character. They act as if they don't know, either because they love their wife and want to keep her, or because they don't have the money to divorce her."

"Can't a man who knows his wife to be unfaithful complain to the Wali and be authorized to divorce her without payment?"

"Yes, in the past he could, but not nowadays. Now a man is not even entitled to beat his wife for her misdemeanor. The Wali will instruct him: 'If you want to keep her, then treat her well. If you cannot do that, then pay her what is her right [that is, *the ghayeb*] and let her go.'"

Clearly, in the minds of these women, a man's honor in the literal sense of the word—his *sharaf*—is often of less consequence to him than are love and money. Although women know it ought to be otherwise, they do not necessarily think poorly of the man who forfeits "honor" in this strict sense. Thus Latifa could relate, without embarrassment, how her father had loved her mother's co-wife so much that he kept her for months after he had learned that she was unfaithful. It was only when she proved utterly incorrigible that he paid her "lots of money" to be divorced. An affluent man, he had the privilege of choice.

THE MALE VIEW

What are male views of honor as they apply them both to males and females? Adultery is inevitably a touchy issue, and we wished to proceed in our inquiry with all possible tact, but we also wanted to be both precise and specific, especially because men are more likely, on such a topic, merely to repeat categorical and absolute normative positions rather than real-life praxis. As so often, it was my husband's closest informant, Ali, who provided us with the most nuanced views. But in all respects, Ali's opinions and attitudes did not differ from those more incompletely expressed by other, less close acquaintances.

Ali insisted that he would never allow his wife, Fatima, to associate with immoral women, who by their abundance constitute a real threat. But when asked what steps he would take to put his principle into practice, he acknowledged: "It is *very* difficult. Fatima cannot refuse to receive a guest. She *must* welcome her and give her coffee. It is impossible to be impolite, and you don't speak offensively to a guest. But there are ways of showing it [your disapproval]: you put out the mat for her, but then busy yourself with other things—clothes, cooking—and let her sit there alone for awhile. Then you serve her coffee. She will notice, leave, and not come back. And you need not visit *her*."

"What makes a woman behave so immorally?"

"If her husband provides for her, takes care of her, then it must be her parents' fault for not looking to what she did, letting her run around uncontrolled, not educating her."

"And if her husband does not provide for her?"

"Then he is responsible. That's why it happens, because he is stupid. He must use his brain and prevent her from doing such things."

"But is a woman not responsible for her own conduct? Is it not wrong to blame her parents or her husband?"

"Perhaps, but if she does not learn the right way, how can she follow it? First her parents, and then her husband, must show her and look after her."

"But what can a man do if he is away all day at work?"

"Then he must set another person to watch her, make a reliable arrangement. It is very dishonorable for him when his wife does such a thing."

"What about *her* honor; is it not at stake?"

"No, it comes from lack of education: how can she know right from wrong when her parents and her husband do not show her and look after her? Maybe she is walking along the road, a taxi driver stops, says 'Where are you going?' offers to take her—but drives into the desert and forces her to have intercourse. How can a woman fight a man? He is stronger. That is the first step. Then her husband brings his friends to the house, lets them talk to her, sit together, have coffee together. One day a friend comes when the husband is out, the wife alone—so they do that thing. That is the second step. Then she gets to know bad women, learns to speak to men and make herself available. That is the third step. There are plenty such women in Sohar, maybe 25 percent of the wives."

"But what makes a man put up with such a wife; why does he not divorce her?"

"Because he does not understand what is happening. If he comes home and finds them there copulating, he will surely divorce her."

"But will not others tell him?"

"No, they will not say a word. It is none of their business to interfere between husband and wife. They will pretend everything is okay, pretend they don't know, even when everybody knows. The man must rely solely upon himself to control his wife; he must take care and make responsible arrangements. He must be a man."

THE TWO SOCIETIES

We see in the male and female reactions to adultery and prostitution that not only are the standards by which woman measures woman different from those by which man measures man, they are also clearly different from the standards by which man measures woman. Thus, in a sense, there are two kinds of "society" in Sohar. There is the multitude of small women's worlds in which men also *do* figure, but only marginally and in partial capacities (as husbands, brothers, sons); and there is the large world of the men, which also embraces women, but does so only in their partial, male-relevant capacities (as wives, sisters, daughters). Both worlds contain standards for both men and women, but one as embraced by men, the other by women.

My understanding is that there are real differences in priorities between men and women, reflecting their different worlds. In the male world, females are interesting *mainly* in terms of their sexual trustworthiness, because this is where they so strongly affect the lives of men. In the female world, hospitality and a number of other qualities are highly relevant and consequently have priority. But a man, why should he *care* about the degree of hospitality of a woman, other than that of his own? I am not simply repeating the point that Soharis are not supposed to censure behavior that is not directed against themselves. In forming an opinion of the honor of another person, one is obviously concerned to see that person as a whole and not merely ask: Is he or she honorable toward *me?* Thus one will use information about that person's dealings with others to form one's judgment. But for a man, in a segregated world, the degree of an unrelated woman's hospitality seems so fundamentally irrelevant to him that it can simply never become a matter of any interest to him. Likewise, to the mutual concerns of women, female sexuality remains marginal; thus, in the standards for female behavior that are applied in women's world, surely adultery is much less heinous (though judged bad) than in the men's world. It remains a key standard for the "rectitude," "integrity" type of honor but becomes a low-priority component in the type of honor concerned with the value of the person in his own and others' eyes.

In societies such as Oman, the "value of a person in her own eyes, but also in the eyes of her society" can be specifically seen as two-fold. The attention of a woman's male society, her husband and kinsmen, is focused strongly enough on sexual integrity for *women*, so that the difference between honor as integrity and honor as esteem is small. Female society measures value by so many acts of female behavior that honor as integrity and honor as esteem come out very different in many cases, as in that of Sheikha.

THE OBSCURING EFFECT OF TACT

Ali confirmed what my friends had maintained; people will not say a word, either to the adulterous wife or her deceived husband. This forces us to confront a further paradox inherent in all the material presented so far: what becomes of the value of a person in the eyes of society if all the members of that society enter into a collusion of good manners and act toward each other *as if* they had the greatest respect for each other? And, likewise, how can a person form an opinion of his own value, when confronted with so bland and polite a reflection of himself?

Although there is indeed such a collusion of good manners in Sohar, it is not a complete or entirely effective one. Facts do become known, and acts are judged and commented upon. A high level of discretion also undoubtedly leads to the development of a high degree of sensitivity to indirect communication and noticing innuendo. It would seem that such a context for the expression of public opinion—if indeed the concept is applicable to a voice so exquisitely constrained and subdued—does not entail an absence of honor, but does greatly confine the impact and consequences of dishonorable acts. The striking way in which past mistakes can be lived down, and people are accepted for what they (genuinely) now are, and not only what they once were, seems logically connected with this.

On the other hand, this does not make life all that much easier for the person. The requirements that must be met to "be a man" in Omani culture, alluded to by Ali in the aforementioned quote, are demanding and manifold. A man is called upon to steer a deft and elegant course with very few signals from that public who are his judges; he must rely heavily, if not wholly, as Ali claims, on himself to set the standards and monitor his own behavior in terms of them. What is more, he can never even be sure that his honor is what *he* thinks it is, as he observes his bland reflection in his polite spectators. At best only cryptic fragments reach him, as when a trusted old neighboring woman once made Ali himself aware of what his position might be turning into by asking him one evening as she passed him in the street; "Ali, are you a man?" And to Ali's "Yes, I am a man," she replied only, "Think about my words" (Ch. 13). Perhaps, indeed, it is those who love you who challenge your honor to your face in Sohar, and not those who are against you.

Certainly in a society where respect for the other person is as sacrosanct as in Sohar, and the threshold of offense so low, it requires a sincere concern for the other person's truly best interest, to the possible detriment of one's own, to commit the transgression of the values of tact and politeness which a challenge of honor entails. Chances are that the other person turns on you in offense. For example, Sheikha's friends maintained that in the improbable situation that a friend of her husband should take it upon himself to inform him of the disconcerting facts, her husband would be truly offended, and retort in anger, *"Zogti, mafihash she*^c*!* [My wife, there is nothing the matter with her!]." It would be an insult, an intrusion, and the end of that friendship. Anticipating the consequences to be similarly disastrous should any one of Sheikha's friends confront her with her shameful behavior, they had all chosen to be silent.

I am reminded of one incident when my husband and I became angry with Ali and scolded him harshly in public—in the presence of a host of women and children. Much to our surprise, Ali did not turn on us, but expressed his gratitude because we had spoken our minds. "People here don't," Ali said. "They hide their anger and go away, with black hearts."

It may be that for a challenge to honor to serve as an expression of love, it must be presented before the other has already committed himself dishonorably—as was the case with Ali when the old woman addressed him. All she did was alert him to the dangers involved should he *not* choose a certain alternative. Perhaps, given such absolute requirements of tact and noninvolvement, any good will expressed belatedly must of necessity translate as ill-will and offense.

WHY BE HONORABLE?

If people are barred to this extent from censuring each other, how then is honor itself secured? How are the ideals that inform honor—for example, tact, hospitality, and sexual chastity—maintained if breaches go unpunished? If a person may serve her own ends while stepping on other people's toes, without reproach—as Sheikha most conspicuously did in the case with the car—what prevents the vast majority of Soharis from being equally self-serving? What is it that ensures the impeccable morality of the great majority of Sohari women when a woman can violate the most cherished ideals with little or no loss of honor?

The answer must be that one of the primary services of these ideals is, indeed, to the woman's own self. They order her own internal controls, which have been instilled in her through all her upbringing. She has been taught to do the right things, not because "otherwise people would say," but because it is *zen*—beautiful, good—to do them. She can, as a consequence, think well of herself. It has been a prevalent view that sex-segregated societies rely fundamentally upon external controls. For example, Hanna Papanek, in a comprehensive and widely cited article, differentiates external and internal controls by the labels of "shame vs. guilt mechanisms," and suggests that "in terms of this differentiation, the purdah system clearly relies more on the use of shame rather than guilt mechanisms of social control" (1973, p. 316). Sohar offers convincing evidence that the above generalization is, to say the least, one with notable and thought-provoking exceptions.

One implication is that of the two faces of honor, "the person's value in his own eyes, but also in the eyes of his society," the former would seem the more fundamental in Sohar. By that I mean that a person's self-regard counts more than the regard in which others hold him or her, in determining what he or she will actually *do* in Sohar. The incredible disregard for, or independence of, public opinion which persons on occasion display, as Sheikha ostentatiously does, would seem to be a corollary of this.

Let another example, told to us as a morality tale, illustrate; it concerns the highly regarded Imam of Sohar's main mosque.

> For a number of years after he was entrusted with the administration of the *waqf* (that is, the mosque property and income), he used part of this property for his own shop and let the mosque deteriorate, never spending money on its repairs. Many people thought he must be using the income for his own purposes only. So it continued, year after year. Then suddenly, he rebuilt the whole mosque, all new. For all those years he had been saving up and reinvesting the *waqf* income. He never told anybody, nor did they ever criticize him to his face. But now, those who distrusted him must say "What a good man!" (Barth, forthcoming)

Unfortunately, in my field work, I was not able to establish concretely how self-regard may differ from the view that others entertain; for example, by eliciting Sheikha's perceptions of her own actions in any detail. It would be of immense interest if a scholar in the future were able to provide also such material.

THE "NEAR" AND THE "DISTANT" PUBLIC AGAIN

There does seem to be an interesting contrast in Sohar between men's and women's relative indifference to "public opinion." My understanding is that the women are the more autonomous, the more self-reliant; the men seem a little less daring in disregarding what people might think or say. I believe that this reflects the greater vulnerability of men's "value in the eyes of society," which stems from the fact that they are measured by more exacting standards, and by many people who do not actually know them.

Reflective of men's predicament is their more "cynical" attitude both to people in general, and to friends and neighbors.

Men quite often complain that "people meddle in each other's affairs"—a grievance I never heard voiced by a woman. It was formulated most poignantly by Ali, who, contrasting the Bedu and the people of Sohar, said:

> The Bedu, if their wife or children quarrel with their neighbors, will not involve themselves. The men remain polite to each other. In Sohar, if a woman tells one bad word that a neighbor has said to her, then her husband becomes angry, abuses the other's husband. Always they meddle in the affairs of their neighbors—make trouble. The Bedu will see other men doing their work, himself do his own and not be dissatisfied. Those people [of Sohar] are only interested in making money. . . . They are not interested in living the right life. . . .

To protect his autonomy and repute, many a man prides himself on "going nowhere but between work and home." Companionship they seek, not among neighbors, whom they politely shun, but from a few friends who have been carefully chosen for their good manners and compatibility. In striking contrast to the women's relaxed association with all kinds of neighbors—be they prostitutes, slaves, or Bedu—the men stress the necessity of exercising care in friendships by quoting proverbs such as "If you sit by the smith, the sparks will burn you," or "A friend is to a friend like a patch to an old garment; if they are of the same kind they go together so that the garment looks new." How circumspect men are in their choice may be glimpsed from what Ali had to tell about his friendships. He reckoned that there were some twenty men who were his friends:

> They are all very close to my age, twenty-five, twenty-six, twenty-seven. . . ., and all of them educated. They are Arab, Baluch, Ajam, all kinds. Only four of them were known to me when I was a boy. We visit each other at home sometimes, but mostly see each other at the market, in the cafés. I, on my part, do not want them to come to my home, for Fatima might see them, and that would be wrong. . . . But among all of these friends I have only one friend whom I trust sufficiently to drink a little bit with, because he is a good person. With the rest, I maintain my reserve. When they offer me a drink, I say no, I do not use it—though in fact I occasionally do buy a little myself. Sometimes with some people I will present, instead of walking away, when they drink, but refuse to take any myself. Who knows, maybe they are *really* impolite people who might one day soil my reputation?

Sohari men are concerned about their own and others' integrity as whole persons. They have an image of themselves that they cultivate and seek to perfect, and an honor and public renown that they carefully build and protect. In a complex society with many arenas and subcultures, rich and poor, freeman and slave, Sunni and Shiah, and where performance is judged by demanding standards of grace and dignity, it is important to be able to anticipate what alternative relations and companionships may entail of honorable or compromising potentialities.

THE FORCE OF PUBLIC OPINION: OMAN VERSUS THE MEDITERRANEAN

It must be rare for people to be so independent of what "people might say," as Soharis are, and to have their own honor—their value in their own eyes—so firmly anchored in their own private conscience. But it must also be rare for anyone to have such good reason not to fear; Soharis *say* remarkably little indeed. On the rare occasions when the phrase *innas yiqulu* (people say) is heard, it may even be used in the sense of what people *think*, not literally say. Thus, when Latifa's husband, Nasr, is said to treat his wife so indulgently for fear that she might otherwise "say" he is not *zen* (good), it is to herself that he worries that she would say it. He surely knows that she can be trusted never to *say* a word to anyone; a wife stakes her honor on a loyalty so uncompromising that her husband must do her grave injustice indeed for her to speak ill of him to an outsider.

It may also be that I myself introduced the concept in its literal meaning into our conversations. Quite early in my field work, I had told them that the Egyptians among whom I had previously lived have *kalam innas* ("people's talk") as an ingrained fear and obsessive concern, and I had inadvertently used the phrase to inquire also about aspects of the Omani way. Thus my friends must have thought that this was a concept I could readily understand, and, in a situation where we were both striving for mutual intelligibility as between our Omani and Egyptian dialects of Arabic, they may well have resorted to it without any clear idea of what the concept meant to me. It is certainly true that the Omani *innas yiqulu* (people say) bears virtually no resemblance as a social fact to the Egyptian *kalam innas* (people's talk). And as the Egyptian phrase seems reminiscent of social phenomena that powerfully shape Mediterranean honor and shame, a brief comparison between Oman and Egypt may serve to highlight those features of Omani honor and shame which differ most clearly from the Mediterranean forms, on which most of the literature focuses, and which my Cairo materials exemplify (Wikan 1980).

Among the Cairo poor, *kalam innas* is portrayed as the most devastating thing in life. Worse even than poverty itself, it has the power, unscrupulously, to transform everything you do and do not do into evidence of *shame*. And you are fully at its mercy. Hundreds of times every day, the phrase recurs, spoken with such concern that the speaker's fear is positively palpable. Soharis, on the other hand, speak of what people will say—*innas yiqulu*—so rarely that the most I think I heard it was once a week or even a fortnight. And they say the words with an unconcern that makes it sound like the most benevolent of institutions.

Egyptians have an obsessive fear of being put to shame, and with good reason. Just as the person time and again every day condemns the conduct of other people as shameful—he or she can full well count on others to do the same to him or her. In Sohar, on the other hand, it is most uncommon for anyone to pass aloud a negative judgment on others. When the word *ᶜaib* (shame) is used, it is usually quickly followed by a positive remark, as if to undo whatever damage has been caused. Thus Sheikha's friends, after they had characterized her adultery as *ᶜaib*, would typically add, in the next breath; "But she is very kind and hospitable."

How different is the Egyptian abdication before "public opinion" from the Sohari woman's proud reference to *nistihi* (I—we—would feel shy) in explanation of why she refrained from compromising acts. Whereas the poor Egyptian must even avoid acts that are inherently honorable, as for a woman to greet her father, for fear that the people's talk would transform them into shame, the Sohari woman may confidently commit acts that are potentially compromising, as to associate with a prostitute, because she trusts her own conscience and therefore trusts that "people know us, and they know her."

The essence of this comparison is to draw out a distinctive feature of the Sohari way: Whereas, among the poor in Cairo, life seems to center on the shaming of others so as to gain value for oneself by contrast, in Oman the concern is to build merit within oneself by *honoring* others. In Egypt the focus is always on other people's faults and weaknesses; they are judged by standards so absolute that they are in fact unattainable. Hence "in the eyes of society"—with the exception of a few friends and kinspeople— every person's value is low. But in Oman the emphasis is on positive characteristics and real-life constraints (for example, my friends' "apologia" for the failure of Sheikha's husband to act up to his honor) on fellow beings' good points and assets. Hence, in the eyes of society, nearly everyone's value is high. The person's honor *requires* that he or she honors others. What seems the only feasible way to achieve value in one's own eyes in Egypt—to aggrandize oneself while denigrating others—would be below every person's dignity in Oman. Thus in Sohar, it would seem that all persons are endowed with value—and thus have honor—through the politeness and respect exercised toward them by *others*.

In Oman, in contrast to the Mediterranean, there is no apparent conflict between honor and legality. To confess publicly that you have been wronged does not place your honor in jeopardy; or Omanis would not so readily appeal to the Wali when they feel that they have been wronged. What a court procedure in Oman can do is precisely "to restore your honor," and not merely to "advertise its plight" (Pitt-Rivers 1965, p. 30).

Even a complaint launched in public, outside the courts, can serve the same purpose. This is the reason why, according to Soharis, all those unfortunate grooms who discover their bride not to be a virgin *must* raise a public outcry: to defend their honor. To request compensation is an honorable act; it proves that you stand up for your rights. If the request is not granted, that merely reflects on your opponent, at least as you see it. Deceived Sohari grooms can therefore confidently press for compensation from the bride's father and yet accept a refusal with grace. Their honor is not at stake.

In striking contrast to the Mediterranean, invincibility is not the issue in regard to the honor of men in Oman. In Sohar, everyone is seen as vulnerable—that is the human condition, inextricably bound up with life in society. To demonstrate that you are invincible is to make false pretenses in Sohar—even a nonsensical maneuver. *Honor*, in this society, does not require that the man assert himself, be aggressive and uncompromising, or take up every challenge, as the case seems to be in Mediterranean societies. On the contrary, it demands of men and women alike that *you* do not offend, but, in a manner unassertive, graceful, and dignified, you must treat everyone as politely—that is, tactfully, correctly, hospitably, morally, and amicably—as possible. That is the essence of honor in Oman.

CHAPTER 9

✤

The *Xanith:* A Third Gender Role?

"Look how Allah made your hand, he gave you five fingers, but each a little bit different. . . . People are the same way, every one of them different."

Any discussion of the social roles of the sexes in Sohar would be incomplete without detailed attention also to a special kind of person, known locally as *xanith* and, for many purposes, regarded by Soharis as neither man nor woman. In English, one might call such persons male transvestites or transexuals. The way they are conceptualized in Sohar and the way they function in that society, they cannot lightly be dismissed as aberrant or deviant individuals, but are better understood, as far as I can judge, as having a truly distinct, third gender role. The existence of such a triad of gender roles—woman, man, and *xanith*—provides as unusually productive opportunity to explore more thoroughly the basic properties and preconditions of male and female roles as they are conceptualized in Sohar, and, in this chapter, I shall discuss the *xanith* mainly with this end in view.[1]

The word *xanith* carries the sense of effeminate, impotent, soft. Although anatomically male, *xanith*s speak of themselves with emphasis and pride as "women." They are socially classified with women with respect to the strict rules of segregation. According to the estimates of informants, in 1976 there were about sixty *xanith*s in Sohar, as well as an unknown number of men who had been *xanith*s previously, but no longer were. In other words, well above one in every fifty males has a past or present history as a *xanith*. In the following I shall seek to develop a role analysis that does not see the *xanith* in artificial isolation, but confronts the role in the

---

[1] The main substance of this chapter has been published elsewhere in the form of the article "Man Becomes Woman—Transsexualism in Oman as a Key To Gender Roles" (see Bibliography).

After I had completed this manuscript, Dr. Frank H. Stewart kindly alerted me to references in the anthropological literature to transvestism, both male and female, among the Marsh Arabs of Iraq. I acknowledge that other references may also have been made, but I have not been in a position to check the literature systematically.

context of the reciprocal roles of man and woman, and the basic constitution of social persons and relationships in this society.

To perform such an analysis, I need to describe both how people classify and think about each other, and how they act and interact. I shall try to show how the conceptualization of each role in the triad reflects the existence of the other two, and how the realization of any one role in behavior presupposes, and is dependent on, the existence and activities of both the other roles. In this manner, I mean to use the role of the *xanith* as a key to answer the following questions: What is the basis for the Sohari conceptualization of sex and gender identity? What insight does this provide into the construction of male and female roles in Sohar, and into fundamental values and premises in Omani society?

Let me first describe some of the concrete behavior enacted by *xaniths* by describing the process by which I myself discovered them. I had completed four months of field work when one day a friend of mine asked me to go visiting with her. Observing the rules of decency, we made our way through the back streets away from the market, where we met a man, dressed in a pink *dishdasha*, with whom my friend stopped to talk. I was highly astonished, as no decent woman—and I had every reason to believe my friend was one—stops to talk with a man in the street. So I reasoned he must be her very close male relative. But their interaction did not follow the pattern I had learned to expect across sex lines, she was too lively and informal, their interaction too intimate. I began to suspect my friend's virtue. Could the man be her secret lover? No sooner had we left him than she identified him. "That one is a *xanith*," she said. In the twenty-minute walk that followed, she pointed out four more. They all wore pastel-colored *dishdasha*s, walked with a swaying gait, and reeked of perfume. I recognized one as a man who had been singing with the women at a wedding I had recently attended. And my friend explained that all men who join women singing at weddings are *xanith*s. Another was identified as the brother of a man who had offered to be our servant—an offer we turned down precisely because of this man's disturbingly effeminate manners. And my friend explained that all male servants (except for slaves), are *xanith*s, that all *xanith*s are homosexual prostitutes, and that it is quite common for several brothers to partake of such an identity. Another bizarre experience now became intelligible: at a wedding celebration, on the wedding night, when no male other than the bridegroom himself may see the bride's face, I was witness to a man casually making his way into the bride's seclusion chamber and peeping behind her veil! But no one in the audience took offense. Later that night, the same man ate with the women at the wedding meal, where men and women are strictly segregated. At the time, I took him to be a half-wit; that was the only reason I could find for such deviant behavior to be accepted. The man's strangely effeminate manners and high-pitched voice, giving him a rather clownish appearance, lent further credence to my interpretation. I then realized that he, as well as the five men we had met that day, were transvestites or transexuals.

This incident also serves to highlight problems of discovery and interpretation in field work which are made acute in a strictly sex-segregated society like Oman. I wonder whether persons corresponding to *xaniths* who have not previously been reported in the anthropological literature on the Middle East may not indeed be found some places there, but have escaped notice because the vast majority of field workers have been men. Barred from informal contact with the women, the male anthropologist might miss the crucial clues to the transvestite/transexual phenomenon. He is likely to meet some effeminate men whom he will recognize as homosexuals (as we did our would-be servant), and others who will strike him as half-wits (like some Omani male singers). The fact that *xaniths* do not assume full female clothing would also give credence to the above interpretations. But the essential feature of the phenomenon—persons who are anatomically male, but act effeminately and move freely amongst women behind purdah—would easily escape the male anthropologist, for the forums and arenas where this interaction takes place are inaccessible to him.

A brief comparative perspective and clarification of terms is helpful at this point. The term *transvestite*, by which such phenomena have generally been known in the anthropological literature, means, etymologically, cross-dressing, and it has come to refer to the act of dressing in the clothes of the opposite sex. The classical anthropological case is the *berdache* of the Plains Indians—men who dressed like women, performed women's work, and married men (Lowie 1935). However, it is not easy to assess, in the anthropological record, the cross-cultural distribution of transvestites, for they are often simply referred to as homosexuals; and homosexuality again is usually equated with a high degree of effeminacy in males. But we know unequivocally that, in a few societies, a transvestite role was a fully institutionalized part of traditional life, as for example, the Koniag of Alaska, Tanala of Madagascar, Mesakin of Nuba, and Chukchee of Siberia. However, I have not been able to find evidence that these institutions are practiced today with their traditional vitality.

On the Batinah coast of Oman, on the contrary, *xaniths* are an integral part of the local social organization and very much in evidence. As we have seen, they cannot be said to wear either female or male clothing, but have a distinctive dress of their own. But Soharis believe that if *xaniths* had the option, they would choose to dress like women. In the event, they are forbidden to do so, as we shall soon see. Does this then mean that they are to be understood most truly as "transvestites"?

The term *transexual* was first introduced by D. O. Cauldwell in 1949. It became well known after the publication of Harry Benjamin's book *The*

A xanith *in ordinary costume, outside his home*

Transexual Phenomenon in 1966. Prior to 1949, transexuals had always been labeled as transvestites—a term introduced sometime around the turn of the century (Dr. John Money, personal communication). Dr. Benjamin's significant discovery was that men who impersonate women can derive extremely different feelings of subjective identity from the act: for some, impersonating women is a way to bolster their subjectively cherished identity as a *male*; for others, it is the way to escape from an undesired male identity and *become* a woman. The transvestite achieves his purpose through the secret fetishistic sexual pleasure he derives from female clothing. There seems to be an emerging consensus in psychiatric and sociological literature today to regard this kind of person as a transvestite. An authority on the topic writes, for instance: "For these men, not only are their penises the source of the greatest erotic pleasure, but they also consider themselves men, not just males. Transexuals, on the other hand, are *never* found to be fetishistic. They have no capacity for episodes of unremarkably masculine appearance. They do not grow out of their femininity. They do not work in masculine professions" (Stoller 1971, p. 231).

According to this usage, it is probable that the Omani *xanith*s are better classified as transexuals rather than as transvestites in that they claim to be women, not men; they never truly grow out of their femininity; and they are assumed by women to resemble themselves in basic sexual attitudes. However, *xanith*s are also clearly analogues to the cases described in traditional anthropological literature as "transvestites" and should be seen in this comparative perspective. Finally, the question remains whether a *xanith* can be illuminated by being classified as either a transvestite or a transexual? As Dr. Money has lucidly observed (personal communication): "In an area of the world where there is no local vernacular or differential diagnostic terminology for men who impersonate women, one has the same problem as existed in Europe and America before the middle 19th century. The Omani *xanith*s have only one way of expressing themselves, and that is as *xanith*s and not as either transvestites or transexuals." In the following, therefore, I shall stick to Omani terminology.

As I have pointed out, the population of Sohar contains not only approximately sixty *xanith*s, but also an unknown number of *former xanith*s. A male's career as a "woman" may have several alternative terminations: (1) the man may be a woman for some years, whereupon he reverts to being a man for the rest of his life; (2) he may live as a woman until old age; (3) he may become a woman, return to being a man, again become a woman, and so forth. To us it would appear obvious that the decisive criterion by which men and women are distinguished is anatomical, and that it is only through hormonal change and surgical modification that one's sex and gender role are changed. Omanis apparently hold a fundamentally different view. But it should be emphasized that this potential for change is a characteristic of males only. Omani females, on the contrary, retain female identity throughout life. I shall return to the reasons for this contrast between the possible careers of men and women.

Let me now turn to a description of the role that we seek to understand. Its character as an intermediate role is most clearly shown in counterpoint to male and female roles.

Women wear *burqa*s before all marriageable males. They need not wear them before *xanith*s and slaves, because they, in their own words, do not feel shy before them. The *xanith*, on the other hand, is not allowed to wear the *burqa*, or any other female clothing. His clothes are intermediate between male and female: he wears the *dishdasha,* the ankle-length shirt of the male, but with the swung waist of the female dress. Male clothing is white; females wear patterned cloth in bright colors; *xanith*s wear unpatterned cloth in pastel colors. Men cut their hair short, women wear theirs long, *xanith*s medium long. Men comb their hair backward away from the face, women comb theirs diagonally forward from a central part, *xanith*s comb theirs forward from a side part, and they oil it heavily in the style of women. Both men and women cover their head, *xanith*s go bareheaded. Men always have their arms covered, women may be uncovered from elbow to wrist in private, but never in public (the specific Koranic injunction on this point makes it clear that the arm above the wrist is regarded as erotic and intimate), *xanith*s characteristically expose their lower arms in public. Perfume is used by both sexes, especially at festive occasions and during intercourse. The *xanith* is generally heavily perfumed, and he uses much make-up to draw attention to himself. This is also achieved by his affected swaying gait, emphasized by the close-fitting garments. His sweet falsetto voice and facial expressions and movements also closely mimic those of women. If *xanith*s wore female clothing, I doubt that it would in many instances be possible to see that they are, anatomically speaking, male and not female. The *xanith*'s appearance is judged by the standards of female beauty: white skin, shiny black hair, large eyes, and full cheeks. Some *xanith*s fulfill these ideals so well that women may express great admiration for their physical beauty.

Eating cooked food together represents a degree of intimacy second only to intercourse and physical fondling. Only in the privacy of the elementary family do men and women eat together; and Omanis are so shy about eating that host and guest, even when they are of the same sex, normally do not eat major meals (as contrasted to coffee, sweets, and fruit) together. Whenever food is offered in public, for example, at weddings, *xanith*s eat with the women.

Women are secluded in their homes and must have the husband's permission to go visiting family or friends. The *xanith*, in contrast, moves about freely; but like women, he stays at home in the evenings, whereas men may spend their time in clubs and cafés.

Division of labor follows sex lines. Housework is women's work. The *xanith* does housework in his own home and is often complimented and flattered for excelling women in his cooking, home decoration, and neatness. He may also take employment as a domestic servant, which no woman or freeman can be induced to do.[2] By this employment he supports himself, as a man must. But wherever tasks are allocated by sex, the *xanith* goes with the women. At weddings, women sing, while the men are musicians; *xanith*s are praised as the best singers. By appearing together with the women singers at weddings, the *xanith* broadcasts his status to a wide public. These performances characteristically serve as occasions to an-

---

[2] In Oman domestic employment is taken only by young boys, *xanith*s, or ex-slaves—before all of whom women may discard their *burqa*s.

nounce in public a change of identity from man to *xanith*. Thus, during my field work, there was a sheikh's son—a married man and the father of three children—who suddenly appeared at a wedding singing with the women. The audience was in no doubt as to the meanings of this act, and one woman of my acquaintance later remarked: "Imagine, the son of a sheikh, married to a pretty woman with very white skin, and yet he turns *xanith*!"

Women are legally minors and must be represented by a guardian. *Xanith*s represent themselves, as do all sane men. Legally speaking, they retain male status.

What then does the *xanith* mean by saying, as he explicitly does, that he is a woman, and why is he socially classified and treated as a woman in situations where sex differences are important? He was born an ordinary boy and acted and was treated as a normal boy until he started his career as a prostitute, commonly at the age of twelve or thirteen. Why then is he classified as a *xanith*—a person with a distinctive gender identity—and not merely as a male homosexual prostitute?

Let us observe closely the process by which the *xanith* returns to a male identity in order to search for an answer to this question. The change from *xanith* to man takes place in connection with marriage. But the critical criterion is more explicit than this: the *xanith* must demonstrate, as must every normal bridegroom, that he can perform intercourse in the male role. Among Sohari Arabs, the marriage celebration has a customary form so that consummation is publicly verified. Intercourse takes place between the spouses in private; but next morning, the groom must document his potency in one of two ways: by handing over a bloodstained handkerchief, which also serves as a proof of the bride's honor, to the bride's attendant (*mikobra*), or by raising an outcry, which spreads like wildfire, and lodging a complaint to the bride's father, and maybe also the Wali, because the bride was not a virgin, and he has been deceived.

If neither event takes place, the impotence of the groom is revealed by default. This will cause grave concern among the bride's family and nervous suspense among the wedding guests. This situation is discussed in greater detail in Chapter 11. The essential point here is simply that such a groom's adequacy as a man is in doubt. Conversely, the *xanith* who does deflower the bride becomes, like every other successful bridegroom, a *man*.

From this moment, all women must observe the rules of modesty and segregation before him,[3] always wear the *burqa*, never speak to him, never let him step into the compound when the husband is absent. Women stress that this does not pose difficulties. The *xanith* himself changes over-

---

[3] A *xanith* groom-to-be usually stops his prostitute activities a few weeks prior to marriage.

night into a responsible man, maintaining the proper distance and, in turn, protecting his own wife as would any other man. In other words, the *xanith* has been transformed from a harmless friend to a compromising potential sexual partner.[4]

But in all his demeanor—facial expressions, voice, laughter, movements—a *xanith* will reveal his past: his femininity remains conspicuous. I consequently expressed pity to some female friends for the poor woman who has such a "woman" for a husband; I felt she could not possibly respect him.[5] "No-no," they corrected me—*of course* she would respect him and love him. He had proved his potency; so he is a *man*.

Here, then, may be the key to an understanding of the gender system in Sohar. It is the sexual *act*, not the sexual organs, which is fundamentally constitutive of gender. A man who acts as a woman sexually *is* a woman socially. And there is no confusion possible in this culture between the male and female role in intercourse: the man "enters," the woman "receives"; the man is active, the woman is passive. Behavior, and not anatomy, is the basis for the Omani conceptualization of gender identity.

Consequently, the man who enters into a homosexual relationship in the active role in no way endangers his male identity, whereas the passive, receiving homosexual partner cannot possibly be conceptualized as a man. Therefore, in Oman, all homosexual prostitutes are ascribed the status of *xanith*.

Such conceptualizations also imply that a person with female sexual organs is a *maiden* (*bint*) until she has intercourse. At that moment, she becomes a *woman* (*horma*). A spinster, no matter how old, remains a girl, a maiden.

Yet Omanis recognize, as do all other peoples in the world, the fundamental, undeniable character of anatomical sex. Girl and boy, female and male, are identities ascribed at birth. This is one reason why the Omani homosexual prostitute becomes a *xanith*, treated *as if* he were a woman. Yet he is referred to in the masculine grammatical gender, and he is forbidden to dress in women's clothes, for reasons we shall return to shortly. Attempts by *xanith*s to appear dressed as women have taken place, but *xanith*s were punished by imprisonment and flogging. But because the *xanith* must be fitted in somewhere in a society based on a

[4] As their motive for an eventual marriage, *xanith*s give the desire for security in sickness and old age. Only a wife can be expected to be a faithful nurse and companion. Significantly, however, our best *xanith* informant, a femininely beautiful seventeen-year-old boy, did not realize the full implications of marriage for his gender identity. He was definite that he would be able to continue his informal relationship with women after marriage, arguing that he was to women like both a father and a mother. This is out of the question in Omani society, but his belief may serve as a significant measure of the *xanith*'s own confused identity.

[5] *Xanith*s fetch their brides from far away, and marriages are negotiated by intermediaries, so the bride's family will be uninformed about the groom's irregular background.

fundamental dichotomization of the sexes, he is placed with those whom
he resembles most: in this society, with women.

It is consistent with these conceptualizations that, in the absence of sexual activity, anatomical sex reasserts itself as the basis for classification.
When in old age a *xanith* loses his attraction and stops his trade, he is
assimilated to the old-man (*agoz*) category. From the few cases I came
across, my impression is that such men tend to avoid large public occasions, where the issue of their gender identity would arise.

Most societies regard sexual organs as the ultimate criterion for gender
identity. It is fascinating to speculate over the origin of the *xanith* status in
Oman. Did it emerge through a clarification of the male role, whereby
Omani men declared, "You act like a woman; you do not belong among
us"? Or was it the *xanith*s themselves who wished to be women and progressively transgressed the gender boundary? The fact that *xanith*s cluster
in groups of brothers suggests the existence of developmental causes for
their motivation. Or the motive may be, as I have suggested elsewhere
(1975), a desire to escape from the exacting demands of the Omani male
role. But, in either case, why is the *xanith* not seen as a threat to the virtue
of women and thus constrained by the men? Physically, there is no denying that he has male organs. Yet, considering the lack of safeguards
observed, it is true to say that he is treated as a eunuch. And, as far as I
know, no documentary sources are available that might illuminate the
origin of the Omani *xanith* status.

Every role, however, also has a sociological origin, which may be identified in synchronic and consequently potentially far more adequate data.
That a role once was created does not explain its continued existence: it
must be perpetuated, re-created anew every day in the sense that some
persons must choose to realize it, and others acknowledge it, as part of
their daily life—whether in admiration, disgust, contempt, or indifference. In how they relate to the role encumbent, they also reveal
something of themselves and their values. The institutionalized role of the
xanith in Oman in 1976 is therefore a clear expression of basic premises
and values in that culture today.

As regards the question of what makes some males choose to become
*xanith*s, we may distinguish two kinds of data that can illuminate it: people's own understanding of the nature of the *xanith* and his relationships,
and why he seeks such an identity, or, on the other hand, objective,
distinctive features, which an investigator may identify in the background,
situation, or person of acknowledged *xanith*s.

The folk understanding of why some young boys turn into *xanith*s is
deceptively simple. Men say that when young boys at puberty start being
curious and exploring sexual matters, they may "come to do that thing"
together, and then the boy "who lies underneath" may discover that he
likes it. If so, he "comes to want it," and, as the Soharis say, "An egg that

is once broken can never be put back together," "Water that has been spilt can not be put back again."

Thus the homosexual activity of the *xanith* is seen by others as a compulsion: degrading to the person, but springing from his inner nature. Although it is performed for payment of money, its cause is emphatically not seen as economic need stemming from poverty. Indeed, informants insist that old *xanith*s who are no longer able to attract customers will end up paying men to serve them.

In the limited material I have been able to obtain, I have been unable to identify any clear social or economic factors effecting recruitment to the *xanith* role. Cases are found in all ethnic groups; they show a considerable range of class and wealth in family background. There is nothing remarkable, to the outsider, about the homes in which they grow up. Closer investigations, however, might uncover some such factors.

Homosexual practices and relationships, of course, have a certain frequency in most, if not all, societies. And, in that sense, there is nothing remarkable about their occurrence in Sohar. Our interest focuses on the crystallization of the distinctive category of *xanith* whereby the passive party to male homosexuality is institutionalized as a recognized role and, for general social purposes, treated as if he constituted a third gender. Are there identifiable factors in the Omani conceptualization of sexuality and sexual relations which give rise to this?

We might go part of the way in answering this question by comparing the role of the *xanith* with that of males practicing homosexuality elsewhere in the Middle East. Homosexual practice is a common and recognized phenomenon in many Middle Eastern cultures, often in the form of an institutionalized practice whereby older men seek sexual satisfaction with younger boys. But this homosexual relationship generally has two qualities that make it fundamentally different from that practiced in Oman. First, it is part of a deep friendship or love relationship between two men, which has qualities, it is often claimed, of being purer and more beautiful than love between man and woman. Such relationships are also said to develop sometimes in Sohar, but very infrequently, and those who enter into them will try to conceal them from others. Neither party to such a relationship is regarded as a *xanith*. Second, both parties play both the active and the passive sexual role—either simultaneously or through time. In contrast, there is nothing in the Omani *xanith*'s behavior which is represented as pure or beautiful; and he does not seek sexual release for himself. Indeed, till he has proved otherwise (most?) people doubt that he is capable of having an erection.[6] Like a fallen woman, he simply sells his body to men in return for money: he is a common prostitute.

---

[6] Women were definite that *xanith*s who were prostitutes on a large scale (*wægid xanith*) were incapable of performing intercourse in the male role. However, one popular *xanith*

Herein lies the other component, I will argue, of the explanation why the *xanith* emerges as an intermediate gender role, rather than representing an irregular pattern of recruitment to the female role. The *xanith* is treated as if he were a woman, and, for, many critical purposes, he is classified with women, but he is not allowed to become completely assimiliated to the category by wearing female dress. This is not because he is anatomically a male, but because he is sociologically something that no Omani woman should be: a prostitute. For such a person to dress like a woman would be to dishonor womanhood. The woman's purity and virtue are an axiom. Officially, there is no such thing as female prostitution. (In practice it exists, but in a concealed form.) By his mere existence, the *xanith* defines the essence of womanhood; he moves as an ugly duckling among the beautiful and throws them into relief. Through him, the pure and virtuous character of women may be conceptualized. One may speculate whether this aspect of the female role would be so clarified, were it not for him.

According to this hypothesis, it would be difficult to maintain a conception of women as simultaneously pure and sexually active, if some among them were publicly acknowledged also to serve as prostitutes. If the public view, however, is that prostitution is an act of *xanith*s, whereas women are not associated with the moral decay that prostitution represents, then women may be conceptualized as pure and virtuous *in* their sexual role. *Womanhood* is thereby left uncontaminated by such vices, even though individual women may be involved. Indeed, the term by which women refer to the activities of female prostitutes (that is, women who are not merely unfaithful for love, but have sexual relations with several men) is *yitxannith*, the active verbal form of *xanith*.

The *xanith* thus illuminates major components of the female role in Sohar. But he can also serve us in a broader purpose, as a key to the understanding of basic features of Sohari culture and society, and the fundamental premises on which interaction in this society is based.

Homosexual prostitution is regarded as shameful in Oman; and all forms of sexual aberration and deviance are sinful according to religion. Boys who show homosexual tendencies in their early teens are severely punished by anguished parents and threatened with eviction from home. So far, reactions in Oman are as one might expect in our society. But the further course of development is so distinctly Omani that any feeling of similarity disappears.

---

whom we interviewed was equally definite that he could, though he had never tried, arguing that he knew several men who had practiced on an even larger scale than himself, yet had been potent. When I reported this view to some female friends, they categorically rejected it. To their understanding, there is an antithesis between performance in the male and the female sexual role; true bisexuality cannot be imagined. Therefore, if an *ex-xanith* proved‘ potent, the modest extent of his activities would thus be proved ex post facto.

If the deviant will not conform in our society, we tend to respond with moral indignation, but with no organizational adjustments. He is disgusting and despicable, a violation of our sense of modesty and a threat to public morality. Strong sanctions force him to disguise his deviance and practice it covertly. But because we do not wish to face up to him, we also fail to take cognizance of his distinctive character. As a result, we construct a social order where men and women who are sexually attracted by members of their *own* sex nonetheless are enjoined to mix freely with them in situations where *we* observe rules of sexual modesty, such as public baths and toilets.

Omanis, on the other hand, draw the consequences of the fact that the sexual deviant cannot be suppressed. He is acknowledged and reclassified as a *xanith* and left in peace to practice his deviance. The condition is simply that he establish his little brothel under a separate roof; he must rent a date-palm hut for himself. But this may be located anywhere in town, and it is not shameful to sublet to him.

This reaction to the sexual deviant is a natural consequence of the basic Omani view of life: the world is imperfect; people are created with dissimilar natures and are likewise imperfect. It is up to every person to behave as correctly—that is, tactfully, politely, hospitably, morally, and amicably—as possible in all the different encounters in which he or she engages, rather than to demand such things of others. To blame, criticize, or sanction those who fall short of such ideals is to be tactless and leads to loss of esteem. The world contains mothers who do not love their children, children who do not honor their parents, wives who deceive their husbands, men who act sexually like women . . . and it is not for me to judge or sanction them, unless the person has offended me in the particular relationship I have to him. It is up to the husband to control and punish his wife, the parents, their children, the state—if it so chooses—the sexual deviant. The rest of us are not involved—on the contrary, we are under an obligation always to be tactful and hospitable to people.

And even the party who has been offended will have difficulties imposing compliance to his rights. For human nature is strong and unbending, and not easily broken. A wife who is unfaithful—the husband may lock her up behind walls of concrete, yet she might break out; he may beat her, but she may persist. Coercion is no answer. A marriage between two who do not love each other can never succeed. Desires, drives, longings, and propensities force their way to the surface despite all constraints. The best way for man is to accept others as they are, while training himself to virtue and gracefulness. That is the way to win esteem.

Such interactional premises provide the preconditions for *xanith*s, as well as female prostitutes, to operate as they do, despite a unanimous agreement that their activities are immensely wrong and sinful. A woman who prostitutes herself deceives her husband, but harms no one else but him and herself. And unless he surprises her in the act, he will never have proof. Neighbors will not inform, for that would be embarrassing, and the matter does not concern them. Thus the most bizarre situations are created; for example, friendships such as those described in the last chapter, where flagrant prostitutes and the most virtuous and innocent women interact and visit.

In other words, Omani society, is one in which the conceptualization of the person is subtle and differentiated. One act or activity is only *one* aspect of the person, and only one facet of a complex personality. No person is branded by any single act committed, and past mistakes can be corrected and ignored. It is bad taste to harp on them later. Perhaps this attitude is the prerequisite for the *xanith*'s ability to reconstitute himself as a man and become a fully respected member of society. Never in my discussion with men or women could I find an attitude reminiscent of the "Once a criminal, always a criminal" assumption. On the contrary, it was only by persisting in asking that I was ever able to locate any former *xanith*s. People did not bring up the subject, even when speaking of biographical matters, and when I finally did ascertain such facts, they were categorical in their view that, "Yes, N. N. once was a *xanith*, but now he is a man."

The fact that persons are not prepared to sanction each other for their behavior toward third persons does not mean that they are uninterested in observing and judging such behavior. Particularly Omani men are concerned about their own and each other's integrity as whole persons, as we saw in the last chapter.

The premises that human nature is unbending and that rights to sanction are restrictively allocated might be thought to provide the basis for a system of social relations where the most unyielding will always triumph. Realities in Oman are very different from this for three important reasons. First, both men and women always try to project an honorable and graceful presence—to embody beautiful manners. Second, persons do have real sanctions over each other in their direct relationships. Thus a wife who wants to remain married and yet desires to be unfaithful may be constrained to behave honorably by the threat of divorce on her husband's part. Third, the state underwrites all social relations and obligations. This last point requires some elaboration.

Every Omani has a court of appeal in the district *Wali* (governor), as noted in Chapter 3. The Wali presides daily in the town's central fort, where he hears cases and settles conflicts. He is assisted by judges who are knowledgeable in Islamic law. The Wali's word is law. No matter is felt to be so personal that it cannot be brought before the Wali. A wife whose husband does not bring her the household goods, a groom who finds his bride to be a "woman" (that is, not a virgin)—they may, and often do, complain to the Wali. And the Wali will call the parties in the case, together with whatever witnesses can be brought; he will have as many aspects of the case clarified as possible, and then make his sovereign decision public. Anyone who does not submit to the verdict is thrown in jail. This sometimes happens, for the Omani nature is so unyielding that not even the people's deep respect for authority is always sufficient to constrain them.[7]

This whole procedure is subject to one very significant limitation: only the concerned party can make the complaint. Thus, for example, parents may not take action on their daughter's behalf if her husband refuses her permission to visit them. Then he has committed an injustice against her, not them, and only she can lodge a complaint. And in this same principle of restricted rights to sanction lies also the explanation of why the Wali does not act against female prostitution, even though such behavior is sinful according to the state religion and he is well aware of its existence. But when a woman deceives her husband, it is he and no one else who suffers an injustice. He has sovereignty over her sexuality, and so has the right to punish her.[8] But no one else has cause for complaint. For the Wali to intervene in the matter would be to encroach on the husband's sovereignty; as long as the woman pursues her unfaithfulness with discretion, the state is not concerned. But if she were to step forth in public and proclaim herself a prostitute—as the *xanith* does—then the state would be the offended party, for prostitution practiced by women in public is unlawful.

Male prostitution in public—that is, the Omani pattern of transvestism or transexualism—on the contrary, is only sinful and not unlawful. What fundamental differences between male and female roles are revealed through these differential constraints on men and women? Earlier in this chapter, I used the *xanith* as a way to uncover basic features of the role of women. Let us now investigate what insights he provides into the role of men.

The state has sovereignty over men and is responsible for upholding law and morality. In view of this, it is remarkable that the authorities of Oman should choose to allow male prostitution to flourish, and I believe the explanation is twofold: the state practices a laissez-faire policy toward persons who are not seen as harming others, while at the same time it acknowledges that *xanith*s have utility: they provide a sexual outlet for men and thus a protection for the virtue of women.

The Omani view clearly sees the sexual drive as a component of man's nature—perhaps that component which of all his nature is the most difficult to control. This is consistent with basic Muslim conceptions that the availability of licit sexual release is vital to the man's protection against *zina* (illicit intercourse) (see Mernissi 1975). Sohari women explain that an

---

[7]In these court sessions, my husband witnessed wild protests from the sentenced, who was taken away by the guards, but later released after intercession by friends and family.

[8]But not *too* severely, for then the *woman* will appeal to the Wali, who, according to my female informants, would command the husband: "Be gentle to her if you wish to remain married to her. If you cannot do that, then divorce her."

adult man needs frequent sexual release. Both men and women argue that satisfaction of this need should be sought with a woman, who should be his wife. But what, then, should an adult, unmarried man do, or a married man who is absent on labor migration? He should not covet his neighbor's wife, much less seduce her. Female prostitutes should not exist, and, to the extent that they do exist, they are difficult to contact. *Xaniths*, however, are everywhere conspicuous. It is highly plausible that they serve to relieve the pressure on more or less faithful women from frustrated single men, and that the authorities are aware of their function in this respect. I therefore assume that they will continue to allow the *xaniths* to practice their trade, although the authorities might fear that they mar the façade that they may wish Oman to present to the world. *Xaniths* are, after all, a lesser evil than female prostitutes would be by Omani standards.

No stigma attaches to the man who seeks the company of a *xanith* for sexual purposes, though both men and women agree that the act itself is shameful. But the world is imperfect, and shameful acts an inherent part of life.

The Omani emphasis on the man's persistent need for sexual assertion may seem reminiscent of the Mediterranean Don Juan complex. But the similarity is superficial, and a brief comparison may be useful to throw into relief some fundamental features of the relationship between man and woman in Oman.

Don Juan seeks to conquer as many women as possible. He brags of his seductions as proof of his virility. Women are prey that can be made into trophies of his self-assertion. But because Mediterranean societies likewise observe sexual shame, there arises a genuine discrepancy between the consequences of the sexual act for a man and a woman respectively. Where Don Juan wins honor, the woman loses it. Yet Don Juan persists in humiliating women in order to enhance himself. The sexual act is principally a mode of self-assertion and a source of social esteem and may be only secondarily a way to satisfy a biological need. To use another male partner would presumably be below Don Juan's dignity, for only women can give the desired aggrandizement and glory.

What do we learn about the man in Oman from the fact that he seems content to go to a *xanith*? Quite clearly it cannot be crucial to him to demonstrate his power over women. In that case, he would presumably search till he found a woman who could be tempted to be unfaithful to her husband, with or without payment. The answer must be that the man primarily seeks to satisfy a biological drive. He needs sexual release because it is part of man's nature, and not to demonstrate his power over women. But why does he choose to go to a *xanith*, rather than to masturbate in private? Part of the explanation may be the Muslim fear of polluting the right hand, part of it may be a feeling that masturbation is an immature act, whereas mature sexuality involves penetration. Of course, it is possible that the Omani man does both; but folk opinion clearly sees the *xanith*, and not masturbation, as the alternative to a woman. Perhaps this is a measure of the extent to which the *xanith* is indeed thought of as a (albeit prostituted) *woman*. It is remarkable that women regard *xanith*s as so similar to themselves that they assume them to *feel* like women, and be "ashamed" (*yistihi*) before men, as are ordinary women.

Granted that the man prefers to obtain his sexual satisfaction in a relationship with another person, economic considerations, besides reasons of convenience, may contribute to making the *xanith* preferable to a prostitute woman. Intercourse with a *xanith* costs only one Rial Omani ($3), whereas intercourse with a woman costs five times as much. But I am inclined to favor another interpretation.

A *xanith* is preferable to a woman because he is his own master, whereas she is another man's property. By means of the *xanith*, a man can achieve his purpose without detriment to others. This is a consideration of great importance in Sohar. Time and again, men would emphasize, in confidential discussions of personal integrity and their own ideals, how they wished to arrange their own life, so that "no one can speak a bad word against me." (See, for example, Ch. 13.) Yet the interpretation I am suggesting might seem contradicted by the Omani statement that it is greater shame for a man to seek a *xanith* than a female prostitute. But this statement, I believe, addresses a conundrum that has been abstracted from its context and is answered by the basic logic that sexual relations are between man and woman and not between man and man. In its real context, judged by Omani values, it seems to me more valid to argue that the favored solution should be one in which a man can satisfy his needs without infringing on the rights of others.

This is in harmony with basic Omani values. "The ornament of a man is beautiful manners, but the ornament of a woman is gold," says an Omani proverb. A man should not commit injustices, nor cause strife, nor seek honor for himself by dishonoring others. To deceive and seduce brings disrepute; bragging about one's virility, or any other aspect of one's person, is vulgar. To brag at all is incompatible with beautiful manners. An Omani Don Juan is unheard of, and this is not because the Omani does not, like Don Juan, seek self-assertion and social esteem. But he does this in a society that admires and values very different qualities in a man. Virility and manliness are minimally associated with the callous conquest of women, and maximally associated with being in command of oneself and one's situation, and acting with grace and integrity toward all—women and men, slaves and sultans.

With this insight into the constitution of the male role, we gain a new perspective on the opportunities for realizing the female role. Different from our expectations of the position of women in Muslim countries—that they are oppressed, subjugated, and unhappy—and in contrast to the stark realities in some such countries, the Omani woman has an honored and respected place in her society. She derives confidence from her knowledge that the man wins honor by treating her gracefully. This does not necessarily mean that he can or will give her what she most desires. Men do not value the ornaments of women—golden jewelry, clothes, and luxury foods for hospitality—as highly as they do. But it does mean that a husband will strive to act correctly and respectfully towards his wife, if he values his own honor at all. To humiliate and mistreat her brings disrepute.

Although a few men seem content to disregard their honor as well as their wives, the majority are praised by their wives for their correct and beautiful manners. Indeed, I very rarely heard complaints about a husband's role performance. No doubt one may question the reliability of negative evidence in this matter, since Omani wives pride themselves on displaying absolute loyalty to their husbands, making them reluctant to confide even in their best friends. However, there were occasions when criticism was voiced, and it is significant that the substance of such discontent always was a wish that the husband would give the wife greater resources for hospitality. But I never heard an Omani woman express dissatisfaction with the basic duties and rights she has by virtue of her status, even though change and modernization are occasionally discussed, and rather exaggerated stories of the new freedoms of women in other Gulf states circulate among them. Indeed many of the constraints and limitations imposed on women, such as the *burqa*, restrictions of movement, and sexual segregation, are seen by women as aspects of that very concern and respect on the part of the men which provide the basis for their own feeling of assurance and value. Rather than reflecting subjugation, these constraints and limitations are perceived by women as a source of pride and a confirmation of esteem.

The stark differences that obtain between wife and husband with regard to sexual autonomy are likewise perceived by Omani women as an unquestionable part of the moral and social order. Women are much preoccupied with sexuality, and they constantly tease each other about how desired they are by their respective husbands and how much these other women enjoy the sexual act. Yet no one admits to enjoying it herself. Nonetheless, no one complains of lack of consideration when the husband demands intimacy when the wife is tired or otherwise disinclined. As far as I could understand, the Omani wife experiences her obligation as a kind of right or privilege, similar to her right and duty to serve her husband food when he comes home hungry. A husband's undeniable right to intercourse thus entails the wife's reciprocal right to receive him. And she herself values her position and defends it. If she suspects her husband of seeking the company of a prostitute (while living at home with her), she will refuse him, saying, "A whore is good enough for you"—and he will not be accepted again till he promises to reform and to abstain from such connections. Sohari women even hold the view that proven infidelity on the part of the husband gives the wife grounds for divorce. Whether the Wali would support them in this is beside the point: the belief is a measure of the kind of recognition to which the women themselves feel they are entitled.

This attitude in regard to the husband's sexual rights is also related, I believe, to what women perceive men's sexual need to be: a biological urge that demands satisfaction. Because the man in the sexual relationship is not seeking dominance or self-aggrandizement, it is not humiliating for the woman to serve him. Marriage implies unequal duties and unequal powers for each of the parties, and this is experienced by both wife and husband as meaningful and proper. In other situations, it will be the husband who has to discipline himself and perform acts that may be inconveniences or hardships, but serve *her* needs—as when working to provide her with ornaments, literally by the sweat of his brow, in the fierce heat of an Omani summer's day. And so it must be in a culture that acknowledges fundamentally different needs for man and woman: each must on occasion be prepared to satisfy some needs in the other which they never feel themselves, if there is to be a reciprocal relationship.

Another reflection of this same respect for the woman in Oman can be seen in attitudes toward sterility. It is a common view in Muslim countries that an infertile woman is a fundamental failure as a human being. She stands in danger of divorce, for a wife justifies her existence by producing children. But not so in Oman. Here many qualities of her person are prominent in her husband's evaluation of her: loyalty and faithfulness, tact and hospitality, love and considerateness. Fertility is desired, but not a condition, and, as we have seen, the whole person is not stigmatized by failure in any one particular respect. If the husband is fond of her for her other qualities, the most that an infertile woman risks—despite a generally high rate of divorce in the society—is that the husband will also take a second wife to provide him with children.[9]

There must be few contemporary societies where law and customary rules combine to define so powerless a position for women as in Oman. They have little say in the choice of spouse, cannot leave their house without the husband's permission, are debarred from going to the market to make a single purchase, often may not choose their own clothes, must wear masks before all males who are marriageable, and so forth. And yet I have never met women who seem so in control of themselves and their situation. Omani women impress with their self-assurance and poise. They com-

[9]Nancy Tapper notes that infertility is also not considered grounds for divorce for the Shasevan nomads of Iran, if for very different reasons than in Sohar (1978, p. 378).

port themselves with beauty and dignity, as if confident of themselves and their position. This is no doubt partly because their tasks and responsibilities are clearly defined and they command the resources to perform them with honor and grace. But above all, it is so because of the fundamental respect that men accord them in the pursuance of their "ornament"—namely beautiful manners, and the preconditions that are thereby created for conceptualizing and realizing a valued identity.

CHAPTER 10

✤

Diverse Interests in Marriage Establishment

"She will be happy because she's well provided for. That was my main con-. sideration."

All Sohari females, with the exception of a few deaf-mutes, get married, and so do all males, with the exception of a few incurable *xaniths*. The fate of the spinster and bachelor is so lamentable that no one is expected to will it. And whereas people recognize that some *xaniths* do live a bachelor's life by choice, they cannot image a woman who would choose to be a spinster. A woman achieves self-realization through being a wife and a mother. Womanhood in fact is thought to inhere in marital status: the fundamental transformation from girl (*bint*) to woman (*horma*) is brought about by sexual experience, and the only legitimate context for this is marriage. The full realization of manhood likewise implies marriage.

Marriage between relatives is a cultural ideal that Soharis share with many peoples of the Middle East. Until 1971, this ideal found partial expression in the legal right of a man to have first option to marry his father's brother's daughter (*bint il amm*); he was even entitled to enforce his right against the will of the girl's male guardian, who traditionally had the right to select her spouse. A certain precedence for male cousins is still recognized today, but it enters as only one among several considerations when a girl is promised in marriage. In real life, less than one third of all marriages are concluded between first or second cousins, counting relatives on both the father's and the mother's side. People explain the choice of an unrelated spouse by the saying "Strangers respect you more [*ilgharib yihtirimu aktar*]."

When two "strangers" marry, they will do so before they have ever met. Each enters into the marriage contract separately. Their first encounter is as groom and bride. How, then, is such a marriage arranged?

SELECTING A WIFE AND A DAUGHTER'S HUSBAND

Every person, male or female, now has a legal right to choose his or her spouse. This right was bestowed upon girls by a legal amendment of 1971,

189

introduced by the Sultan, whereas previously it had been the prerogative only of men. In practice, however, the male and the female are both prevented from exercising their rights to the full. But the circumstances that constrain them are very different for the two.

In the case of the girl, there is a strongly entrenched and shared view that her male guardian can better choose on her behalf. He has the required experience and wisdom. Considering the low marriage age for girls and their history of seclusion, this view may seem warranted. On what basis would a thirteen-year-old girl who, for the latter half of her life has hardly been within sight of an eligible man, much less talked to one, make her choice? The ideals of modesty, which have been inculcated in her throughout her life, further inhibit any expression of opinion or preference on her part. It takes only a trifling show of interest and initiative to make a girl seem eager and shameless. Fear may also enter. Guardians are expected to punish disrespectful behavior with mental and physical coercion. One sheikh was quite outspoken about this:

> If the girl refuses, we will speak to her patiently, explain that she is now grown up, and must marry. If she still refuses, we will speak to her harshly, shout at her. If she still refuses, we will beat her, to force her. She may be just afraid, or in love with someone, or something. . . . But if she still refuses after being beaten, we will not force her. There's no use. She would see to it that the marriage did not work.

The mental pressure exerted by the guardian and other relatives need not amount to more than subtly expressed displeasure to make a shy and susceptible girl feel that she has been improperly assertive. Thus organizational patterns and cultural premises—wherein are embedded the girls' conceptions of their own identity and of the male role—work together to prevent them from exercising their legal right. During the period of my field work, girls exerted little or, more commonly, no influence upon the choice of their husband.

Very different is the male's situation. He may be under various pressures and influences, particularly from close female kin, but it is recognized that the decision of whether to marry at any particular time, and whom to marry, is ultimately his own. However, he will be impeded, in his exercise of free choice by other constraints, stemming from the practice of sexual segregation and the values of tact and integrity. His decision therefore will have to be based upon piecemeal and second-hand information.

A marriageable man has few chances to observe unrelated girls, and none to become personally acquainted with one. Cousins are more familiar, especially if they live nearby. But even when a cousin seems attractive, the male tends to be too apprehensive of the feminine mystique to rely fully upon his own judgment. Thus he solicits the advice of close female kin, who, convinced of the naïveté of the men in this matter, are happy to lend their wisdom and knowledge.

In search of a bride, they will make inquiries to neighbors and itinerant vendors about marriageable girls in distant places. (Grooms prefer to fetch their brides from afar to reduce interference from in-laws and protect their authority.) On the basis of such secondary information, they attempt to patch together pictures as detailed and reliable as possible to present to the prospective groom. He, in turn, may encourage them to try to catch a glimpse of one or more of the candidates. But however much they would like to do so, both to still his anxiety and their own—for family members share a profound concern about a new bride's appearance and demeanor—such a mission can be accomplished only with great difficulty, if at all. Omani values of tact and grace are so exacting as to preclude any move whereby representatives of the prospective groom approach the girl's family and ask to have a closer look at her. Such a procedure is institutionalized in some Middle Eastern societies; for example, in the form of a tea-serving ritual, where the girl is scrutinized while serving tea to family members of the prospective groom. Not so in Sohar, here the maiden's sensibilities are respected, and norms of interpersonal conduct are so exquisitely polite that the embarrassment of rejecting a bride-to-be must be avoided for the sake of both parties.

Other factors exacerbate the difficulties of gathering second-hand information. The seclusion of females is, as we have seen, so pervasive that there are no public forums—for example, a well, a brook, or a kiosk—where women congregate and which the suitor's female kin could frequent in the hope of catching a glimpse of one "candidate." Nor can a woman take an occasional walk into the neighborhood where she lives, with the same hope in mind. Norms of visiting preclude a Sohari woman from embarking on a visit to a distant neighborhood—unless she has been specifically invited by someone living there. The combined effects of all these factors is that only in those rare cases where the women have a close friend who is also a close neighbor of a bridal candidate can it be arranged for them to be simultaneous guests at a coffee party. Then, if the girl does not measure up, the proposal can be shelved without offense. But considering the length to which suitors literally go to fetch a bride, as well as the limited character of female networks, such a convenient friend is not often at hand. Commonly, the groom must be satisfied to select his bride while knowing her looks only at third hand, and her character from hearsay.

NEGOTIATIONS

When a preference for a bride emerges, the proceedings begin: an elder male kinsman of the groom (preferably a paternal relative) approaches a close male kinsman of the girl's guardian. Constrained by the Omani distaste for boasting, to go-between can praise the groom's qualities in a very low-keyed manner; he also hints at the size of the bride price that the groom is ready to pay. This crucial information is passed on to the girl's guardian. If he is pleased with the proposal, the negotiations proper can begin. A delegation of the groom's kinsmen (preferably men related in the paternal line) meets with two or three of the guardian's kinsmen to negotiate an agreement. The most important matters to be settled are the exact size of the bride price and various other material benefits to be paid by the groom, such as the *mashtara* (furnishings); also to be decided are the size and elaborateness of the wedding celebrations, and the manner of residence for the couple (for example, whether they will occupy a room in a joint household, or build their own house). If the bride's parents know that the groom's parents are difficult, they may ask that the couple have a separate house as a condition for the marriage. No females take part in these negotiations, though backstage their influence may be significant.

Because Sohari marriage negotiations are pursued with such privacy, I am not sure at what point in the proceedings a binding agreement emerges, or whether its two main parties—the groom and the guardian—meet at all before an effective agreement is reached. I am inclined to think that by the time the prospective groom, accompanied by his close kinsmen, makes his first visit to his prospective father-in-law, it has already been decided that a marriage will ensue. Inconclusive negotiations would seem incompatible with the Omani's respect for woman, because bargaining over her would implicitly be to treat her like a commodity. Such bargaining would also be incompatible with a man's cherished self-image of poise and control. As a result, the guardian may well never see a suitor before he accepts him as his son-in-law. However, when one considers the more extensive range of men's movements, the chances of this happening are in no way comparable to the odds that the suitor faces in stealing a second-hand glimpse of his bride-to-be. We should also note that the guardian has the *option* of observing a suitor's looks and comportment. If he chooses to disregard physical appearance, it must either be because he deems it unimportant, or because it is secondary to other, more important considerations.

EVERY MARRIAGE HAS ITS PRICE

A chief consideration is the bride price (*mahr*). Every marriage requires one. The actual size in any case varies with many factors. Essentially it is a result of the bride's desirability for the groom, and his desirability for her guardian. Rank, physical attributes, ethnic status, and degree of kinship are important considerations. One quality supersedes all others in a bride: her reputed condition as a virgin (*bint*) or a woman (*horma*). Other things being equal, a virgin usually costs three to five times as much as a woman. Every girl who marries for the first time is reputed to be a virgin—at least within the delicate context of the marriage arrangement, where to make a reference of even the most oblique kind to that epitome of honor—a maiden's virginity—would be inconceivably scandalous. Generally speaking, the most esteemed and expensive bride will be a maiden of high rank, of light skin, endowed with property, and of Arab descent. The least attractive one is a divorcee or widow of slave origin and black skin. However, the actual price paid for a particular bride depends upon the highly personal judgment of the particular parties involved. In marriage agreements, as in most other aspects of life, a remarkable diversity persists.

With reservations, a few general trends may be indicated. It costs to cross boundaries. Relatives should pay less than strangers, sometimes only a token fee. Men of other ethnic status who want to marry into the dominant Arab group should pay extra for the privilege, as should an already married man for the privilege of acquiring a second wife.

Because no boundaries are absolute, a man's financial status influences his range of choice in brides more than any other factor. A poor man must be content to look for a dark-skinned widow or divorcee—unless a relative agrees to accept him. A rich man may even aspire to have a snow-white virgin of Arab descent as his second wife.

The bride price is paid to the girl's guardian. It is up to his discretion how to use it. In 1973 the bride price was limited by law to a maximum of 300 Rials ($1,000), allegedly in response to a complaint from the soldiers to the Sultan that they could never hope to marry on a salary as low as 40 Rials. The Sultan acted promptly; he nearly doubled the soldiers' salary and decreed a reduction of the bride price to a fraction of its previous level. A range of 1,000–3,000 Rials had been common. It still is, despite the threat of severe punishment for the guardian guilty of extracting, *and* for the groom who acquiesces to pay, a bride price exceeding 300 Rials. If detected by the Wali's spies, the groom and the guardian are both thrown in jail. But the groom may gain an over-priced bride, and keep his money and freedom through the following procedure. He can pay the excess demanded, but after the marriage report his extortioner to the Wali, whereupon the excess money is returned, and only the guardian is jailed. Cases of either kind are rare.

Soharis claim that the *mashtara* has nothing to do with the bride price and thus is not constrained by the law. But the Wali asserts authoritatively that *mashtara* is an illegitimate concept. There should be no such thing. The groom should pay a bride price of maximum 300 Rials. Then, after the marriage, the bride and groom together should save for furnishings, the specifics of which they should decide together.

THE CASE OF MEIMONA

This brief outline of procedure and prerequisites for contracting a marriage may serve as a preliminary background for an actual case. This case exemplifies the variety of considerations and dilemmas that Soharis face when they seek to translate their ideal preferences into real practice.

Meimona was a pretty and lively fourteen-year-old girl when we first met her in 1974. She lived with her parents and five younger brothers and sisters in a large date-palm garden, with no close neighbors. But her twelve-year-old sister, Badriya, kept her good company, and at school she had many friends. Her father, Abdullah, was an intelligent and ambitious autodidact, who was widely traveled and spoke English beautifully. He had eagerly embraced the educational opportunities provided by the government, and enrolled Meimona in her thirteenth year into the first grade of elementary school. Most fathers would consider it unnecessary to educate their daughters at that age, for marriage would presumably be imminent. But Abdullah reasoned that some education was better than none and, besides, he was in no hurry to marry off Meimona. He seemed to have a genuine attachment to each of his children, as well as for their mother, a quiet and contented woman; and he repeatedly stressed his concern that his daughters make a happy marriage. Education, he said, would further that end, because it broadens the horizon and equips a girl to make a *good* life with her husband.

A year and a half later, when we returned, Meimona had been married. "It all happened so suddenly, some three months ago," her mother, Rahmeh, regretfully told us. "Along came this one suitor from Salan [a neighboring village], and Abdullah wanted him and no one else."

"What about Meimona, what were her feelings in the matter?"

"She was very unhappy, for she wished to continue school. And she cried, and we [her mother and sisters] cried. And I pleaded with Abdullah to let her wait only one more year so she could finish third grade. But he and the groom were both adamant."

Rahmeh went on to relate how there had been dozens of suitors before this last one, Mubarak, so that there was no need to accept him. Yet her husband had judged him the perfect groom. She did not quite understand the reason: her son-in-law is educated, has a good income, and takes religion seriously; he prays and fasts. But in this he is no different from other suitors who came before him, and he has one grave handicap: he lives very far away. A return fare to Salan costs one Rial by taxi. So the most they could hope to see Meimona is once a month or fortnight.

Rahmeh was unhappy indeed, because reality had proved worse than the gloomiest expectations. Only once after the marriage had she seen Meimona, for her husband had moved her all the way to Muscat, when he found a job and apartment there. By so doing, Rahmeh felt he violated an implied condition of the marriage, for surely they would never knowingly have married Meimona so far away! How much better life would have been if her husband had heeded her warnings and chosen a husband for Meimona from among their own relatives in the same neighborhood. "All our kin live here, and here Meimona should have lived too. Both I and Meimona wanted it that way, and my brother was eager to marry Meimona to his younger son. But Abdullah said no, both to this relative and to several others who signaled their interest. And this even though he cannot fail to know that relatives make the happiest marriage," laments Rahmeh. "Abdullah and I are cousins—our mothers were sisters—and have always been very close and very happy."

Asked what Abdullah had against her brother's son Rahmeh explained: "My nephew fools around, drinks, and does not pray, whereas the one who married her is educated and serious; he goes nowhere but to his work and home. He is just like my brother's elder son—*mustaqim* [straightforward]. The elder boy is married to my older sister's daughter. If only the younger boy had been like his elder brother! Now my brother and his family are very angry because they did not get Meimona, so angry they did not even attend the wedding! And they are most angry with me, not with Abdullah. They say, 'You are from our family, you should have persuaded him.' But I really tried. And what can a mother accomplish anyway? It is the father who decides."

Rahmeh became so distraught thinking about her brother's wrath that I asked if she could not remedy the hard feelings by explaining to her brother about his son's irresponsibility? She said that she could not, because that would make him very angry, and he would point out that Meimona would have come to live in his own house; he himself would have been responsible for her and provided for her, so that she would have suffered no harm. "As if that is all a husband should do!" Rahmeh woefully exclaimed. "What does he think that marriage is?"

To appease her brother, she has said that her husband will give their second daughter, Badriya, to his son instead. "But my brother answered that it was Meimona they wanted. And besides, Abdullah says that he will surely not give them Badriya either!"

"HIDDEN COSTS" IN MARRIAGE

This case highlights some problems in Sohari marriage arrangements which are crucial to our understanding of woman's life. One question that arises is whether marriageable girls are just pawns in a male-dominated game. Why else would Abdullah impose a marriage upon his daughter that she (reportedly) was unhappy about, and the girl's uncle demand that she enter into a different one, of his choice? What male attitudes to females and married life find expression through such acts? And how do they match female expectations?

Rahmeh criticized her brother for his narrow conceptions of the husband-wife relationship, yet generously offered her second daughter as a substitute wife for his son. Did she imply that one cousin-wife is as good as any other? Furthermore, she offered her second daughter while fully conscious of her nephew's deplorable character traits. What did *she* conceive marriage to be? It seems reasonable to assume that the degree of harmony or dissonance between male and female expectations must significantly affect the dynamics of marital life. If, for example, the bride and the groom enter into marriage with incompatible aspirations and resentful of what the other considers his or her rightful expectations, or even solid rights, then sources of endless discord have been provided. If, on the other hand, each aspires to play a role that is consistent with the other's expectations, a basis for harmony is established (if not necessarily for happiness—considering that people may resign themselves to conventional fates, not because they like them, but because they see no way out).

In Sohar, decisions are made on the girl's behalf by the men who represent her. Thus Abdullah turned down dozens of suitors before settling for one. What considerations may have determined his choice? How does his son-in-law compare with the preferred husband as judged by the bride-to-be's point of view? What I am seeking are some clues to the relationship between a maiden's aspirations for her married life and the criteria used by her elders in selecting a husband for her. To what extent do their considerations seem in accordance with her preferences or her real advantage and objective interests?

One major difficulty is determining "real advantage" and "objective interests." But it is precisely this kind of judgment to which the' men themselves refer in Sohar (as in a multitude of Middle Eastern societies) when they give explicit justifications for arranged marriages. The identification of a truly suitable spouse *is* important, they claim, and the guardian alone commands the requisite skills and responsibility to make an optimal choice.

The basis for such a view may be that the crucial issue in marriage negotiations is not in fact what people say it is—to further the happiness of two young spouses—but rather to forge or cement alliances between larger kin groups—in which case a maiden would surely be unfit to decide. The anthropological literature on the Middle East gives ample evidence of societies where political interests—both explicitly and implicitly—channel marriage arrangements. Sohar is definitely a case to the contrary. Political alliances may have loomed large in the past, but at present they are not in evidence. Relationships between in-laws in fact are so uncompelling and distant as to be virtually nonexistent, except in a purely formal sense. Today the overwhelming focus of marriage, as people see it, is on particular persons and the creation between them of that indispensable relationship through which man and woman can realize themselves.

That being the case, is there anything in the material to indicate that guardians do in fact possess *and* exercise a judgment more apt to further a young girl's happiness than her own? Let us return to Meimona's case for an illustration. Her husband was reportedly chosen because of his sound education, piety, and material prosperity. Is there any evidence that such qualities are essential to marital happiness, yet would not be perceived, or would be deemed insignificant, by Meimona herself, were she given the power to choose? If, on the other hand, her mother's preferences had been heeded, Meimona would have married a cousin who lacked all of these attributes, but distinguished himself as a close relative from the same neighborhood. What prerequisites would thereby have been secured for her marital happiness? Could it be that cousin-marriage, from a maiden's vantage point, confers so many benefits as to compensate for a variety of human failings?

If one follows this way of reasoning, guardians will be judged to possess superior evaluational skills only if they apply criteria that an examination of married life reveals to be conducive to happiness, but that the young girls underestimate. A significant difference between the judgments of long-married women and brides-to-be would consititute important evidence. However, if the factors that guardians take into consideration do not differ from the girls' ideas, there seems no logical reason why the guardian's should not abdicate in favor of the girls. Another possibility exists. Guardians may be found to apply criteria that are unrelated to everyone's conceptions of the prerequisites for a happy marriage and instead serve their own private interests. In that case, their "superior judgment" is revealed to be self-interest.

THE PREFERRED HUSBAND FROM THE GIRL'S POINT OF VIEW

What qualities does a girl desire in her husband? My material embraces the ideals of seven marriageable girls and five newly married women; their answers show overwhelming consensus.

The preferred husband is kind and generous. He gives amply, according to his means, of all the things that a woman values: clothes, jewelry, and foods, including fruits and biscuits for entertaining her friends. He also gives her money, so that she can buy small things for herself from itinerant vendors. He does not interfere in feminine pursuits, but leaves his wife free to visit her friends and entertain them as generously as she likes. He lets her visit her parents. He is even-tempered and understanding, guiding her by means of instructions and reprimands, not beatings.

Beauty is also desired, the ideal husband has white skin, a strong body, and youthfulness.

Strongly emphasized, if only implicitly, are the husband's material resources. The more affluent he is, the more capable he will be of realizing this female dream of the good life—expensive as it is. Even a wife's visit to her parents may be, as Meimona's mother pointed out, a costly affair. Indeed, women believe that affluence nourishes the qualities of kindness, generosity, and understanding, by easing the pressures of work and worries: an affluent man will be more relaxed and responsive to the needs of his wife and children. Because a woman derives much of her personal happiness, and most of her social esteem, from the generous expenditure of foods for entertaining and the abundant possession of clothes and jewelry, a loving husband sees to it that she is generously provided with such assets.

No preference for either a cousin or an unrelated husband was stated. An explicit question elicited that Solomonic reply so revealing of the Sohari outlook: "Sometimes a relative will be good, and sometimes a stranger. You know, people are different." They did, however, voice one cryptic condition for marital happiness: "A marriage between two who do not love each other will never succeed."

Brides-to-be and newly married women stress the importance of affluence more than older women do. My impression is that young girls in Sohar resemble their Western sisters in harboring simplistic and naively romantic ideas about the sources of marital happiness. But they emphasize different things. Western girls tend to believe that love can overcome all material obstacles; once it is present, happiness is secured. Sohari girls have a nearly opposite view of cause and effect: they tend to believe that affluence fosters love and soothes discord. In both cultures, views become modified with age and experience.

THE LOCUS OF DECISION

A father's responsibility to select his daughter's husband seems to be regarded by young girls as entirely natural and just. A father commands the required knowledge and understanding. A girl has been brought up to defer to his decisions in all major areas of life, and she feels secure that she can also trust him in this matter: a father is expected to ensure his daughter's happiness in a selfless manner.

But no other male is ascribed such unselfish motives. If the father is dead, the man acting in his place is required to ask the girl for her explicit consent before finalizing a marriage agreement for her. As a double precaution, the *mutawa* (scribe) asks her for her consent at the time of writing the contract. It is not considered shameful for a girl to speak her mind. "But we did not," Latifa and Feyza, two fatherless girls, told me.

"We would feel shy to express our view." By her acquiescence, Feyza became married to a cousin whom she resented, whereas Latifa made a most satisfactory match. My impression is that shyness prevents most young girls from voicing a view, although I was told of one very brave girl who refused when her guardian (her father's brother) insisted that she marry his son. He ignored her and had a fake contract written, whereupon the girl appealed to the Wali, who annulled the contract. She then married the man of her choice. The Wali told us that cases like this one were becoming more frequent as girls embrace the new ideology of exercising independent judgment.

THE AVOWED CONSIDERATIONS OF MEIMONA'S FATHER

Let us return to Meimona's case, keeping in mind the girls' picture of the ideal husband. In trying to illuminate the factors that determined her father's choice, we face serious difficulties in obtaining adequate data. Soharis are notably reticent about marriage negotiations, preferring to keep as a family secret "why" and "how" a particular bride or groom was *actually* chosen. Men do not engage in ex post facto discussions. Reasons as to why a particular suitor was chosen may be put forward, but they are unlikely to constitute the full answer. And for an outsider to search for this, even though he or she be a close relative, is considered bad manners. This discretion is also reflected in the substance of women's informal talks, which contain frequent references to the "who's who" of recent marriages, but rarely to the "why." When the latter is discussed it is typically only because of some unusual circumstance connected with the marriage, such as that the groom is reported to have paid an exorbitant bride price, or that the bride proved not to be a virgin. Probing for Abdullah's reasons in choosing this particular son-in-law, we were therefore compelled to exercise restraint and to refrain from arguing or pressing him. To act otherwise would have been an offense to his dignity. However, Abdullah was exceptionally prepared to speak with us on these topics, for he recognized our interest in understanding Sohari ways.

Abdullah volunteered this information. He was sad to have married off Meimona when he did, but he felt that it was the only sensible thing to do. Personally, he would have liked for her to continue her education, and, given a different time and place, that would have been in her own interest. As it was, she was too old when she started; it would have taken ten or eleven years before she could obtain the training that she would need for a job, and most likely her husband would not let her work anyway. So it was better for her to be married. So many men asked for her, including a cousin from her own family, to whom she was almost promised. But the last suitor, Mubarak, was the best one. He has a good job in the Army High Command (actually the Ministry of Defense, see Ch. 12), which provides a monthly salary of 100 Rials ($300) and a flat in Medinat Quaboos (a suburb of Muscat). He comes from a good family of six brothers, who get on very well. They live together in adjoining houses and are so well-off that they buy all food by the sack. Their father is dead, and their mother has remarried, so Meimona will not live with a mother-in-law. Sometimes living with one's mother-in-law is good, for the older can guide the younger, but most often they fight, like children. This way Meimona will be in charge of her own home, and happy.

Abdullah explained as follows:

> You see, prices have gone up in the last five years, not two times or ten times or sixty times, but a million times. So life is difficult unless you have much money. Meimona will be happy because she is well-provided for; that was my main consideration. The government gives them a good house with electricity and air conditioning and even a carpet on the floor. She will be happy. But we are sad that she lives so far away. I had thought she would be close, and that, since her husband and his brothers have a car, she could visit all the time.
>
> So with Badriya I will wait, and not let her marry before she has some education and has become wise so she can make a good life with her husband. And then I will marry her to someone nearby, so she will visit often. And then Meimona will come to visit her sister often, thereby we shall see her too. . . .

A PRELIMINARY EVALUATION OF THE
FATHER'S CONSIDERATIONS

Judged by the young girls' preferences, Abdullah appears to have made a thoughtful and intelligent choice. He stresses his son-in-law's material affluence and harmonious family residential arrangement; he takes due account of the troubles inherent in a wife living with a mother-in-law.

Abdullah, in his statement to us, made no reference to his son-in-law's intellectual and religious qualities, those very traits that his wife claimed had decided the matter. It is possible that Abdullah had stressed these moral aspects to Rahmeh and merely left them out when speaking to us. It is equally possible that she herself had selectively overestimated their importance in Abdullah's considerations. Reflected in either case may be Rahmeh's views of what makes for a happy marriage. She herself has the personal experience of a long and happy marriage to a man who has only recently become prosperous. She is aware that in today's booming Oman nearly everyone can enjoy material abundance, and therefore what counts in a son-in-law is the quality of the man himself more than his financial solvency. It is probable that Abdullah is well aware of her views and that, when presenting his own preferred suitor to her, he has played up to her values. Unfortunately, I cannot tell to what extent he himself may actually have been influenced by the suitor's moral excellence.

To the outsider unfamiliar with Omani society, Abdullah may appear to have an inflated idea of the happiness that money can buy—indeed, in the manner of the young girls themselves. But seen within the context of his own experience, and judged by the standards of Sohari male culture, his priorities are justified. Abdullah has struggled to earn his living since he was a small boy. Through hard work and prudence he has succeeded in establishing a position so respectable that, in his own words, his relatives, who used to be harsh and disrespectful toward him when he was a boy, now pride themselves with being related to him (Barth, forthcoming). His status seemed stable and secure until the present runaway inflation began. Convinced of the importance of material things, he is intensely fearful of material want. Typical of Sohari men he also believes that material goods hold the key to a woman's heart. Thus it is his judgment that Meimona will be happy because she is well-provided for.

His choice was less than perfect in one respect, which he himself also recognized; the location of his daughter's future home. Even if her husband had not moved her to Muscat, she would still have lived too far away for visits to her parents to exceed the legal minimum of one a week. But in failing to marry his daughter close, Abdullah is not guilty of any major sin of omission. More than half of all spouses in Sohar come from places as far apart as those of Meimona and her husband. Keeping to Meimona's case and her father's avowed motives for selecting this particular man, he appears to have provided her with a good husband.

MEIMONA'S INITIAL REACTIONS

Yet Meimona is reported to have cried and to have resented her father's choice. What are we to make of such statements? Unfortunately, I was not able to discuss the case with Meimona herself. My interpretation of her reaction must rest upon a general understanding of the responses of young brides.

Meimona may well have cried, but I doubt that she did so in reaction against any particular groom. Her crying more likely expressed her feeling of sadness at the imminent parting with family and friends. For Omanis, crying expresses heartfelt sorrow and is appropriate only in a few, circumscribed situations. Proper demeanor requires graceful self-control. It calls on the girl to acquiesce to her guardian's choice of husband with courteous deference—except when there are gravely aggravating circumstances connected with him—such as that he already has one wife, or is extremely old—in which case her resentment may be expressed. Otherwise she does not cry—or not excessively. Instead, she struggles to conceal misgivings she may have to avoid being suspected of illicit feelings. Omani men believe that resentment against one suitor must spring from attraction to another one. And no decent Omani girl "falls" in love. Love is the privileged emotion of spouses; it is conditional upon marriage. A maiden is neither lured by the charms of any one man nor repelled by his failings. She properly has only one overt reaction toward all marriageable males: polite noninvolvement.

Realities fall short of ideals. Girls do develop sympathies and antipathies toward the males with whom they are familiar. Meimona's mother claimed that her daughter had preferred her cousin for a husband. She may, and she may not. Nearby cousins have ample opportunity to get to know each other well, and Meimona may well have developed a definite attraction—or, equally likely, a repulsion—toward this particular one. Love apart, she may have wished to marry him for the security of moving in with well-known relatives who have pervasive, if diffuse, commitments to each other, and could be counted on to treat her well. The match would have afforded easy access to her parents, and she could have enjoyed the additional privilege of continued close relationships with her sisters and brothers—ties that are usually severely impaired by marriage to a stranger. Consonant with Omani values, she may not have worried or even thought about love, but confidently expected it to blossom automatically, as the only natural response between husband and wife.

If Meimona had truly hoped to remain close to home, she encountered a very different fate. Like nine in ten young brides, Meimona, on her wedding night, was transferred, shielded behind a cloak of black and a veil of opaque green, several scores of miles along the coast to a house and place she has never before seen. From this moment on, she may never revisit her childhood home (her lawful right notwithstanding) without explicit permission from her husband.

A REEVALUATION OF THE CONSIDERATIONS

It was precisely the issue of visiting that was to cause Meimona's family such perturbation. When we met them again, three months after the marriage, the old-time atmosphere of relaxed contentment was gone. The father, despite serious efforts to comport himself, looked painfully distressed. The mother's face was anguished; the older daughter, Badriya, looked dispirited and sullen; and the younger children were tense. What had gone wrong?

A combination of unfortunate circumstances was responsible, all connected with Meimona's marriage. Not only had Abdullah failed to anticipate the prospect of his son-in-law, Mubarak, moving to Muscat, he had also assumed a nonexistent desire on his part to cultivate close relations with Abdullah's family. In fact, Mubarak showed a strong, although not atypical, reluctance to have his wife associate with her parents. To this unfortunate end, Abdullah had alienated his wife's and children's closest kin, who were also his own close relations. In addition, there was reason to believe that he had been forced to hasten his daughter's marriage, in order to hush up some "dark secrets" connected with her.

On her wedding night, Meimona proved to be an experienced woman, not a virgin. "It is a terrible shame for her family," a close friend of mine remarked, "so much so that they will never reveal this truth to you, though they know that you and everyone else knows. For the groom *must* make the outcome of the virginity test public and create a scandal."

What other aspirations Abdullah may have nurtured for his daughter, I have no way of knowing. Furthermore, I do not know in what measure his choice reflected an earnest concern for her happiness, or the pursuit of his own. He did provide his daughter with a *good* husband, as measured by the standards of young girls. But it does not follow that a good husband for her was what he was primarily concerned to obtain. The result may have been a by-product of quite a different striving. Because of the strong value that both young girls and grown men (but not older women) put upon material wealth, though for very different reasons, a guardian may be strongly (but not wholly) motivated by pure self-interest, yet obtain a husband who is desirable to his daughter. In this I am not saying that Abdullah was so motivated, or that such a fortunate outcome need be the result when the guardian acts in self-interest. My concern is to point out a serious methodological difficulty in providing answers to a major question raised above: To what extent are guardians in fact motivated by a genuine concern for the best interests of their wards?

The son-in-law, Mubarak, did have certain attributes that could only have been seen as conducive to Meimona's happiness and irrelevant to the interests of a father-in-law, as perceived by Abdullah. The absence of a mother-in-law was clearly to the young wife's advantage, as was the (reportedly) harmonious relationship between the co-residing brothers.

If it is also true, as Meimona's mother claimed, that "Mubarak goes nowhere but to his work and home," I think Meimona is likely to count herself fortunate indeed. Provided she has *not* fallen in love with her mother's brother's son, the evidence so far indicates that she has much to be happy about.

As to the benefits that Abdullah might derive, the affinal connection, though it entailed no alliance, confers a certain prestige. A son-in-law from a well-to-do family confers esteem. It is even possible that with sanctions on disclosing the bride price size, the impact of a suitor's family renown increases. His home, if distant, was within reach: Abdullah had many acquaintances in the area and could always feel that he had the opportunity of paying his daughter a visit in connection with some other errand (though actually he is likely to refrain so as not to impose himself). The difference between his and his wife's situation in regard to visiting was cogently brought home to me one day when she felt especially frustrated and wearily confronted him: "It doesn't matter to *you* if Meimona lives far away, for you can always go there by taxi to see her! But we, her mother and sisters, we suffer. For we must remain where we are seated [*ihna qaᶜdin*]."

On a similar occasion, after the family had waited fruitlessly for hours for an expected visit from Meimona, the usually compliant woman let out a poorly disguised accusation, "That's what we get for marrying her to a stranger" (see Ch. 12).

Our evidence suggests that Abdullah came to regret his failure to marry Meimona to a nearby groom as much as his wife did. But when, at the time of decision, he had other preferences, the following considerations seem to have weighed on his mind. First, as is characteristic of Sohari men, Abdullah held an ingrained conviction that "Strangers respect you more." An orphan in early life, Abdullah had been cheated of his inheritance by more powerful relatives, and so he is cynical of the value of kinship, feeling that it creates complications rather than security. He may have resisted the further kinship involvement that a marriage would imply. Second, a higher bride price may legitimately be demanded from a stranger, and Abdullah is, like so many men in today's Oman, a small and ambitious entrepreneur with more plans and projects than he can ever hope to finance. He could hardly have resisted this chance to acquire major capital. I would assume that the suitor's material wealth, with its effect on the size of the bride price, was the most important factor in his decision. In this, Abdullah is a telling example of Sohari guardians.

THE INSTITUTION OF THE BRIDE PRICE

Generally speaking, the decisive factor in whether a marriage will take place is if a bride price can be negotiated that is agreeable to both parties. The constitution of the two parties varies. The bride's guardian and the groom are always included; the bride's mother may have more or less say in the matter, as may the groom's parents or other close relatives, if he is economically dependent. Or, if the groom himself supports kinsmen (for example, a single mother or sister), they may put pressure upon him to keep the bride price low.

The bride price (*mahr*) is divided into two parts: the *hader* (present) and the *ghayeb* (absent). The *hader* is paid before the wedding, whereas the *ghayeb* is held in reserve in case of death or divorce.

Because the *hader* constitutes the major fraction of the bride price, commonly as much as 75–100 percent, it is referred to by women as *the* bride price; they speak of it as *il mahr*. One reason may be that it is often the only part that is handed over. It is given to the guardian a few weeks prior to the marriage, as proof of the groom's intent, and also to cover the major expenditure of the bride's gold jewelry. The jewelry is bought from either Muscat or Dubai by the guardian in person. In rare instances, he may be assisted in his selection by an elder female relative.

The *hader* is paid in full in money, to the guardian in person. Although there is an entrenched ideal that the father should hand most of it over to the bride in the form of gold jewelry, there are no sanctions for the father who appropriates most of it for himself. The money is considered compensation for his expenses in raising the girl, and payment for his relinquishing certain rights; for example, on her labor. However, only when her father serves as guardian is such a retention appropriate. Another male, acting as guardian in the father's stead, should hand all of the money over to the bride, though I was told that practice frequently deviates from the ideal. I also was told that a woman who marries for the second time will claim the whole bride price for herself, saying to her guardian, "You have already once eaten it. Now it is my turn."

Generally speaking, Sohari fathers seem to pocket 50-75 percent of the *hader*. The remainder goes to cover a variety of expenses, not only the bridal jewelry but also one dress for each of the bride's closest relatives, as well as a token bride price for her brothers and father's brother's sons. Justification for the latter practice is that these cousins must be compensated for relinquishing their right to marry her. However, when we pointed out to Ali, one of our male informants, that also "compensated" are her brothers, who have no such right, he reflected a moment, then concluded that the practice is wrong, a popular misconception.

The monetary shares given to these diverse agnates may amount to considerable sums; it is common for brothers to receive 50-100 Rials each, whereas cousins receive 25-50 Rials each, depending upon their age and the size of the bride price. A small boy receives less than a grown one. The father may, however, legitimately appropriate the money that is nominally given to his dependant sons.

The *ghayeb* is a kind of insurance that the husband must pay in case he initiates divorce. However, if the woman takes the initiative to end the marriage, she must return the *hader* to him; consequently, the larger the size of the *hader*, the easier for a husband to initiate divorce, the more difficult for a wife. With a larger *ghayeb*, the case is reversed.

The *ghayeb* also serves as a kind of death insurance. In case of the husband's death, it should be paid from his estate, or by his heirs. The size of the *ghayeb* is written on a piece of paper, which is handed to the bride on the day she leaves her father's house to move in with her husband. Men say that the bride will not leave until she receives this promissory note. But one would think that if this were true, women would show more interest in the amount. No married woman I spoke to had the faintest idea of the size of her *ghayeb*. The *mahr*, as they saw it, was synonymous with the *hader*.

In addition to the *hader* part of the *mahr*, the groom before the wedding must also provide a *mashtara* (which may be roughly translated as "furnishings"). This includes the bride's wardrobe—for years ahead—and home furnishings; it is specified in detail by the bride's mother. Certain basics are always requested: a closet and a chest in which the girl can store

her possessions; a double bed with mattress, pillows, and cover; kitchen-
ware; cosmetics. Clothes are specified to the minutest detail as to their
number, quality of material (silk, cotton, wool), and design of material
(flowered, plain, checked). Demands for thirty to fifty outfits are commonly granted. The *mashtara* consequently amounts to a considerable
sum, typically 100–200 Rials, or the equivalent of one third to two thirds
of the legal *mahr*. Indeed, its chief function since 1971 seems to be to serve
as a licit way of evading the bride-price ceiling. The concepts of *mahr* and
mashtara seem to be acquiring new meanings, at least in the minds of
women, whereby the *mahr* comes to mean, literally, 300 Rials, or the *legal*
size of the bride price, and the *mashtara* to refer to any amount paid in excess of this. Thus one mother, when I asked her, told me that her
daughter's *mahr* had been 300 Rials, but the *mashtara* was 800 Rials!

What Meimona's *mahr* and *mashtara* were, I do not know. Her
jewelry, which was described to me in detail, must have cost 700–800
Rials, and the total sum paid for her (judging from the sums paid for girls
of similar status with whom I was more familiar) could have been
1,500–2,000 Rials. It would have been impertinent for me to ask her
parents about the sum. I did, however, ask my closest friend, Latifa,
whom I expected to know, for her cousin is married to the brother of
Mubarak, Meimona's husband. Her answer brought home to me the profundity of Sohari tact and restraint: "I do not know," Latifa said.
"Sheikha [the cousin] would have told me had I asked her. But I did not
ask her."

Although Abdullah might have expected to make a sizable profit on his
daughter's marriage, he probably gained only half the expected amount.
This is because, in the Wali's words, "When a man marries, he gets his
bride on certain conditions [ʿala shurut]. If they prove not to be true,
he has the right to retrieve half of the price." The "conditions" is the
bride's virginity. Why it is so highly prized, and what reciprocal conditions are presumed in a groom, are questions we will address in the next
chapter.

How are we to interpret the practice of fathers pocketing most of the
bride price, which, in popular conception, should become the property of
the bride herself, to give her joy and a sense of security and esteem? The
Baluch, fellow citizens of the Arabs, regard it an utterly selfish act. When
they want to extol their own culture, they allege that a higher regard for
Baluchi women is evidenced in different bride price customs (as in a variety of other behaviors; see Ch. 3). A Baluch father obtains no personal
benefits from the bride price: the groom gives it all to the bride, in the
form of jewelry. It is a father's duty to check that this jewelry is of acceptable quality and value; therefore, the groom must present the jewelry for
inspection some days prior to the marriage. However, every bit of it becomes the bride's personal property.

Baluchis see no connection (or at least they do not express it) between this difference in bride-price customs and another conspicuous difference: among the Baluch, the bride remains resident with her parents—it is the groom who must move—whereas among the Arabs it is the other way around. I should think, however, that the two are connected: Baluchi parents do not "lose" a daughter. She continues to be a member of their (extended) household—a source of joy and labor. Her husband acquires the exclusive right to her sexuality and fertility, for which he expresses his gratitude through the jewelry he gives her. But Arab parents come close to "losing" their daughter; from the moment she marries, they have no more rights in her. *She* has the right to visit them. But *they* cannot demand that she do so, and she is highly dependent on her husband's good will for the exercise of her lawful right. Her father may indeed feel that a "compensation" to her family is called for.

However, by this mode of comparison, we confuse—as the Baluch seem to do—two separate and distinct levels of behavior. The fact that Arabs have a *custom* whereby the groom pays a bride price to the bride's father, who may dispose of it at will, does not imply that the majority of Arab fathers must choose (as they actually do) to appropriate most of it for themselves. Baluchis seem to regard the latter an automatic consequence of the former. And maybe it is—but in a very different sense from what they imply. Maybe the practice is an unavoidable consequence in a society where business acumen is so pervasively and acutely developed as in Oman?

If the Baluch had a custom as the Arabs have, would Baluchi fathers also become more "selfish"? This hypothetical question is not to be understood as an apologia for Arab fathers, who, we should also remember, differ greatly among themselves in how they dispose of the bride price. Instead, my point is that if we seek to understand behavior, rather than to pass judgment, then a close examination of the contraints and incentives under which people act cannot be dispensed with.

I contend that, among Sohari Arabs, these customs tend to have the consequence of serving to divert the guardian's attention away from the bride's point of view or best interest, through a seductive appeal to his own interests. When Sohari Arab marriages are usually as harmonious as they are, I believe this is due less to the guardians' foresight than to the impressive skills that Sohari women themselves bring to bear in coping with marriage and making it work for them (see Ch. 14).

THE PREFERRED WIFE FROM THE MALE POINT OF VIEW

We have examined some of the qualities that girls find most desirable in grooms. We shall now pay attention to the preferences of the male, and explore his image of the sort of wife he prefers. His ideals will constitute standards for measuring wifely behavior and thus significantly affect married life.

Courtesy and graciousness are the chief considerations. They inform the quality of absolute loyalty, which is the essence of wifely love. A wife should defer to her husband and elders and act tactfully toward all. She should be quiet and compliant. Beauty is desired, and a light complexion is highly esteemed. Negroid features, even in light-complexioned girls, constitute drawbacks. Literacy is desired; education is believed to foster intelligence and moral behavior.

Men seem to harbor another strong preference, which is only partly conveyed by the saying, "Strangers respect you more." The bride should come from afar. Like Meimona's husband, Mubarak, most men do not seek out the girl next-door or the girl from their own district or village; they search in remote places. The consequences of such a practice are clear: the wife is cut off from easy access to her kin, and her dependence upon her husband is enhanced. But the consequences of an act may differ from its motives. What could they be in this case?

Courtesy is perhaps the most cherished ornament of the male. This valued style of self-presentation presupposes personal restraint and is facilitated by autonomy and lack of involvement with others. Much of the male's behavior can best be understood as his effort to actualize this honorable style. This would naturally be taken into account in his choice of wife. Fetching her from afar minimizes the dangers of discord with in-laws—dangers so easily bred in close associations. Indeed, the Sohari saying, "Strangers respect you more," seems essentially an inversion of "Familiarity breeds contempt." Or, put another way: it seems an appreciation of controlling or attempting to control the familiarity of one's audience. It also enhances the wife's dependence upon him, thus strengthening the marital bond. And it facilitates that process of wifely education and discipline which males value highly, and females placidly accept.

STRANGER-MARRIAGE VERSUS COUSIN-MARRIAGE

In theory Sohari males embrace the view that it is desirable to marry cousins, in practice they tend to avoid them. Having explored the factors affecting the groom's choice of bride, and the guardian's choice of son-in-law, we should now be in a position to understand why a prevalence of stranger-marriage is generated in a culture in which cousin-marriage is the explicit ideal. Protagonists of the Sohari way, the men feel obligated to advocate the ideal of agnatic and tribal loyalties. But they maximize the values of autonomy and tact. Thus the two main parties, groom and guardian, share an interest in steering clear of that further kinship involvement which a cousin-marriage entails. Yet there are many exceptions, creating a certain frequency of marriages between close kin (approximately 30 percent). Some men have stronger kinship commitments; others desire a cousin-wife for financial reasons; yet others marry a cousin because they love her, and a father may feel his daughter is best cared for by a cousin.

As one may expect, because women abide by somewhat different standards and priorities, they also tend to take a different view of cousin-marriage versus stranger-marriage. Less committed to the cultural order, women do not affirm the ideal of cousin-marriage. Their view of marriage, as of everything else, is pervaded by a remarkable emphasis upon the singularity of each case. They say that marital happiness ultimately depends upon the particular personalities of the spouses. What they have in mind, however, is not that kind of tenuous personal compatibility which we seek and value. Rather, they seem to urge the necessity of judging each particular suitor on his own merits, irrespective of whether he is a relative or a stranger, and denying the preeminence of his material status.

Women of all ages make this argument. But in their actual preferences, brides-to-be and their mothers are more often apart than together. Young girls often resent marrying a cousin. They appear to conceive of strangers as more exciting and worthy of respect, more likely to trigger that unique response of wifely love and devotion. Of course, it may happen that cousins fall in love and want to marry. However, a cousin generally seems a far too ordinary person for the exalted position of husband. He has the qualities of ordinary mortals; some may even be distasteful. The crucial point is, I think, that a girl has interacted with a cousin *before* the marriage and developed a set of specific attitudes toward him. These must necessarily color her role as a wife. She is not, and will never be, only his wife, for their relationship as cousins will continue to affect their marital roles. But a girl who marries a stranger obtains a complete husband, so to speak. She has no expectations of him other than that she should love and honor him.

So it is that brides-to-be resemble guardians in their predilection for strangers, parting ways with their own mothers. What is it in the mothers' situation that predisposes them to take a different view of comparative benefits and drawbacks?

THE PREFERENCES AND INFLUENCE OF MOTHERS

A conspicuous feature of the mother's situation is her immobility, or "seatedness," as Rahmeh termed it. This is due to the combined effects of seclusion, a severe climate, and the expense of taxi fares. Another important feature is a suspicion on her part that the motherly love she so strongly feels is less fully reciprocated. She cannot count on the daughter to go to the trouble of visiting her. So the single most desired quality in a son-in-law comes to be that she herself should be a welcome visitor into his home, so that she may continue to nurture the relationship with her daughter. If the son-in-law is a kinsman from the same neighborhood, it is likely to further that end. This is because the affinal tie itself confers no privileged access, but only a mute understanding to keep out of one another's way. Only when the son-in-law is also a close relative does the mother gain easy access to her daughter's home. One might think that because the men are away for most of the day, the mother could easily visit a daughter married to a stranger. In fact she stands little chance—for strangers prefer to fetch their brides from afar. Only relatives occasionally present themselves as suitors from within the same neighborhood. The reason may either be that as close kinsmen they have had a privileged opportunity to see the girl and become attracted to her, or their main concern may be the advantages of a reduced bride price over those of autonomy.

The preferences of the groom's mother are more difficult to evaluate. She seems torn between two opposing wishes: to have a daughter-in-law who is modest, graceful, and a dutiful worker, in which case a stranger is likely to be appealing; or to have one who provides pleasant companionship, in which case a relative would be better. A relative is also preferable from the point of view of the bride price; the bride's father can hardly demand a fortune. I am inclined to think that the latter two considerations prevail, so that the groom's mother usually shares the bride's mother's predilection for a relative.

The effect of the mothers' efforts to enhance their own life quality is to make them appear advocates of cousin-marriage. However, this preference (which is nothing more than a tendency) does not reflect a closer adherence on their part to the cultural *ideal* of cousin-marriage. On the contrary, it is a by-product of their striving to secure *other* goals within a life situation that is so patterned that cousin-marriage seems to them the means most likely to bring about such a desired end.

Part of a mother's earnest desire may be to secure her daughter's happiness, for which she may also regard cousin-marriage as the better course. Meimona's mother is one case in point. It may seem strange that she should favor a son-in-law whom she regarded as irresponsible and given to gambling and drunkenness. But the reason may be that she herself had experienced a long and happy marriage to a cousin, as had three of her sisters. The fourth sister, who had married a stranger, had not been so fortunate, and because this was the only stranger-marriage with which Rahmeh was closely familiar—it being below a woman's dignity to reveal marital secrets to outsiders—she may have sincerely believed that cousin-marriage was the better fate, irrespective of the particular cousin's attributes. She may also have felt that by being nearby she could contribute to her daughter's happiness. Where deference to elders is as deep-seated as it is in Oman, and the attitude that age brings wisdom is so deeply ingrained, mothers can hardly escape the conviction that they know better than their daughters what is best for them. In one case with which I am familiar, a young girl's fate was sealed by her mother's absolute preference for a cousin-marriage. Feyza's father was dead, and her mother was convinced that Feyza should marry her brother's son, strengthening in the process the foundation on which most of the mother's own security depended. The second and less favored wife of a man whom she adored, Feyza's mother was constantly at odds with her co-wife and needed her brother's support. Feyza resented the cousin in question very much, because he is "very weak," but she was also fearful of the displeasure of her mother and uncle—"that the world would be all hard feelings." She was destined for unhappiness either way and chose the most graceful alternative—of submitting to her mother. Two years later she had resigned herself to her fate, not through dull listlessness, but by an active (impressive) effort to make the best of it. The reason for this change of heart was obvious to her friends: Feyza had developed the only sentiment that befits a wife—*hubb* (love).

MEIMONA'S REACTIONS AFTER THE EVENT

So it was with Meimona: whatever feelings she may originally have had toward her husband, she radiated loyalty and devotion when, accompanied by her husband, she paid her parents a visit some three months after the marriage. We were present and were forcefully impressed with her manner and poise. The event is presented in detail in Chapter 12. Suffice it here to note that her solidarity with her husband was so manifest as to cause a suppressed sigh from her mother once they were gone: "You see how life is; when a daughter marries, she transfers *all* of her affections to her husband. That is not right. There should be one part for him, and one for the parents."

CHAPTER 11

✦

The Bride Should Be a Virgin, the Groom Should Be a Man

"And he said to me. . . . 'You are not my wife for tonight only. We have a whole life ahead of us!' "

Marriage, as we have seen, is an occasion for major celebrations. But the groom's and the bride's families conduct their festivities separately, and the groom's part of the wedding is much more substantial, lasting for three days, whereas the bride's part is limited to one or two days. It is the groom who pays for both.

The dramatic first encounter of the newlyweds takes place at midnight, when they are brought together in the honeymoon hut. The bride is said to be so overcome with embarrassment and fear that she desperately clutches her green veil, and only rarely do the couple see each other at all. The *mikobra* (bridal attendant) places the bride's right foot on top of the groom's, and underneath both she puts an egg, which they break to promote fertility. Then they are served a light meal, but it is the groom alone who eats. The bride is too ashamed to partake. Thereupon the groom should pray, ideally on his bride's green shawl. But she hangs on to it so forcefully to conceal herself that he generally must content himself with only a trifling corner of it. Thereafter, the marriage should be consummated, and crucial proofs procured of the bride's honor, as well as that of the groom.

The wedding celebrations, and the particular reactions of individual grooms and brides and those close to them, tell a great deal about the meaning of marriage and about crucial features of gender roles. In Chapter 2, I gave an external view of the groom's part of the public proceedings. In the present chapter, I shall concentrate first on the bride's part, and on a more personal view of events and their significance for participants. These provide a basis for grasping those aspects most revealing of gender roles, important to the future life of the bride and groom, both in their mutual relations and toward society at large.

The sequence of wedding events for the bride and her relatives is as follows:

1. about one week of preparation immediately preceding the marriage
2. one or two days of festivities
3. the departure of the bride to the groom's home
4. the entry into the honeymoon hut and the union with the groom
5. a visit by her closest female relatives and friends (excluding her mother) three days later
6. a visit by the bride, the groom, her in-laws, and closest new neighbors to her parents' home seven days after the marriage.

I shall describe these events as they unfolded in the case of one particular bride, Mariam, on the occasion of her marriage to an unrelated man living some ten miles away from her natal home. Then I shall address the questions of what is at stake for the bride and the groom on their wedding night, how the proofs of their respective honors are established, and what the consequences are of a failure to fulfill these requirements of honor.

THE WEDDING OF MARIAM

Mariam was the first bride whose wedding I attended, and she has come to personify to me what otherwise easily becomes a lifeless abstraction of "the bride." One afternoon, as I was walking along the beach, three of my best friends, Latifa, Feyza, and Khadiga, called me into a nearby house. Here wedding preparations were in full swing, and a score of women—my friends included—and children were busy lending a helping hand. My friends turned out to be close paternal relatives of the prospective bride; others present were her neighbors. But none of the bride's maternal kin were present. On this, the third last day before the wedding, my friends were making clothes for the bride and proudly displayed five finished outfits. Mariam was to have twelve in all, they told me. Knowing that thirty is common, and that both Latifa and Feyza had received fifty each, I reasoned that either Mariam's groom must be quite poor, or her father must be particularly greedy, leaving Mariam only a small fraction of the bride price.

She was a sparkling young girl with proud composure, golden-brown skin, large expressive eyes, and the most snow-white teeth I ever remember seeing. Beautiful indeed, by my conceptions. But by Sohari standards, she fell short. This was made clear to me the day after the wedding, when Latifa and Khadiga were eager to know whether I had found the groom handsome. *"Nuss-nuss* [so-so]," I said. And they nodded affirmingly, "Yes, for he is *asmar* [brown-skinned]!" "But so is Mariam!" observed Latifa. I wondered how Khadiga must have reacted to Latifa's verdict, for she herself is of even darker complexion.

To return to the prewedding activities: I was impressed with the dignity and grace with which Mariam moved amid this excited turmoil of women and children. Although hardly more than thirteen years old, and the cause and natural center of all the excitement, she nevertheless made strenuous efforts to give an unaffected and calm impression, and she succeeded admirably. However, now and again I thought I could sense her excitement and anticipation breaking out from behind her graceful composure.

Her father was also present, in expectation of an imminent visit from the groom. He had sought refuge inside the house with his brother Hamid (Latifa's and Feyza's father's brother and Khadiga's husband). Hamid was the one the groom first contacted in the matter of the marriage, rather than the bride's father, in keeping with Sohari conventions. Today they were to decide on the exact time for the signing of the marriage contract, where the bride herself would not be present.

Seven of the women were making *yas*, a yellow paste that is used to decorate the bride's forehead and the part in her hair. They were merry and frivolous, amusing themselves and others with pantomimes of what the groom does with the bride on the wedding night. Mariam gave no sign of being the least bit affected by their antics. Latifa and Feyza commented that they did not wear *yas* as brides, for it soils the clothes when one perspires and makes one very dirty. Mariam also did not wish to wear it, but the groom's family insisted that she should. "You see, they come from a *village*," Latifa and Feyza explained derogatorily.

All they knew about the groom was his name, Khalfan, that he was five years or so older than Mariam, and that he lived "among the Bedu." When I asked Mariam about him, she said that she did not know any more either, but she avoided the pejorative reference to the Bedu. About his looks, she said she knew nothing, but her cousins explained that she has nothing to fear, "for her male kinsmen have seen him and they know how to judge." This seems cold comfort; Khadiga, for one, knows how much male kinsmen can be trusted in such matters. She had given me a vivid account of the shocking revelation that her own husband's looks were: "They had told me he was old, but not that he was stone old! I was so disappointed and so terrified." Maybe the statement expresses the efforts of girls to adjust emotionally to what they experience as an unresolvable dilemma by seeking consolation in the male ideology, for in the next breath, they added: "Besides, it would do the bride no good to see her future husband's face, for she could not show dissatisfaction in any case. If she did, her father would punish her by letting her remain unmarried." It is revealing that a failure to marry is conceived of as the most deplorable outcome of all, to be avoided at all costs for a female.

After a short while, the drone of an approaching motor could be heard, and the children started shouting, "Here comes the groom, the groom is coming!" while the women excitedly hustled Mariam into the house and crowded along the inside of the compound wall to peek and eavesdrop. A date-palm wall is so constructed that if one puts one's eye to the cracks it is possible to watch without being observed. The groom and his companions sat down in the sand outside the wall, with Mariam's father and uncle. After a meeting of hardly five minutes, the groom left again, and Mariam was let out of her sanctuary—a superfluous precaution, for the groom stood no chance of glimpsing her through the fence. Perhaps the real intent was to prevent *her* from seeing *him*?

Encouraged by my friends, Mariam's father offered to show me the bridal jewelry. It comprised all the customary items—necklace, bracelets, rings, a forehead decoration, *burqa* rings, and a watch—all of medium quality. He also showed me, without being prompted to do so, a bill for 268 Rials from a jeweler's shop in Dubai. All the items were specified, except the watch and the *burqa* rings, which were bought from a different shop. "As you can see," he said proudly, "I have bought gold for a total of 300 Rials." His brother Hamid later told me that the bride price (that is, the *hader*) excluding the *mashtara*, amounted to 800 Rials. His own two sons, aged two and four, had received 25 Rials each, whereas Latifa and Feyza's two brothers, because they were older, received 50 Rials each. The sons of a third brother, with whom they were not on speaking terms, received nothing. Mariam's father thus seems to have made a sizable (but, by Sohari measures, not unreasonable) gain from his daughter's marriage.

The bride's new wardrobe was kept in a very large cupboard that stood in the yard, itself a part of the *mashtara* and worth 50 Rials. The doors contained two large mirrors, each protected by a sheet so that they would not be damaged. The cupboard also contained two *burqa*s, one with golden rings for formal wear, and a plain one for everyday use. Mariam became bashful when I asked if she looked forward to assuming the *burqa*—a meaningless question to her, I presume, as no respectable woman goes without it. She merely nodded affirmingly.

It was evident that Mariam was thrilled on the occasion. Her face glowed at the sight of the jewelry, and she comported herself with the unassuming self-awareness of a queen. From time to time she inspected the dressmaking efforts of her friends, and the cupboard's contents, but she herself took no part in the sewing. On the feelings of "the bride," my friends explained: "She is happy every day of the preparations, and likewise on the wedding day, up until the moment when the groom comes to fetch her. Then she cries. And during that night with the groom in the honeymoon hut she is terrified. But the following day she is happy again. For then she loves him."

Love and life in Sohar are hardly so simple, however. My friends seem to be giving the ideal as the real, though they had often expressed their awareness of the gap between the two. It is the culturally expected, right course of events that they depict. Feyza, for one, did not love her husband when she awoke after her wedding night. Mariam, as we shall see, did not cry when she was fetched by the groom. But others, Latifa among them, have experienced the true-to-life quality of these expectations. Entrenched ideals, the proper and the honorable, may have a self-fulfilling character. It is therefore significant that Soharis have an ideology that love is *created* through consummation of marriage.

The day before the wedding celebration, the marriage contract was signed by the groom and the bride's father at the *qadi*'s (judge's) office in the fortress. From this moment on, Mariam followed the Sohari tradition of carrying a silver knife in her hand at all times—to fend off *jinn*, my friends explained. *Jinn* are envious, supernatural beings which Soharis greatly fear. Mariam played and fussed with the knife, making drawings in the sand, swinging it distractedly in the air; and she seemed to appreciate this highly tangible symbol of her own importance and propitiousness.

Around sunset—six o'clock—of the evening preceding the wedding day, the main celebrations started. A group of six singers—five women and one *xanith*—provided the entertainment. There were no musicians, ostensibly because Mariam's father did not wish to have any for moral or religious reasons, but actually because of the expense. As the singers approached, Mariam was again hustled into the house. A bride is not allowed to take part in her own wedding festivities, but must stay indoors until they have come to an end and the groom presents himself to take her away. On this afternoon, Mariam had embellished herself with some massive silvery anklets, borrowed from a neighbor. Not many women own these nowadays, because silver has become outmoded. But according to time-honored tradition, silver offers the best protection against *jinn*, and, because a bride is particularly vulnerable to their attacks, she borrows the anklets in return for a small payment.

Secluded in her place of refuge, Mariam was kept company by the children. Her role-playing those days was striking: she vacillated between attempts to look indifferent and blasé, and clear expressions of anticipation and delight.

The female guests constantly tried to tease her, and amuse themselves, with pornographic stories and mimicry. Mariam remained unmoved, however, even by lengthy dramatizations of the agony and panic the bride undergoes when, on the wedding night, she is locked in the *kille* (honeymoon hut) by the groom from the inside and the *mikobra* from the outside. Intercourse, the women averred, is the most terrifying experience imaginable. They mimicked how the panic-stricken bride fights desperately with the groom to prevent him from removing her veil, and how she breaks out in fever and rash from pure fright when the exasperated groom finally carries her fully veiled and clothed, but with her trousers all torn, to the marriage bed. For additional effect, the storytellers interspersed an occasional "Remember Aisha!" or "Fatima—she came out even worse."

Mariam surely remembered them. She must have recognized that the pantomimes, though theatrical in form, had a real life experience as their reference. But she also knows that the ordeal of the wedding night is an integral part of every female's life. It is indeed the way, and the only way, that a girl becomes a woman.

The *kille* had in the meantime been prepared at the groom's home. It is built by the groom's male friends out of palm fronds (*barasti*), consists of one room (rarely more than two meters by four meters), and is richly decorated by his female kin. Here the bride and groom spend seven days, in solitude, with no chores; they are waited upon and have their clothes washed by the *mikobra*. The first week of marriage is indeed thought of as a honeymoon, when the newlyweds should devote their full attention to each other. When the honeymoon is past, the *kille* is torn down.

On the afternoon before the wedding day, Mariam's father suddenly vanished from the scene. It did not take me by surprise, as I had already learned that the bride's father becomes increasingly shy and embarrassed as the time approaches for his daughter to be fetched by the groom. Thus, he usually chooses the solution of acting as if he knows nothing about the impending event. Yet I feigned surprise and asked my friends where he had gone. They excused him, saying he had had to go on urgent business to Muscat and would be away for three days. On a Thursday night (the night before the Muslim holiday), I thought, that would have been a very strange coincidence! It is revealing that my friends chose to pretend that the bride's father absents himself on account of his work. Sohari accommodations to this unspoken dilemma are reminiscent of reactions reported from some other Middle Eastern societies.[1]

In Sohar, according to our informants, the absence of the bride's father can extend from three days to one week, depending upon the acuteness of his embarrassment. But when the bride and groom, accompanied by relatives and neighbors (at least five carloads full), pay her parents a ceremonial visit on the seventh day after the marriage, her father is present again "and feels shy no more."

On the wedding day, I came to Mariam's home around 10 A.M. She was lying outstretched on her back inside a *barasti* hut while her cousin Latifa decorated her with *hennah*—a red, propitious color. This was the sixth time in four days that the bride was thus decorated. Her face was completely covered with the green shawl, otherwise she wore everyday clothes. Surrounding her were a number of little girls, similarly outstretched. Incense burned. Latifa was busily painting the hands and feet of the bride

---

[1] For example, the Bedouin of Cyrenaica (Peters 1965) and the Pathans of Swat in Pakistan (Barth 1971), with the essential difference that among the Bedouin it is the groom's father who acts as if he knows nothing about the wedding; among the Pathans, it is the groom himself.

and the small girls with patterns of flowers, trees, rings, and stars, according to their individual preferences. Older girls threw sweets over the bride's head, and smaller ones shrieked and scrambled to grab them. The occasion is evidently joyous for the little ones. Around 11 A.M., the singing began and neighbors assembled to take part in the celebration. Everyone was dressed in their best finery, except for the bride and her mother. The mother wore clothes that were exceptionally ugly and conspicuously worn. My friends explained that it would be shameful for her to dress up, "for she is unhappy to lose her daughter's assistance in housework."

At this time, the bride's maternal grandmother and aunt arrived from their village, which was fifty kilometers south of Sohar. Although mother and daughter, grandmother and granddaughter, had not seen each other for the past year, their greeting was a perfunctory handshake. Had I not known better, I would have taken them to be complete strangers.

After half an hour's entertainment, the guests were served spiced porridge with melted butter and then a sweet—*halwa*. There was more entertainment until 12:30 P.M. when lunch was served. In her secluded hut, Mariam spent the whole time seated on a new plastic mat—green for good fortune. She was kept company by the children and occasionally an adult. She acted completely calm and unaffected by the seriousness of the occasion. As the hours passed and the time approached when the groom would arrive, I waited observantly, expecting her to show signs of increasing nervousness, fear, or anticipation, but I detected none. Mariam persisted in her calm role presentation as if in perfect control of herself and the situation. Around 5 P.M., and only an hour before the groom was expected, her mother bathed her and dressed her in her wedding clothes (which were green from top to toe, but otherwise undistinguished from everyday dress). I was sure that Mariam would be shaken, but her polished composure remained intact. The only trifling sign of emotional excitement, whether from anticipation or nervousness, was her preoccupation with the silver knife, which she played with constantly, as also with the keys to her chest. The chest contained perfume, incense and an incense burner, a pair of sandals, *yas*, *hennah*, and *dihan* (another red color). Her clothes and jewelry had been transported in the large cupboard to the groom's home in the morning, by three of his kinsmen, along with a large red mattress for the *kille*.

As sunset approached, and with it the hour when the groom was expected, the wedding guests became increasingly excited and pornographic. They produced increasingly vivid accounts of the terrors awaiting the bride. Mariam did not bat an eyelid, while the women enjoyed themselves so much they were in stitches. Fatima expanded on how *zen* (good, beautiful) blood is as a sign of honor, but Mariam remained unmoved.

The sun set, and the minutes dragged on and turned to hours, yet there

A bride, shown during the last half hour before the groom comes to fetch her

was no sign of the groom. Not till 9 P.M. did the cars arrive, and we never did learn the reasons for the delay. I, for one, had become quite nervous because of the delay, but not so the bride, at least not noticeably so. Or did she play somewhat more distractedly with the knife? During this last hour, she also got up from time to time to inspect the chest. The *mikobra*—who in this case was her father's sister—had likewise been checking that everything was in order. Shortly before the groom appeared, she put an extra pair of sandals into the chest.

Immediately on hearing the sound of motors, Mariam pulled the green veil over her face. Her younger sister started crying. The wedding guests crowded around Mariam to catch a last glimpse of her. Among them was a *xanith*. Ten cars made up the groom's convoy. The first eight were packed with men, while the women were relegated to the last two. The groom glowed with impatient expectation as he stopped at the gate to wait for his bride and the procession of women. But as Mariam lingered more than he thought necessary, he threatened to go in and fetch her himself and made much fuss. Finally she appeared, an enveloped black bundle, from which her feet and hands protruded. Only her head stood out in contrast, shrouded in the distinctive green of her marriage shawl. I could not hear her cry, and, considering her composure throughout the day, I would have found it "unnatural" if she—at the spur of the moment—burst into tears.

The bride's mother, who was still wearing worn old clothes (although in the afternoon she discarded the dirty ones for a clean outfit), likewise did not cry. But she was evidently concerned to insure that women whom she trusted would escort Mariam on the departing trip, and she dashed about to secure this. The trusted ones—three neighbors—huddled in the back seat of the groom's car with Mariam in their midst. Mariam's paternal cousins and grandmother, and the *mikobra*, followed in another car. No maternal relatives were included, nor the mother herself. A mother may not even visit her daughter's new home until one month after the marriage, when the bride's parents pay their first, and last, ceremonial visit to their son-in-law's family. As previously mentioned, relations between the bride's and the groom's kin are infrequent and optional.

The wedding convoy took an extremely circuitous route to the groom's home. It is important to be observed by a maximum of spectators, as the number of cars is an indicator of status. On arrival the bride and her company were taken into the groom's mother's house, which was strewn with clothes and crockery. Mariam's grandmother asked the groom's female kin if this was the *kille*, to which the blunt reply was, "As if *any kille* looks like this!" It was oppressively hot inside and more than the 100°F outside, and Khadiga and Feyza charitably set about fanning Mariam, who was swathed in her green marriage shawl, as well as the formal *abba* and the usual set of dress, headscarf, and long pantaloons. After awhile the female hosts took pity on her and removed her *abba*, leaving her head and torso wrapped in the shawl. It looked as if she was distracting herself by toying with the knife under the shawl. Otherwise, she showed no sign of unease and certainly did not cry. The *xanith* who had peeped behind Mariam's veil at home was also present with this all-female group.

Those of us who had accompanied the bride were served sweet tea, rice stew with meat, and coffee. The very moment we had finished eating, we got up and departed, honoring Sohari customs by offering no word of farewell. On our way out, we briefly inspected the *kille*, which the women judged to be of poor quality; the jewelry should have been of gold, the cushions should have been the ready-made kind from Dubai, rather than homemade, the mirrors should have been more plentiful, and so forth. "But what can you expect, when the groom lives among the Bedu," was the commentary. When I remarked that I did not see any Bedouin around, my friends explained: "The Bedu are not exactly here, but all around in the vicinity. And, as you can see for yourself, this is the *kind* of place that Bedu prefer—*sih* [desert type], with one house here and one there. It is *not* a *harah* [town quarter]."

Two days later, when I visited Mariam's cousins again, they were bursting with news: Mariam had not yet had intercourse with the groom! (*Ma ᶜarrisit*; literally, not yet gotten married). For she is menstruating! It was the grandmother who sprang the news last night when she returned from the groom's place. (In addition to the *mikobra*, she had stayed behind to lend support and comfort throughout the trial.) On the wedding night, according to my friends, she had slept close by the *kille* and had been awakened by a fearful racket in there. She had rushed to the door and found a moaning groom who insisted on having intercourse with his bride. Grandmother absolutely forbade this; the groom insisted it was absolutely necessary. Grandmother repeated her refusal and threatened to make a scene, and leave the place immediately, and go home to sleep unless he stopped. Only then did he resign himself.

"But the marriage *must* be consummated before the groom must return to work, in three days' time," my friends said, "even if the menses have not come to an end. Otherwise the groom's situation becomes unbearable, for he is burning with desire."

The next day—that is, the third after the wedding—we paid Mariam the customary ritual visit, on the occasion when the bride first steps out of the *kille*. She spontaneously broke down in tears at this reunion with her relatives and friends. The singers also came along to congratulate her. We were served bread, canned pineapple, sweetened rice and coffee, and we were invited to help ourselves freely to the perfume and incense. The groom was also present, but stayed at a distance from the women. Whenever he entered the *kille*, Mariam had to stop whatever else she was doing and follow behind. So did the children, trotting along after them.

Mariam did not eat with her guests, but subsequently and separately from us, along with her female in-laws. Thus the new allegiance, and the severance of old ties, are potently expressed.

Mariam seemed unruffled and content in her new position. She comported herself with grace and confidence; even in the company of her mother-in-law and sister-in-law—who until three days earlier had been complete strangers to her—she betrayed no sign of awkwardness or shyness. Perhaps such a striking absence of disorientation and change reflects the general constraint practiced in all social interaction, even among the closest family members. Had I not known better, I might have thought I was seeing Mariam in her natal home.

(Though if contentment it was, it was of a transient kind. Within six months Mariam—with her husband—had moved back to her childhood home, reportedly because of continual bickering between her and her mother-in-law.)

Two days later (the fifth day after the wedding), an eagerly awaited bloodstained handkerchief (*xalaq*) was brought by the *mikobra* to the bride's mother, along with 30 Rials in cash. Mariam's paternal grandmother and cousins, whose spontaneous reactions to the news I witnessed, drew a sigh of relief and joy: "*Ilhamdlillah* [Praise be to God], she was a virgin." Not that they had suspected anything else, I would think; yet that long wait had been wrought with suspense. An awareness that "many brides turn out not to be virgins," as well as a recent distressing family event—Mariam's father's brother's daughter, Feyza, had brought dishonor to the family by being a *woman* (*horma*)—had taught them to be on their guard.

The 30 Rials given to the mother are referred to as *kalam il ʿaros* (the message of the bride; that is, the sign of the bride's reputation). It is a time-honored custom by which the groom rewards the bride's mother for having maintained the daughter's honor. Because of the mother's continual presence in the home, and also her role in training and raising girls, the men credit her with the main responsibility for the preservation of the daughter's virginity.

THE CONCEPTS OF VIRGIN AND WOMAN

The antithetical concepts of *virgin* and *woman* deserve some attention. The Arabic word for *virgin*—*bint*—is also the standard term for *girl*; another connotation is *unmarried*. These three meanings are ideally inseparable. Because there is no legitimate context for sexual intercourse except marriage, every unmarried female should be a virgin; and because marriage is regarded as the natural and desirable state for all adults, only the immature—girl—should be unmarried. But reality is more complex. A few females never marry. In Sohar, all deaf-mutes are denied the privilege, even when they are considered "very intelligent and understand everything that goes on," for the reason that they cannot communicate and make themselves understood.

In this, we also see an implicit statement of what the relationship between the spouses is thought to be—not so much one of sexual intimacy as one of personal, communicative intimacy. I would presume that the deaf-mute's unlucky fate is shared by persons with other serious physical or mental handicaps, although no other cases were brought to my attention. There is no separate word for a spinster or an old maid; she is spoken of as a *bint*—a "girl." Yet the essential meaning of the word is again revealed when a bride who marries for the first time is discovered to be sexually experienced. The devastating disclosure is all conveyed in one unequivocal utterance: "*Hiyya til ᶜit horma* [She proved to be a woman]."

Woman—*horma*—has connotations both of respectable woman and (sexually experienced) wife. The concept itself has no inherently derogatory meanings. Richard T. Antoun points out that its triliteral root form means "to forbid, and in its other verbal forms, to be forbidden, to be sacred, and to declare inviolable. The word *haram*, of course, refers to the woman's quarters and their occupants. Finally the term *haram* has the meanings sin, dirt, violation, sacred and forbidden by the Sacred Law." Antoun argues that "the clear connotation of all these meanings is that the virtuous woman (*horma*) is one who is protected or fortified or concealed, and in the last set of terms, inviolable and in that sense sacred" (1968, p. 679).

A girl who, unauthorized, acts the woman, breaks fundamental injunctions and becomes dishonored in the act. Her act is *haram*—a violation of the Sacred Law, for which she will be severely punished in the afterlife. To become a woman unsanctioned is to become an anomalous and discredited one.

THE PROOF OF VIRGINITY OR WOMANHOOD

How is the honorable condition of virginity, or its opposite—womanhood—publicly established? In Meimona's case, it was rumored that a young man had been caught in compromising circumstances in her garden and taken to be her potential or actual lover. But his seizure, crucial though it would have been, would not have sufficed to establish anything whatsoever about Meimona's honor—at the time. Islamic law requires four eyewitnesses to the act itself to establish guilt of fornication or adultery. To my knowledge, there is also in Sohar no standard procedure whereby parents who suspect a misdemeanor may have their daughter examined and possibly "mended."[2] Sohari Arab women deny that the hymen may be broken as a result of any kind of honorable accident (although a Baluch father, in his explanation of why the Baluch do not make virginity a public issue, affirmed precisely that). Arab women also disclaim that the hymen may be broken without shedding blood.

Thus the critical test is the bloodstain on the wedding night. A bride who bleeds when she is penetrated is honorable; one who does not is dishonorable. A virgin whose hymen is broken with no trace of blood is unheard of; she is by definition a woman. Yet every bride who does not bleed is not a woman. The symbolic meaning of the blood on the wedding night is, in Sohar at least, much more intricate and comprehensive than any reading of the ethnographic literature of the Middle East would lead one to suspect.

This became clear to me only very slowly and indirectly. One day, on my second visit to Sohar, a young masked woman, whom I did not know, joined our circle of friends. When she had left, I asked who she was. "But don't you recognize her? She is Rowda," came the reply. I protested that Rowda was so young, I would never have expected her to have assumed the *burqa*. To which my friend replied, "Not only has she married since you were here last, she has also been divorced." There was a moment's hesitancy and then an explanation: "For she did not bleed."

Well conversant with the meaning of an absence of blood on the wedding night, I immediately knew what my friend had meant. Poor Rowda, she had lost her honor. And I marveled at the lack of reprobation in my friend's tone of voice. She had put her remark as casually as if its content—heavy with implications—was of no concern to her. And I thought to myself: how telling of Omani grace and tolerance.

Not till much later did I learn that I was guilty of a crucial misunderstanding. There was nothing the matter with Rowda's honor. Marriage notwithstanding, she was still a virgin. That was precisely the problem, and the cause of her divorce. It was the groom who had failed—by being impotent. He had claimed that he was ill, and the bride's family had given him a chance to restitute himself. But not more than five days. When he still did not succeed within such a period of grace, they demanded their daughter back and returned the bride price.

---

[2] In some other places in the Middle East, suspecting mothers may take their daughter to a doctor on the pretext that she has fallen down a staircase; if the hymen is found to be ruptured, a simple skin transplant suffices to undo the damage. El Saadawi observes: "The murky fate which awaits a girl who loses her virginity often forces her to find some way out of the dilemma. The daughter of a rich family can go to a gynaecologist and pay a large sum of money to undergo a plastic repairal of the hymen. Whereas a poor village girl will depend on the subterfuges of the *daya*, which include fixing the date of marriage at the time of menstruation or placing a small bag full of chicken's blood at the opening of the vagina to ensure a red flow at the time of defloration" (1980, p. 30).

My friend must have thought she had made the cause of the divorce perfectly clear to me when she used that loaded phrase "For she did not bleed." I on my part associated the concept "blood" when juxtaposed with marriage, only with the bride's honor. Not till the misunderstanding had been clarified did I reflect that my friend's phrase had not even been ambiguous, but fully unequivocal in its meaning. If the reference had béen to Rowda's honor, the only natural expression would have been "For she was a *woman*."

This incident is a telling example of how expectations may color interpretations and give rise to serious misunderstandings cross-culturally—as, indeed, within cultures. In all my reading on the Arab Middle East, the notion had never struck me that the wedding night may be an agonizing experience for the *groom*. The ethnographic literature, although rich in descriptions of weddings, usually focuses exclusively on the condition of the bride. She alone, we are to believe, undergoes fear and suffering and faces the threat of dishonorable disclosure. Sohari women, however, stress that the groom's fate is the more precarious.

It was made quite explicit to me in the conversation that also served to clarify the misunderstanding mentioned above. Intrigued with the not infrequent occurrence of nonvirginal brides, I had occasionally pursued the topic with my best friends in an effort to understand the consequences that ensue from a dishonorable disclosure. Then one day, when we were pondering the fact that, among Arabs, "the groom *must* make a scandal" and will never keep the bride's dishonor a private secret, like the Baluch do, Khadiga impatiently reproached me: "You talk as if it were only the groom who makes demands about the bride's sexual condition. I can tell you that the bride's family is equally exacting of him." There was a moment's pause, and she continued: "You remember that girl Rowda? Didn't you understand *why* she did not bleed? Because the groom could not penetrate!"

This crucial divulgence having been made, other cases were recounted. My friends soon convinced me that impotence occurs with such frequency as to make the wedding night a real trial for many a groom: "Five days, imagine: five days, was all they gave him!" One eighteen-year-old woman said she was certain it must have been better in the old days—that the bride's family was more compassionate and more patient then. Nowadays, one week is the normal period of grace, she said. And some, like Rowda's groom, got even less. My friends apparently did not feel that a week's honeymoon, with no chores or obligations other than to consummate his marriage, gave the groom reasonable chance to prove himself, or that the bride's family were justified in thinking so. Their explicit criticism was exclusively directed toward the bride's family, in a manner so emphatic that I feel convinced it was their true feelings that they expressed. They claimed to know several unfortunate grooms who had failed the potency test, yet—in more congenial circumstances—remarried and fathered children. Twenty days, they said, was the maximum they had ever heard having been granted an "ailing" groom, and then only because he was a close relative of the bride. Yet the issue's crucial significance and their own ambivalent feelings on the issue are reflected in the fact that the woman who was most vocal in criticizing other families' lack of compassion gave a vivid description of the tormenting suspense at the marriage of her husband's brother's daughter, Latifa:

"Four endless days dragged on, with no sign or word from the groom. And we," she nodded teasingly to Latifa, "started to fear that maybe you were a woman. So I cannot describe our joy when the fourth day appeared with the *xalaq* [bloodstained handkerchief] and the *kalam*."

Latifa rushed to her husband's defense: "But how *could* Nasr have managed before? He was ill on the wedding night, with a fever and rashes. And he said to me: 'There is no hurry. You are not my wife for tonight only. We have a whole life ahead of us!'"

THE DISCLOSURE AND CONSEQUENCES OF IMPOTENCE

Thus a wedding tests the qualities of the groom as well as the bride. The marriage is privately consummated; how then is a case of impotence established? By the effective requirement that the groom must provide proof the next morning of his potency in one of two ways: either by the bloodstained handkerchief, which also serves as proof of the bride's honor, or by raising a public outcry and launching a complaint to the bride's father and perhaps also to the Wali, because the bride was a woman and he has been deceived. In the absence of either action, his impotence is revealed by default.

The possibility of an impotent groom concealing his failure by accusing his bride of being sexually experienced was never mentioned by anyone. Considering the women's delight in talking about sexual matters, I feel quite convinced that had this been a possibility, they would surely have mentioned it.

Women's compassion for a nervously incapacitated groom indicates the fact that he stands to lose much more than the nonvirginal bride. Not only is he divorced, he also suffers severe financial loss. The *hader* is returned to him, but no other expenditures—for example, the *mashtara*. Also wasted are considerable expenses connected with the wedding festivities. But most important of all, his honor is at stake. Impotence is a shameful condition; the impotent man's very masculinity—his manhood—is compromised. Women say that the impotent groom is so shaken by the public disgrace that he will never dare to marry a maiden again, but content himself either with an Omani "woman"—that is, a widow or divorcee—or a foreigner—for example, an Indian or Egyptian—in which case the marriage rite does not entail public proof of potency. His fate is indeed "second-rate."

SUPPOSED CONSEQUENCES AND REAL CONSEQUENCES OF NONVIRGINITY

Not till my last day in Sohar did I have occasion to elicit the Wali's authoritative views on what actions a groom may take when he discovers that the bride he thought to be a virgin is in fact a "woman." Until then, I had depended upon my friends to tell me. To my surprise, they had to resort to guessing and came up with a number of disparate views. But before exploring the reasons for this lack of consensus, let me report some of their suggestions.

They agreed on two things: chances are minimal that a groom will divorce his bride. He forfeits too much money, and besides, how can he be sure that the next bride will be different? What he will and "must" do, however, is raise a public outcry, which spreads like wildfire in defense of his honor, and lodge a complaint to his father-in-law. But what the complaint was all about, the woman were less able to specify.

The most extreme view, expressed by a sizable minority, was that the groom would refuse to pay the 30 Rials kalam il ᶜaros, but that this would not be allowed; they also believed that should he want a divorce, he would have to pay the ghayeb in full. However, a father-in-law who wanted to demonstrate his good will could reduce the kalam in half. This statement is most astonishing, for the kalam is the very symbol of recognition of virginity; to demand it for a "woman" is a contradiction in terms. The protagonists of this view thus would have it that the kalam is nothing but an empty gesture, devoid of real significance. Most women, however, believed that the elimination of the kalam constituted the only financial concession to the groom. Some believed that the groom would demand return of part of the bride price, for he had definitely, if unintentionally, been deceived. No one had any idea about the relative size of the amount. All they knew was that the Wali would settle the issue if the two parties could not agree.

The Wali, when I questioned him on this, authoritatively stated that as the groom has been given his bride "on certain conditions," it is a breach of promise if these conditions are not fulfilled. In case of such failure, two recourses are open to him: either to divorce the bride and reclaim the whole bride price, or to keep the bride, but retrieve half the bride price. By choosing the latter course, he pays in fact no more for her than he would if her womanhood had been known beforehand; for example, if she were a widow or a divorcee.

No woman with whom I spoke was properly aware of these rules and practices. How can it be that women are so ill-informed about what their own virginity is worth, so to speak? They are definite that it is shameful and sinful for an unmarried girl to have sexual intercourse, and they know that a groom must pay much more for a virgin: why, then, do they not perceive him to acquire definite rights?

Part of the explanation may be that the women recognize the elusive character of rights that are not supported by sanctions and rightly perceive the groom's weak bargaining position, divorce being an unattractive alternative for him. If so, one might have expected the Omani emphasis on tact and beautiful conduct to put the bride's family under pressure to act fairly and compensate the groom. On the other hand, the code of tact and consideration for others does not obtain in trade and money-matters in Sohar; and the presence of substantial sums of money as part of the transaction between groom and bride's family may cast their relations more in the mold of the market than in the graceful, tactful mold. But the main explanation of the women's confusion and vagueness about the prevailing rules would seem to be the women's exclusion from all major decisions and negotiations, coupled with the privacy and secrecy with which such matters are pursued. Women have minimal knowledge of the way bride-price negotiations are conducted and seem content to be left out of them. The deeply ingrained values of tactfulness and politeness further deter inquiry. Finally, it would seem that it is to these values we must turn for a key to that most astonishing of positions—that the deceived groom is not even excused from paying the *kalam*. If nearly all of life is pervaded by extreme tact, and the actors themselves are consciously acting their part in what at times amounts to massive make-believe maneuvers, is it not only reasonable that they should expect the groom to do likewise, once his honor has been protected through the public outcry? The fact that a nonvirginal bride faces few if any public sanctions makes it more understandable why women do not expect her disgrace to have serious consequences, such as a return of half the bride price would be.

NONVIRGINITY AND SHAME

Unfortunately, I do not know what the consequences are for the bride. All agree that her fall from grace is *haram*—sinful in the extreme—and women characterize her situation as a *fadiha*—a scandal. But they are quick to add that the frequency with which such scandals nevertheless occur proves that many girls do not respect or care a bit about what people might say. What the women do not stress, however, is the premise so self-evident to them, which permeates all social life: that "other" people hardly say a word. Nor do they even reveal by action or avoidance what may be their judgment or opinion in such cases. Again, as noted in Chapter 8, we came up against the paradox of the possible meaning of honor or shame in the absence of public sanctions and even articulated public opinion. A nonvirginal bride's prospects of esteem amongst those who confer it—her friends and neighbors—are hardly impaired. Indeed, the attitude of the virtuous ones is that it *ought* to be of no consequence whether the bride is a virgin; the groom should keep the outcome a secret, as do the Baluch. On several different occasions, a story in support of this view was related to me:

> Once, long ago, there was a groom who discovered his bride to be seven months pregnant, although it was not apparent from her stomach. He showed her love and compassion and kept the disgrace a secret. When the baby was born, he carried it in the darkness of the night to a nearby mosque, where he put it down. The next morning he went there again, to find a large excited crowd, who were wondering from where the baby had come. So he said to them, "Let me who have no son, raise it as my own." This way the child could remain with its mother, who was not discredited, and her husband derived much honor from the Prophet. But that, alas, was long ago. . . .

But if the nonvirginal bride goes clear of censure in her relationships with neighbors and friends, she must expect to pay the price of her frivolity in her marital relationship: her husband will supervise her very strictly, and never let her visit her parents alone. He will stay close by her during such visits, to insure that she does not stray, as she has done before in her father's house. Though through time, women say, he becomes more lenient.

What consequences does it have for a man that his wife is publicly known to have had sexual experience? Is not *his* honor affected? Soharis—both males and females—say that the purpose of his outcry is to cleanse his name. Would he not better do so by concealing his wife's disgrace, by producing that crucial bloodstain by other means—an acknowledged technique in many parts of the Arab world? For him, it would not be better, as the bloodstain serves as simultaneous proof of the bride's virginity and his own potency. Then it would be beneath his dignity to resort to subterfuge in a society that does not blame him for having misjudged the bride. It is her family who is dishonored, so Soharis say. And it may be more difficult for the family to marry off a second daughter, who might attract fewer suitors and a lower bride price.

As in other Muslim and Arab societies, in Sohar the honor of men depends heavily on the moral conduct of their women. Segregation, propriety of manners, virginity of daughters, faithfulness of wives, proof and maintenance of potency of grooms—all are issues of great importance to both woman and man, but where, characteristically, failures reflect above all on the *man* responsible for the woman who fails.

This is reflected in four salient facts:

1. A woman's legal right to obtain an immediate divorce if her husband proves impotent. In Oman, this is the only legal ground on which a woman can obtain an immediate divorce.

2. The prevalence of male pressure on a related woman, whose husband is absent for a long period of time—for example, on labor migration—to instigate divorce. Thus, one of my friends complained that her male kin placed great pressure on her to do so, when her husband had been gone for two years continually. They were not content that she loved him and wanted to wait.

3. An expectation that if an "elder" girl (about eighteen or older) fornicates, the Wali will punish her father, or other male guardian, not the girl.

4. The case of Sheikha—which should need no further comment.

But there is a paradox here: On the one hand, it is the woman who commits the destructive act. But because men do not grant a woman the ultimate responsibility for herself, she goes free, and there is that absence of stigma and other consequences, which we have noted for the woman who falls short. Yet we also have difficulties in identifying the dire sanctions for the *man* whose female ward fails in these supposedly terrible ways. He may suffer some economic loss, but where is the "honor" or other aspect of the person which is supposedly devastated?

To judge from the ethnographic literature, there can be little doubt that potency in Oman is a more explicit and emphatic theme than in most other parts of the Middle East. It seems reasonable to see a connection between this fact and another one that seems also peculiar to Oman: the high frequency of male transexuals. A man is a male who *acts* the masculine sexual role. No wonder the bride's family becomes struck with fear when their son-in-law fails in this test. And no wonder the groom, who knows how much is at stake, is inclined to become paralyzed. And again, those ultimate sanctions that one expects to find behind absolute rules elude us. *Xanith*s *are* tolerated, grooms *are* given a long period to succeed, cuckolds are *not* publicly shamed, and so forth.

The themes that receive fundamental emphasis in Omani gender roles, and culture in general, stand out clearly—but their ultimate force, how compelling and crucial for a person—remains an enigma.

To give more complete answers to these questions, we shall have to develop our analysis further in the following chapters. But it is quite clear that in a comparison between male and female in Sohar, the rhetoric of female chastity notwithstanding, it is male potency that is really consequential, and, *in the judgment of women*, it is the male who faces the more exacting demands and ordeal.

CHAPTER 12

✤

The Visit of an Undutiful Daughter

"That is what we get for marrying her to a stranger!"

One would think it a terrifying experience for a thirteen-year-old bride to be abruptly uprooted from her family and home, where she has spent her whole life, and transferred to strangers: a husband she has never met, and his relatives, whom she does not know. To her parents as well, the separation and loss of the daughter would seem painful. Yet we remarked about how Mariam moved with (apparent) grace and confidence among her new relations, only three days after the marriage. And, in Meimona's case, we commented upon the impressive loyalty to her husband that she displayed on their visit to her parents, only three months after the marriage.

Noted, too, has been the Sohari saying, summarizing their life experience and expectation, that the bride on the wedding night fights desperately with the groom, but, on the following morning, he is her husband and she loves him.

This chapter examines the transformation that takes place in a young Sohari girl upon her marriage, and the accompanying changes in her relationships to those closest to her. Until the event, her self-presentation is characterized by unquestioning obedience and submissiveness to all elders; modesty, gentleness, and tact toward everyone; and an unequivocal identification with parents and siblings. Marriage implies new tasks and new responsibilities and a wholly new status or position in society: How does the young girl accommodate to the change? What self-image does she construct for herself and present to the world?

Statuses (like daughter, mother, father, wife, husband), are in one fundamental sense always reciprocal: they occur in *relationships*. A girl is a daughter only so long as her parents are alive, and she is a wife only provided she has a husband. Each reciprocal pair of statuses is characterized by distinctive mutual rights and duties that determine what each may rightfully expect of the other. But because every person, at every stage of

life, occupies many, more or less compatible, statuses, special problems
may arise when he or she is called upon to *act*—and particularly when
several statuses have to be acted out simultaneously. Only rarely are rights
and duties unequivocally defined. Expectations and demands are usually
more diffuse and do not provide the person with clear-cut guidelines for
behavior in all exigencies of life. It is up to the individual to review the
situation and find a practical solution. Thus in each *role*—the actual
behavior associated with a status—the person has to consider more than
the particular rights and duties of that status: he or she has to pay attention also to limited resources (like time, affection, money) that will be
needed in other relations, and to the qualities required in other contexts.
Particularly when acting in one capacity before an audience to whom one
relates in another capacity (for example, Meimona talking with her
parents in front of her husband), a person could otherwise easily discredit
himself or herself in their eyes, in terms of the commitments he or she has
to these other persons.

And some statuses are best understood as identities that affect the person's relationship to all others. Thus, in the case that concerns us here, a
maiden's marriage not only makes her the wife of a particular man, it also
transforms her into a *horma*, a "woman," and this is now the identity in
terms of which she partakes in all social relationships, also those to her
parents, her siblings, and so forth. Although her rights and duties in these
relationships are to a considerable extent unchanged, she must nonetheless shape her role performance in them differently, because of her changed
identity.

The young Sohari wife might thus come under cross-pressures to satisfy
the legitimate rights of husband and parents simultaneously, and she will
be faced with the continuous task of always acting in the for her new ways
becoming to a *horma,* a woman.

Role dilemmas of this kind have received much attention from anthropologists, and the solution a person chooses is thought to reveal his or her
priorities and self-image. For example, a Bengali husband chooses to
shower all attention on the mother and to let the expression of his relationship to the wife be suppressed (Roy 1975). The wife's only "solution" is
never to be together with her parents and her husband at the same time,
such a situation being inherently unresolvable.

The case of Meimona's first visit to her parents after three months of
marriage provides the necessary material for a concrete discussion of these
changes in a young Sohari wife's identity and relationships. January 2,
1976, marked the first day of the Muslim New Year, followed by a long
two-day weekend. Meimona had two months previously moved all the way
to Muscat and had been wholly without contact with her parents during
the interval. They missed her painfully and were worried about her well-
being—so wholly on her own and far away from everyone she had known

and loved before. Taking it for granted that her husband would return to spend the holidays with his family in neighboring Zaffran, they were high-spirited on the morning of Thursday, January 1, expecting to see their daughter that very afternoon—Muscat being only a two-hour ride away.

We were also eager to see Meimona; she had been a good friend. But so as not to impose ourselves on the family, we waited till next day, at noon, before we dropped by their home in the date-palm garden.

We found no Meimona, but a very despondent family, getting ready to have their lunch—alone. The mother was cooking, the father was praying, and the four children were tense and noisy.

The reason for their distress was promptly disclosed: as they had discovered, Meimona had arrived as expected in Sohar the previous after-noon, around 5 P.M. But she had not so much as stopped by to see them for a moment on her way to Zaffran, though the road passes close by their home. They might not even have known that she had arrived, had not her father, Abdullah, run into his son-in-law, Mubarak, by chance in the market that morning. The son-in-law had excused himself, saying they had planned to visit that very morning, but then his brother had, unex-pectedly, driven off with the car. At noon, however, they would surely come.

So everyone was waiting, dressed up in their best attire, but becoming more and more tense as the minutes dragged by. Abdullah showed visible signs of annoyance, bordering on anger. "It is plain nonsense, this excuse about how the car had disappeared. There are dozens of cars in Zaffran," he commented. "Mubarak could and should have asked one of his friends for a lift. Besides, there are also plenty of taxis. Mubarak is not poor; he should have hired a taxi."

Because lunch was ready, and it was clear Meimona would not arrive, we were invited to partake. But we politely excused ourselves and went walking in the gardens while the family ate. Immediately afterward, Ab-dullah declared that he had urgent business in town, but would return shortly. It seemed to us that this was his way to escape from a situation of rapidly escalating emotional distress.

So we waited with the rest of the family and tried to provide some dis-traction and consolation. Rahmeh was visibly restless and unhappy. She repeated again and again how a daughter *should* visit: all day every Friday if she is close, a week every month if she is far away, a month a year if she is abroad. When she and Abdullah lived in Kuwait, they flew into Oman for a month's vacation every year and stayed with *her* family—no, not with *his* family, but her mother was his aunt, so that was really the same thing. Meimona *must* visit them now. Abdullah had become very angry that she has not yet arrived.

The children, too, were agitated. They ran purposelessly about, clashing and fighting and trying to pass the time by being boisterous and clowning. Rahmeh remarked how they had hardly slept the night before from excitement and anticipation because of their sister's impending visit.

About 4 P.M.—standard time for Omani afternoon visits—Abdullah returned. He was tense and asked for coffee. Both he and his wife clearly tried to remain polite and controlled in front of us, but their deep disquiet broke through in the tone and content of their own exchanges.

"Mubarak had a moral duty to bring Meimona here this morning and was perfectly able to have done so," argued Abdullah. "This brother of his could have taken them here in the car first and *then* done whatever business he had afterward. Besides, it is plain nonsense that she could not come even if he had taken the car. What if they sold the car! Would she then never visit her family at all!"

Rahmeh answered softly, "Maybe the real reason is they do not wish to bring her."

As sunset approached, the tension mounted noticeably. Everyone listened for the sound of cars to note which way they were coming; Abdullah distractedly kept looking at his watch. They spoke disjointedly, if at all. Shortly before 5 P.M., and only a few minutes before Meimona actually arrived, Abdullah again addressed his wife, harshly:

"Perhaps the Ministry doesn't have vacation tomorrow, and they will return to Muscat without Meimona visiting us at all, or merely dropping in on their way. This business about his brother's car is just an empty excuse. There are cars passing by that house twenty-four hours a day, and he has plenty of money for a taxi. . . . Think of poor Meimona, sitting there in an unfamiliar place and never seeing her own relatives at all. . . . But she *herself* should have insisted on being taken here; *she* should not have accepted this!"

Rahmeh, in a low voice: "That is what we get for marrying her to a stranger!"

Finally, shortly before 5 P.M., a car arrived. The children rushed to the gate while the parents remained motionless on the sitting platform. Too disappointed and probably also humiliated, they did not go to welcome the longed-for visitors.

Meimona was dressed in the *abba* and the *burqa* (she later explained that she only uses the *burqa* here in Sohar, not in Muscat). Her husband was dressed in fashionable Gulf-style clothes. With the children clutching them and dancing around them, they slowly walked the thirty-yards-long path up to the house. Not till they were a few steps from the sitting platform did the parents arise. Meimona embraced and kissed, in the formal fashion, first her father, then her mother, on both palms of the hands and then on the forehead. Her parents remained passive. We were amazed at the unemotionality of the scene; had we not known better, we would have taken this to be a meeting of complete strangers. Abdullah and Mubarak also embraced in ritual fashion, as did Meimona and myself.

Then we all sat down on the sitting platform, in a circle, with Meimona and myself in the seats of honor. She looked markedly shy and uneasy and kept on the *burqa*. Abdullah opened the conversation with elaborating for his son-in-law how they had been waiting for hours and hours, the son-in-law ought to have come a long time ago. This was definitely a reproach, but voiced with sufficient control and induction so it remained, barely, within the requirements of politeness. There was no explicit criticism, and his face revealed no annoyance; there was only a slightly noticeable nuance in his voice.

Mubarak could not have failed to sense the message, however, and he defended himself by saying that the car had been used constantly that day (four brothers share one car). Someone urgently needed to go to the market, another to visit a business associate; besides, there was his grandmother, who's sick in the hospital, to visit. Rahmeh could not constrain herself and remarked that surely there must have been taxis and other available cars—after all, cars pass by that house twenty-four hours a day.

Upon hearing this, Meimona became annoyed and stubborn—and defended her husband:

"*Wallahi* [By God], there was no car. We *did* try, in vain, to find one. Also, there were a lot of people we had to visit!"

"Who?" asked her mother.

"Well, Mubarak's grandmother in the hospital."

"Well, your grandmother is also ill and expecting you to visit her!"

The topic was dropped, but the scene was noticeably tense, despite the efforts of all to control themselves. Then Abdullah asked how Meimona liked it in Muscat.

"I'm fine."

"But Said [the husband of Abdullah's niece] said you looked tired."

(Sharply) "Why should I be?"

"Because you are by yourself and don't know anybody."

"I'm *not* by myself. I know a lot of people."

"Who then?"

(Manifestly irritated) "Some Zanzibaris,[1] and some from Oman [that is, interior Oman]."

"And they speak Arabic?"[2]

"Yes, they do!"

"And they come to you, and you go to them?"

(Moodily) "Yes, of course!"

Throughout this exchange, Meimona emphasized her distance by keeping on the *burqa*. She seemed shy, embarrassed, and annoyed at the parents' marked display of concern.

Not till half an hour had passed and her mother headed for the kitchen

---

[1]Zanzibaris are Omani citizens from Zanzibar in present-day Tanzania.
[2]Zanzibaris often do not know Arabic, but only Swahili, their mother tongue.

to prepare snacks—followed by the children, who seemed glad to get away from the strain of the situation, and thereupon by Meimona—did Meimona take off her *burqa*.

The hospitality was rather modest by the standards of Soharis of their economic level, but ample by those normally practiced by Abdullah. We were served three plates: canned cherries, sliced oranges, and cookies. The children were instructed to sit in the background and wait for their turn, while Meimona's eldest brother, aged twelve, was included, with a remark about being adult now. Both Meimona and Mubarak were visibly shy and uneasy, causing Abdullah to remark that surely no one is shy about eating with their own family (*ahlu*)! Mubarak had two pieces of orange and one cherry and then put down the spoon. His father-in-law put the spoon back in his hand, to make him take more, but had to repeat this several times—with little success. Meimona also helped herself very modestly, with embarrassment.

The conversation kept flagging, though Abdullah tried being vivacious. But he was nervous and started suddenly shaking his right thigh, though sitting cross-legged. He made occasional attempts to play up to me, who had so wanted to see Meimona again; to my husband by talking of the importance of his work for Oman; and to little Feisal, Meimona's two-year-old brother, who had asked ceaselessly for Meimona the day before. Meimona also played up to me by sitting very close to me and telling me how she had missed me. Her younger sister, aged twelve, who had always been her closest friend, kept staring at Meimona and smiling to her, but was too shy to utter a single word.

After coffee (the son-in-law drank one cup only), Meimona disappeared with her mother and sisters and brothers. Father-in-law and son-in-law sat passively and said nothing. After a long pause, we tried to break what to us was an embarrassing silence by asking Mubarak about his work, and which Ministry employed him. Abdullah was clearly surprised to hear that it was the Ministry of Defense (he had thought it was the Army High Command) and inquired what were the tasks and responsibilities of this ministry.

At the conclusion of this desultory conversation, we prepared to leave. The length of our stay had extended to an hour. Meimona hugged my arm and insisted that we must come and visit her in Zaffran the next day. Her mother overheard this and asked, surprised, if Meimona was not coming back to visit them then? To which Meimona answered that she was not. When her mother inquired why, she received an abrupt reply: "*Bass*" ("Nothing doing!" or "Stop it!"; it is difficult to find an adequate translation for this very meaning-loaded word). The mother exerted much self-control to hide her disappointment. I felt embarrassed and told her that in case we went to Zaffran, we would surely drop by and fetch her.

The son-in-law took the opportunity to get away by driving us to the market, claiming that he had to buy petrol.

The next day, we arrived at Abdullah's home around noon, anxious to see whether Meimona had in fact come back. Her mother told us that Meimona had said the day before that she would come by 11 A.M. and have lunch with them. Meimona and Mubarak had stayed only till 7 P.M. the previous night; they left immediately after supper.

Abdullah was out on some errand or other; Rahmeh did not know where or what. When he returned a half hour later, his first remark was, "Meimona did not come?" By 1 P.M., Rahmeh observed again that Meimona had asked them to make lunch, saying she would arrive around 11 A.M. "What is the use of saying and not doing?" And, with a sigh of resignation, "Oh well, let's make lunch for us at least."

We left, but returned at 5 P.M. to find a sad Rahmeh, all alone. The father and children had gone to the fort where an army bagpipe band was performing for the festival. But she had preferred to stay behind, in the hope that *maybe*, against all odds, Meimona would appear.

My husband excused himself, and I remained with Rahmeh, who seemed so disconsolate and in need of company. In the privacy of this setting, she confided in me in words roughly as follows:

She is terribly disappointed that Meimona did not come today. And also that yesterday all she did was stay for two hours. They, the parents, had wanted her to spend the night. But the son-in-law had refused, saying he himself had to return home and he would naturally not allow his wife to stay behind alone. However, in this he is not to blame. It is only natural for the man to want his wife to be with him. The fault lies entirely with Meimona. *She* should have said "No, I will not go with you. I want to stay with my family." But Meimona said no such thing.

When I asked her if she has any idea of the reason why Meimona is so happy with her husband's family, Rahmeh answered:

"Yes, she is happy; she likes it there."

"So there *are* girls who are more fond of their husband's family than of their own?"

"Yes, there are *many*; for example, Meimona's cousin Aisha. She hardly ever visits her parents, even though her mother says to her, 'I have small children, I cannot come to you, so you must come to me.' But Aisha does not like to."

"Why not?"

"*Bass. Hiyya kida, bi rohha* [Simply, that's the way she is, that's her nature]."

"And Meimona, why do you think she does not want to visit?"

"I do not know. *Bi rohha kida* [That's just her way—her nature]."

As it turned out, Rahmeh's vigil was purposeless and only aggravated her disappointment and distress. Meimona returned to Muscat that very evening without stopping by to tell her parents goodbye.

This case reveals some fundamental features of how persons in Sohar experience themselves and others in their most intimate relations. Thus it provides premises that are basic to our understanding of Sohari society. Although the case is concerned specifically with the transformation that takes place in a young girl upon her marriage, it reveals both basic aspects of how she conceives of her own most important relationships, how she evaluates and adjusts to the claims of persons close to her, and also how they in turn respond to her transformation.

In my own field experience, this encounter with undutiful daughter cum devoted wife, distressed parents, and detached son-in-law constituted one of those "enlightened moments" when vaguely sensed intuitions, statements never quite believed or understood and assimilated, and observations waiting for their interpretive context suddenly come together and are transformed into clarifying insights and a new basis for understanding.

A number of themes stand out and deserve individual discussion. Some have already emerged in previous chapters. But they are so fundamental to the constitution of persons in Sohar, that additional evidences serve to clarify the distinguishing features of this society and to throw it into relief.

First, it is an axiom of Omani culture that persons are endowed with different natures, which determine the way they behave. It is for others to acknowledge and accept this—no matter how painful the consequences. The only exception is where the behavior in question violates the legal or moral rights of the other person, in which case counteraction may be taken.

We have seen repeatedly how this view of behavior permeates Sohari understandings and provides people with an ever-ready answer when they are called on to explain the acts of others. In the present case, Rahmeh resorted to it when I asked her about her daughter and volunteered her niece Aisha as another example. More importantly, in the behavior of each of the main actors we can recognize the effects of this way of understanding others; rather than directly or indirectly putting pressure on others to change unwanted behavior, one seeks to keep up appearances and acquiesce, despite one's discontent.

A corollary of this way of conceptualizing fellow human beings is that it also serves to relieve some of the hurt caused by the acts of others and thereby to shield the cherished self-image of the "offended" one; this is so because acts that might otherwise be insulting can be understood to arise in or from the other's nature, rather than being a response to one's own acts and qualities.[3]

[3] I am indebted to Professor Vilhelm Aubert for this interpretation.

Second, implicit in this view of the connection between human nature and behavior is the premise that each person is accountable for his or her actions (with the one exception of women's sexual conduct, for which, in the *male* view, their guardians are responsible). Although Meimona's parents were truly angry with their son-in-law's "nonsensical excuse" for not visiting, they placed the ultimate blame upon their own beloved daughter: *she* should not have accepted the situation; *she* should have demanded to come before; and *she* should have refused to accompany her husband back to his home in the evening. What a remarkable emphasis upon the individual's power and ability, and possibly even duty, to shape the events of his or her own life!

I do not seem to find comparable attitudes described in the anthropological literature on other parts of the Arab world: on the one hand, a *woman* being regarded so completely as an actor in her own right, and, on the other, that one's own daughter or other close kinsperson should be faulted when there is a likely candidate for blame close at hand who is less closely related (in this case, Meimona's husband). Rather, the characteristic pattern in most Arab tribal and village societies is summed up in the saying, "Me against my brother, me and my brother against my cousin, me and my brother and my cousin against the outsider."

Similarly, in an urban situation like Cairo, where kinship solidarity is not particularly strong, one nevertheless finds a pattern of accusations of *taslit* (manipulation), whereby the close person is absolved from direct responsibility for undesired acts by the hurt person constructing often elaborate explanations of what pressures or deceptions he or she has been subjected to by more distant and less cherished third parties (Wikan 1980). In Sohar, however, an unsentimental objectivity is generally practiced toward those dearest to you.

This leads to a third point, noted but not stressed before: a spectacular ability to empathize with third persons and take their point of view. Thus Rahmeh's comment, "It is only natural for a man to want to have his wife with him." The world is regarded an imperfect place where people pursue their own interests, which is another way of saying that they act according to their nature—that is natural and right. But why, then, was there no *expressed* attempt to take Meimona's point of view—beyond "poor Meimona sitting there all by herself . . ."—when they no doubt accept the rule that a woman should defer to her husband (cf. how Rahmeh criticizes and distances herself from, yet accepts, Abdullah's acts and decisions)? It was perhaps due to the unsentimental and true reasoning that Meimona had been away for three months and had a legal right to see her parents—and her right was ideally compatible with their wish.

Fourth, we had been struck, long before this event, by the uncompromising loyalty that Meimona displayed toward her family. Whenever we met her—about every other day—she appeared cheerful and content, with a genuine affection for her sisters and brothers. If reality backstage took on a somewhat different aspect, we had no inkling of it, and no way of knowing. Only three months after her marriage to a complete stranger, she had been literally transformed in her relationship to those previously dearest to her: from a respectful and obedient daughter into an autonomous, self-aware wife and woman; she is visibly annoyed and embarrassed by her parents' display of anxious concern for her, and for their controlled but clear criticism of her husband. She comes out in *active*, avowed defense of him—so there can be no doubt where her loyalties lie. Her parents' disquiet for her own person she answers with staccato comments voiced with all overtones of "Stop it!" or "Leave me alone!" The only sign that she still identifies with her family of origin is her getting up and following her mother into the kitchen, but only after her siblings had already gone before her.

So it is that in this situation, which embodies all the characteristic components of a typical role dilemma, Meimona acts *as if* there were, for her, no dilemma at all. Had she indeed experienced it as a problem—of how to satisfy simultaneously her parents' and her husband's expectations of loyalty (that is, affection) from her—she might, with offense toward none, have chosen the easiest way out: remaining entirely passive. But Meimona did not. She chose to make it perfectly clear where she stood, where her priorities, wholly and singly, lay, by overemphasizing or *demonstrating* her unequivocal loyalty to her husband.

Elsewhere in the Middle East, it is characteristic that when predicaments arise in any meeting between a newly married couple and his or her parents, it is the marital relationship that is suppressed (see Barth 1971, and Peters 1965). Not so in Sohar: spouses prefer to confirm their relationship with each other, even at the cost of those with their parents and other close kin (for a male case, see Ch. 13).

Fifth, we have seen how Meimona's parents felt hurt and humiliated and how they criticized their son-in-law, but put the blame on their daughter. How did they accommodate to the "loss" of a daughter? Mainly with sighs of resignation. During the twenty days that we remained in Sohar after the event, we heard scarcely a mention of Meimona, beyond Rahmeh's reflection, "When a daughter marries, she transfers all of her affections to her husband. That is not right. There should be one part for him, and one for her parents."

This generalization, that daughters transfer all their affection, I take as an empirical and statistical statement of fact, as Rahmeh understands it, not her statement of custom or norm. The way in which Meimona's parents reacted throughout the incident demonstrates that they desired and expected it differently. This is in accordance with Sohari views. Persons are expected to cope with their difficulties and resolve them with grace. Meimona's parents recognized that her husband also had rightful claims

over her; had we challenged her parents, they would doubtless have
agreed that for her to resist his will and insist on being with her parents
might constitute a breach of wifely loyalty. But such is life, in the Sohari
view; real life *has* such complexity.

If I were to summarize my understanding of these aspects of the Sohari
world view it would be as follows: no categorical right and no perfect rule
can provide the simple solution that will fit a complex and imperfect
world. Indeed, apart from those cases that fall specifically under the rules
and injunctions codified in the Koran and the Shariah, there is probably
no true and perfect answer to *any* concrete life situation. Each person
must judge and exercise fairness and tact and be responsible for the
results. As the Wali said: "What some may think I did well, others will
think I did poorly. One can never satisfy everyone."

Meimona's parents believed that had their daughter insisted on her
rights, and her obligations to them, she would have had her way, the
powers of her husband notwithstanding, and the outcome would have
been better, in their view.

Sixth and finally, we can try to confront the major question that arises
out of this chapter: How can such a transformation take place in a young
wife, so profoundly and so rapidly?

One set of preconditions must be sought deep in the structure of personality and temperament: in how individuals in this society fundamentally relate to other persons and to fateful events. Highly suggestive parts
of an answer lie deeply embedded in child-rearing practices common and
peculiar to this culture.

We have seen how the two year old is abruptly and simultaneously
separated from the mother's breast and the consoling opium extract, then
handed over to the care of a sister or grandmother, because a rival baby is
calling for the mother's full attention. He is gradually treated as no longer
an irresponsible baby, but a child who will be expected to do as instructed.
Surely, it is reasonable to expect a person, after such an experience, to
repudiate the relationship to the previously beloved one, to respond actively
to detach himself so as to ease the feeling of loss that has been inflicted.
The experience may be so traumatic that in the future the person will fear
any further attachment and seek to keep other intimates at an emotionally
safe distance. This *might* explain the daughter's lack of pain as a bride at
the separation from her parents. Obviously, this provides only a gross
outline of a hypothesis, but the facts seem striking enough to warrant its
formulation. Any elaboration, or deduction from it, would naturally require that a comprehensive and professional study of personality development be made in this culture.

I have, however, one observation that fits into the puzzle of the construction of the individual in Sohar—and that, judging from the literature, is so unique to all of the Middle East that it cannot fail to reflect

distinctive Omani conditions. All over the Middle East, the concept of "the evil eye" is well known, and most villagers and tribesmen strongly fear it. Soharis maintain that their people are envious and hence easily prone to cause the evil eye. If an envious person looks at another while complimenting him for some quality or other, the spell is transferred from the eye of the envious person to the person or object of envy, causing the latter to suffer any and all kinds of illnesses, accidents, and even death itself. As is common in the Middle East, the evil eye belongs to a non-relative, but the better known and closer this person is, the greater is the danger.

Soharis also have a conception of another kind of evil eye, which is even more powerful and dreadful, namely the "lover's eye" (^{c}en ilmuhibb). In contrast to the ordinary evil eye, this is not a special power with which only some persons are endowed. Every person is prone to it, toward relatives, if their love is strong enough. Consequently, the mother is the most dangerous source, followed by other close relatives. According to Sohari belief, the effect is caused quite inadvertently, indeed very much against the agent's will. All a loving mother need do is look at her child and think of him or her as the most wonderful child in the world. The child instantly falls sick.

Does this mean that a Sohari mother must consciously try to suppress her feelings of love and affection for her child while in eye-to-eye contact with him? And if so, with what effect?

We have noted the general absence of overt affect in all intimate relations, and the deemphasizing of its very existence. It hardly seems adequate, for example, in view of the pleasure that mother and unmarried daughter seem to take in each other's company, to say that a mother is sad on her daughter's departure as a bride for the loss of labor that is entailed. Yet that is the explanation conventionally given—never a mention that the *person* of the daughter will be missed. The formal restraint on greeting when close relatives meet, noted previously (Ch. 11) and also exemplified in this case story, is likewise evidence, though ambiguous in its meaning: Are deeper emotions merely being shielded from public view? Are they being constrained from fear of "lover's eye"? Are they being genuinely suppressed? Are they absent?

In reflecting on these perspectives one cannot but be struck by the ambivalent character of all close kin relations in Sohar. They often seem to have basically contradictory features in the behavior that they enjoin. Let us consider each relationship within the close family in turn.

The father is responsible for his daughter until she marries; particularly, he must be concerned about the intimate matters of her modesty and virginity, yet his relationship with her should not entail intimacy. He has great legitimate powers to command and control her, yet it is only by treating her with gentlemanly restraint and grace that he can win approval for his own behavior toward her.

In relation to his son, likewise, the father has responsibility and almost unbounded authority during the son's minority. Yet he can only permit the son to excel by leaving him free to act on his own responsibility, and he earns approval in his paternal role only if he succeeds without making use of the powers vested in him.

The mother should love and serve her children, yet not harm them with her "lover's eye" and abandon them for a newborn in need of nurturing.

Brothers are one. Their acts reflect on each other, as do those of fathers and sons, and the senior should be as a father to the junior. Yet as small children, the younger displaces the older as the object of maternal attention and love, and they are rivals. Each can only become a man by exercising autonomy and foresight.

Brother and sister should love one another, and the former should protect and take responsibility for the latter, yet they are divided by sex into the separate segregated worlds of men and women, from which places they can damage each other by their respective acts (for example, the brother by making concrete decisions on behalf of his sister if the father is dead, and the sister by proving to be a "woman" on marriage). But they can hardly establish any common field of assertion or interaction.

The relationship between sisters, uniquely, may be one not structurally predestined to become contradictory. From being legally under the same master, they pass into different spheres of authority. From being together, they become separated by physical space, which is difficult for either to cross. Their lives run parallel courses, and they readily retain similar interests without being at cross-purposes. Consistent with this, Abdullah and Rahmeh concluded from their sad encounter with Meimona that they would marry their next daughter to a close neighbor and relative, "and then Meimona will come to visit her sister often, thereby we shall see her too."

Except under the fortuitous circumstance that sisters live geographically close, however, the strength and importance of this relationship will be drastically reduced with marriage. And certainly, during Meimona's brief visit the cleft of experience between her and her sister who was two years younger seemed to separate them, so that embarrassed uncertainty was all that remained. And the sister spent the entire two hours in silent, shy, smiling admiration of Meimona.

Of all social relations, in fact, that between husband and wife may be the only true exception to this general character of ambivalence. Between them, sexuality unites instead of separating and segregating; they are mutually dependent for realizing the cherished identities of man and woman: their strong mutual vulnerability in their struggle to think well of themselves makes for constraints on the husband's exercise of authority and paves the way for mutual trust to develop and wifely loyalty to be proved. Sohari men say, "A woman should be spoiled and indulged; only insofar as household economics and movements are concerned, should she be constrained."

The women, in turn, pride themselves on unconditional, wifely loyalty (for verbatim statements, see pp. 263, 289). All the evidence underscores the point Fatima once made, "Even *if* Ali acted unreasonably toward me, would I ever say anything, but Ali is *z-e-e-n* [very good]." The complementarity and mutual give-and-take is also expressed in women's common saying, "The wife respects the man, that the man shall respect her." "And give her things," some add.

Returning to Meimona's parents sitting there desolately in their garden, brooding over their lost daughter and promising that next time they marry a daughter, she shall live close, it remains to be said that only *one* woman I ever spoke to mentioned that close contact with the parents or the mother was a precondition for a happy life. What each and every one of them stressed, on the contrary, was the importance of having a *house* of one's own. It is autonomy that counts.

If my interpretation is correct, then a full fifteen years may come to pass before Meimona can empathize with her mother: the day when time has come full circle and it is she who sits there waiting in vain for her own undutiful daughter.

CHAPTER 13

Portrait of a Marriage

"When I get my month's salary . . . I show Fatima and say, 'Do you know why it is so little, much less than before? And she answers, 'It is not the money I want, I want you to be with me!'"

Fatima was one of the first women we came to know personally in Sohar. When in the evenings we used to go up on the roof of our house to watch the sunset and enjoy a refreshing breeze, Fatima would see us from her neighboring *barasti* hut, smile, and give a friendly wave to us. She was a young girl, approximately fourteen years old, with a rather Negroid appearance: dark skin, a flat nose, and kinky hair. She was always dressed in gaily colored and strongly patterned materials, more in the style of Sohari slave women than Arabs. On her family background, some of my friends later remarked: "Though her parents look white, Fatima is of slave descent. Her grandparents were dark, and therefore God made Fatima dark so that her family will remember their true origin and not pretend to be better than they are."

Fatima was living with her parents, two younger sisters, and a younger brother in a very ordinary *barasti* compound, and we assumed her to be unmarried because of three typical indicators. First, she wore no *burqa,* and though our neighborhood, Higra, was a mixed one, including residents of slave descent, we rightly assessed Fatima as not counting herself among them. Second, Fatima wore no golden jewelry, apart from a golden button in her nose, whereas married women in general are richly adorned. Third, she had a childlike, naive appearance, which contrasted to the self-assured looks of young Sohari wives her age. However, as soon as we became acquainted, Fatima proudly told us of her marriage to Ali.

They had been married for one year. Ali was her distant paternal cousin (their paternal grandfathers were brothers), fourteen years her elder. At present he was working with Petroleum Development Oman (PDO) in the oil fields at Fahud some three hundred kilometers away. About once a month, he came home on a long weekend visit, which Fatima evidently looked forward to and cherished. She spoke of her husband with a combination of shyness and admiration, which we found typical of Omani wives. She emphasized his qualities of intelligence, education, and knowledge of English. It was plain that she also wanted him to be proud of her, because one day she asked me to teach her to write her name in English. She put so much perseverance into the task that within one day she could write "FATIMA SAID BAXIT" from pure memory. I was impressed with her memory and steady handwriting, as this was the first bit of schoolwork Fatima had ever done. She had never attended Koranic school. Another day, she brought me a stamped envelope, a piece of paper, and a pencil and asked me to write a letter from her to her husband. She sent him her best wishes and hoped he was in the best of health and that he would soon come to visit. She signed the letter herself. As I suspected Fatima's judgment of her husband's command of English—mainly I think, because I could not quite believe that a man *so* well educated would marry a girl *so* unsophisticated—I wrote in simple style suitable for reading by a person with a superficial knowledge of English. Ali's reply came a few days later—in beautiful handwriting and rich, impeccable English. Even then I was not convinced. I suspected that somebody had helped him write the letter. Not until Ali himself appeared two weeks later did I realize that Fatima's description of her husband had been true.

Ali spoke beautiful English indeed—if one overlooked his startling use of the invective "fucking" for emphasis. He was small and slight, probably even lighter than the 114 pounds of the average Omani man. His build was fine-boned, his skin color was on the light side, and his features had the classical perfection frequently seen among pure-blooded Omani Arabs. He was clean-shaven and dressed in the traditional Omani *dishdasha* and *kummi*.

Ali seemed thrilled to have English-speaking neighbors, and, in the course of the next fourteen days, my husband and I became close friends with the couple.

At first they seemed a strangely incongruous pair. Ali had great self-assurance, cosmopolitan behavior and outlook, and great facility of expression; Fatima looked childish, not-so-clever, and was very passive. While Ali enjoyed intellectual activity and took pride in trying to give detailed and comprehensive answers to all our questions, Fatima emphasized her ignorance by replying "I don't know" to all questions, no matter what the topic. When I struggled to make her "think" by suggesting "Is it maybe like so or so. . . ?" she would mumble disinterestedly, "Maybe." In her husband's presence, Fatima acted the normative Omani role of reverent, submissive, and obedient wife. She rarely spoke, but sat quietly, motionless, and seemingly content even through hour-long conversations in English. When I felt pity for her, thinking she must feel left out, and translated parts of the conversation into Arabic, she smiled shyly, giving the impression that the conversation was of no concern to her, and she persevered in her passive pattern. Later I reflected that she probably had not felt ill at ease, for her behavior was consistent with the role she had played time and time again as a child and guest.

She interrupted her passive posture only to fetch things for her husband at his bidding: his cigarettes, matches, a glass of water, a book he wanted to show us. This is also consistent with the division of labor between husband and wife. A wife is expected to do all the housework, while the husband's realm of work is wholly outside the home. With development and modernization, however, these roles are very slowly changing. Fatima later reflected: "Ali does not do any housework at all, doesn't even fetch himself a glass of water. He says I am tired, you go, and so forth. There are a few husbands who do a little, for instance wash their own clothes and even their wives' clothes. But not Ali."

Ali expressed annoyance with the trouble he had brought upon himself by marrying an uneducated girl: "I must teach her everything, what is good and what is the right way. But even so, it is better to marry a close relative than an educated woman from strangers. Then what you do for your wife is not for strangers; you do it for yourself because she is your family." Ali seemed to imply that marrying a close relative entails greater assurance of reciprocity, greater trust, and more comprehensive sanctions. He told a morality tale of a friend who had advised him to marry an educated stranger, and did so himself. Within one month, the friend was in trouble. So he divorced his wife and married a relative. Then he had to admit that Ali was right.

Ali had also learned his lesson the hard way. His marriage to Fatima was his second. He had married a distant, paternal relative two years previously, but from the very beginning there were problems. "She would not obey me, but quarreled incessantly." When he discovered that her mother was immoral, divorce was inescapable. "For when a woman has been taught the wrong way, how then can she follow the right way?"

He was proud that to this day his former in-laws had not managed to obtain the *ghayeb* from him, despite their strenuous efforts. (Their failure to do so might indicate that Ali's wife had in fact been discovered in adultery.)

Ali's first marriage had been arranged by his father, as it took place at a time when Ali had just returned from a stay of eleven years abroad and so knew nobody in Sohar. When it failed, Ali decided that he must arrange the next one himself. Some female relatives recommended Fatima as a potential wife, so during *ʿid* he paid her family a ceremonial visit, met Fatima, talked to her, and liked her. She seemed humble, obedient, and kind, and though she was completely uneducated, Ali believed he could train her. So he disclosed his wish to Fatima herself and made her agree to marriage before he sent his father to ask her father's consent. Fatima's father refused, giving as his reason that "Ali does not know

Arabic." Ali purports that this was a camouflage for his real reason—namely, fear of loss of authority, because Ali's father is the senior man of the family and responsible for it. In case of a dispute, the Wali would call on him as the authoritative representative of the family. So Ali himself went to Fatima's father and talked him into agreeing.

We asked him whether he saw much of Fatima during the months preceding the wedding. Ali explained: "Yes, a few times in her home. That I could do because she is my relative, but never, had she been a stranger. When the two are of the same family, they should see each other, speak together, and know each other one full month before they marry, so that they will know each other's character."

"What about touching, or physical caresses?" I asked impudently. Ali recoiled at the mere thought:

"No, no, unchastity is not practiced here! Before marriage, you should not touch her. If you asked her to do such a bad thing with you, and she consented, how could you think she would not do it again, and choose her to be the mother of your own blood? One must think to the future."

Ali had indeed been out of contact with the Arabic language and Omani ways for a number of years. He was only eleven years old when he ran away from home and left Oman to seek an education abroad. His departure was triggered by his mother's death and his father's subsequent remarriage, shortly after. His stepmother mistreated him in a manner reputed to be typical of Sohari stepmothers. "When in the presence of my father, she was friendly and kind, but in his absence she scolded me and spanked me and gave me second-rate food. See how tactical [siyasiyyan] they are, such women!" Ali endured life with them for two years, mainly thanks to the warmth and support given him by a neighboring woman. Then he left for India. He worked in the daytime as a waiter in a Bombay café and went to school at night. After four years, he went to Saudi Arabia, and some years later, to Zanzibar. Everywhere, he combined daytime work with night school.

When twenty-two years old, he returned to Sohar. He had been away for eleven years and nobody recognized him. He found a job with PDO, where he was, as of May 1974, in charge of stores and he earned a good income (4 Rials a day, plus overtime, which amounted to about 160 Rials a month). On this income, he supported not only his wife but also his father (25–30 Rials) and his fifteen-year-old brother (15 Rials). Ali's father who was old, sickly, and uneducated, claimed that Ali was responsible for him. Ali objected to his argument, saying, "It should be the other way around, a father must be responsible for his son." But at the same time he felt he had to help his father and brother, because they are his family and he is fond of them. He also recognized a kernel of truth in his father's argument. "The father feeds the son when he is small, so when he is grown, the son must reciprocate by feeding his father." Ali was annoyed, however, with his brother because he did poorly at school, wasted his time, and kept bad company. Ali said he would support him only until he grew up: "Then every man must be responsible for himself, seek education, and use his time to gain knowledge, not just fritter time away smoking and drinking and talking and fighting about nothing."

Ali idealized the trust and obligations binding relatives, while recognizing that reality may sometimes fall short of ideals. His view of the people of Sohar and of the Batinah coast in general (in contrast to the Bedu and mountain people) is that they are basically egoistical, intent on earning money, jealous of each other, concerned with their rights, and unobservant of their obligations. "They are not interested in living the right kind of life at all." Relatives were no exception to this. He was bitter with his father for his claim to support in old age, when he had neglected Ali as a child. But above all, he thought poorly of Fatima's father:

> Being a close relative, he should not behave like he does. He is my father's cousin, and his sister is married to another cousin of my father. Yet he appropriates the twenty-five to thirty Rials a month that I send to Fatima in care of her father. Fatima has complained about this so often, but she gets nowhere, and I don't want to interfere, because that only creates more trouble. In fact, he also kept the whole bride price and did not even give Fatima a ring for her finger. And I could say nothing, because the bride price goes to the bride's father, and it is up to his discretion to use it. Fatima complained once, but I instructed her not to do it again.

Fatima's father was atypical in keeping the whole bride price for himself. Ali was, on the other hand, atypical in paying no more than the government-regulated amount of 300 Rials. Most likely this low amount reflected a combination of several factors. First, because Ali was a relative, he should pay less than a nonrelative. Second, Ali had great respect for laws and regulations—for doing things the correct way. Fatima's father must have known this and feared that, if Ali was pressed to pay more, he might complain to the Wali after the marriage, and the Wali would punish Fatima's father with imprisonment and demand that he return the excess money. Third, Fatima's father stipulated, as a condition for the marriage, the unusual claim that the couple take up residence with the bride's family. The reason for this stipulation is not entirely clear; the concern of Fatima's parents for her well-being and happiness may have been part of it. But Ali believes that economic considerations were uppermost in their mind.

By settling with his parents-in-law, Ali would contribute to the upkeep of their family. The two families would pool their resources and share expenses. Although Ali was legally responsible only for two persons, his wife and himself, he would be morally responsible for the whole extended family, of which he was a member. Ali was angry with Fatima's father for pressing this claim, but found himself in such a predicament that he had to accept. He had become infatuated with Fatima and did want to marry her. He could not take her to live at his father's place, for that meant residence with his stepmother, who could be counted on to make trouble for Fatima, as she had done for himself. Separate and independent residence was a most uneconomical alternative, for the government had put a ban on building with concrete in the area where Ali owned land, and erecting a provisional *barasti* hut (which must later be torn down) implied great economic loss. Moreover, separate residence would also prevent him from working outside of Sohar, for a young wife cannot be left alone at night. Thus Ali acquiesced. By so doing, he alienated his father, who had insisted that Ali and his wife live with him. His father also became angry with Fatima's father, who had been his close friend, and a nonspeaking relationship (*xisam*) developed between the two men. As proof of his ac-cusation of material self-interest as his father-in-law's motive, Ali cited several cases, of which the following is representative:

> When Fatima and I had been married for six months, I went to work with PDO, so I left Fatima in the care of her parents. I made arrangements with a shopkeeper to give her credit for foodstuffs, which her father would buy for her, as it is shameful for women to enter the market. When I returned after one month, the shopkeeper presented me with a bill of 50 Rials! Forty Rials more than I reckon was spent on Fatima! So her father must have bought food for the whole family and charged it to my account. I had also sent 30 Rials pocket money to Fatima in care of her father. When I came home, I discovered that Fatima had only received half this amount. So I asked her father what had hap-pened. He said he had had to buy new car tires, so he had borrowed the money. I pressed him to pay back the money. Nothing happened. Next day I asked for it again. Her father said, "What money?" So I repeated the story, and next day he gave me 5 Rials. I waited a week, then I asked for the remaining 10 Rials. So he gave me five more. But when I pressed for the last five, he said, "Ali, your character is changing, you used to give freely, as the Koran enjoins." I retorted, "Then I must give my alms to the blind and the poor, not to you. . . ."

Ali said this incident and similar ones had caused him so much trouble that he had been thinking of divorcing Fatima. But whenever he threat-ened, she cried, and so he felt pity for her and put up with his situation.

Difficulties between Ali and his parents-in-law also arose due to differ-ing views on the value of traditional versus modern ways. The *burqa* was one such matter of disagreement, as has already been described (in Ch. 6).

In rejecting the *burqa*, Ali was most atypical of Sohari men. Other men who have traveled extensively like Ali and lived abroad will sometimes change their personal dress for the more fashionable and cosmopolitan Gulf style (for instance, they discard the Omani *kummi* for the Gulf head scarf), but insist at the same time on a strict adherence to traditional dress for their wives and daughters. Ali, on the other hand, dressed traditionally—perhaps a reflection of the fact that his travels had not brought him to the rich and modern Gulf states, which today set the style that people in Sohar seek to emulate. It is strange that Ali should be categorically opposed to the *burqa*, when in most other respects his behavior toward his wife in no way deviated from the traditional role. The only tentative explanation I can find is that he might have remembered that his mother did not wear it, for she came from south of Kaborrah, where women go unveiled.

According to Fatima, in the beginning of their marriage, Ali was very strict in his demand for deference and correct behavior; he allowed her very little freedom and enforced harsh discipline. "He did not even allow me to stand at the gate and talk to my friends, or let me go visiting any place at all. All the time I sat in my room and cried." "But I complained to nobody," she proudly added, "not even to my parents." It is even unlikely that Fatima would have been indiscreet enough to commit this disloyalty toward her husband before me, were it not in the context of happy praise of him for how good he has become, now, two years later. It is no exaggeration to say that loyalty above all is what Omani wives pride themselves on, and they will submit to quite extreme exercise of authority and power without complaint to any outsider, not even to their parents.

Our observations of husband-wife relationships in general, and that of Fatima and Ali in particular, confirmed Fatima's evaluation of Ali's behavior. He was firm and strict, as could be seen one day when Fatima rushed to the gate of the house to fetch her siblings, who were fighting in the street. In her haste, she forgot to put on her *wiqaya* (top head shawl). Although her head and hair were completely covered by the *leeso*, Ali became furious and harshly scolded her. When we questioned him on the cause of his anger, he explained: "It is a matter of principle. With uneducated persons, you must be firm and consistent or they develop bad habits."

Lest the reader think that Ali used Fatima's lack of education merely as an excuse for being authoritarian, let me add that only three months later, when the government opened an evening school for married women, he insisted that she enroll. When we returned to Oman, in December 1976, Fatima was in her second year, had learned to read and write simple Arabic, do arithmetic, and had just begun English lessons. She complained that she did not like school and would not have gone of her own accord, but that Ali demanded that she do so. So she spent three hours a day, four days a week, in school and a couple of hours a day doing homework. Classmates praised her as being a very clever pupil. Fatima proudly told us that Ali helped her with her homework, but she complained that he had insisted that she continue school even after the birth of their baby (she was then six months' pregnant), and that she place the baby with her mother during school hours. Division of labor is categorical between husband and wife, and it is beneath most men's dignity to baby-sit even for their own children.

On whether he wanted a baby boy or girl, Ali was quite definite: "A boy of course! . . . If I get sick or old, perhaps the boy can work and support us. What good is a girl? You feed her for fifteen years, then she marries somebody else."

"But you get *mahr* for her—"

"Money is no good, it is like smoke and disappears without a trace. I am not interested in money."

In taking the role as his wife's teacher and disciplinarian, Ali acted in accordance with Sohari values. Married women are often heard to emphasize their own illiteracy and lack of understanding. All Soharis, irrespective of sex, age, and station in life, have an immense—one might say inflated—regard for education. Women think it natural that their husbands, who are better educated than themselves, should teach them. A deeply ingrained respect for rules and regulations, and the benefits deriving from them, is also widely shared among Omanis. Men in particular express the view that education is a means to self-control that reduces the need for external sanctions, and discipline is a means to understanding and education. Time and again, Ali expressed this view. A woman, he held, must be instructed and guided—first by her parents, then by her husband.

Ali held Fatima's parents responsible for her lack of understanding and knowledge. Moreover, he felt that they had not only failed to do her good, but by their ignorance had done her positive harm: "They interfered with Fatima, beat and abused her. That's wrong. Women should be spoiled and indulged, and given their responsibility. Only insofar as movement, hospitality, and housekeeping are concerned must they be controlled."

This view seems representative of Sohari men. Because Fatima had not learned the right way, she could not be expected to follow it, and Ali must teach her by patient instruction, discipline, and control. But he realized that even with education there were limits to the control she could be expected to exercise over herself. For such are the ways of women.

When Ali had to be away from Sohar on work in Mattrah in the second and third month of marriage, he was happy to be able to leave Fatima in the custody of her parents. But because he did not fully trust them, he began an active search for a *barasti* hut to rent in Mattrah, so he could bring his wife there. In the third month he succeeded and came to fetch his wife. According to Ali, the following incident took place:

> Her parents said no, absolutely no. I was in a weak position, I had no money, I was a new man. I could not complain about the bride price they had taken, or the money—about 60 Rials in all—that they had spent on food for themselves and charged to my account. But Fatima was my wife, and I wanted to take her with me. Her parents refused and brought me before the Wali. The Wali asked me to explain what the complaint was about. I said I had no complaint, it was

my in-laws who complained. So the Wali said, "What is it that is wrong?" Father-in-law answered, "This man is taking our daughter away from us." The Wali, on establishing that we were married, said "How can you say that? If they were not married, then it means that he is stealing your daughter. When they are married, then he must be responsible for her." Father-in-law claimed it had been a special condition of the marriage that Fatima would be allowed to remain in his house. The Wali said, "This is a serious charge; you must go to Muscat to the Sultan if you want to make it." Father-in-law refused. So the Wali scolded him: "How can you live in this country if you do not listen to me? I say you or I or even the Sultan cannot keep a man from taking his wife with him. That is my ruling, and if you do not accept my ruling, how can you stay here?" So the Wali ordered me to remove Fatima. I got a taxi and called Fatima out; her mother cried and followed, she climbed onto the taxi, but I caught her by the leg and pulled her down. So Fatima and I went on and lived six months in Mattrah.

Life in Mattrah was very expensive. Ali paid half his monthly income of eighty Rials in rent for a two-room *barasti* hut. This made saving impossible, and he needed to save, both to pay installments on his land and to be able later to build on it. He calculated that a two-room concrete house with a fence would cost approximately 4,000 Rials. So he felt forced to leave his job in Mattrah and seek something better. From a friend, he learned that PDO paid very well, and although employment with that company would entail working in Fahud and leaving Fatima with her parents again, he saw no other way. He discussed his plans with Fatima, who agreed that, as a temporary expedient, this was the best.

When we met the couple, Ali had been working for six months with PDO. He was content with his work and happy to make a considerable income, approximately 160 Rials a month. But Fatima was far from happy. Ali says he sensed it the moment he entered the house; though she smiled and tried to give a cheerful impression, he knew it was playacting. But because he had come home on a month's sick leave and had a husband's right to selfless care and attention, she brought up no uncomfortable topics. On the contrary: Fatima surrounded Ali with warmth and comfort and seemed to savor her role as a needed and wanted nurse. Ali fussed a great deal about his health—a tendency we often found among Omanis. But he did not really seem so unhappy about his sickness, for it resulted in much attention and comfort. About the cause of it he liked to tell how the English company doctor had vindicated his own diagnosis over that of the medical orderly: "I have a surfeit of hot foods in me and will die if I continue to drink tea with sugar. I also need a rest. One needs to eat cold foods, such as fresh vegetables, to counteract the hot foods. Sugar is the strongest of all hot foods, and one night I kept drinking tea with sugar in large quantities without thinking. Now I stay completely off it."

Ali spent most of the time the following week in bed, and much of it tightly wrapped in woolen blankets, though the temperature was 100–110°F. Fatima all the while sat by his side with a loving expression on her face, ready to anticipate and fulfill his slightest request. It is a folk belief that one can rid one's body of a surplus of hot foods through sweating. But the measure did not work in Ali's case; he one day related to us: "Today I did something very bad—I do not understand why, I have never done it before. I asked Fatima to help me find someone who could cure me. She sent for a neighboring woman, who came and said she could tell immediately at a distance what was wrong: 'Do not ask me; I know what you need.' So she took a thin steel rod and heated it fifteen minutes in the fire till it was red hot, then she cauterized the biceps of both arms." The next day Ali said that the burns hurt him a good deal, but he was still confident that they were helping. And the following day he claimed to be cured.

On that very day, Ali subsequently reported to us, Fatima abandoned her cheerful façade and disclosed the cause of her unhappiness: she wanted a house of her own. The request did not take Ali by surprise; men are aware that such is the ambition of every woman. Sohari women are expected to be independent, strong-willed, and sensitive to criticism; they like to be second to no one other than their husband. "I could well understand that Fatima wanted to be in charge of a home of her own, where she would make the decisions, be responsible, and be able to receive guests without interference. But as she very well knows, it is impossible to build on our plot of land for the time being, until the government has decided where the course of the main through road is to run." So he had brushed aside her request as a stupid demand not to be taken seriously. To his astonishment, Fatima was adamant and would not be deflected. "Then we can build a *barasti* house," she countered. "Foolishness!" Ali exclaimed. "Only a woman could talk rubbish like that!" He scolded her for having no sense of economizing (a frequent accusation in confrontations between husband and wife) and impatiently explained to her—one more time—the loss involved in building a *barasti* house, which must later be torn down to give way to a concrete one. As everybody—Fatima included— must know, used *barasti* materials will sell for a fraction of their current value: everybody now wants to build in concrete. Ali told her that if they waited only one year, they themselves could also build a cement house. Annoyed at what he considered thoughtless stubbornness on Fatima's part, he was brusque in his manner. Halfway through his reprimand, Fatima started crying. Ali became confused and regretted his harsh tongue. She was, after all, an uneducated woman. He asked her to explain what was wrong. Had her parents ill-treated her? Fatima's mouth was tightly shut, and she would not tell a word.

The following day, Fatima reintroduced the subject. What about it, (when) had he decided to build? Ali answered that he was thinking about the matter, but that he had had a relapse and did not feel quite well. He was dizzy and had a stomach ache, so he needed rest.

During this phase we were in daily contact with the couple and were able to watch their interaction at close quarters. To our understanding, Ali used his illness as a pretext to postpone a serious discussion and decision. In the meantime, Fatima played the role of respectful and obedient wife, but she seemed more restless and determined than usual. One could sense that she had put her mind to something that she was determined to achieve. Ali said he also detected a tenseness in her relationship to her parents and siblings, but whenever he tried to inquire about the matter, she was evasive and refused to tell.

Ali played the role of authoritative husband and stressed his disciplinarian and teaching role, but though he tried to act calm and controlled, his nervousness showed. He also complained, in general terms, about the nature of women, how they are unreliable and irresponsible, extravagant and demanding, unreasonable and stubborn.

Three or four days later, Ali had recovered again and started to move about. That same evening, Fatima dressed up and declared they should go and visit her father-in-law. Ali sensed a danger—that she wanted to complain about him—but to refuse to take her would be a disgrace. So he slowly made himself ready, and they were in the process of leaving when we accidentally dropped by. We tried to excuse ourselves, but with the graceful hospitality of Soharis, they insisted that we sit down and have coffee.

When Fatima left to prepare the coffee, Ali hinted that we need not hurry to leave—quite the contrary. But when we were not quite as brief as Fatima had hoped, and Ali leaned back in a relaxed posture to light his second cigarette, Fatima playfully, but determinedly, put out his match! Ali got the message, put his cigarette away, and said apologetically that they would have to leave for his father's house.

Early the next morning, Ali rushed to the market to buy *barasti* building materials, while Fatima wore a big smile. But though her triumph was great, she did not gloat, but behaved toward her husband in her usual deferential and humble manner. Her strategy had proved effective, and Ali's fears had been well-founded. She had indeed complained about him to his father, but perhaps even more importantly, she had threatened to complain to the Wali if Ali did not immediately build her a house of her own. Ali's father had strongly advised him to fulfill her request—a separate house for the couple being in his own interest. But Ali claimed that the prospect of being brought before the Wali was of greater weight in his decision. He gave the impression of having panicked, thinking a house of her own is a right that a wife has according to Shariah, and therefore expecting that the Wali would support Fatima's demand. He said that after thinking the matter over thoroughly, he had come to the conclusion that extended family residence of any kind is against Shariah, as it reflects a failure of the husband to provide adequately for his wife. He believes that Shariah *enjoins* a man to give his wife a house *separate* from his father's and her father's.

Ali's statement seems remarkable, considering that in Oman, as in the rest of the Muslim world, extended family residence is a time-honored ideal, and in Sohar it is practiced by two out of every three families. In this he may have been less than candid. His previous conflict with Fatima's parents, when he had obtained the Wali's support for removing his wife from her parents' house, may have made him all the more uneasy to be called before the Wali for this, the opposite failure. But if that were his main consideration, I would have expected Fatima to know and anticipate it, and to resort to the simple course of merely threatening him with going directly to the Wali. Instead, she chose to confront Ali before his father—though she had never before shown any inclination to involve him in their affairs, and though Ali had never given much weight to his father's opinions or judgments. Why then did she turn to him; why was her move effective; and what were the deeper reasons for Ali's change of heart?

I think two factors, in combination, both with a potentially compromising effect on Ali's reputation, were decisive in giving her victory. "The ornament of a man is beautiful manners, but the ornament of a woman is gold," says the oft-quoted Omani proverb. We have noted the great importance attached to a very demanding code of graciousness, style, and integrity among Omani men. A man wins respect in his own eyes, as in those of others, by behaving toward everyone, including his wife, in a polite and morally correct manner, and by being completely in control of his own life and situation. By calling Ali before his father, Fatima chose the audience that would actually harm his reputation least, yet show the seriousness of her threat. Going to the Wali would be a serious but reasonable escalation; and even if the Wali were to dismiss her complaint, Ali's failure to give his wife what public opinion deemed reasonable would by then have been made irretractably public. Furthermore, it is quite possible that the Wali would have advised Ali to comply with his wife's wish, even though Shariah does not compel him to do so. As some of my female friends commented to me: "The present time is woman's time. Even when the man *has* the right, the woman *is given* the right."

But behind these threats to Ali's position loomed a greater one, now that the extent of Fatima's unhappiness had become clear. As previously noted, Ali explained the necessity of "spoiling" women with material goods lest they become unhappy and inclined to shame their husbands through infidelity. Once he realized the extent of Fatima's misery, there could be little doubt that a shadow of fear would haunt him if he forced Fatima to live unhappily in her parents' house. But as he would not admit that his own wife could be feared to commit such a horror (cf. his change to general terms in his mode of speech when explaining why he would not let Fatima go to the market, Ch. 4), nor that she had the power to impose her will on him, he tried to give us the impression that his decision was his own, triggered by his own insight that this was the optimal course to take.

The following days, Ali's manner vis-à-vis Fatima when in our presence was more forceful and authoritarian than before. He evidently tried hard to pretend that he was in charge. Fatima played up to his role by tolerating his irritable mood without signs of impatience and by stressing her admiration for his kindness and efficiency. It was not easy for Ali to collect enough building materials for a two-room house. *Barasti* materials are in short supply during winter and spring, so that owners are unwilling to sell. They gamble, with the tough business mind so characteristic of Sohari people, on an even higher demand and correspondingly increased gain. Once Ali made his decision, however, he set about realizing it with thoroughness—and in three days' time he had obtained what he wanted—at the cost of more than 300 Rials ($1,000).

Ali gave a new version of the reason why he had decided to move: "When I came visiting here, one old woman in the neighborhood said to me, 'Ali, are you a man?' I said, 'Yes, I am a man.' She said, 'Think about my words.' So I thought about it that night, and I spoke to Fatima about it. It was then that I decided to move her to a separate house."

Another day he told us that he had decided to move because of the excessive heat in town in summer. The new site is located inland, where the humidity is lower and the climate more tolerable; and he seemed to make a point of complaining more than before about the weather.

Fatima happily told me, on the same day that Ali had collected the building materials, that the building would start the next day, with Ali, his father and father's brother, and her father working together. Ali simultaneously told my husband that he would pay for all transport and building, but do no work himself. As it turned out, Ali asked his father-in-law to do the transport (gratis), and the next day he went off to work together with hired men at building the house.

The work lasted one week. During this time Ali was tense and restless and talked much and inconsistently about the house he was building. One day he said that he would build in cement during the next month, another day, that he would close it up and leave it, and so forth. Evidently his real problem was that he was afraid of Fatima living in the house by herself, which she must of necessity do if he was to keep his PDO job. Thus he had various schemes. One was to take a six-month compassionate leave, during which he would take a job as a clerk in the hospital, even though the salary would be only half that of his PDO income. Another was to use delaying tactics so that Fatima would not be able to move (how?).

He still did not know the full story of why Fatima and her parents did not get along, but he had a strong impression that part of her problem was lack of privacy vis-à-vis her siblings: they interfered when she had friends visiting, and she had no private possessions, food, and so forth. He had tried asking Fatima several times about the cause of her unhappiness, but she absolutely refused to confide in him.

Fatima's secrecy was not unexpected, for it is a strong value of Omani culture that a conflict between parties in a relationship is to remain within that relationship; it is of no concern to outsiders, and to involve other persons is not only to exacerbate the conflict, but more importantly, to act beneath one's dignity, where self-reliance and ability to cope constitute essential elements. (For example, Fatima took pride in not complaining to her parents when Ali, in her view, mistreated her.)

Another day, Ali told us that contributing to the conflict between Fatima and her parents was the fact that, in a disagreement long ago between him and them, she sided with him, and this they could not forgive and forget. He also complained that his father was angry with him. When Ali set Fatima up in her parents' house, his father warned him that the arrangement would give him trouble later. Now, said Ali, his father had asked him if he remembered what he had said. Ali answered that he did, but not exactly, so his father repeated it. This seems to have been the whole exchange and the sole basis for Ali saying that his father was angry—indicative of the self-restrained and low-keyed quality of Omani relations.

Ali had never discussed with his parents-in-law his plans to move. He just proceeded with the building without saying a word and ignoring their curiosity. With characteristic polite disinterest they on their part refrained from asking about it. However, when he was ready to move the furniture, Ali said to his father-in-law,

"Are you free to drive it for me tomorrow morning?"

His father-in-law replied, "Yes, I am free." Later he said, "Ali, it is better to wait till evening."

Ali said, "No!"—seeing this as an attempt to postpone the move indefinitely. Fatima's father also said that he would have to see Ali's father about the matter.

Ali said, "See him, but it is for me to tell him that I am moving."

As it turned out, his father-in-law did transport the furniture the next morning. But on the third trip, when Ali moved Fatima, her ten-year-old sister came along and spent the first night in the new house!

Ali's own father came visiting in the morning and in the evening. He had never come to the other place. But Ali was happily confident that Fatima's parents would not come, because they were and would remain angry. And "his own heart was black" still for what they had done. But he said that he hid it and just agreed with everything they said, did not listen to them, would not involve himself with them. When we joked that Fatima's family would all move in with them, starting with Fatima's sister, who had left that day "to fetch her clothes," he enjoyed the idea as black humor, saying that of course her family must be allowed to come and visit once a month, even once a week, but if they impose themselves on him, he would complain to the Wali!

When we left Sohar a couple of days later, Ali was nervous and restlessly searching for a job in Sohar: to go back to work in Fahud and leave Fatima alone would be impossible. Fatima was radiant, obviously happy at the prospects of having her husband permanently with her. She must have known that establishing a separate home would result in such an arrangement on Ali's part, and it is even likely that the wish for them to live uninterruptedly together was one factor behind her insistent demand. Ali, however, gave no impression of happiness and contentment. On the contrary, his face these days wore an expression of despair, and he sighed with resignation as he repeated over and over again, "Look at Fatima, she is not yet a complete woman, she is really still a child. . . ."

One-and-a-half years passed before we met Fatima and Ali again. They were still living in their *barasti* house by the main road, but it looked desolate much of the time. As soon as we arrived, we made several attempts at contacting them, at different hours of the day, but in vain; either the gate was locked from the outside, indicating their absence, or it was locked from the inside, indicating "visitors unwanted." The former was surprising; a woman should stay in her house and make her own absences brief in order to honor her moral duty of hospitality to potential visitors. The latter was extremely surprising, for whatever the time and place, a guest should be honored.

One day I happened to meet Fatima on her way to the hospital; she seemed delighted at the encounter and insisted that I visit her at once. We made a date for the following afternoon. When I arrived, the gate was again locked from the inside, but when I knocked, she hastily opened it and heartily welcomed me. An elderly female vendor was with her, seated outside the house on a dusty plastic mat, with Fatima's schoolbooks spread all about. The scene gave the impression that Fatima had been interrupted in the midst of her homework and made me think that she might be exceptionally conscientious about such work and that this would explain the locked gate. I was aware, however, that it might be the other way around, that homework was used as an excuse to avoid obligations of hospitality.

Fatima fetched a new, green-patterned plastic mat (made in Japan) for me, and gold-embroidered cushions for the back (made in Dubai), and the vendor joined me in this prestigious seat of honor. Fatima then brought the treats: tea with powdered milk and sugar, followed by the ever-present rich and spicy Omani coffee. These beverages, delicious though they were, confirmed my impression that Fatima practiced an atypical hospitality pattern. In Sohar, all foods are ranked on a scale of prestige; judged by these standards, Fatima's entertainment was so stingy, it bordered on the offensive under the circumstances. My momentary unease turned out to be misplaced however; over the next two months, I came to recognize this modest style of hospitality as a characteristic of hers, which also may serve as a clear indication of qualities in the relationship between her and Ali, and the extent and nature of their joint aspirations.

Perhaps the simplest way to characterize her pattern of hospitality toward female friends is to say that it is the way most men in Sohar wish that their wives would act. While men pride themselves on being generous, with moderation, in their own relations, they strenuously object to women's admitted tendency to lavishness and extravagance. So opposed are the views of men and women that a wife's hospitality is a prominent, and maybe the most prevalent, cause of marital conflict in Sohar. Fatima's loyalty to her husband is irrefutably shown in how she chose, in his absence and even on such a special occasion, to fulfill his wish to the letter.

We also have reason to believe that Ali in his educating zeal had lectured her on the mode of hospitality among "civilized" people, like the nonextravagant English who let be with a cup of Nescafé. Fatima's choice of milk tea would be the Omani equivalent of Nescafé.

What is more, Ali's own consumption choices are somewhat unusual in Sohar. He had acquired a power generator, a color television, and a car (used and very cheap; it soon broke down). It may have been no coincidence that he had singled out items that, with few guests coming to his home, were readily visible to a large public: the sizable television antenna by day (seen by hundreds of people what passed by daily on their way to the hospital), the sound and lights from the generator when in use at night, the car (when it worked) all about town. Reflected is, to my understanding, an admiration, still uncommon in Sohar, for modern consumer goods, combined with an inclination toward conspicuous consumption. Fatima's restraint in hospitality was no doubt easier for her the more she came to share these consumer aspirations. But such a development of shared aspirations is in itself unusual and reflects the closeness of the couple.

It is not that Ali actively discouraged Fatima from the normal pattern of cultivating the neighbors' friendship; in fact, he was very critical of her parents for having done precisely that: "They interfered with her and gave her no chance to see her own friends. That is wrong. I myself don't meddle in women's business: Fatima must be allowed to have friends here, they should dance here if they like; when I see them I go to the other room, I do not interfere."

Our observations, however, give evidence that his statement was only partly true. Although Ali did not forbid Fatima to see friends, he did want to have a say in *whom* she should befriend and to limit her contacts to a few chosen or approved by himself. On another occasion, he inadvertently admitted to harboring such an attitude:

Yes, Fatima receives visitors and gives them hospitality. Many husbands punish and beat their wife when they find out that she wastes money on visitors, but that is wrong and shameful. Hospitality is a reciprocal thing, but I on my part do not want Fatima to go much to them [neighbors], and anyway, how can these employed people [that is, poor servant people] reciprocate for what they receive? But when I point that out, Fatima answers, "We receive everything from God, how can we refuse to give to others?"

By referring derogatorily to their neighbors and admonishing Fatima to play the role of hostess on a permanent basis alone and not reciprocate by being a guest, Ali indirectly and effectively reduced her opportunities for cultivating friendships. Reciprocity is the very foundation for visiting patterns in Sohar, and a failure to reciprocate between equals is the most effective way of discontinuing a relationship.

Adhering so faithfully to her husband's instructions in this matter was not likely to have been accomplished by Fatima without some feeling of sacrifice, though she never alluded to this. When Ali was away and she lived with her parents, she met daily with several neighbors. In her new home, however, she had only two persons with whom she visited daily. Both were old-time neighbors from Higra, who also had recently moved into this new neighborhood. But the most striking feature about these two women, to my mind, was that they were the only older women who voluntarily attended evening school; they were Fatima's schoolmates. By Ali's values, the choice could not have been better, had he made it himself! And he probably did all he could to encourage the tie.

Finally, we may note that Fatima and Ali had settled in an area of recent and still only incipient urban growth, mainly inhabited by people of Bedu origin. Although Ali extolled many of their virtues, in contrast to the character of townspeople (see Ch. 3), he and Fatima shared the feelings of contempt for Bedu typical of the townspeople. Their neighbors were therefore not very important to them ("significant others") in giving or withholding esteem, and this must have made it easier to disregard them and ignore appearances, such as closing the gate from the inside. But again, for Fatima to be content with this reflected her unusually strong identification with her husband, and, no doubt, their practice of spending more time together, and speaking together on a wider variety of topics, than most couples.

It also bears mention that Fatima's long and frequent absences from home, signaled by the locked gate, had their legitimate reasons: she went to school at 2:30 P.M. four days a week and did not come home till 9 or 10 P.M, after Ali picked her up from her parents' house, where she went to stay until he finished his overtime work. Both her own fear of supernatural agents, such as *jinn*, and of highly natural ones, such as thieves and drunken men, as well as his fear of women's infidelity, made it impossible for her to stay alone after dark.

Fatima's self-presentation had changed much during the previous one-and-a-half years: she moved with self-confidence and style and seemed in graceful control of herself and her situation. Gone was her childishness and clumsiness; her face and manner had matured considerably. She was five months' pregnant, which certainly must have contributed to her confidence, but it is my impression that it was above all her position as respected wife, in charge of her own home, that accounted for her new ease and happiness. She proudly showed me her home. It consisted of two rooms and an outdoor kitchen; a well and simple bathroom were located in the back of a spacious compound. The rooms were almost identically furnished, except that one contained the bed and the other the television. The floor was completely covered with colorful plastic mats, and the walls were covered with them, as if they were wallpaper. This gave a cozy and intimate effect and made the rooms tighter against the wind and dust, which would otherwise have become a real hardship, because the house was so close to the heavily trafficked, unsurfaced main road.

Her home had the beautiful simplicity and unpretentious functionality so characteristic of Sohari homes, but it differed a little in being both more spartan and more extravagant in style than homes commonly found among people of her economic level. She owned no decorative plates and bowls, or a small woolen carpet (all items used mainly for hospitality); however, the house was equipped with a power generator and a fan—fashionable status symbols that mainly serve the family's private needs. Their home thus reflected the modern, Western, and perhaps male priorities noted above.

Fatima's kitchen was provisional. It had walls on three sides only and a corrugated iron roof as shelter against the sun and rain. Wooden boxes served as shelves for her small selection of pots and pans, plates and saucers. A small *butagaz* stove, with two burners and no oven, was its central pride. Everything had been bought by Ali.

She kept her home tidy and clean; the rooms and the yard were meticulously swept. Sitting on the plastic mat outside the house, one could look above the *barasti* fence to a view of scattered trees on a wide and open plain. It would have been a peaceful and relaxing sight, had it not been for the constant hammering noise and whirling dust clouds from passing automobiles on the road. Ali often complained about it: "As long as the road is not surfaced, it is terribly dusty. The dust penetrates everything; we cannot sit outside at all. Maybe, in the name of my brother, I will apply for a lot on the other side of the hospital and build there, then if they surface this road in the meantime I will rent out the other house."

Ali was rarely at home during these evenings; he worked overtime, because this was the last month of the year, and the bank at which he worked was preparing its annual accounts. When we first met him at his home, he told a long story about how he quit his former job, claiming his boss would not release him, though he demanded honorable release for family reasons. It was necessary for him to find work in Sohar, because Fatima could not live alone:

"If a woman has three or four children [later he also specified, "if she has a thirteen- or fourteen-year-old boy who understands what is happening"], then her husband can leave her, but not otherwise. Someone must be responsible for her."

My husband asked him, "Why? What are you afraid might happen?"

Ali explained, "If someone climbed over this fence and Fatima was alone, could she fight him? He could steal and take away anything he wished. . . ."

Despite this explanation in terms of security, our impression strongly remained of an unspoken understanding that a woman cannot be trusted alone.

Ali claimed that it was much better to be in Sohar and to look after one's family than to work elsewhere. We suspected his contentment to be dictated more by dire need than preference; he was sorry indeed about his lowered income: "When I get my month's salary, 120–30 Rials, I show Fatima and say, 'Do you know why it is so little, much less than before?' And she answers, 'It is not the money I want, I want you to be with me.'"

In so decidedly wanting her husband to stay with her, Fatima differed from many Sohari women, who complain that men are nagging and demanding, their presence entails much work, so life is better when they are gone (see Ch. 14). Fatima, however, felt herself respectfully treated and had nothing but praise for her husband:

Ali has become *very* good to me [*W-æ-g-i-d zeen*]. Many husbands forbid their wife to visit neighbors, but I may go as I like. He was very bad the first month we were married, did not allow me to stand by the gate or go any place at all, so all I did was sit in my room and cry. But now. . . ! Even though Ali does not like my parents, he requires me to visit them *every* Friday. Last Friday I was lazy and did not want to go, but Ali insisted. So I went. . . . Most husbands try to cut off all contact between the wife and her parents, so to obtain her right she must complain to the Wali, who will instruct her husband to take her on a one day visit once a month. [Note this further example of a woman's lack of knowledge of her legal rights; cf. Ch. 14.] Many women complain about their husband to the Wali, but I never would. Even if Ali beat me or bothered me, I would never say anything but that Ali is *z-e-e-n*—very good. And the first difficult month I did not even tell my parents. Every month now he gives me 10 Rials pocket money to spend on clothes, perfume, and the like, and two months ago he gave me a golden watch worth 25 Rials. He is very good to me.

If Fatima's portrayal is true, Ali was indeed good by Sohari standards— giving her the three things in life that a woman values most: freedom to visit neighbors and friends, resources to entertain them, and access to her own family. Women generally share Fatima's opinion that many men fail to provide their wives with these essentials for happiness. Without knowing just how exceptional Ali is in this, there is no doubt that Fatima con-

sidered herself very fortunate and was also considered so by her friends
and acquaintances, who spoke very favorably of Ali. But we should also
recognize that some of her praise may primarily reflect her strong sense of
loyalty. With regard to her supposed freedom to visit neighbors, for example, Ali did constrain her. It is possible, however, that she herself did not
sense this restriction, either because she was only happy to please him, or
because Ali communicated his interference in a manner so subtle that
Fatima saw in it no unpleasantness, but only a loving regard for her own
best interests. Ali himself mentioned one such instance: "Shortly after we
moved here, Fatima told me something, bad things that a neighbor
woman had said. I said, 'Have nothing more to do with them, *all* the
neighbors, both she who talked and those she talked about. Just sit in your
own house and mind your own business.'" Fatima later related the same
case as one more illustration of Ali's affectionate concern for her.

I suspect, however, that the reasons why Ali, and men generally, encourage or instruct their wives to avoid contact with neighbors are egoistic
in their intent: on the one hand, a strong dislike of the monetary expenses
involved (cf. Ali's own saying p. 261), on the other, a pervasive fear of the
potentially immoral influences at work, so often alluded to by men (cf.
Ali's statements of this, p. 108).

Passively sitting in her own house and minding her own business must
be much more trying for a woman with no children than I think Ali could
ever fathom. How much business can a woman in this position find to
mind, and how satisfying? Although Ali spent significantly more time
with his wife than Sohari husbands generally do, it still amounted to no
more than three to four waking hours a day. For the rest of the day, he is
away. He has his work, shopping to do, the attractions of a humming
market; and he has his friends, whom he cultivates as he likes. Due to the
unequal rights of spouses, he is free from wifely injunctions about minding his own business, or restraining hospitality, with only his own judgment to guide him.

The relative closeness that characterizes Fatima's and Ali's relationship
may partly reflect the absence of other close ties. Not only does Ali claim
that he sees his friends less because his house lies so far out of town. More
importantly, Fatima has, by quarreling with her parents, intensified her
dependence upon Ali. In case of marital conflict, she has no real refuge
except the Wali. Her chosen option is to make Ali content and to live happily with him. Ali has also broken away from his family and, because of
his long absences from Sohar, has no strong personal involvement in the
community. His strong sense of responsibility and his determination to
educate Fatima make him further inclined to spend much time with her,
training and disciplining her.

Ali's decision that Fatima should honor her parents by visiting them
once a week, on the other hand, is remarkable. We came across no similar

instance, but often the contrary attitude, as exemplified by Meimona's husband in the previous chapter. Denying the wife access to her parents is seen both as a safety measure against the potential complaints and appeals that she might launch to them, as well as being an effective means of dramatizing authority. It is also the cheapest course; geographical distances and taxi fares combine to make most such visits a considerable expense. Fatima's parents, however, lived within walking distance, and Ali felt absolutely confident of her loyalty. Having nothing to lose and esteem to gain, he insisted that she make use of the right that Omani law gives to a woman, of one weekly visit to her parents.

It is not that the married daughter has a duty to visit her parents, only a privilege; but Ali may well have reasoned that it was in Fatima's own best interest to give this evidence of salutary respect for her own parents. As her guardian and husband, he should show her the right way and see to it that no one could judge her wanting in good qualities; he quite clearly wants to be proud of her. And the importance he attaches to such appearances is clearly attested by his own guiding principle: "I don't want anyone to be able to speak bad things about me. Now I have worked, I have taken care of my life, I have a job, I have a family; no one can say a bad word against me. I want to protect that reputation."

Not only does Ali want to protect his reputation, once established. He clearly realizes that it is a precarious thing that needs constant tending and forethought—something that can, with great difficulty, be enhanced, but can also be very easily damaged. To enhance his reputation he wants to excel, morally speaking, to be extravagant in his moral commitments, to fulfill more than his ordained share so that people will admire his style and beautiful manners and say, "Ali, he is a man." On his own relations to Fatima's family, Ali related:

> Her parents drop by once a month on a brief visit, but her sisters [age ten and fourteen] come once a week and stay overnight. That's okay, but if they stayed more than one night I would kick them out. Fatima's little brother [age five] comes daily and often sleeps here, but that's okay, because I am often late from work and Fatima does not like to be alone. I also make Fatima visit her mother every Friday for three or four hours, after she has cleaned up the breakfast. It is right that she should visit her family, according to religion. But I cannot forget how they acted and will not see them much myself, but sometimes I drop in for two or three minutes. When I work overtime at the bank, I tell Fatima to go to her mother's after classes and wait for me there. I drop by when I am finished, stay a moment and then take her home.

About his relations to his own family he explained:

> My father never comes here, because he is still angry, not with me, but with Fatima's family. I visit him sometimes and give him money, fifteen Rials every month, for he is an old man. When my brother lived with him, I used to go more frequently. Poor boy, he has not his own mother [only a stepmother]. I offered to take him in my house and give him an education, but no, he wanted to

fool around, he got bad friends, drank, and quit school. So I made him think
about an occupation; he considered driving, but could not get down to it. Finally, I arranged for a group of soldiers on leave to abduct him, on the lieuten-
ant's, my relative's, orders—they caught him in my father's garden and took
him to a recruiting station, said the government had heard complaints about
him, and made him enlist. Now he has finished six months' training and is sta-
tioned in Jebel Akhdar.

Fatima gave a more complete version of their distant relationship to
Ali's father:

I have been angry with him for six months because once when he came to fetch
a goat I politely asked him to sit down and have coffee while waiting for Ali, but
he was brusque in his manner and said he did not care for coffee. All during
^c*id* [feast] we planned to swallow our anger and go to greet him, but we
didn't get further than to a relative's in Higra [a ten-minute walk from Ali's
father's house] before we changed our mind and went back home. . . . "

Fatima's story substantiates the generalization given previously of how
easily persons feel insulted and how fragile relationships are. It is also
evidence of the intimate character of her marital relationship. For Ali to
abstain from visiting his father on the feast, at which time the Koran enjoins people to show forgiveness and reconciliation, and custom obliges
them to honor their parents, is a clear message of his predominant loyalty
to his wife.

The behavior adopted by Fatima and Ali in regard to their parents and
parents-in-law, and the attitudes they express, are highly revealing of the
character of close relationships generally in Sohar, and consistent with
other data already presented. But in the present context, Fatima and Ali
are particularly interesting for the light they shed on the character of their
relationship as spouses.

Fatima's indifference to visiting her family can be read as an unequivocal statement of what Ali means to her. Admittedly, her childhood home
may not have been particularly dear to her, and till her last day there she
had been made to do more than her share of housework, whereas in her
marital home she had greater leisure. But her status as a Friday visitor to
her parents was no doubt one of privilege and few duties, whereas Ali
tended to be particularly demanding of attention on his day off—yet that
was where she wished to be.

The strength of Ali's identification with her is also revealed: rather than
savor how she favored him before her parents, he felt as deep a concern for
her esteem in the eyes of others as he did for his own, and so chose to
forgo his own enjoyment for the enhancement of her reputation. Yet he
respected her sufficiently to suffer the loss of esteem and self-regard that
must have been entailed in his own failure to perform the annual, ritual
affirmation of filial piety by visiting his own father, so as to affirm his

primary loyalty to her. Their respective acts speak clearly of a primary identification with each other, before all other coexisting relationships.

Fatima was never talkative—a trait she shared with most Sohari women—but on the rare occasions when she did spontaneously share her thoughts and feelings with me, she never failed to praise Ali: "Ali is *wægid zen* [very good]" was her recurrent brief but meaningful phrase. To identify the bases for this judgment—which I must manage alone, for Fatima could inadequately help me due to her own inarticulateness—I venture the following interpretation.

Ali's "goodness" consisted mainly in his practice of treating Fatima with real respect. He was firm and determined with her, exercising his authority as a husband and never leaving doubt as to who was master of the house. But because Fatima managed to make him feel secure about her loyalty and admiration, he rarely felt the need to dramatize his authority and superiority: he was convinced that she struggled to the best of her ability to please him, and that her shortcomings were due to a lack of knowledge and understanding rather than will. Consequently, he responded with considerable patience and consideration to her weaknesses, and he succeeded on the whole in making her feel that his sanctions and occasional loss of temper were fair and in her own best interest. He did not hold Fatima herself responsible for her failings, but put the blame on her parents. To make up for their sins of omission, he spent more time talking with Fatima about life and people than husbands were wont to do, sharing many of his daily experiences with her in an effort to widen her horizons. He often elicited her opinion before making decisions in matters concerning them both, and he sometimes even followed her views when they differed from his. One such instance that Fatima proudly related was the question of whether to rent their house while they lived in Mattrah a few months after Ali had quit his PDO job. Ali was much in favor of it, because it meant a monthly income of four Rials, but Fatima was strongly against it, because "it is not good letting strangers move into your home." The house being part of Fatima's domain, Ali respected her wish. He was determined that she should be responsible for her own house, considering this a prerequisite for learning and growth.

Ali seemed to want to portray the burden he had brought upon himself by marrying an uneducated girl as particularly heavy and demanding. But his plight was indeed shared by most Sohari men, for girls are married as young as thirteen to sixteen years old. Till then, they have spent all their life in the narrow world of home and neighborhood, performing roles that put a premium on passive obedience and imitation. Thus they must seem immature, unreflective, and in need of training from the point of view of their husbands. Not only is a groom usually nearly twice as old as his bride, he has also lived a life that has given him a chance to develop creative qualities, like initiative, judgment, and exploration, which were suppressed in her. He has had freedom of movement and is usually widely traveled; he has been responsible for himself and has faced courses of action that necessitate selection and choice; he has made independent decisions, participated in an uncertain world to build up a social identity and gain the esteem of his fellows; he has been faced with myriad impressions and allowed to exercise and satisfy his curiosity. In short, he has moved in an open, potentially limitless world that he could explore at will, where courses of action are not fixed and custom and tradition provide only a guide, but no watertight solution, to all complexities and eventualities. He has had to rely upon his own intellectual and emotional capacities to shape and create his individual life.

This world has been completely closed to his wife. When she was a small girl, her brothers were allowed to play in the gardens and the sea and to run errands to the market, she had to stay within the narrow confines of her home; while they were given the right to exercise body and mind in (sometimes reckless) exploration, she was impelled to discipline herself to become quiet, shy, respectful, and reserved—the manner expected of a decent and well-behaved girl. Thus both boy and girl are selectively prepared for the roles they play in mature life, as this life has been shaped until very recently. This is the pattern of experience and background that also characterizes Ali's and Fatima's lives. Despite Ali's criticisms, Fatima's parents are moral and responsible people who clearly had not neglected their parental duty to inculcate the feminine virtues and values in their daughter. The extended portrait I have sought to give of these two persons, and of their relationship, can thus serve as our personification of husband and wife in Sohar—strikingly unique in all particulars and in the way they have developed their relationship, yet undeniably children of the circumstances and values that affect the lives of most Soharis.

The portrait of Fatima and Ali, and of the relation of many spouses in Sohar today, is not complete without considering those suggestions of changes in the future that can only dimly be sensed in the present. This is a future for which parents have largely, and naturally, failed to prepare their daughters. It is therefore more visible in nuances of the wifely role that some young husbands, Ali among them, are beginning to visualize for their wives. The vision of a changed wifely role arises among these husbands in response to the swift and pervasive spread of a new government-sponsored ideology of development and education for all, and a bettered life for women. Because of the men's greater perceptiveness and cosmopolitan exposure, they are the ones most receptive to this. The new wifely role I am speaking of does not yet differ significantly, if at all, from the old one with respect to tasks and functions. Rather, the innovation, if such diffuse beginnings may be given such an ambitious name, concerns the qualities and attributes a wife ought to possess, and *how* she should go about carrying out her tasks, not *what* she should do. The desired qualities are all thought of as implied in, or deriving from, the one magical adjective "educated." Omani men seem to regard education as the source of every conceivable virtue. Superior moral insight, as well as conduct and a purification of mind and body, are thought to spring from it. Consequently, education for the wife is expected to have beneficial, if unspecified, repercussions in all areas of a couple's life—at least by the *husband*. It is significant that women either do not share this conviction, or do not aspire to such height, as revealed by the fact that of the twenty or so married women in Fatima's class, only three attended by their own choice. The remaining wives went unwillingly, on their husbands' command. Women's lack of interest is understandable when one considers the curriculum. It contains little of practical interest to their lives, and much that seems a direct nuisance, such as writing, arithmetic, and English. Not only can this education, as they see it, not benefit them in their daily work of homemaking and child rearing, it also interferes directly with their favored activities by being very time-consuming. The time available for visiting and for sewing and embroidering (women's cherished income-bringing work, which can also easily be combined with visiting) is thereby drastically reduced. Although men seem to value such work and encourage their women to pursue it, those with modern aspirations, like Ali, put an even higher value on education and its positive effects on home life and child care. Child raising is, as we have seen, entirely the woman's task, both her privilege and responsibility. The mother is the major influence in children's lives, until the age of ten for boys, and marriage for girls. Omani folk theories of personality development further underscore the importance of environmental factors, as opposed to inheritance; children and grownups alike are regarded as dangerously susceptible to molding through social interaction. Because children's conduct also to some extent affects the father's life and honor, it seems highly likely that men's aspirations for their own future, as well as that of their children, are major factors behind their determination to have their wives educated.

If Ali is representative of such modern men—and our evidence indicates that he is—then one additional factor should be considered: the desire for a fuller, personally more satisfying marital relationship. In traditional Omani culture and society, husband and wife are persons with different but complementary qualities who interact in limited capacities, but live the remainder of their lives in separate worlds. A wife does not even have the right to *ask* her husband about his life outside the home, because he is hers only within it. I do not think Ali intended to relinquish this privilege, but I have a strong impression that he wanted Fatima to be able to partake in his world when and where he chose to let her in. He seemed to desire a marital relationship with a potentiality for personal living and sharing, and the quality of companionship with a wife whose capacities were not limited to those of homemaker and sexual partner, but who was a more complete and developed person as well.

Unfortunately, I have no parallel evidence of Fatima's aspirations for her marital relationship. I believe she would have faltered had she known of Ali's longings and plans, for they would have threatened the security of the familiar world for which she had been socialized. But throughout the period we knew them, her willingness to accommodate his wishes and accept his standards seemed unflinching.

CHAPTER 14

✤

Role-realization
in Marriage

"See how life is; when a daughter marries, she transfers all of her affections to her husband. That is not right. There should be one part for him, and one for her parents."

The closer one looks into the life situation and behavior of two persons in a marital relationship, the more singular and exceptional they become. Nowhere can this be truer than for married couples in Sohar. So the central problem of this chapter is to depict the relations between particular spouses, as I have had the opportunity to come to know them, and yet arrive at statements that also capture their common features and the shared premises and circumstances of married life in Sohar, without brushing aside, or doing violence to, this individuality.

Fatima and Ali's relationship, as portrayed in the preceding chapter, seems to me to epitomize both the individuality and the features basically Sohari. Two briefer, contrastive portraits of other couples may serve to illustrate the diversity that confronts us—and give a first sense of the common ground that underlies this variation—before we attempt a more systematic analysis of marital patterns and their possible determinants. The first case concerns the same Sheikha already discussed in Chapter 8, and her husband, Suleiman.

When I knew her in 1974, Sheikha was considered by all her neighbors the most unfortunate of wives. Said her friends Latifa and Khadiga:

"Her husband is very stingy and never lets her entertain at home. Once he even acted so offensively that we swore we would never set foot at her place again. She had invited us, Latifa's mother and grandmother over, and just as we sat down to have coffee, he appeared. Before our very noses he grabbed the tray! Even though all she was offering us was a dish of candies and a plate of biscuits, he was furious and commanded her to the other room, where he wildly scolded her and beat her for wasting his hard-earned money. For a whole year we never went there again."

Of my closest friend, Latifa, I asked, "Why does he act like that, is he so poor?"

"No, just stingy, like so many men. But he is not well off, he works as

271

an orderly [*farrash*] at the hospital. And he is very uneducated. He has not even traveled outside of Sohar and seen the world, neither been to Dubai or Muscat and gained knowledge."

"What does he look like; is he handsome?"

"He looks just like their daughter, so you can judge for yourself!" (There is a mute agreement between us that she can hardly be called pretty.) "He is like the wife," adds Latifa, without scorn, in a matter-of-fact way. "She too is not much to look at."

"Why do you think Sheikha's parents married her to him?"

"Because her folks are no better than his, and so they could reach an agreement." Sheikha's own version or understanding was that the sheikh of her village had been bribed into lying about her future husband's qualities.

"Can she not divorce him?" I asked.

"No, he demands his 500 Rials back [that is, the *hader*], and her kin cannot or will not pay the money."

In the course of the subsequent year and a half, Sheikha's life changed drastically, in the way we have already seen. Knowing my interest in understanding Sheikha's situation and keeping abreast with developments, Latifa had news for me one day in January 1976 as I arrived at her home:

"You should have heard the racket last night! Sheikha's husband threatened her with divorce, upbraiding her so fiercely that we could hear it all through the wall! His patience is finally and definitely at an end, he said. Never is lunch ready on time; the house is filthy and messy; the clothes, always soiled. If she doesn't instantly and radically improve, it's out and finished! And it is true," commented Latifa gently, "her house is very dirty, for she is never there to do the work." There was an instant's pause, and then she continued, with emphasis:

"But you should have seen Sheikha before, how good she was; she was z-e-e-e-na [very, very good!]. When her husband told her 'Don't go there,' she didn't go. When he said, 'Don't entertain guests,' she didn't entertain. In everything she obeyed him. She was so kind that she even helped prepare the cement from which they built the house! Man's work! She was always hard-working and thrifty, whereas he was impossible to make content, he scolded her and beat her—for no reason. And despite all that, she never complained to her kinsmen, never said a word to anyone. Just went into her room and cried. Sometimes we would hear her and feel so sorry for her that we wept on her behalf. Her mother-in-law lived with them then. When she died, two years ago, Sheikha turned bad, and her husband turned good. Not till then did she finally complain to her kin, who came and quarreled with the husband. So now he treats her very well, because her kinsmen stand by her. But now that he has become good, she has turned bad."

I asked Latifa, "Why didn't Sheikha complain to her kin before?"

"I don't know. . . ."

"Do you think that perhaps she was afraid of her mother-in-law's anger in case she did such a thing?"

"Maybe. . . ."

"Maybe she wants to get back at him now for all those bad years?" I suggested.

"Maybe-e-e . . .," mused Latifa.

"Or maybe she is working at provoking him to divorce her?"

"Oh, no!" Latifa was suddenly definitive and unequivocal in her reply: "She doesn't want a divorce, for another man might not let her carry on the way she does, and that's the way she wants to have it. She even says that she loves her husband. But would a wife who loves her husband bring shame upon him like she does?"

And she reminded me one more time of the predicament of Sheikha's husband: he is trapped—due to the monetary expenses involved in getting a divorce, along with other hardships.

This excerpt from marital life, when juxtaposed with the extended portrait given in the previous chapter, highlights three matters of importance to our understanding of marital roles in Sohar. First, the extreme spectrum of variation that the behavior and relationship of different couples display, and the similarities that are discernible across such a range of variation. Second, the difficulty of identifying simple causes for these differences, and the form each relationship takes. And third, the characteristic way one can see, where the facts are known, how the parties to a marriage, by their own particular choices and acts, have shaped, and occasionally entirely transformed, their lives and their marital roles. What could be more contrastive than the immoral, rebellious, and assertive Sheikha of 1976 from the abused and loyally submissive Sheikha of 1974? And who could imagine a happier transformation than the proud and contented Fatima, living in her own house with her husband, from the insignificant and exploited daughter living in her natal home, with her husband far away?

The lives of these two women have undergone more radical changes in the course of one year than many Sohari wives experience in the course of a lifetime, with the result that the behavior and life styles of the two are very different. Yet if we compare their wifely roles in 1974, there are certain striking similarities. Perhaps most notable is the unswerving loyalty of both. They had complained to no one, not even their closest kin or friends, when too harshly treated by their respective husbands. Both had obeyed the husband's word to the letter with respect to hospitality and visiting. And both had the means to change radically the course of their lives and ultimately took the steps to do so. Thereby both have, if we are to trust the judgment of Sheikha's friends, realized the kind of life that they wanted, though these lives could not be more different. Contrast Fatima's "It is not the money I want, I want you [Ali] to be with me" with Sheikha's pursuing her prostitute career in utter defiance of her husband. Nonetheless, both wives could be said to have had their way at the cost of the wish of their husbands: Ali regrets having had to leave his job with PDO and wasting money on a *barasti* hut; the fate of Sheikha's husband is so pitiful by Sohari standards as to need no further comment.

I do not think that it was because of any unusual force of personality that these two women were able to compel their husbands and effect such dramatic changes in their lives. I think rather that each had made a reasonably adequate estimate of her husband's probable reactions and a realistic calculation of what she stood to gain or lose by pursuing her respective course. Such calculation is both evident in Fatima's careful timing of her request for a house, and in Sheikha's spacing of her amorous rendezvous. Needless to say, not all Sohari wives are so fortunately placed as to have the scales weighted in their favor. To provide a further contrast to these two, let us focus briefly on another woman who seems if anything to have more mettle than them, yet has not (yet?) found a way to change her unhappy situation.

This unfortunate one is Khadiga, a gracious and willful woman of nineteen years and the mother of three little boys.

Khadiga and Hamid had been married for six years in 1976, and Khadiga was expecting her fourth child. The age difference between the spouses is great: Khadiga was nineteen years old, Hamid was forty-five, but the difference appeared even greater. Khadiga, with her exceedingly youthful manner and slender build, looked no more than fourteen. Hamid's face was furrowed by age and hardships, his posture was stooped, and he looked like an old man. Other incongruities of looks, personality, and background aggravate the gap between the two. Hamid, though himself rather poor, comes from a well-to-do and fairly influential large family. Khadiga's kin are all poor. She has noticeably Negroid features, whereas he is light-skinned. In manner, Khadiga is very sweet and gentle, even by Sohari standards, and she seems unusually intelligent and observant. Hamid, for all his respectable manners, can be a bit crude and awkward, and he is clearly not so bright.

Their marriage had not been successful. There were slight nuances in behavior that told of the cleavage between the two. Khadiga was less discreet about her husband's family secrets than other, more happily married wives (for example, in revealing to me which girls had not been virgins at marriage). She was also less loyal to him personally (for example, in being prepared to disclose to me that her husband occasionally beat her). Hamid did not sufficiently respect Khadiga to let her take charge of that which, by Sohari conventions, is the woman's realm: the care of small children. Whenever one of his sons would cry in his presence, he told Khadiga to stop his crying by popping some sweets into his mouth. And when Khadiga mildly objected that such leniency was no feasible disciplinary measure, he ignored her and forced his own will.

It is difficult to say whether Khadiga and Hamid were not from the beginning too poorly matched for their marriage ever to succeed. Khadiga's remark about their first encounter is telling in this respect, "They had told me that he was old, but not stone old." As it is, coresidence with a mother-in-law who makes no secret of her dislike for Khadiga has been an effective deterrent to marital accommodation. She put pressure on Hamid to divorce Khadiga.

I had been present only two days on my second field visit when Grandmother, amidst a group of kinswomen, asked whether I did not think that Hamid ought to divorce Khadiga.

"No," I said emphatically, "is he thinking of such a thing?"

"Yes, for all the children are dark like their mother and none have the fine features of their father."

I remarked that we think that brown skin color is beautiful.

"How can you," retorted Grandmother, "when it generally goes with a broad nose, large lips, and kinky hair. We think such looks are ugly!"

When my disapproval continued to be evident, Grandmother amended her own statement and said that if Hamid takes a new wife, he will divorce Khadiga.

"Why did he marry her in the first place," I asked, "did he not know that she was brown-skinned?"

"Yes, he did, we told him that, but a go-between swore otherwise and stressed, moreover, the family's great fertility, and Hamid chose to believe her. Now he regrets it."

Later I asked Latifa whether it was true that Hamid is thinking of taking another wife. She said that she does not know, but that in any case he cannot afford to do so. He has only two rooms in his house, and one is occupied by his mother. To take a second wife, he would need a third room. But he is so poor he does not even have the funds to complete the house he has; the walls are unpainted and the ceiling is corrugated iron only.

On the quality of her life with a mother-in-law, Khadiga, in a comparison between Latifa and herself, observed:

> Latifa has such an easy life because she lives with her mother. And even when she moves to her own house down the street her mother will continue to take care of the child. For a grandmother loves her daughter's children. Look at me! I work not only for my own children and husband, but also for my mother-in-law, who does nothing but sew and never lends a helping hand. On the contrary, when a child cries, she becomes sour and annoyed. Had my mother lived close, she would have helped out. A grandmother ought to prefer her son's children, as you yourself heard my mother-in-law say the other day when she complained that Mariam [a son's daughter] never visits her, whereas her daughter's daughter does. But reality is just not like that.

I suspect that Khadiga was aware of her vulnerable position, as may be indicated by the following incident: Latifa and I were visiting her when her three-year-old son was restless and demanding. Khadiga hit him and told him to run off and play. Then, as if she had just noticed what she had done, she asked me whether we spank our children, and before I had had time to answer, whether in my country the husband beats the wife? When I answered "No," she and Latifa both immediately remarked that in Sohar there are *many* men who beat their wives. When I, incredulous, repeated "*many* men?" they modified their statement, saying that men do not beat their wives so much any more, because the Wali disapproves of it, but previously it was very common.

"Does it ever happen that the wife hits back?" I asked.

"No," answered Khadiga, "when Hamid beats me, I never answer in kind, just cry by myself, for I am afraid that he might divorce me. . . . A woman with small children is always afraid, for it is only the child that she nurses that she may keep. [Another instance of a woman's unawareness of her legal rights.] And it is impossible for a stepmother to love her stepchild, therefore women like me who have small children, must always be accommodating—that is, those who *love* their children."

Khadiga loves hers dearly. Because there is no male kinsman to appeal to in time of crisis and no deferred bride price to act as a deterrent on her husband in case of divorce, I would not be surprised if the marriage eventually breaks up.

In what these three women, in 1976, were realizing through their wifely roles, Fatima can be said to have embraced hers as the dominant component of her whole identity; Khadiga to have accommodated to hers and sought self-realization in her relationship to her children; whereas Sheikha comes close to having discarded hers, fulfilling only the barest minimum of her obligations in it. She seems in the process of shaping an identity wholly her own, as a truly autonomous person, in explicit revolt against her wifely role. Or is it perhaps best understood as a revolt against the basic woman's role in Sohar?

In either case, we do not seem to come very far if we seek to homogenize such different lives into a standardized description of "the marital relationship in Sohar." Nor would it seem promising, or satisfactory, to search for particular explanations of "deviance" in the more aberrant cases, so as to be left with a more unitary, customary form. What we need is a more dynamic way of describing the lives of Sohari spouses in terms of the meanings that different acts and activities have within the context of the marital relationship in Sohar, and in terms of the factors—within the persons and in their environment—that limit and channel their choices and acts.

ROLE-REALIZATION

The key concept that may enable us to understand such diverse lives and relationships under a unified perspective is that of *role-realization*.

The simplest anthropological construction on the concept of role sees it simply as the behavior whereby a person acts out the rights and duties entailed in his or her status (Linton 1936). Although the rights and duties of wife and husband clearly affect their behavior vis-à-vis each other, it is quite unrealistic to try to imagine that all regularities in their behavior derive from this simple source. Indeed, all life has the dynamic and indeterminate character that requires every individual to find solutions to the existential problems of his or her life, and so to some extent shape his or her own behavior and fate. And because no two situations are identical, neither will the solutions be so. But in many relationships and life situations the constraints that impinge on people and influence their responses are so powerful and pervasive that the variation between different persons occupying the same status in a relationship is relatively small: not only because of the rights and duties of the status, but also because of the environment in which the behavior must take place, the assets and skills commanded by the actors, rules of polite demeanor, and so forth. Examples from Sohar of relationships where these constraints produce a high degree of standardization of behavior would be merchant and customer, father and daughter, son-in-law and parents-in-law (if the two are not related by kinship), and neighborhood relations between women. In each of these cases, the reciprocal roles are composed of a few characteristic and general features of behavior.

Why should not this be equally true of the marital relationship? Soharis themselves would probably seek the answers in individual personality differences. Because the marital relationship is so intimate and many-faceted, such differences are given scope to assert themselves more profoundly than in other, more narrowly focused relationships. Soharis often interpret marital behavior to be directed toward achieving concrete and specific goals, and to be part of very long-term strategies, while at the same time they recognize that there are great differences in people's "nature"—that is, what they value and seek. But in essence, this amounts to little more than saying that people act as they do because that is how they are.

Perhaps a more productive insight can be developed by giving due attention to the profound *difference* and *interdependence/complementarity* that obtain between wife and husband in Sohar. This interdependence gives rise to accommodations and strategies whereby the behavior of one party is conditioned by that of the other party to the relationship. But the language of strategies is most illuminating where there exists a clear conflict of interests—and such conflicts do take place, as we saw between Fatima and Ali in the matter of house-building. In Sohar, however, it would rather seem that for many purposes wife and husband, and indeed woman and man, regard each other as supplementary and interlinked rather than opposed: they are so basically different that they do not think of themselves as competing, but rather that each party, by his or her very existence and distinctiveness, provides the occasion for the other to realize what is of value to him or her. This kind of complementarity is certainly physically embodied in their first encounter as wife and husband, where the bride—by having her virginity intact, and thereby providing public proof of her honor—also provides the occasion for the groom to document his. If this kind of complementarity of function is general—and I shall provide ethnographic evidence in the following that it may be—we may have part of the key to the wide variation of role behavior in marriage. What unfolds of behavior between any particular couple will depend on the particular constellation of mutually relevant traits, interests, and endowments, *and* the particular history of interaction between the two, whereby these potentialities have or have not been made relevant and developed. Such a model, composed both of confrontation and complementarity, is much more difficult to apply than a model that depicts the marital relationship as a tug of war, but it is also, I believe, much more true to life.

An additional factor contributes to the explanation of what seems an extreme range of variation. In Sohar, more than most other places in the world, the solutions to the problems of married life must to a great extent be designed, one might even say *invented,* by the persons themselves. This is partly due to the exclusiveness and insulation of each couple (noted in Ch.13), which means that they cannot serve as role models for others to emulate. Marital interaction takes place in highly secreted privacy; and because loyalty reigns supreme, what takes place between any two particular spouses is effectively shielded behind a near impregnable barrier. Friends of the woman, her neighbors and kin, have no more knowledge of the actual behavior that takes place between husband and wife than what they can see with their own eyes (for example, Sheikha's husband grabbing the tray), or hear with their own ears (for example, Sheikha sobbing), and in most cases this does not add up to very much. Some things they may gather as second-hand information (for example, that Ali is building a house for Fatima). But what motivated him to do it? I am sure Fatima told no one, nor that any of Ali's friends know what he confided in my husband. In consequence, Fatima, despite her successful maneuver, left her neighbors as unenlightened as before about how *they* might act to obtain the same advantages. For they would never ask her about it, and she would never brag or explain.

The cherished selves that Soharis want to present to the world are constituted so as to preclude gossip, curiosity, and inquiry about the lives of others. Such little gossip as there is, is weakly interpreted and presented as confidential news of an untransformed kind, interesting matters of fact to enliven a humdrum life, and not as inquisitive and censorious infringements on the life and integrity of others. For example, when Latifa uttered the phrase, "When she [Sheikha's mother-in-law] died, Sheikha turned bad and her husband turned good," I thought to myself: aha, finally a clue. The mother-in-law's presence and Sheikha's goodness were connected, and Latifa knew it. But when I asked her to explain the connection, she was at a loss. If she had sensed it at all, she had never pondered what its nature might be. To her, the mother-in-law's death and Sheikha's commencing with prostitution were just two events linked in time. It may even have been fortuitous that she happened to mention the two together.

All this means that there are only a few, fragmentary and poorly generalized, role models. The two strangers who come together at their wedding and have thrust upon them the statuses of husband and wife are equipped with little insight, experience, or progressive guidance to cope with all the eventualities of a complex relationship and to realize the roles of husband and wife. In most respects, they must shape their roles by trial and error through private assessment and intuition in counterpoint to each other.

This is very different from the wide public knowledge of people's life in most societies of the world, and reminiscent rather of the insulation and privacy enforced on married couples in urban Western society. But compared to them, Soharis are left even more to their own devices. Young girls must cope with marriage entirely without the insights offered by books, movies and other mass media; without the perspective provided by gossip, confidences, and reminiscences; and without any formal or informal advice and counseling, apart from the questionable aid of the *mikobra* during the seven-day honeymoon. As far as I can ascertain, even one's own mother generally fails to furnish one with much perspective, for parents would not stoop to the indignity of quarreling in front of the children, or commit the indiscretion of exposing their own situation to them.

The absence or paucity of role models implied in the loyalty/noninterference syndrome also helps to account for the startling phenomenon that we have encountered time and again, namely women's lack of knowledge of their legal rights—exemplified in connection with virginity and the rights to visit parents.

The most extreme example of the latter that I came across was poor Khadiga, who visited her mother no more than two days a year and believed that should she complain to the Wali, he would affirm that the wife *belongs* to her husband, so she has no reason for complaint. I pondered long before I found what I believe is the clue to women's ignorance of their lawful rights: loyalty and lack of gossip must provide the answer. When women enhance their pride by refraining from complaints about their husband, and never, in their circles of friends and neighbors, discuss the relative merits or impropriety of different behaviors or pass judgments and provide tactical advice, then no consensus about proper ways and lawful rights can materialize. So unless Khadiga had been instructed by her mother before marriage—"Remember that you have the right to be taken here on a visit once every fortnight!" (her mother lives rather far away)—she may never come to know her privilege. Nor will the fact that others, such as her neighbors, make regular home visits be likely to enlighten her. As in the case of Fatima's success of obtaining a house: what leads to success for one is not revealed to others, and Khadiga would likely as not have no way to discover what is her right, and what is just other people's good fortune.

This unavailability of role models has another aspect that I must emphasize: it is not only the married person, but even more the enquiring anthropologist, who is left with little generalizable material. How can you, as an outsider, hope to penetrate behind the façades that family members and friends of a lifetime have not breached? In the course of my six months in Sohar, I never once had the opportunity to meet the husbands of my close friends Latifa and Feyza, for they were absent on labor migration. I never caught a glimpse of Sheikha's husband, though he was in residence throughout my stay, nor did I see the husbands of numerous other acquaintances who do not figure by name in this book.

So it is no coincidence that Fatima and Ali were chosen for the extended portrait in the preceding chapter. Due to the fortuitous circumstance of Ali's long sick leave, and his delight in having English-speaking neighbors, we were uniquely fortunate to see him and Fatima interact frequently and for extended periods. Of equal importance, Ali's articulateness and his confidence in my husband provided us with the data that lend some detail and depth to the portrait. If I had had to rely upon Fatima alone for information, with her taciturn and ubiquitous "maybe," there would have been little to portray.

Otherwise, the material on which this chapter is based includes considerable observation of interaction, between Rahmeh and Abdullah, and some between Khadiga and Hamid—both alone and in the presence of Hamid's resident mother. A dozen or so of other couples who do not figure by name in this account, I have seen together during brief visits in their homes. Finally, I have information and commentaries, both from the wives themselves and from third parties, on the marital life of Latifa, Feyza, Khadiga, Rahmeh, and Sheikha.

With such limited material, I shall not be able to penetrate and expose the inner workings of married life in Sohar. But, for once, I do not say "unfortunately." Let Soharis keep their secrets. The dignity with which individuals and couples struggle to comport themselves, so that their lives will embody the gracefulness and style they so value, deserves to be respected.

What is more, the resultant picture may in many respects be more true to life than a more searching dissection. Life in Sohar, even more than most places, *is* surface and appearance. The imperative of tactfulness, which entails the acceptance of others at face value, also means that social reality is constituted by these appearances. Pretenses that others see through, and realities with which others are familiar, are part of that world on which I am reporting, but the private joys, doubts, and miseries that are not made visible to other Soharis are not necessary for my description either.

SOME GENERALIZATIONS

Soharis often remark that on the wedding night the bride struggles desperately against the groom and cries much. But the next morning she is happy again, for she loves him. If she does not love him then, she never will, and a marriage between two who do not love one another will never succeed. This is no doubt an oversimplification: Feyza, for example, is said to have been very unhappy about her marriage to her cousin, both before and for a considerable time after, but to love him now. Nor is it possible to grasp the particular meaning of the kind of attachment referred to as *hubb* (love)—by a standard Arabic-English dictionary. Is it primarily what we would term loyalty, or solidarity, or affection that Soharis have in mind, or is it all of these? It is important to note, however, that an attachment called love should be there, according to Sohari views; that they do not see love as depending on personal familiarity or shared experiences; and that, if it is lacking, it is both justified and possible for either party to obtain a divorce.

My observations of interaction would lead me to formulate the following generalizations. A high degree of mutual loyalty is practiced by nearly all couples, and wives generally radiate a confidence and dignity that seem at odds with their legal rights and obligations. This does not mean that most wives and husbands are utterly satisfied with their life and are not striving to achieve something different and better. But before analyzing this striving, let us focus on a third portrait of a married woman who seems to personify the good life as it is realistically conceived by the ordinary woman in Sohar. It would clearly not be right to represent her situation as ideal from everybody's point of view. And it is striking that different aspects of her situation are variously valued by her friends according to what they themselves miss the most in their own marriage. But I am confident that she can exemplify what will be generally accepted in Sohar as an enviable position.

Latifa is this fortunate one, and a description of her situation leads us directly into one general feature of marital life in Sohar: the disparity of the man's and the woman's worlds. Latifa's husband, Nasr, has lived and worked in the rich, modern Gulf states for the last fifteen years, since he was about ten years old. Latifa has never traveled further from Sohar than to her husband's native village, Ghel, some thirty kilometers south along the coast. Immensely proud of him as she is, she cannot remember exactly in which of the Gulf States he works, and she does not know what his work is.

In this Latifa is displaying proper modesty and respect: a wife should not ask her husband about his activities outside the home, for he is properly hers only within it.

They are a well-matched couple, by Sohari standards. There is the right age difference—nearly ten years—between them. She is beautiful (very pale, slightly chubby, with unfailingly polite manners), and he is very meticulous and much concerned about his repute. He has a very good income, approximately 250 Rials Omani per month, and according to Latifa, will not consider taking employment in Oman owing to the lower salaries there. Both spouses are of well-to-do, respectable families, and the marriage was arranged because Nasr was a younger personal friend of Latifa's (now deceased) father. Nasr is now a personal friend of Latifa's elder brother, Ali, who is roughly of the same age and is employed in a nearby company. In 1975, Latifa had been married for three years and had a two-year-old daughter. She was three months' pregnant with her second child.

On how fortunate Latifa was, Sheikha commented:

> So much does Nasr love her that even when Latifa's own mother tells him not to be so indulgent with Latifa and let her go wherever she likes [Sheikha at this time was virtually held prisoner in her own house by her husband's strictures], he says no, he will not constrain her lest Latifa will say/think that he is no good. He is *very* kind to her and gives her all the good things.

All the good things . . . lucky indeed the woman who has such a man for a husband. And Latifa did consider herself very lucky. This was plain whenever she spoke of her husband, which was rarely, as becomes an Omani wife, and also from the relaxed self-confidence and contentment that encompassed her whole composure. Whenever she did speak of her husband, her whole expression lit up, and only shyness seemed to constrain her from displaying her love uninhibitedly. Those qualities about him that she would commonly extol were his generosity, affluence, and education. As for his looks, she made no mention of them. From others we picked up the comment that he was rather short and heavyset. Latifa was proud that she, alone in her neighborhood group, felt no need to do income-bringing work, so lavishly did her husband provide for her. In the characteristic fashion of Omanis, however, she did not brag about her good fortune. It was disclosed quite by coincidence in the following dialogue between us:

"Why doesn't Khadiga come visiting much any more?"

"She does come sometimes, like yesterday, she was here. But usually she is busy sewing, for Hamid doesn't earn much, and as you know, they have just built the house, which cost 4,000 Rials."

"What about Grandmother [who lives with them], who provides for her?"

"She provides for herself by sewing. Hamid gives her only the food. Feyza too, the reason you rarely see her is because she sews to help on the economy. Her husband doesn't earn much and doesn't give her much. But besides, she wants him to *save* his money so that they can build themselves a house. So she tells him *not* to give her gifts of clothes and gold, and sews to keep herself provided with such things."

"Is that why Aisha Baluch and Sheikha always bring embroideries along, to sell for money?"

"Exactly. Have you ever seen them come without them? But they sell for so much that no one in the neighborhood will buy from them. . . . Before I married, I too used to sew to buy myself clothes, but not any more. Why should I tire myself when I do not need to? Nasr is so kind and generous, he gives me everything that I need. To spare me work, he buys his *kummi* ready-made from the market, and he has his washing done at the laundry. He is *very* good to me. . . ."

"But you do sell materials?"

"Yes, but that is only to guests. That is not work."

Among other good things about her husband that Latifa drew my attention to—intermittently throughout my field work—was his consideration in sending money directly to *her* via a friend who works with him in the same company, and comes back to Sohar regularly, once a month. She emphasized that Nasr sends letters to her in care of her father's brother, Hamid. But he sends money directly to her. She did not explain this statement, and I might not have grasped its significance, had I not remembered all too well Fatima's unhappy experience when her husband used to send her money through her father. To Latifa, Nasr's choice of delivery must have been seen both as an expression of his concern for her and of his respect for her autonomy.

This was one of the ways in which Latifa felt that Nasr expressed his love for her. Another was by inviting her to join him eating, rather than what could have been natural for him: eating with her elder brother and leaving her to eat with her mother and the children. She remarked that Nasr himself, and educated men in general, would not eat out of a plate with children. They say that children are dirty and have bad manners.

Latifa was also proud that Nasr chose to sit at home during the evenings he spent in Sohar, instead of joining other men at the cafés.

She and her family and friends saw yet another unequivocal expression of his love in the fact that when Nasr went away to work, three months after the marriage, he moved her from his own family's home, where they had lived until then with his brothers and their wives, to her mother's home. "He did so to make sure I would be happy," Latifa said.

The only thing she mentioned that she did not like was her husband requiring her to attend women's evening classes. She saw no use in it, and derived no gratification from it. I never encountered Latifa engrossed in homework, unlike Fatima, and suspect that she did only a bare minimum of it. Had Nasr lived at home and spent time instructing and helping her, as Ali did with Fatima, she might have undertaken the task with somewhat more zeal.

Latifa did not see much of her husband. He was home for only one-and-a-half months a year, divided between two vacations. As for his long absences from Sohar, she never expressed regret. I believe that she did not experience them as a loss (for example, the way in which Fatima missed Ali). But then her marital relationship had developed quite differently from that of Fatima, and it seems that she regarded Nasr as a stranger. Her neighbors teased her by saying that she used to run and hide when Nasr came home on leave. And she admitted that she did so, "because we are so newly married and I feel shy." They had been married two-and-a-half years by then.

Once I asked Khadiga whether she did not think that such long separations must be trying for Latifa.

"Not at all," replied Khadiga. "Men are demanding and nagging; so many wives are happier to have them gone. Take Nasr as an example. When he is away, Latifa has no work to do. Her mother does the washing and cooking and helps her with the child. When Nasr is home, Latifa has to be perpetually ready to serve him. He is terribly clean, washes himself several times a day, and she must bring him water, soap, and towel. . . . Not all men are like that, Hamid [her own husband] does it himself. Latifa must shake the bed sheets several times a day, for Nasr cannot bear a grain of sand. And when the child plays in the sand he gets angry, complains that she gets dirty, and insists she must stay on the sitting platform. When the food is served, he inspects the plates *underneath* to see if they are clean, and, if there is a grain of sand on the *outside* of the coffee cup or the tray, he gets angry and returns the food. For he is *muta^callim* [educated]" she explained with admiration.

"But Latifa, doesn't she get angry in turn when he is so finicky?"

"Not at all. Why should she when her husband doesn't let her lack anything, but gives her abundantly of all the good things?"

THE BALANCE AND COMPLEMENTARIES OF
THE HUSBAND-WIFE RELATIONSHIP

Khadiga's commentary on her friend Latifa's married life implicitly expresses what seems a prevalent view point: that there should be reciprocity and fairness in the marital relationship and that there is nothing inherently repressed or unjust about the position of women. The situation of

Latifa and Nasr (as also elaborated below), and that of Fatima and Ali, give clear evidence both of efforts from each side to make the other happy and content, and of the presence of potential sanctions in the hands of both parties in case they do not feel satisfied. This also agrees with our general observation of the relative power between spouses, which indicates a pattern of daily mutual accommodation and a balance in the influence they wield over each other in joint concerns.

How can this be, considering the profound inequality in jural position that obtains between husband and wife? To summarize briefly, we have seen that the husband is his wife's legal guardian, with full authority and responsibility for her as a minor. He has the unilateral right to control her movements and property transactions. He has sole sexual access to her at will and has the right both to practice polygamy (he can have up to four wives) and to have sexual relations outside marriage. He can dissolve the marriage without giving causes, whereas her only legal right to divorce arises from proved impotence on his part, or his protracted failure to provide for her. The children that result from the union are his alone. How, when the basic premises for the relationship are so unequal, can even a subjective, much less an objective, balance and reciprocity emerge?

The answer can only be grasped if we look closer at the real life context where these unequal rights have to be acted out and realized. Two major circumstances affect this: the very authority of the husband and his social aspirations to live with grace and have a claim to pride, and the fact of the much wider field of activities and involvements of men than women. These circumstances have rather unexpected implications. First, the formal pre-eminence and authority of the husband has the counterbalancing draw-back for him that just because he has such power, he is expected to govern his house and its members and can be held responsible for the result. With the exacting standards of grace and dignity that exist in Sohar, this means that his self-image and social esteem are highly vulnerable and can be damaged considerably by actions of his wife, which do not essentially damage her own self. This could, of course, be counteracted by constant supervision and control on his part, given the powers he has. But a man's activities of necessity involve him in many different areas and relation-ships to which he must also attend. This discrepancy in the size and diver-sity of the husband's and the wife's worlds means that she is prepared, and able, to mobilize far more time and effort to secure influence in her home life, central as it is to her whole existence. He, on the other hand, will be tempted to adopt a policy of compromise and accommodation so as to reserve more of his time and resources to a larger public, and by com-mon consent more "important" arenas. Our friend Said, when we asked him why so many men, himself included, shower their wives with dresses by the dozens, explained; "A dress is so cheap, only three Rials—it is nothing to quarrel about." The prevailing pattern of formal authority, mutual interaction, and control, as well as the resultant balance of influence, is summarized in the Sohari women's saying: *"Irragil biyuhkum, walakin ilhorma siyasiyyan* [The man rules, but the woman maneuvers]."

Elucidating this statement, women explain: "Women learn the habits and the predilections of their men—when they come and when they leave, what they like and what they dislike, whether they sleep heavily or lightly, and what a wife can do without arousing their anger. Men are too wrapped up in their own problems to work out such things, or see through them."

Behind a husband's readiness to please and satisfy the wife by accommodating to her wishes is also, I believe, a more or less conscious and ever-present fear of a wife's ultimate sanction: infidelity. Said's choice of example reflects this; and the standard explanation among men of the occasional occurrence of infidelity contains the same specifics: "The wife wants something like all the neighboring women have. He says I cannot or will not give you three Rials for that; the wife goes and does bad things to get the money" (see Ch. 4). Some other men deny this interpretation of the causes of unfaithfulness (as do also the women) and point out that though money for clothes and hospitality is very highly valued by women, there are other ways of obtaining it if the husband fails to give it than by infidelity. Indeed, as we have seen, most women supplement their husband's provisions with income they themselves earn from embroidery or sewing. One day as I arrived at Latifa's place, she was sewing dresses for her daughter and little sister on the machine, and she remarked:

"These materials have been lying around for so long, for I have not been in the mood to sew. But I will not pay others to sew for me. They charge too much."

"Why doesn't every woman sew herself?"

"Some don't have a machine, others don't know how to, yet others have many children and no time. They earn a lot, those who sew for others. Others, such as Aisha Baluch and Sheikha, earn much by embroidering *kummi*s. As you have noticed, they always bring embroidery along."

"Do their husbands earn little?"

"Not at all; they both work as doorkeepers in a company and have a salary of perhaps 100 Rials a month. Many women do income-producing work who do not need to. And the men are happy for the economic help."

The factors so far noted bring out major features of the actual interdependencies and asymmetries of the husband-wife relationship. On the one hand, he is dependent on her to realize his cherished self as competent master of his life and his home, displayed with the beautiful manners that are the man's ornament. Particularly, he must have her loyalty and fidelity to achieve this. She is less dependent and, in a sense, more self-sufficient; although she needs him to provide her with basic support, a house, and a minimum of leisure, she can, if need be provide herself with the assets most needed for esteem in her social world: the resources for hospitality.

On the other hand, the husband is in a position, if he so wishes, to provide his wife with essentially all the requirements for the good life: house, leisure, clothes, jewelry, and food for hospitality. She on her part, cannot provide him with most of the things he needs for his life. He must work, though he values leisure as much as she does. He must make his own way through the labyrinths of politics, business, and friendship in a variety of public arenas. At best she can provide him with affection and advice, with regular meals and a place of rest and refuge from these contests while at the same time being the greatest potential threat of all to his public esteem.

This also provides us with the realistic premises that govern the option of dissolving the marriage. The power to do so lies in the hands of the husband, but the cost of doing so is great, entailing both payment of the *ghayeb* (the deferred dowry) and of a new bride price to establish a new complete household. "And how will he know that his next wife will be better?" as Soharis candidly observe. The wife, on the other hand, provided she does not have small children, has less to lose, for the responsibility to support her reverts to her own family until she is remarried—a marriage in which, unlike her first, her own willingness and choice carry much weight or even are decisive. And if she is caught up against her will, in a truly unwanted marriage, the threat that an unhappy wife poses to a husband's interests and aspirations is such that the only wise course for him is to acquiesce to a divorce. For these reasons, women are probably correct when they unanimously say, "It is very easy for a wife to obtain divorce," explaining that "all she has to do is run home to her parents constantly until the husband tires of fetching her back." This knowledge cannot but contribute to the woman's feeling of confidence and control over her own situation.

What is more, these general tendencies are further reinforced by the Sultan's present public policy of systematically improving the status of women. This policy is actively adopted by the Wali of Sohar, so I frequently heard women comment that "even if the husband *has* the right, the wife is *given* the right."

MARITAL MANEUVERS AND STRATEGIES

What are the actual actions entailed in such a marital game of discreet mutual influence and pressure? Schematically, one might say that the alternatives open to a person to improve his or her position in a marital relationship and life situation must take one of the following courses:
1. Each may put greater effort into one's own behavior
2. Each may seek to modify the behavior of the spouse, by
   a) positive sanctions (encouragement, reinforcing desired behavior by reciprocating with behavior desired by the other, and so forth)
   b) negative sanctions (criticism, threats, or punishment for unwanted behavior), or

c) the mobilization of third parties to put pressure on the spouse (one's own kinsmen, the spouse's kinsmen, the Wali)

3. Each may withdraw from the relationship when it is unsatisfactory, either temporarily, or permanently, by divorce.

If it is so that "the men rule, but the women maneuver," by what maneuvers do women seek to achieve and protect their interests, and by what means and to what extent do men effectuate their rule?

Folk generalizations are rather clear on this point. Women say, "It is the man who rules, and the woman respects the man, otherwise the man would not respect her and give her things." Men say, "Women should be spoiled." Looking closer at the case materials I have available to me, is it also true to say that these are the kinds of actions that the parties have chosen when there is disagreement or conflict between them?

I have gone through my notes carefully and counted a total of about forty incidents of response to disagreement, disappointment, anger, and the like. They reveal a few cases of a person losing his temper: Sheikha's husband removing the tray (p. 271), Ali upbraiding Fatima for her impatience in the house question (p. 254), and Latifa's husband smashing a radio (p. 289). Other reactions are predominantly positive, trying to elicit good by being good. Sheikha offers an extreme example: despite her husband's maltreatment, "She was so kind that she even helped make the cement with which they built the house." Maybe she thought that by being excessively kind she could induce her husband to be good also. The measure did not work in her case. It seems to do so in most others.

I will take as an example the marriage between Rahmeh and Abdullah. Rahmeh would have preferred to stay in their house in Higra. It was Abdullah who was in favor of moving out to the gardens. When Rahmeh realized how much the change of life would mean to him, who so loves horticulture and "country life," she made no fuss, and now seemed at pains to convince herself that life there is not so bad: "Here there is plenty of water and vegetables are nearby, so there is little work." But, and then comes the sigh, "In Higra there were neighbors." When she differed with Abdullah in her judgment of the better son-in-law, she tried to reason with him and, when that failed, accepted his decision without remorse. At other times it is he who has given in to her wishes, as in the matter of his last job. Abdullah was employed as a clerk at the hospital when he was offered a much better job as an accounts assistant at the new bank. He asked Rahmeh's advice and she counseled against it, fearing both the responsibility involved and the loss of free access to medicines that his quitting the hospital job would entail. Although Abdullah's own arguments weighed in the other direction, he decided to follow Rahmeh's advice and later praised the wisdom of her decision.

Other couples provide similar cases, as we have seen for Feyza and her husband (Ch. 10), or the persistent attempts of Latifa's father to secure his wife's love (Ch. 8). Let us look closer at the marriage between Latifa and Nasr as an example. As to the nature of the issues and conflicts that arose between them, I have only sparse and incomplete evidence. Latifa revealed only one such incident to me, and it was one that she seemed to find more amusing than discreditable, for the next day she was interested to know whether I had recounted the story to my husband and if he, too, had found it entertaining.

Her husband had been taking a shower and, when finished, called on her to bring him the towel. But the radio was turned on very loud, and the baby was crying, so she did not hear him. He yelled louder and louder, and had been standing there soaking wet for a full ten minutes before his voice finally got through to her. When he got out of his seclusion chamber, he was so enraged that he slammed the radio against the cement wall; it broke into dozens of pieces. "A radio worth 40 Rials!" exclaimed Latifa with awe and exhilaration (and also with a touch of pride, I imagine). He neither reproached nor censured Latifa.

When I asked what other things could make him angry or annoyed, she came out with one kind of incident only: "When Nasr comes home from the market, carrying a heavy load, he is in a very bad mood, and it is important that I rush to the gate the instant he appears and relieve him of his burden, and smile and am very grateful and cheerful." (Carrying a heavy load—second only to exposure to the sun—is believed to be a major cause of illness.)

Questioned as to what she does when she gets angry with him she answered: "Don't talk to him, refuse to do any work for him, etc. But it never lasts long—maximum one hour." She would not, however, specify what could provoke her anger.

Latifa said that she always strove to avoid Nasr's anger, and disagreements with him, and to make him content. She said that she tried to be sensitive to his bad moods, caused by his involvements in the world outside of home, and to offer consolation through her considerateness. "If it happens that he is displeased and harsh with me, I keep quiet and complain to no one, I don't tell anybody. Even if Nasr were to beat me, I would not complain. . . ."

Latifa did find Nasr's demand for cleanliness and neatness excessive, yet never complained about it; he was an educated man, therefore it was only natural that his standards would be superior and it was for her to accommodate. She disliked attending school, yet would not dream of protesting.

Nasr, on his part, exercises much forethought and consideration to make Latifa feel loved and pampered in ways that we have already seen.

His mother-in-law, with whom the couple reside, plays her part in this. According to Latifa, she never interferes in a disagreement between the young spouses, "for she is afraid not to treat Nasr well enough for fear he might move me back to his kin the next time he goes off to work [in the Gulf]. So my mother does all she can, so Nasr shall be happy with us."

This summary shows a clear pattern: a considerable amount of behavior between spouses has the strategic purpose of influencing the acts and attitudes of the spouse, and the means selected are predominantly positive. Even where conflicts of interest arise, the response of Sohari spouses seems to a large extent to be an effort to be more considerate and to increase efforts and attentions, and to make use of positive sanctions. This is not to say that other reactions never take place. Latifa's husband did lose his temper and smash the transistor radio, Fatima did complain before her father-in-law, and so forth. But the selection of means is weighed in the positive direction, and this creates the characteristic climate of accommodation, and mutual respect and support, which seems to characterize the relationship.

Are there factors that can explain this pattern? I am not implying by this question that it is particularly inexplicable that spouses act constructively toward one another, but rather that there must be factors in the social and cultural context of Sohar that particularly favor this type of response. Some such factors can be identified. We have returned repeatedly to the emphasis placed by Soharis on the practice of interpersonal tolerance and noninvolvement. Bad acts by one party are not regarded as justification for the relaxation of such standards by the other party. The person who refrains from attempts to punish the (unwanted) behavior of a spouse is thus acting in accordance with explicit collective values and will be rewarded by enhanced reputation and self-esteem, even if the spouse persists in his or her unwanted behavior (for example, Latifa's praise for Sheikha enduring twelve lean years, Ch. 13). What is more, by maintaining one's own standard uncompromised in this way, one also in fact presents the spouse with a standing *offer* of better relations. Considering the prevailing influences from the surrounding society, such patience may perhaps offer a better chance of being rewarded than it would in many other places. Men are in fact sometimes criticized by women for going so far in this passivity that they lack *axlaq* (character, strength, honor), to the extent of even being willing graciously to receive their own wife's paramour if he is socially prominent.

The selection of sanctions to modify the behavior of one's spouse will be affected by these same pervasive ideals. The point is simply that in this society positive sanctions will tend to affect the actor's own social position positively, whereas negative sanctions will have negative effects. Positive sanctions will often be indistinguishable from the kind of unperturbable observance or overfulfillment discussed above and will benefit the actor directly in terms of public esteem: the husband who rewards his wife is considered liberal; Fatima, who was studiously respectful and attentive after forcing Ali on the issue of the house, was acting in ways that could only benefit her in the eyes of others. Negative sanctions, on the other hand, are rarely fully compatible with high standards of politeness and grace and thus are unlikely to benefit a person's reputation. What is more, there is a prevalent view that attempts to change a person's behavior are essentially unavailing, certainly where the behavior in question is deeply motivated in the "nature" of the other. This is put most forcefully in the extreme case of faithfulness–infidelity: "A wife's fidelity or lack of it is independent of her husband's actions. If a woman wants that thing, there is nothing a husband can do. He can beat her, and she will persist, he can lock her up and she will break out." Thus negative sanctions, being thought both costly to the person who adopts them and probably ineffectual for the purpose adopted, are largely shunned. An apparent exception is the use of physical punishment: "many husbands" reportedly beat their wives, though the women who provided this information generally agreed that it was less frequent now than previously because the Wali has forbidden it. Without any actual measure of prevalence, or standard by which to compare Sohar with other societies, however, any discussion of this question must be inconclusive. We might note two points, however: such sanctions take place in private, and so will not really be known to others (and affect reputations), except in the excessive cases where neighbors hear the rumpus. What is more, dispensing physical punishment may have been regarded as a natural part of the responsibility of the head of a household, and its decrease at present, when its justification is being questioned, can be seen to reflect precisely this reluctance of Soharis to adopt negative sanctions.

The avoidance of negative sanctions, we should note, is also conditioned by the Sohari fear of anger and quarrels. Soharis say, "If two bottles knock together, both will be broken, and then who can mend them?" The truth of this saying is illustrated for them by numerous known cases where relationships among neighbors or kinsmen that were once close have become estranged, and for years the parties have not been on speaking terms. Not only is the Sohari attitude that it is impolite and undignified to quarrel. Soharis, I believe, tend to dread the potential consequences of a quarrel blowing up to disproportionate dimensions. Thus Latifa says about herself: "Like Khadiga, I too would never quarrel with my husband, for fear he might divorce me. I would be afraid, for I have a small child." I cannot imagine that Latifa has much reason to fear, even should she occasionally quarrel. Her husband's love for her is clearly profound. But I also think that she herself is not aware of this secure position. Her fear is genuine, so deep-seated is the attitude that quarrels should be avoided if at all possible.

The final alternative of bringing in third parties clearly violates Sohari virtues of discretion and loyalty, and it also demands interference in a society that extols noninterference. The relative frequency with which the Wali is brought in to settle intimate family disputes is a measure of this latter point: his function is precisely to relieve others of the need to maintain control and justice. But calling in third parties of any kind remains an extreme and last resort, and it is generally done with great care and consideration both of what would be the propitious moment and who would be the least challenging third party for the spouse.

There would seem to be fewer ideological obstacles to the third major course, that of withdrawing from interaction temporarily or even by severing the relationship, though both can no doubt be regarded as negative sanctions from a certain perspective. Yet one can see how, in the Sohari context, they may seem more readily practicable. Although it is hardly polite to refuse to interact, to do so entails no abusive action, no loss of poise and self-control, and no interference with the other. As an occasional recourse it seems to be practiced by the woman in the form of "not being on speaking terms," by the man even more painlessly by physically absenting himself.

As for permanent breach, threatening divorce may be regarded as abusive, whereas carrying it out is not regarded as an improper act, though practical and financial considerations may militate against it. Some female friends of mine also maintained that a woman ought to exercise effort and patience to make her marriage work, "not like nowadays, divorce if she is just a little dissatisfied." Self-control, accommodation, and ability to cope are major values.

As for the calm consideration of divorce as a possible course, it is sufficiently consistent with a valued Sohari self-image, so Ali was prepared to tell how he had mentioned it to Fatima as a last-resort course out of his troubles, and he seemed discreetly proud of the fact that she had cried at this suggestion.

VARIATIONS OF ROLE

There are thus clear and pervasive circumstances and pressures in the general cultural and social context of Sohar that canalize the choices of strategy in married life toward overfulfillment, positive sanctions, and occasional resort to passivity and avoidance, and away from negative sanctions, quarreling and expressed acrimony, and the mobilization of support from others. It is reasonable to identify a self-reinforcing potential in such a pattern of interaction: if sensitivity and attentiveness on one's own part are answered by a similar response in the other, it breeds more of its own kind and a growing trust and loyalty. This, presumably, is an essential component in the Sohari experience of marital "love" (see Ch. 10). Fashioned by such forces, one would expect marital relationships in Sohar to tend to share a number of characteristics, despite the absence of more intimate role models: the context should favor mutual efforts of accommodation, the graceful fulfillment of reciprocal tasks and responsibilities, and—particularly in its overt aspect—the practice of loyalty and solidarity.

But the concrete content of the relationship—what spouses actually do together, and for each other—can, apart from the standard guidelines of the division of labor between the sexes, become rather particular and idiosyncratic in each case. Presumably, it will depend heavily on the individuality of each party, the accidents by which they discover each other's personal needs and dispositions, and the private meanings that thereby emerge between them. And, on the other hand, relationships that deteriorate or never achieve the self-confirming basic structure of loyalty and positive reciprocity (for example, Sheikha's marriage), may well develop in very different directions. Every particular relationship will thus call for a uniquely biographical explanation to account for its form, fashioned as it had been by two strangers, coming together and becoming progressively somewhat attuned to each other.

CONCLUSION

The perspective of role realization developed above has allowed us to describe common features and variations and, within limits, explain the forms of marital relationships in Sohar. The picture that emerges is one of a relationship progressively fashioned by the parties themselves through their marital history and normally transcending its restrictive and unequal jural bases to become one of greater mutuality and reciprocal accommodation. As a result of such histories or biographies, the particular forms exhibited by "the marital relationship in Sohar" are highly various and difficult to characterize in terms of specific content. This is not only true in terms of the overt behavior that routinely takes place between spouses: I have also suggested that the *meanings* carried by acts of behavior may likewise be particular and relatively private to a relationship. This thesis is difficult to substantiate, particularly as between couples who, by their tact and loyalty, defend and keep their own secrets. But the assertion may be illustrated by an example contained in the case material presented. With my woman informants, I have emphasized the importance of mutual respect: "The woman respects the man, otherwise he would not respect her." By women, such respect is primarily expressed through deference and submission, and acts with these connotations are readily recognized and their meanings widely shared, though their presence and frequency vary between sets of spouses. For example, Fatima fetches each and every glass of water for her husband; Rahmeh lets her husband buy all her clothes; Khadiga abstains from visiting her mother. But how does a husband express his respect for his wife? This is an essential aspect of their reciprocity, and I think an aspect of the relationship that depends heavily on biography and private meaning. Thus Rahmeh emphasizes how her husband, Abdullah, always took her along when he lived abroad on labor migration. Latifa, on the other hand, sees her husband's genuine and deep respect for her expressed in the fact that he moved her to her natal home when traveling. My own feeling is that Rahmeh, by temperament and interests, is if anything less naturally disposed toward traveling than Latifa, but she knows her husband's ideals and values and correctly sees his insistence on her companionship as a strong affirmation of respect. Latifa, with probably equally well-founded insight, sees the same being affirmed in the opposite behavior. Thus what characterizes both couples, and many others in Sohar, is that existence of the abstract quality of mutual respect, not agreement as to how this quality is expressed, or similarity in the acts performed between them. Thinking of Khadiga's misfortune, I wonder whether a major reason for her unhappiness is not that her husband, Hamid, seems incapable of expressing his respect for her, if indeed this is one of the feelings he harbors. Had she found only one, personal signal that such a quality is to be found in his relationship to her, I think her position would have seemed to her much more bearable.

Watching couples interacting in Sohar, it becomes apparent that such qualities in their relationships are achieved, if at all, by the exercise of much self-control, patience, and attentiveness, and an active accommodation by both parties, but perhaps particularly by the wife. Although the result of this effort is highly valued, the effort may yet only be possible because it does not dominate the day: segregation, and the separate worlds of women and men, reduce the interaction of spouses to perhaps three hours per day, or, in the case of labor migration, fifteen to forty-five days a year. There may be a great deal of insightful realism in Khadiga's commentary on Latifa's husband's absence.

The cast of all my observations is such that I have placed major emphasis on the *complementarity* of the wife-husband relationship, as it unfolds in interaction between spouses. Despite this, it certainly retains a fundamental inequality—in the unilateral authority and responsibility assigned to the husband and the comprehensive restrictions and impediments imposed on the wife. To what extent can the affirmation of mutual respect and value eliminate a subjective experience of suppression in these aspects?

The answer is perhaps best indicated in the reaction of women to the new opportunities offered through the present reforms, and their conceptualization of possible future freedoms. Most clear and consistent is their reaction to education at present: despite strong encouragement from their husbands, most wives are at best dull and uninterested pupils, and many do not attend classes. On the other hand, children of both sexes attend school, and women see this as a clear indication that the *burqa*—presumably the epitome of segregation—will never be adopted by the coming generation of girls. As for other aspects of freedom, accounts circulate among them of the prevailing sexual emancipation of women in Bahrain, who are said to choose their own husbands "and even to be allowed to sleep with them before marriage!"

Such future seems to hold no attraction to them, judging not only from their comments before their husbands and in larger gatherings of neighbors but also in private and unconstraining conversation. Their general contentment with the instituted forms of married life as they practice it is fundamentally attested by their eagerness to enter into marriage: their positive evaluation of the independence of own kin that marriage entails and the frequency with which they discontinue visits to their childhood home; their assurance of having the option of divorce; but most of all, the self-confidence and serenity with which they pursue their tasks and interests and live their graceful lives.

APPENDIX

✤

A Framework for
the Analysis

In trying to subject myself to the "rigor of rethinking the world in everyday terms" in the preceding text, I have been precluded from entering into lengthy and explicit discussions of the anthropological theories of culture and society that informed my thinking on Sohar. This has not been a hardship: I generally find the technical concepts both ugly and cumbersome and recoil from the schematism in observation and thinking that they easily invite. This does not mean, however, that I have not been aware that particular concepts, premises, and biases have informed my perception and analysis. What is more, my field-work experience in Sohar has inevitably drawn my attention to some methodological issues and thereby been reflected in the positions I have taken when trying to make sense of my data. It may therefore be useful, particularly to readers familiar with current anthropological literature and debates, that I give some account of my position, as I see it, on some of these issues.

I believe I am in harmony with a lasting current in social anthropology, though perhaps not one particularly emphasized in the discipline's current rhetoric, when I have seen the main object of my endeavor as that of gaining insight and providing information on people's lives, their selves and their identities, and how they represent themselves to themselves and to each other. To do so, I would argue that we must focus on *whole* persons, and their performance in all those trivial and fateful events of life where their behavior cannot be simply represented as the enactment of statuses and roles, and that the material that best equips us to do so is that which allows us to give a close and accurate description of the details of the real lives of real people. With Roger M. Keesing, I agree that "it may be precisely in exploring the phenomenological world of the familiar and immediate, the everyday and mundane, that we stand to gain the most crucial knowledge of how humans perceive, understand and act" (1974, p. 63). Gaining this knowledge requires, to my understanding, intimate field material obtained by participant fieldwork and used to construct such a close picture of real lives, described in experience-near terms (see Geertz, 1974, p. 223), rather than as an intake to social structure, institutional norms, or abstract analyses of symbolic systems.

My priorities and fundamental premises in this respect have no doubt been shaped both by my particular training in anthropology and by my own temperament and experiences. My basic training in anthropology was at the University of Bergen, under the auspices of Fredrik Barth, not long after he formulated the ideas contained in his *Models of Social Organization* (1966). This is not the place to spell out the "generative model" that he articulated, but only to highlight the stamp that it left on my thinking about social life, both when I have seen myself as working in line with him and in opposition to him.

Briefly, the perspective he taught allowed me to focus my attention on real people, rather than the nonhuman abstractions of systems and structures which then, and still today, figure so prominently in the literature. With Jules Henry, "I have to see *that person* before me; and what I cannot see as *that actuality*, what I cannot hear as the sound of *that voice*, has little interest for me." (Henry 1973, p. xv). The patterns that emerge in society I identify as ways to describe a multitude of behaviors performed by living individuals in the pursuit of their various goals. Second, Barth's transactional and strategic model did not entail the structural-functionalist's one-sided interest in the normative, customary, and conformist acts, in contrast to rule-breaking and deviant ones. Both kinds of behavior may be equally "rational" when seen from the point of view of the performing actor. This suited my temperament and gave scope for a form of analysis that I have pursued throughout this text: a close attention to the purposes that behavior may serve to the actor, the priorities revealed by acts and the advantages they secure, not just how they differ from cultural norms. Third, I was alerted to the way in which acts and patterns could be not only described but also explained by elucidating the actors' own, perceived opportunity situations: the constraints under which people labor while pursuing desired ends.

It remains essential for me to be able to give an account of acts in these terms, and I do not see that the main criticisms that have been directed against the concepts of choice and maximization have reduced the importance of such an account (for example, Asad 1972). Choice normally enters as an essential component of any act; there is rarely anything inevitable about the things that people do, and there are usually a number of alternative courses they could have chosen to follow. To understand why people act as they do, and what the portent of their actions is, we need to know "the genuine alternatives of behavior—concretely, what the actor in a case did *not* choose to do, though it had been possible" (Barth in Pehrson 1966, p. xi). And the idea of value maximization I read as an admonishment to identify the proximate goals toward which behavior aims, rather than an obviously unsupportable thesis that people are perpetually and relentlessly struggling to wring the last fraction of advantage from every encounter and incident. I would allow much room for the operation of habit and lethargy in human behavior and also for a tendency to refrain from expending energy on "rational" maneuvers that could bring value when it might be easier to sit back and hope that things will, somehow, turn out one's own way. But the axiom that people are maximizing value in the sense of choosing courses of action that they judge apt to further their ends have been a guiding principle in all my work. When I emphasize the importance of how people conceive of themselves and their identities, how they present themselves to themselves and to one another, this is not in opposition to generative and strategic perspectives, but very much in the spirit of those perspectives. Presenting oneself is not a matter of mere symbolic expressive playacting; it is an often pragmatic and swift-moving contest of self-presentation and transaction.

Likewise, when I embrace a basically generative viewpoint in this study, it in no way prevents me from raising questions about rules, norms, and ideals. Much of the present work has been concerned to problematize the relationship between Omani ideals—including those Muslim theories and injunctions they incorporate—and Sohari actions on the ground. My reflections on the relationships betwen the ideal and the real, or norms and practice, may be a useful entry into the model that underlies the present work. The question of how, to what extent, and in what way the latter reflect and are shaped by the former cannot be ascertained a priori, but is a matter for empirical investigation. Indeed, we can also use discrepancies between the two very fruitfully to explore the nature of each, and their interdependence. *What* is regarded as a breach reveals the critical limits of the ideal; *how* the breach is conceptualized and criticized tells us a great deal about the logic of the ideals. On the other hand, the circumstances and correlates of concrete breaches reveal practical preconditions for the observance. Culture provides people with guides to behavior and frameworks for interpreting their lives and world; it defines for them what is worth striving for—the honorable and praiseworthy. But the world is so complex and life so complicated that no people anywhere manage to put all their values and ideas into simultaneous practice. Constraints may be of various sorts, economic—having to do with limited resources—ecological—having to do with physical and technical conditions—and social—consisting in the obstacles people create for each other in a social environment as they all go about the pursuit of their often conflicting goals. But often, too, the cultural framework itself presents people with insoluble dilemmas; it may define norms and values that are ambivalent, disjunctive, or even mutually inconsistent—and simply cannot be realized at one and the same time. And even when no glaring discrepancies are visible, it must be recognized that cultural imperatives are always generalized and do not provide people with concrete guides for all the exigencies of actual life. They must be *interpreted* by each actor to apply to his or her own circumstances. In other words, cultural norms, values, and ideals represent only one set of influences on people's actions, along with economic, ecological, and social factors. Any consistency between ideal and real is the outcome of personal decisions made by individuals as they pursue their various goals, constrained by external circumstances. Their goals must be empirically investigated, and this is the case whether the real is consistent with the ideal or widely discrepant. The two call equally for an explanation.

The program of description and analysis that I have been espousing in the preceding pages of this appendix, and attempting to realize in the preceding text, requires field data of a particular kind, unusually broad in coverage of whole persons and intimate in its sensitivity to *their* perceptions and purposes. Such data can only be obtained, to my understanding, through thorough participant observation.

Participant observation is connected with our basic goal: as Bronislaw Malinowski has formulated it, "to grasp the native's point of view, his relation to life, to realize *his* version of *his* world" (1927, p. 25). As a participant you disturb that life as little as possible by your presence, and you can observe it as it naturally unfolds. The most genuine information to us is that which naturally flows as if we were not present.

Let us question the term chosen to name this method: *participant observation*. It might give the impression that anthropologists are visually oriented; I submit that we are not. Anthropologists are in fact auditively oriented; we are trained to use our ears more than our eyes. Perhaps what most anthropologists do as "participant observers" could more appropriately be called "inconspicuous listening." It is from hearing people talk, and talking to them, that we chiefly get our information. We *depend* upon the spoken word, which *expresses* the native's point of view, and it is precisely for this reason that we are disdainful of the elicited response, so prized by other social scientists: because it will be cast in the mold of scientists, and not the speaker's world.

Now, let us go back to Oman. Field guides to anthropology speak as if words in various forms, as talk, chatter, and gossip, were always available. In their absence, what does the anthropologist do, especially if she is concerned with gaining insight and providing information on people's lives, their selves and their identity, and how they represent themselves to themselves and to each other? Had one better give up the idea of doing anthropology—at least on such topics, under these conditions?

My work extended over two visits with more than a one-year interval. During the first six months that comprised the first stay, I tried dutifully to conform to the canons of participant observation, as I understood them. This meant that I struggled to be as unobtrusive as possible while participating as much as possible in women's lives. When I found that they hardly talked, I understood that I must play the role of interlocutor much more than I should have liked. But when my probing questions had met with the standard "I don't know" or "maybe" an endless number of times, I realized that this was no way out, or I should rather say, "in." So I reverted to "participation" in that I spent endless days observing the women as they gazed out into space, all the time trying to figure out what the world looked like from behind those eyes. And all the time I was being overcome by boredom and frustration.

The second trip of field work took a very different course, and not because of any conscious planning or superior insight on my part. Most important of all, owing to a combination of circumstances, I arrived in a state of near exhaustion. And what did I find? An atmosphere of pervasive acceptance and tolerance, peace, no need to talk, no need to prove yourself—beyond extending the same reassuring acceptance to others. Temporarily relieved of my impatient need to know and understand everything, I was able to participate in a silence that was truly "being" rather than "nothingness."

It was one of the more rewarding experiences of my life. And I feel sure I should have missed it were it not for the very special state I was in. Had I arrived in Oman directly from Norway, fully fit and equipped with a myriad of questions and problems that I *must* now—for it was my last chance—absolutely solve, no doubt it would have eluded me. And in this I am not saying that what I experienced then was what Omanis themselves experience. With Clifford Geertz, I think that we as anthropologists largely cannot perceive exactly what our informants perceive (1974, p. 224). But I feel convinced, judging both from their largely nonverbal reactions to me, and my own intuitions, that they felt we were much more in tune.

I am making so much of this very personal experience because I think it has a point. As the psychologist Abraham Maslow has observed: "Any clinician knows that in getting to know another person, it is best to keep your brain out of the way, to look and listen totally, to be . . . receptive, passive, patient and waiting, rather than eager, quick and impatient . . . Freud's term (free-floating attention) describes well this non-interfering . . . receptive, waiting kind of cognizing another person" (1966, pp. 10–11).

Anthropologists, I suggest, could well benefit from developing and exercising more of these qualities. Indeed, having skimmed a large number of American field-work guides, I am appalled at the extent to which the contrary attitude seems to rule the ground; that as anthropologists we have the right to act the part of "the man with the note-book and a thousand questions," going about our task so egoistically that, as the author of one such guide recognizes, the local inhabitants "must surely wish that for once they could enact a small bit of local custom without having to explain it all to the anthropologist" (Pelto 1970, p. 225).

Due to the congenial atmosphere I found in Oman, it took me no time at all to regain my strength, and with it, alas, my impatience and drive to penetrate and understand. But I had learned something essential: I had realized how very different I was from the Soharis, how secure and confident they were of themselves, and that I too, in being myself, would be accepted. There was no need to *play* the part of "participant"; the need was rather to be genuine.

So I reverted to being myself. I displayed my curiosity, my appetite for gossip, my need to understand. It worked. I started to obtain the little snippets of crucial facts, the discrete suggestions of evaluation of the performance and persons of others, and the gentle reprimands to myself on which I have built my understanding of women's lives in Sohar.

I should point out here that most of what figures as gossip in this book has been initiated by myself. If parts give the impression that Sohari women gossip much, it is because I have played a major part in negotiating reality so that gossip and talk would ensue. I have also, I feel, *squeezed* my field notes and have not been able, as anthropologists usually are, to choose between several nicely illustrative pieces.

Yet I was not properly aware of a deeper insight that was within my reach. So afterward, at my desk, trying to write my analysis, I was exasperated at the lack of data with which to back up my understandings and intuitions. I combed my notes for verbal data, sayings, informants' statements—this essential evidence which anthropologists use to illustrate, exemplify, prove their interpretations. And I had neither key informants nor questionnaires, neither life histories nor answers to psychological tests. But then, what could be the source or basis of the things that I intuitively felt were true? What *were* the situations when I had felt that things had been clarified to me? What was it that I must have forgotten to note down? I felt that I had a wealth of data somewhere that was somehow escaping me.

In retrospect, I now believe that what I had done in the field was slowly and unconsciously to orient myself by means of the nonverbal cues and expressions that passed between the women in Sohar. These became that hidden source of insight which escaped me when I sat at my desk trying to substantiate my understandings in writing.

Why did I go so wrong? Chiefly, I suggest, because I operated on two assumptions, which are unquestioned or self-evident to a Westerner, but are quite misapplied to Oman, and I was also blinded by taking all too literally the connotations evoked by that all too evocative conception of "participant observation."

The first assumption concerns silence. We equate silence with emptiness, with the absence of something. We are afraid of it, as seen by our frantic efforts to fill it, to erase it, when we find ourselves in the presence of someone we know. Talk, chat, chatter is our resolve. An anthropologist from Oman could thus be well-advised not to pay too much attention to the words as such, as, for example, in talk about the weather, but rather to the "meaning" in terms of our conceptions of self, person, and the other that are being expressed when we fill the space between us with noise and chatter.

Why did it not strike me that the endless silences in Oman might yet be pregnant with meaning—full of the assertion of security, confidence, and acceptance that provided the context for the meaning of tiny acts, gestures, and movements—and even a few words? Partly, I suggest, I remained unconscious of this because I was trained in a discipline that overemphasizes the spoken word at the expense of all else. Silence to us *is* emptiness. The sociolinguist Benjamin Whorf has given a vivid example of the dangers of labeling something as nothingness: there is his famous story of men working at the gas station, handling full and empty gas barrels. They *knew* that the empty barrels were by far the more dangerous, yet they acted as if the full barrels were the ones with which they had to be careful. An "empty" barrel means empty of liquid petrol—whereas they are full of dangerous vapor. Likewise, once you have classified something as silence, you stop thinking that it may contain something else.

Second, I came equipped with conventional notions of what social reality really is. A whole battery of concepts, dichotomously arranged, warns us of the danger of believing in appearances. We must, we are taught, distinguish between what people say and what they think, between ideals and reality, norms and practice, rules and behavior, self-presentation and self, façade and inner emotions, performance on stage versus backstage. Unconsciously, I believed that the true Omani was somehow *behind* the impeccable manners. But because *we* act on the assumption that a graceful and polite composure must somehow conceal the "self," is there anything to indicate that others in this must resemble us? Why not view behavior as *being* the person rather than as something that conceals something else, only indirectly accessible, that is the "real person"? When I finally recognized that Omanis may be primarily concerned with what people do, rather than what they covertly feel and think I turned on Erving Goffman's *Presentation of Self* for having misled us, only to find that the book *opens* with the following lines, a citation from George Santayana: "Masks are arrested expressions and admirable echoes of feeling, at once faithful, discreet, and superlative. Living things in contact with the air must acquire a cuticle, and it is not urged against cuticles that they are not hearts; yet some philosophers seem to be angry with images for not being things, and with words for not being feelings" (1959, p. vii).

I had done precisely that, I had urged it against cuticles that they were not hearts; against beautiful manners, that they were not concealed reasons. I had been obsessed with somehow obtaining accounts—meaning unreflectedly, verbal accounts—of this inner reality, the "real" self. So I reluctantly tried to abandon the self-evident dichotomies and regard the self as that which is expressed, not as something *behind* that which is expressed. Only afterward did I find Geertz's beautiful expression of similar difficulties:

> Only when you have seen, as I have, a young man whose wife—a woman he had in fact raised from childhood, and who had been the center of his life—has suddenly and inexplicably died, greeting everyone with a set smile and formal apologies for his wife's absence, and trying, by mystical techniques, to flatten out, as he himself put it, the hills and valleys of his emotion into an even, level plain ("That is what you have to do" he said to me, "be smooth inside and out"), can you come, in the face of our own notions of the intrinsic honesty of deep feeling and the moral importance of personal sincerity, to take the possibility of such a conception of selfhood seriously and appreciate, however inaccessible it is to you, its own sort of force. (1974, pp. 227-28)

In retrospect, I now think that what I should have done in the field was to focus much more consciously on these other modes of expression through which Omanis represent their selves to themselves and to one another—through silence, accepting behavior at face value, unobtrusively entering and leaving a house, and so forth. This would have entailed greater attentiveness to nonverbal or expressive aspects of behavior. Anthropologists, of course, have done much research on nonverbal communication, but of a special kind: dramatic, symbolic *activity*, as in ritual, trance, artistic expression, where something is clearly being *said*—or, alternatively, nonverbal expression as a check on verbal, where there is clearly a discrepancy, for the former is taken to be "truer"—less subject to conscious manipulation.

Perhaps it is necessary to become impressed with the power of *silence* in human communication to become aware of the need systematically to attend to nonverbal communication. Ray L. Birdwhistell observes, in a fascinating essay, how "a research experience I had about 20 years ago destroyed my earlier confidence that words were central to communication" (1974, p. 211). In research about "happy" marriages, he discovered that "The *median* amount of conversation between these couples came out to the astonishing figure of 27½ minutes per week. Certainly far less conversation than any of the standard descriptions of behavior available would have suggested. The reader is warned that we did not count silences then. I now am much more aware of the unavoidable importance of not talking" (1979, p. 212).

I think that there are a number of reasons why most anthropologists have treated nonverbal aspects so casually. The human being's capacity to record and observe is limited, and an anthropologist is faced with a vast

flow of communication, both verbal and nonverbal. We are forced to select; and, when we concentrate on the verbal aspects, it is not only because
we are word-mongering academics. We need a notational system, which
we have for the verbal, but lack—because it is poorly developed and we do
not command what there is—for the nonverbal: in such matters we are
truly illiterate. Speech is also convenient because it is linear, single-chan-
neled, discontinuous, and often transmitted by one person at the
time—whereas the nonverbal is multichannel (Birdwhistell uses a score
with nineteen channels, for eyebrows, hands, and so forth), continuous,
and transmitted by everyone present simultaneously. We may learn to be
sensitive to it, to "read" it, but are physically unable to record it unaided,
even while interacting with a single other. But most essentially, we have
not learned to *look*.

I am not suggesting that all anthropologists become kinesticians, or
that this would solve the problem. But I strongly urge that we need to at-
tack problems that we regard as important, even if we can only do so provisionally and poorly. I find authority for this in the dictum of Maslow,
who, having found that many scientists disdain what they cannot cope
with, what they cannot do well, coined the aphorism, "What needs doing,
is worth doing even though *not* very well. . . . 'You must love the questions themselves,' Rilke said" (1966, p. 14).

References

Antoun, Richard T. 1968. On the Modesty of Women in Arab Muslim Villages: A Study in the Accommodations of Traditions. *American Anthropologist,* 70(3).

Asad, Talal. 1972. Market Model, Class Structure and Consent: A Reconsideration of Swat Political Organization. *Man* (N.S.), 7(1).

Aswad, Barbara. 1971. *Property Control and Social Strategies: Settlers on a Middle Eastern Plain.* Ann Arbor: University of Michigan Press.

Baroja, Julio Caro. 1965. Honour and Shame: A Historical Account of Several Conflicts. In J. G. Peristiany (Ed.), *Honour and Shame in the Mediterranean.* London: Weidenfeld & Nicolson.

Barth, Fredrik. 1966a. *Models of Social Organization.* London: Royal Anthropological Institute Occasional Paper No. 23.

Barth, Fredrik. 1966b. Preface. In Robert N. Pehrson, *The Social Organization of the Marri Baluch.* Chicago: Aldine.

Barth, Fredrik. 1971. Role Dilemmas and Father-Son Dominance in Middle Eastern Kinship Systems. In Francis L. K. Hsu (Ed.), *Kinship and Culture.* Chicago: Aldine.

Barth, Fredrik. 1978. Factors of Production, Economic Circulation and Inequality in Inner Arabia. In George Dalton (Ed.), *Research in Economic Anthropology.* Greenwich, Conn.: Jai Press.

Barth, Fredrik. Forthcoming. *Sohar: Culture and Society in an Omani Town.* Baltimore: Johns Hopkins University Press.

Beck, Lois, & Keddi, Nikki. 1978. *Women in the Muslim World.* Cambridge: Harvard University Press.

Benjamin, Harry. 1966. *The Transsexual Phenomenon.* New York: Julian Press.

Beny, Roloff. 1976. *Persia—Bridge of Turquoise.* London: Thames & Hudson.

Birdwhistell, Ray L. 1970. *Kinesics and Context.* Philadelphia: University of Pennsylvania Press.

Birdwhistell, Ray L. 1974. The Language of the Body: The Natural Environment of Words. In A. Silverstein (Ed.), *Human Communication: Theoretical Explorations.* New York: Wiley & Sons.

Cosar, Fatma Mansur. 1978. Women in Turkish Society. In Beck & Keddie 1978.

Darlow, Michael, & Fawkes, Richard. 1976. *The Last Corner of Arabia.* London: Quartet Books.

El Saadawi, Nawaal. 1980. *The Hidden Face of Eve.* London: Zed Press.

Fischer, Michael M. J. 1978. On Changing the Concept and Position of Persian Women. In Beck & Keddie 1978.

Ford, C. S., & Beach, F. A. 1951. *Patterns of Sexual Behavior.* New York: Julian Press.

Geertz, Clifford. 1968. *Islam Observed.* New Haven: Yale University Press.

Geertz, Clifford. 1974. From the Native's Point of View: On the Nature of Anthropological Understanding. In Keith Basso & Henry A. Selby (Eds.), *Meaning in Anthropology.* Albuquerque, N.M.: School of American Research.

Goffman, Erving. 1959. *The Presentation of Self in Everyday Life.* New York: Doubleday Anchor Books.

Hamilton, Alexander. 1727. *A New Account of the East Indies.* London: 1930.

Henry, Jules. 1973. *Pathways to Madness.* New York: Vintage Books.

Hershman, P. 1974. Hair, Sex, and Dirt. *Man,* 9(2).

Joseph, Suad. 1978. Women and the Neighbourhood Street in Borj Hammond, Lebanon. In Beck & Keddie 1978.

Keesing, Roger M. 1974. Theories of Culture. *Annual Review of Anthropology,* 3(73).

Leach, Edmund. 1954. *Political Systems of Highland Burma.* London: G. Bell & Sons.

Levy, Reuben. 1965. *The Social Structure of Islam.* Cambridge: Cambridge University Press.

Linton, Ralph. 1936. *The Study of Man.* New York: D. Appleton-Century-Crofts.

Lowie, R. H. 1935. *The Crow Indians.* New York: Rinehart & Co.

Malinowski, Bronislaw. 1927. *Argonauts of the Western Pacific.* New York: Dutton.

Maslow, Abraham H. 1966. *The Psychology of Science.* New York: Harper & Row.

Mead, George H. 1934. *Mind, Self, and Society.* Chicago: University of Chicago Press.

Mernissi, Fatima. 1975. *Beyond the Veil: Male-female Dynamics in a Modern Muslim Society.* Cambridge, Mass.: Schenkman.

Miles, Col. S. B. 1919. *The Countries and Tribes of the Persian Gulf.* London: Harrison & Sons.

Nadel, S. F. 1947. *The Nuba.* London: Oxford University Press.

Paine, Robert. 1970. *Second Thoughts on Barth's Model.* Royal Anthropological Institute. Occasional Paper No. 32.

Palgrave, W. G. 1865. *A Year's Journey through Central and Eastern Arabia* (2 vols). London: Macmillan.

Papanek, Hanna. 1973. Purdah: Separate Worlds and Symbolic Shelter. *Comparative Studies in Society and History,* 15(3).

Pelto, Perti J. 1970. *Anthropological Research: The Structure of Inquiry.* New York: Harper & Row.

Peters, Emrys Lloyd. 1963. Aspects of Status and Rank among Muslims in a Lebanese Village. In Julian A. Pitt-Rivers (Ed.), *Mediterranean Countrymen.* The Hague: Mouton.

Peters, Emrys Lloyd. 1965. Aspects of the Family among the Bedouin of Cyrenaica. In M. F. Nimkoff (Ed.), *Comparative Family Systems.* Boston: Houghton Mifflin.

Phillips, Wendell. 1971. *Unknown Oman*. Beirut: Librairie du Liban.

Pitt-Rivers, Julian A. 1965. Honour and Social Status. In J. G. Peristiany (Ed.), *Honour and Shame in the Mediterranean*. London: Weidenfeld & Nicholson.

Qatar. *Dunhill Guide to Living and Working in 1978*. Bahrain: Hilal.

Rassam, Amal. 1980. Women and Domestic Power. *International Journal of Middle East Studies*, 12(2).

Reiter, Rayna R. 1975. *Toward an Anthropology of Women*. New York: Monthly Review Press.

Rosen, Lawrence. 1978. The Negotiation of Reality: Male-Female Relations in Sefrou, Morocco. In Beck & Keddie 1978.

Roy, Manisha. 1975. *Bengali Women*. Chicago: University of Chicago Press.

Stoller, Robert J. 1968. *Sex and Gender*. London: Hogarth Press.

Stoller, Robert J. 1971. The Term "Transvestism." *Arch. Gen. Psychiatry*, 24(3).

Tapper, Nancy. 1978. The Women's Subsociety among the Shahsevan Nomads of Iran. In Beck & Keddie 1978.

Wellsted, J. R. 1838. *Travels in Arabia* (Vol. 1). London: John Murray.

Wikan, Unni 1975. Hustyrann eller kanarifugl—Kvinnerollen i to arabiske samfunn. [Domestic Tyrant or Pet Canary—Women's Roles in Two Arab Societies]. *Tidsskrift for samfunnsforskning*, 16(4).

Wikan, Unni. 1977. Man Becomes Woman—Transsexualism in Oman as a Key to Gender Roles. *Man* (N.S.), 12(3).

Wikan, Unni. 1978a. The Omani *Xanith*—a Third Gender Role? *Man* (N.S.), 13(3).

Wikan, Unni. 1978b. The Omani *Xanith*. *Man* (N.S.), 13(4).

Wikan, Unni. 1980. *Life among the Poor in Cairo*. London: Tavistock.

Williamson, Andrew. 1973. *Sohar and Omani Seafaring in the Indian Ocean*. Muscat: Petroleum Development.

Index

Abba, 5, 22, 35, 54, 121, 220, 234
Abdullah, 8, 11, 20–22, 52–53, 194–96, 199–204, 206, 233–44, 288, 293
Abu Dhabi, 29, 30, 31, 35, 37, 107
Affinal relationships, 120–21, 133, 196, 200, 202–4, 207–11, 220, 222, 228, 232–41, 249–50, 252–59, 263, 265–66, 272, 275, 283, 289
Aisha Baluch, 40, 80, 113, 115, 117, 118, 134–35, 283, 286
Ajam, 4, 35, 40, 41, 45, 46, 114, 164
Ali, 45, 61, 103, 120, 159, 161, 162, 164, 205, 244, 245–70, 271, 273, 278, 280, 284, 292–93
Amin, Kacem, 57
Antoun, Richard, 142, 223
Asad, Talal, 297
Aubert, Vilhelm, 238 n
Autonomy, of person, 38, 163–64, 208–9, 240, 243, 244, 254, 258, 262, 276, 283, 295
Avarice, 133–35

Bachelors, 189
Badriya, 136, 194–96, 200
Bahla, 4, 126, 134–35
Baluchis, the: *burqa* of, 94–95; language and customs of, 4, 17, 41; marriage customs of, 25, 40, 41, 42, 45, 108, 116, 125, 164, 204–11, 224, 225, 229; occupations of, 35; women's dress among, 40

Baroja, Caro, 151
Barth, Fredrik, 27, 31, 32, 34, 40, 43, 163, 201, 217, 240, 297
Batinah coast, 3, 4, 29, 30, 51, 105, 107, 170, 249
Baydawi, 56
Beck, Lois, 105
Bedu, 43–45, 164, 214, 221, 249, 261
Beni Omar tribe, 32
Benjamin, Harry, 170–71
Beny, Roloff, 107
Birdwhistell, Ray L., 303–4
Bride price, 22, 25, 85, 158, 192–93, 203–7, 210, 213, 215, 224, 226–27, 247, 249, 252
Brother-sister relationship, 85, 194–95, 202
Brothers, relations between, 248, 262, 265–66
Bukhari, Al-, 51, 56
Burqa: as beautifying device, 98–101, 215; design of, 88–91; impressions of, 10, 14, 88–93; male attitudes toward, 101–8; practices of wearing, 5, 35, 54, 68, 86, 94–98, 122, 127, 136, 147, 172, 184, 234–36, 245, 250–51; as symbol of womanhood, 3, 86, 174, 215, 224

Cauldwell, D. O., 170
Children: breast-feeding of, 76; crying of, 77; dress of, 76, 78–79; education

309

Children (*continued*)
  of, 80–83; ethnic identity of, 45; and
  food, 132; play of, 79; protection of,
  76; responsibilities of, 81; swaddling
  of, 76; tact of, 113, 144–45; weaning
  of, 77; in women's gatherings, 112–
  13
Circumcision, 44
Climate, 12, 29, 54, 114, 123, 257
Clothing: of children, 76, 78–79; of
  men, 53, 250; of women, 53, 121–22,
  128, 250–51; of *xaniths*, 172–73
Commensality, 132–33. *See also* Food
Conflicts and their resolution, 31–34,
  166–67, 180–81, 193, 203, 227, 238–
  41, 249, 250–53, 255–57, 258, 264,
  272–73, 279, 285, 287–92. *See also*
  Wali
Conformity, concept of, 67
Conspicuous consumption, 22, 260
Cosar, Fatma Mansur, 106
Cousin-marriage, 189–90, 193–95, 196–
  99, 202, 208–11, 247
Crying, 22, 76, 82, 201, 215–16, 220,
  221, 254, 272
Cultural pluralism, 4–5, 14, 39–45, 114
Custom, concept of, 67, 157, 207, 221

Darlow, Michael, 74
Deaf-mutes, 223
Deviance, concept of, 67, 179, 276, 297
Divorce, 83, 103, 110, 158–60, 181, 185,
  205, 224–30, 247, 250, 272–73, 275,
  281, 287–88, 291–92, 295
Dowry. *See* Bride price
Dubai, 27, 30, 34, 35, 37, 70, 87, 107,
  115, 123, 128, 130, 259, 272

Education: of men, 246, 249, 268, 282,
  284; of women, 159, 194, 199–200,
  207–8, 246, 247, 251–52, 259–61,
  264, 267–70, 284, 294
El Saadawi, Nawaal, 56, 57–58, 224
Esteem. *See* Honor; Reputation
Evil eye, 75, 242–43

Fadiha, 51, 228
Fahud, 259

Father-daughter relationship, 56–57,
  62–63, 75, 81–82, 190, 194–201, 203–
  7, 214, 234–38, 242, 250, 251, 252.
  See also Parent-daughter relationship
Father-in-law/son-in-law, relations between. *See* Affinal relations
Father-son relationship, 75, 81–82, 84–
  85, 236, 243, 247, 248–50, 252, 255–
  56, 258, 264, 265, 266, 274
Fatima, 61, 103, 116, 118, 120, 121,
  159, 164, 244, 245–70, 271, 273, 278,
  280, 284, 292–93
Fawkes, Richard, 74
Feasts, 117, 128–29, 247, 266
Fertility, 185, 275
Feyza, 110, 114, 117, 118, 121, 127,
  198–99, 211, 213–15, 220, 280
Field work, 4–15, 16–26, 65, 80, 146–
  49, 152–54, 156–60, 169–70, 199,
  224–25, 238, 280–81, 296–97, 299–
  304
Fischer, Michael, 54 n, 101 n
Food, 109–11, 124, 129–34, 173, 236,
  248, 258–60. *See also* Hospitality;
  Visiting
Friendship: between men, 39, 45, 116,
  164; between women, 116, 120, 138–
  40

Geertz, Clifford, 59, 297, 300, 303
Ghayeb, 158, 204, 227, 247
Ghel, 115, 282
Goffman, Erving, 57, 60, 68, 302
Gossip, 10, 14, 64, 65, 85, 125–27, 136–
  37, 146, 157–58, 160–62, 165–66,
  228–29, 278–80, 299–301. *See also*
  Honor; Tact
Gwadar, 40

Hader, 204–5, 226, 272
Hadira, 114–15
Hamid, 214–17, 274–76, 280, 282–84,
  294
Hamilton, Alexander, 74
Handicrafts, 34, 125
Harrit alSheikh, 115
Hennah, 20–22, 217–18

Henry, Jules, 297
Hershman, P., 54 n
Higra, 96, 114, 125, 245, 288
History of Sohar, 27, 39, 46-48
Homes, description of, 36-37, 262
Homosexuality, 169-70, 174-75, 177, 178
Honor: anthropological concept of, 141-43, 148-49, 150-55; in contrast to shame, 149-53; of men, 70, 72-73, 142, 147-48, 150, 158-60, 161-62, 163-65, 183-84, 193, 208, 213, 226-30, 278, 290; methodological problems of, 150-57, 160-63; in Oman versus the Mediterranean, 141-43, 165-67, 183-84; as self-regard versus social esteem, 151-53, 154-56, 162-63; two senses of, 153-54, 160-61; of women, 71-73, 143-67, 193, 213, 223-24, 228-30, 278, 290
Hospitality, 110-11, 115, 118, 124-25, 129-35, 141, 145-49, 152-53, 157-59, 167, 236, 252, 259-61, 271, 286. *See also* Food; Neighbors; Visiting
Households, 192, 249-50, 252-57, 283
Housing in Sohar, 8, 10, 27, 36

Ibadhi, 42, 45
Illness, 75-76, 137, 224, 226, 252-54, 289. *See also* Evil eye; *Jinn*
Impotence, 174, 224-27, 229-30
Indian community, 10, 34, 39, 40, 42, 46, 52-53
Individuality, 33-34, 45, 65, 179, 238, 241, 271, 277, 293
Infidelity, 61-63, 66, 70, 102, 113, 115, 136-37, 143-53, 157-61, 166, 179-80, 185, 223, 230, 247, 256, 261, 263, 264, 274, 279, 286, 291. *See also* Sexuality
Istakhri, 4, 27

Jinn, 75, 76, 77, 216, 261
Joseph, Suad, 117 n

Kaborrah, 107, 251
Kalam ilᶜaros, 222, 226-28
Keddie, Nikki, 105 n

Keesing, Roger M., 296
Khadiga, 117-18, 121, 124, 127, 146, 156, 213-14, 220, 225-26, 271, 274-76, 279-80, 284, 293-94
Kille, 19, 88, 215-18, 220-21
Kinship relations, outside elementary family, 39, 85, 117, 120-21, 124, 151, 189, 192, 199, 202, 204-5, 213-15, 220, 247-48, 249-50, 272
Kuwait, 128, 233

Labor migration: from Sohar, 9, 30, 35, 83, 280; to Sohar, 42, 134
Latifa, 13, 110, 115-18, 121, 124, 127, 129-31, 133-37, 145, 156-57, 165, 198-99, 206, 213-17, 226, 271-73, 278-89, 291, 293
Latifa's grandmother, 114-15, 117, 118, 124, 135-36, 220-22, 271, 275, 280, 283
Latifa's mother, 115, 118, 135-36, 156-57, 271, 282, 289
Leach, Edmund, 58
Leisure, 64, 111-12, 126-27, 287
Levy, Reuben, 56
Love, 45, 62, 64, 157-58, 185, 190, 198, 201-2, 209, 215-16, 231, 242-43, 273, 276, 281-83, 289, 291-92
Lover's eye, 242-43
Lowie, R. H., 170

Mafraj, 115
Mahr. See Bride price
Majlis, 36
Makran, 40, 41, 107
Malinowski, Bronislaw, 299
Mariam, 136, 213-22, 231
Market, 9, 16, 27, 34-35, 39, 51, 64, 81
Marriage: across boundaries, 44, 46, 193; bride's identity after, 139; consummation of, 22, 212, 214-17, 221-30; establishment, 189, 247-48, 272; negotiations, 189-228; power of choice in, 189-91, 194, 198-99; between relatives, 189, 193-95, 196-99, 202, 206-11, 247; between strangers, 189, 194-95, 198, 208-11. *See also*

Marriage (*continued*)
Bride price; *Kille*; *Mikobra*; Wedding
Mashtara, 192–93, 205, 206, 215, 226
Maslow, Abraham, 300, 304
Mattrah, 4, 7, 8, 29, 61, 92, 252–53
Mead, George H., 154
Meimona, 135–36, 194–97, 199–204, 206, 208, 210, 211, 223, 231–44
Menstruation, 221
Mernissi, Fatima, 56, 57, 58, 181
Mikobra, 19, 174, 212, 216–17, 220–22, 279
Modernization, affecting women, 69, 72, 108, 128, 199, 268, 276, 287, 291–92, 294–95
Moharram, 41
Money, John, 171, 172
Mother-daughter relationship, 22, 75, 117, 194–95, 203, 204, 209–11, 218, 220, 222, 234–37, 241–42, 244, 247, 251, 275. *See also* Parent-daughter relationship
Mother-in-law/daughter-in-law, relations between, 200, 203, 210, 222, 272, 275
Mother-son relationship, 75, 190–91, 210, 241–42, 269, 275–76
Mubarak, 194, 199, 202–3, 206, 208, 233–37
Muscat, 4, 27, 29, 47, 70, 87, 103, 194, 201, 204, 232, 234–35, 272

Nasr, 136, 165, 226, 281–85, 289
Neighbors, relations between, 110, 114–21, 125–27, 129–40, 144–48, 152–53, 155–56, 159, 220, 235, 251, 260–61, 263–64, 271–73, 278
Noninvolvement. *See* Conflicts and their resolution; Tact; Tolerance
Nonverbal communication, 60, 300–304
Nuptial hut. See *Kille*

Occupational structure of Sohar, 35, 44
Oman, foreign experts in, 3, 6
Opium. See *Soukour*

Palgrave, W. G., 59
Papanek, Hanna, 105, 163
Parent-daughter relationship, 53, 81, 207, 232–44, 251–53, 257–58, 260, 263–64, 266
Participant observation, 9–11, 13–15, 19–20, 24–26, 65, 146–47, 152–54, 156–60, 169–70, 199, 224–25, 280–81, 299–304. *See also* Field work
Pelto, Perti J., 301
"People's talk," in Egypt, 165. *See also* Gossip
Persia, 47, 54, 107–8
Persians. *See* Ajam
Person, inherent nature of, 234, 238–41, 277
Peters, Emrys Lloyd, 106, 217, 240
Phillips, Wendell, 46
Photographing in Sohar, 19, 68, 162
Physical appearance: of men, 213–14, 246, 272, 274, 282; of women, 135–36, 213, 245, 272, 274–75, 282
Pitt-Rivers, Julian, 141, 154, 166
Politeness, 16, 129–30, 135, 137, 141, 156, 159, 162, 164, 166, 179, 208, 228, 235, 258, 278. *See also* Tact; Tolerance
Prostitution: female, defined, 143 n; male, 169, 174–75, 177–79, 181
Public opinion, 33, 68, 72, 144–45, 147–48, 156, 160–67, 179, 228–30. *See also* Honor

Qaboos bin Said, 6, 33, 37, 190, 253, 287

Rahmeh, 52–53, 120, 125, 194–96, 200, 202–4, 209, 210, 233–44, 288, 293
Reciprocity, 120, 131, 247, 261, 284, 293
Reiter, Rayna, 126
Reputation: of men, 147–50, 153–54, 160–61, 163–65, 256, 265–66, 285, 290–91; of women, 145, 151–54, 266, 290–91. *See also* Honor
Residence patterns. *See* Households
Respect, 64, 156, 161, 166, 190, 192,

208, 209, 244, 255, 256, 274, 282–83, 288–94
Role dilemma, 21, 217, 231–44
Role-realization, discussion of, 276–81
Rosen, Lawrence, 56 n
Roy, Manisha, 232

Said, 45, 102, 285
Said bin Taimur, 6
Salan, 16, 40, 194
Saudi Arabia, 51, 152, 248
Self-confidence, of women, 71, 139–40, 165–67, 185–86, 240, 281–82, 295
Self-realization, 141, 151, 186, 189, 295
Sexuality, 54, 56, 57, 60–65, 68–71, 136, 160, 175–78, 181–85, 189, 216–18, 221, 225, 230, 248. See also Infidelity; Prostitution
Sexual joking, 85, 118, 129, 136–37, 146, 214, 216, 218
Sexual morality, 71, 149
Shame, 68, 70, 141–51, 153–55, 163, 165–66, 203, 226, 273. See also Honor
Sheikha, 63, 113, 115, 118, 121, 127, 130, 135, 137, 143–53, 155–58, 162–63, 166, 230, 271–80, 282–83
Shiah, 41–42, 45, 165
Shizaw, 114–15
Shyness: of children, 69; of guests, 69, 131, 133; of men, 70; of women, 68–72, 95–96, 149, 172, 190, 199, 235–36
Siblings, relationship between, 78, 82, 85, 194–95, 200, 202–3, 205, 220, 234, 236, 240–41, 243, 248, 251, 255, 258, 265–66
Silence, 11, 13, 15, 17, 77, 80, 109, 111–12, 123–27, 137, 236, 278–80, 299–304. See also Gossip; Nonverbal communication; Tact
Sinbad the Sailor, 7, 46
Sind, 42
Sisters, relations between, 200, 202–3, 220, 258, 265
Slavery, 43, 45, 47, 96, 116, 135, 172, 193, 245
Sobara, 115–18

Soukour, 77–78, 241
Spinsters, 175, 189, 223
Spouses, relations between, 51–54, 56–57, 63, 82, 103–4, 111–12, 114–15, 118, 120, 126–27, 143–45, 147–49, 157–60, 184–85, 194–96, 197–98, 200–201, 207–9, 211, 212, 215–16, 221–23, 226, 229–30, 231–33, 234–37, 239–41, 243–44, 245–70, 271–95
Stepmother-stepchild relationship, 83, 158, 248, 250, 265, 276
Stewart, Frank H., 168 n
Stoller, Robert, 172
Sunni, 41–42, 45, 165

Tact, 10, 13, 24, 33, 43, 45–46, 74, 86, 110, 127, 129, 135–37, 141–47, 155–57, 161, 162, 163, 167, 179, 185, 191, 206, 208, 228, 231–41, 256, 278–80, 302–3. See also Gossip; Honor
Tapper, Nancy, 116 n, 185 n
Tolerance, 6, 10, 33, 45–46, 48, 65, 127, 144, 145, 147, 168, 179–80, 224, 228, 238–41, 290. See also Politeness
Trade, between women, 133–35, 281–83
Transsexuals, 168, 170–72, 230. See also Xaniths
Transvestites. See Transsexuals; Xaniths
Tribes, 42–43

Veiling, 104–8. See also Burqa
Vendors, 72, 120, 134, 259
Virginity, 136, 167, 192, 202–3, 206, 222–30, 242, 278
Visiting, among women, 109–11, 118, 120–27, 129–40, 191, 251, 258–61. See also Food; Hospitality; Neighbors

Wali, 7, 8, 32–34, 35, 54, 62, 151, 158, 174, 180, 181, 185, 199, 226, 227, 230, 241, 248, 249, 252–53, 255–56, 259, 263, 276, 279, 287, 291–92
Wedding: bride's part in, 22, 213–30; groom's part in, 16–26
Wellsted, J. R., 39
Whorf, Benjamin, 302
Widows, 150–51, 193, 205

Wikan, Unni, 165, 239
Williamson, Andrew, 4, 30, 39, 47
Women: freedoms of, 69, 72, 108, 199, 294-95; inherent nature of, 67, 71-72, 148-49, 153, 237-40, 255, 291; in Islam, 55-58, 62; rights of, 53, 56-57, 62, 140, 151, 158, 181, 184, 189, 202, 207, 227-28, 232, 233, 239, 256, 263, 276, 279-80, 285; self-determination and responsibility of, 238-41, 252, 254-57, 260, 267, 273-74, 292; structure of society of, 113-21, 137-40

Xaniths, 46, 78, 130, 168-86, 189, 216, 220-21, 230
Xalaq, 222, 226

Zaffran, 40, 124, 133, 233, 236
Zanzibaris, 40, 235, 248
Zatut, 31, 44
Zidgali, 4, 42, 46

Unni Wikan is tenured associate professor of social anthropology at the University of Oslo and curator at its Ethnographical Museum. She is the author of *Life among the Poor in Cairo*.

This book was composed in Times Roman text and Oracle display type by Action Comp, from a design by Lisa S. Mirski.
It was printed on S. D. Warren's 50 lb. Sebago Eggshell paper and bound in Holliston Roxite A by Universal Lithographers.